The *Catecismo* of Martín Pérez de Ayala

The *Catecismo* of Martín Pérez de Ayala

A Window into Christian–Muslim Relations in Sixteenth-Century Spain

Lincoln J. Loo

FOREWORD BY
Luis F. Bernabé Pons

☙PICKWICK *Publications* • Eugene, Oregon

THE *CATECISMO* OF MARTÍN PÉREZ DE AYALA
A Window into Christian–Muslim Relations in Sixteenth-Century Spain

Copyright © 2024 Lincoln J. Loo. All rights reserved. Except for brief quotations in critical publications or reviews, no part of this book may be reproduced in any manner without prior written permission from the publisher. Write: Permissions, Wipf and Stock Publishers, 199 W. 8th Ave., Suite 3, Eugene, OR 97401.

Pickwick Publications
An Imprint of Wipf and Stock Publishers
199 W. 8th Ave., Suite 3
Eugene, OR 97401

www.wipfandstock.com

PAPERBACK ISBN: 978-1-6667-3805-6
HARDCOVER ISBN: 978-1-6667-9826-5
EBOOK ISBN: 978-1-6667-9827-2

Cataloguing-in-Publication data:

Names: Loo, Lincoln J., author. | Pons, Luis F. Bernabé, foreword writer.

Title: The *Catecismo* of Martín Pérez de Ayala : a window into Christian–Muslim relations in sixteenth-century Spain / by Lincoln J. Loo ; foreword by Luis F. Bernabé Pons.

Description: Eugene, OR: Pickwick Publications, 2024 | Includes bibliographical references and index.

Identifiers: ISBN 978-1-6667-3805-6 (paperback) | ISBN 978-1-6667-9826-5 (hardcover) | ISBN 978-1-6667-9827-2 (ebook)

Subjects: LCSH: Pérez de Ayala, Martín, 1504–1566 | Christianity and other religions—Islam | Christianity and other religions—Islam—History | Religion and culture—Spain | Spanish literature—Classical period, 1500–1700—History and criticism

Classification: BP172 L66 2024 (print) | BP172 (ebook)

01/10/24

"Scripture taken from the NEW AMERICAN STANDARD BIBLE®, Copyright © 1960, 1962, 1963, 1968, 1971, 1972, 1973, 1975, 1977, 1995 by The Lockman Foundation. Used by permission."

In loving memory of my parents—Delio Asen Murgas Loo (1920–77) and Rosa Mariana Ung de Loo (1928–2019).

Contents

List of Tables | viii
Foreword by Luis F. Bernabé Pons | ix
Preface | xiii
Acknowledgements | xv

1. A New Search | 1
2. Martín Pérez de Ayala and Juan de Ribera: Two Reformers, One *Catecismo* | 6
3. Overview of the *Catecismo* | 31
4. The Religious Context of the *Catecismo* | 55
5. The Content of the *Catecismo*: The Need, Request, and Criteria for a New Catechism | 102
6. The New *Catecismo*: Audience and Format | 112
7. The New *Catecismo*: The Gospel and Reaction | 151
8. The New *Catecismo*: Experience and Evidence | 167
9. The New *Catecismo*: Heart, Mind, and Behavior | 201
10. The Content of the New *Catecismo*: Apologetics and Polemics | 220
11. Juan de Ribera's *Catecismo*: Martín Pérez de Ayala's Legacy | 249
12. Reflections | 280

Maps | 288
Appendices | 290
Bibliography | 303
Index | 309

Tables

Table 1. Type of Content | 53
Table 2. The Competition | 109
Table 3. Results of Round One, All Six Events | 150
Table 4. Summary of Round Two, Events 2 and 3 | 162
Table 5. Results of Round Two, All Four Events | 166
Table 6. Results of Round Three, All Four Events | 200
Table 7. The Symbol | 207
Table 8. Results of Round Four, All Two Events | 219
Table 9. Questions and Statements | 266
Table 10. Final Results | 277

Foreword

FROM THE MIDDLE AGES to the present, there are few subjects that have so affected the European mentality as its relations with Islam. Ever since Muhammad's prophetic message caught on among the Arab tribes and quickly spread beyond the Arabian Peninsula, Jews and Christians, soi-dissant custodians of Abraham's monotheistic faith, have been wondering about the nature of that faith and that of their followers. Today, when Muslims number in the millions as citizens in Europe, those medieval questions still hold true.

In this continuous interrogation about Islam, a handful of territories in Eastern and Southern Europe also have a past of which Muslims have been an important part. What kind of part is something that remains subjected to discussion, as a proof that relations between Europe and Islam have always been closer to suspicion and mistrust than a dispassionate approach. Even the—very visible—legacy that Islam has left in some of these societies continues to be subject to disparate interpretations, as if its presence continued to be an inconvenience for the recreation of a certain idea of the West.

In the case of the Iberian Peninsula, moreover, the continuous presence of Islam from the seventh to the seventeenth century, that is, throughout its stage of political formation and development, is at least impossible to ignore. Its presence is resoundingly dominant between the eighth to twelfth centuries. At that time, the Christian kingdoms, which had already been conquering Iberian Islamic territories before, began their most powerful expansion at the expense of successive Islamic powers. The presence of a notable Islamic population under Christian power—the Mudejars—together with the no less numerous Jewish presence, would give the Hispanic Middle Ages a very peculiar panorama.

Although politically tolerated by the authorities, the Mudejars were always the target of the Church, which always saw the presence of three religions on the Peninsula as a complete anomaly that had to be fought. The fall of Granada and the arrival of a new mentality regarding the belief that the king's subjects must have (cuius regio eius religio) caused the forced conversions of 1501 (Castilla), 1515 (Navarre), and 1525 (Aragon), putting an end to official Islam in Spain.

Of course, no one at the time assumed that these conversions led to a sincere change of belief. Rather, it was hoped that by prohibiting manifestations of Islamic idiosyncrasy, exercising some control over the now-called Moriscos, and above all an adequate evangelization, it would be possible for the new generations of new Christians to grow up as sincere believers.

It is in this context that the book by Lincoln Loo is framed, devoted to one of the most interesting figures in charge of Christian teaching to the Moriscos, Martín Pérez de Ayala, an important Spanish ecclesiastical figure of the sixteenth century and also an eminent theologian. Let's say right away, along with the author of this book, that the evangelization of the Moriscos was a failure. Perhaps not a complete failure, but a resounding defeat because the hopes that had been placed since 1501 in an adequate Christian religious instruction for the Moriscos were never fulfilled. Many reasons have been given for this failure: lack of educated and motivated personnel, lack of interest on the part of the clergy assigned to Morisco towns, the appearance of an aggressive anti-Islamic polemic, underestimation of the religious resistance of the Moriscos.... Possibly all these reasons had their role and it is clear in this book. But this does not prevent us from recognizing that some special characters from the sixteenth century in Spain did become actively involved in this catechetical work.

Undoubtedly one of the most prominent was Martín Pérez de Ayala, successively Bishop of Guadix in Granada, Bishop of Segovia and Archbishop of Valencia. A trusted man of King Carlos V, for whom he participated in several Diets, he was a professor at the University of Granada and an influential theologian who took part in the Council of Trent. If we consider his whole career, what perhaps stands out the most about him is the fact of being a, say, "professional" in religious instruction. His concern for the ministry to the believers and the role of the ecclesiastics in it is revealed in his catechetical works, regardless of whether they are addressed to the Moriscos or not. The fact, indicated by Loo, that Pérez de Ayala hesitated whether to accept his posts in Guadix and Valencia (that Morisco "Babylon" that horrified him) because he felt that he was not prepared for this challenge with the Moriscos, indicates that he was a man who took his mission very seriously from both a spiritual and an intellectual point of view.

For this reason, mainly his *Catecismo para la instrucción de los nuevamente convertidos de Moros* (1566) is one of the most interesting works that emerged from this evangelizing effort. Its structure implies that Pérez de Ayala reflected deeply on what could be the best way to bring Christian doctrine to the Moriscos. Firstly, it is one of the three catechisms that uses Arabic—the language of the Moriscos from Granada and Valencia—to bring Christianity closer to neophytes. This implies an effort to link two languages, one identified with Islam and the other with Christianity, in a task that is by no means easy. Although Pérez de Ayala's effort to use both languages was criticized as aberrational in the sixteenth century, his use of translations for religious exchange has recently been vindicated by some scholars. Secondly, the dialogue form of the *Catecismo* between a Moro and a character representing Pérez de Ayala himself tries to avoid long and often incomprehensible doctrinal excursions. Third, despite obviously containing negative views against Islam, Pérez de Ayala's *Catecismo* attempts to tone down the aggressive bias present in other polemical works of the sixteenth century, especially against Muhammad. Lastly, its way of presenting Christian doctrine strikes a difficult balance between accuracy and an understandable exposition.

These are the topics that Lincoln Loo is studying and clearing up throughout this book. The fact that the Archbishop of Valencia, the Patriarch Juan de Ribera, chose the unpublished *Catecismo* of Pérez de Ayala among all the material at his disposal for the catechism of the unattainable Moriscos in Valencia, indicates that for the intellectual who Ribera, was, the *Catecismo para la instrucción de los nuevamente convertidos de Moros* was a valuable tool. Before Ribera lost hope on the conversion of the Moriscos, he saw in the work of Pérez de Ayala one of the last possibilities of getting Christian teachings to penetrate the interior of the Moriscos in Valencia.

Was Juan de Ribera right? Was Pérez de Ayala's *Catecismo* a good instrument for his purposes with the Moriscos? Lincoln Loo dedicates an important part of his book to this, clearing up all the elements of the catechism, extra and intratextual, contextual and co-textual, personal and stylistic, in order to analyze the true value of Pérez de Ayala's text. And he does it with an original and novel methodology, applying to the text an almost anthropological scheme of competition that makes it stand out from other similar texts and that shows the advantageous characteristics of the *Catecismo*. Through his novel method, the author manages to make us appreciate the benefits of Pérez de Ayala's book and realize some of his drawbacks for indoctrinating the Moriscos. Loo rightly concludes that Pérez de Ayala's work was undoubtedly a good text to bring the dogmas of the Christian faith closer to the Moriscos, but that elements outside the book—the atmosphere of oppression, the lack of balance on occasions between the style of the text and its adaptation to its Morisco audience, the absence of preachers who knew how to take advantage of it, etc.—ruined its potential as an evangelizing text.

This book by Lincoln Loo will shrewdly show the reader that a good religious text does not necessarily succeed if its application and context are not adequate. Pérez de Ayala's experience as a theologian and as a man concerned for his faithful were not enough background to solve a problem that had become entrenched over the decades. As can be seen in this book, his work used all the elements, linguistic and religious, that he considered pertinent to achieving success, but by 1599 the fate of the Moriscos had already been cast.

Luis F Bernabé Pons, PhD
Professor, Department of Arabic and Islamic Studies
University of Alicante

Preface

MARTÍN PÉREZ DE AYALA—ARCHBISHOP of Valencia from 1564 to 1566—wrote a catechism titled *Catecismo para instrucción de los nuevamente convertidos de Moros*,[1] which remained unpublished when he died in 1566. The present book assesses the significance of the *Catecismo* by investigating two related questions: (1) What was the potential of the *Catecismo* as an evangelistic tool addressed to Moriscos? and (2) Why did Juan de Ribera—Archbishop of Valencia from 1568 to 1611—publish the *Catecismo* thirty-three years after Pérez de Ayala had passed away and ten years before the decree of Philip III in 1609 that launched the process to expel the Moriscos from Spain? The present book examines the religious, social, and literary contexts of the *Catecismo*. The content of the *Catecismo* is analyzed together with the content of thirteen other catechisms and polemical treatises published in sixteenth-century Spain.

---

1. *Catechism for the instruction of the newly converted among the Moors* or *Catecismo* from hereon.

Acknowledgements

My profound appreciation to Dr. Peter G. Riddell and Dr. Luis F. Bernabé Pons for the guidance they gave me during the entire process of completing my doctoral thesis, which is the basis of the present book. They offered numerous suggestions and fresh perspectives. They opened doors to impossible to access academic books and journal articles. They were always eager to help and prompt to respond to my requests for assistance. I am immensely grateful to have had both of them as my supervisors.

I am also grateful to the institution that hosted my PhD program, Melbourne School of Theology, an Affiliated College of the Australian College of Theology, for the support and encouragement given to me throughout the course of my research.

I would also like to express my heartfelt thanks to my son Jeremy Daniel for his care and creativity in designing the maps and fine-tuning the images in the appendices. My wife Esther also deserves a giant "Thank you!" Her love and support are impossible to calculate. She made sure that nothing would interrupt my schedule so that I could meet deadlines and stay on track. I am indeed most blessed to have her as my faithful spouse through this journey of life.

Chapter 1

A New Search

MARTÍN PÉREZ DE AYALA was born in 1504. He earned undergraduate and graduate degrees from the University of Alcalá and a doctorate from the University of Granada. Charles I of Spain appointed him to attend the Diets of Worms, Speyer, Augsburg and Regensburg and the Council of Trent. The king also appointed him to the bishoprics of Guadix and Segovia. Philip II appointed him to the archbishopric of Valencia. Pérez de Ayala died in 1566. His *Catecismo* was novel in its approach, conciliatory in tone, and shared parallels with two of the most popular catechisms of sixteenth-century Spain[1]—the Counter-Reformation works of Jerónimo de Ripalda and Gaspar Astete.

The *Catecismo*—written for Muslims who had recently been baptized into the Catholic Church—is composed of two books. Book One covers topics such as God, human nature, sin, the true path to God, Islam, the life of Muhammad, and the Qur'an. Book Two teaches five basics of the Christian life—faith, hope, charity, obedience, and the sacraments—and defends the Bible against accusations of having being corrupted. The two objectives of the *Catecismo* were to help these "new converts" understand why Christianity is the true path to God and strengthen their grasp of the basics of the Catholic faith.

Questions

The present book is a cross-disciplinary study that offers insights into the relations between Christians and Muslims living in Spain in the first half of the sixteenth century by investigating two related questions: What

---

1. Framiñán de Miguel, "Manuales para el adoctrinamiento de neoconversos en el siglo XVI," 14.

was the potential of the *Catecismo* as an evangelistic tool addressed to Moriscos and why did Archbishop Juan de Ribera choose the *Catecismo* to bolster his own evangelistic task in 1599—thirty-three years after Pérez de Ayala had passed away and ten years before the decree of Philip III in 1609 that launched the process to expel the Moriscos from Spain? The answers to these two questions are drawn from the analysis of the *context* and the *text* of the *Catecismo*.

Context

The analysis of the context of the *Catecismo* focuses on *the environment of the Catecismo*; that is, literary context; style (is it unique and how does it compare with the critiques written by contemporaries of Pérez de Ayala?); historical context (Pérez de Ayala lived when Charles I and Philip II fought the armies of the Ottoman Empire); religious context; social context; audience (the *Catecismo* was addressed to Muslim converts); and Pérez de Ayala's legacy.

Text

The analysis of the text of the *Catecismo* focuses on *the content of the Catecismo*; that is, Pérez de Ayala's biblical apologetics; the evidence he used to support his argument that Christianity is the true path to God; the way he defended Christianity; what he defended; his polemical approach to Islam; the evidence he used to support his argument that Islam is not the true path to God; the manner in which he critiqued Islam; what he critiqued about Islam; the structure of his arguments; and his plan for teaching new converts.

Contemporary Works

Catechisms and polemical treatises were written with the dual purpose of teaching Christian doctrine to *mudéjares*[2] and *moriscos*[3] while opposing Islam. Thirteen works are examined—those written by Hernando de Talavera (*Breve doctrina y enseñanza*), Antonio García Villalpando (*Instrucción de la vida cristiana*), Juan Andrés (*Confusión o confutación*), Bernardo Pérez de Chinchón (*Antialcorano* and *Diálogos Christianos*), Lope Obregón (*Confutación del alcorán y secta mahometana*), Alonso de

---

2. Muslims who stayed in Spain after the *Reconquista*, but were not converted to Catholicism.

3. Muslims who converted or were forced to convert to Catholicism after Spanish authorities proscribed the open practice of Islam by the *mudéjares*.

Orozco (*Catecismo provechoso*), Pedro Ramiro de Alba (*Doctrina Cristiana*), Pedro Guerra de Lorca (*Catecheses mystagogicae*), Jerónimo de Ripalda (*Catecismo de la doctrina cristiana* or *Doctrina Cristiana*), Gaspar Astete (*Catecismo de la doctrina cristiana* or *Doctrina Cristiana*), the anonymous *Catecismo del Sacromonte*, and Pérez de Ayala's other catechism (*Doctrina Cristiana en lengua arábiga y castellana para la instrucción de los nuevamente convertidos del Reino de Valencia*).

Scholarship

The history of the scholarship on the *Catecismo* consists of a doctoral thesis submitted in 1955 (which is not dedicated solely to this work, but considers it alongside a group of other catechisms) and five journal-length studies published between 1980 and 2005.[4] The doctoral thesis "Catecismos para la instrucción religiosa de los Moriscos" presented by Antonio Sánchez Hernández to the Universidad Pontificia de Salamanca also examined five other catechisms—*Arte de sauer ligeramente la lengua arauiga y vocabulista arauigo en la lengua castellana* by Pedro de Alcalá (Granada, 1505);[5] *Libro llamado anti-alcorano que quiere decir contra el alcoran de Mahoma, repartido en xxvi sermones* by Bernardo Pérez de Chinchón (Valencia, 1532);[6] *Confutación del alcoran y secta Mahometana sacada de sus propios libros y de la vida del mesmo Mahoma* by Lope de Obregón (Granada, 1555);[7] *Catecheses mystagogicae pro aduenis ex secta Mahometana*[8] by Pedro Guerra Lorca (Madrid, 1586);[9] and *Manuductio ad conversionem Mahumetanorum in duas partes divisa*[10] by Tirso González de Santalla (Madrid, 1687).[11] Pérez de Ayala's *Catecismo* was published in Valencia in 1599.

Sánchez Hernández's doctoral thesis compared the content of the six catechisms to determine how they prepared clergy to minister to Muslims.[12]

---

4. Framiñán de Miguel, "Martín Pérez de Ayala," 211–12.

5. Sánchez Hernández, "Catecismos para la instrucción religiosa de los Moriscos," 64–88. The page number refers to the page in the digital copy of this doctoral thesis archived at the Universidad Pontifical de Salamanca www.summa.upsa.es.

6. Sánchez Hernández, "Catecismos para la instrucción religiosa de los Moriscos," 89–133.

7. Sánchez Hernández, "Catecismos para la instrucción religiosa de los Moriscos," 134–62.

8. *Catechisms of instruction for those coming from the Muhammadan sect.*

9. Sánchez Hernández, "Catecismos para la instrucción religiosa de los Moriscos," 163–205.

10. *Leading to the conversion of the Muhammadans divided in two parts.*

11. Sánchez Hernández, "Catecismos para la instrucción religiosa de los Moriscos," 247–95.

12. Sánchez Hernández, "Catecismos para la instrucción religiosa de los Moriscos," 3.

Chapter Five of this doctoral thesis focused on the *Catecismo*.[13] Sánchez Hernández's methodology consisted of examining the content of the *Catecismo* and making observations.

The five studies on the *Catecismo* are García Cárcel (1980), García Cárcel (1981), Medina (2001), Resines (2002), and Framiñán de Miguel (2005).[14] García Cárcel regards the *Catecismo* as a skillful blend of aggressiveness in refuting Islam and intelligent presentation of grand themes such as the concept of God, the corruption of the human nature, the immortality of the soul, and life after death.[15] García Cárcel also highlights three characteristics of the relationship between Christians and Moriscos: the belief among liberal Moriscos in Valencia that Moriscos and Christians could each find salvation in their respective religion; the disinterest of the Inquisition in open dialectic confrontation with Moriscos, which led to the banning of Pérez de Chinchón's *Antialcorano* and Juan Andrés' *Confusión o confutación*; and Moriscos spying on and betraying each other at the instigation of the Inquisition.[16] Medina in his overview of the ministry of the Jesuits among Moriscos living in Andalucía, Aragón, Granada, Valencia and Sevilla mentions that Pérez de Ayala's endorsement of a plan to establish a professorship in Arabic at the University of Valencia did not materialize due to his death and Ribera's opposition to the idea of priests using Arabic to preach.[17] Resines consults Pérez de Ayala's *Catecismo* in his analysis of a catechism used in the evangelization of Moriscos in the Iberian Peninsula—*Catecismo del Sacromonte* (Granada, 1588)[18]—and one catechism used with Indians in the Americas—*Doctrina Cristiana de Fray Pedro de Feria* (Mexico, 1567).[19] Framiñán de Miguel evaluates the catechisms written by Hernando de Talavera, Pedro de Alcalá, Bernardo Pérez de Chinchón, Lope de Obregón, Pedro Guerra de Lorca, Martín Pérez de Ayala, and Tirso González de Santalla to understand the linguistic, cultural and spiritual barriers that the Catholic Church faced in its pastoral work of Muslims who converted to Catholicism.[20]

---

13. Sánchez Hernández, "Catecismos para la instrucción religiosa de los Moriscos," 206–41.

14. Framiñán de Miguel, "Martín Pérez de Ayala," 211.

15. García Cárcel, *Herejía y sociedad en el siglo xvi*, 59.

16. García Cárcel, "La Inquisición y los Moriscos Valencianos. Anatomía de una represión," 414.

17. Medina, "Apostolado Morisco," 2747.

18. Resines, *Catecismo del Sacromonte*, 47.

19. Resines, *Catecismo del Sacromonte*, 57.

20. Framiñán de Miguel, "Manuales para el adoctrinamiento de neoconversos en el siglo XVI," 25–37.

Pons Fuster (2013) can be included besides the above studies mentioned by Framiñán de Miguel. He divides his examination of the *Catecismo* into five areas: historical context; authorship and structure; the *Catecismo* as a work of religious polemic; the use of natural and divine reasons in Dialogue XIX of the *Catecismo* to refute the Qur'an; and the influence of Pérez de Chinchón's *Antialcorano* and Juan Andrés' *Confusión o confutación* on the *Catecismo* and the usefulness of the *Catecismo*.[21]

Significance

There has been a limited amount of academic work devoted to Pérez de Ayala and his *Catecismo*. There is a need for a wider approach that considers the context and the text of this catechism. Sánchez Hernández, Resines, and Framiñán de Miguel do not analyze its environment (context) and content (text). Sánchez Hernández only examines and makes observations about its content. Resines focuses on comparing the similarities and differences between *Catecismo del Sacromonte* and *Doctrina Cristiana de Fray Pedro de Feria* and uses the *Catecismo* primarily to highlight those similarities and differences. Framiñán de Miguel only provides an overview of six catechisms used during the sixteenth century, including Pérez de Ayala's *Catecismo*.

An original approach

The present book uses an original methodology that has never been used in this type of cross-disciplinary study. The process of evaluating the content of *Catecismo* adapts the process used in competitive sports to determine a winner; that is, athletes compete against competitors in a series of events arranged in several rounds.

This original approach includes **Competitors** (the *Catecismo* and the thirteen catechisms and polemical treatises), **Events** (the sixteen criteria used to evaluate the content of the *Catecismo* and its competitors), and **Rounds** (the criteria divided into four rounds). This approach has three steps.

Step 1. Use the criteria to evaluate the content of the *Catecismo* and its competitors.

Step 2. Analyze the apologetics and polemics of the winner of Step 1.

Step 3. Answer the two questions.[22]

---

21. Pons Fuster, "El patriarca Juan de Ribera," 189–220.

22. A full explanation of this approach is presented in Chapter 5. The Content of The *Catecismo*: The Need, Request, and Criteria for a New Catechism.

Chapter 2

Martín Pérez de Ayala and Juan de Ribera

Two Reformers, One *Catecismo*

Overview

THE GOAL OF THIS chapter is to introduce Martín Pérez de Ayala and Juan de Ribera. Pérez de Ayala lived when Muslims no longer dominated the Iberian Peninsula yet continued living there. This section of the present book offers a brief and broad overview of the military, political, and religious changes of his era. It is likely that Pérez de Ayala wrote his *Catecismo* when he had close contacts with Muslims while serving as bishop of Guadix (1548–60), a town in Granada with a large Muslim population.[1] Muslims ruled Medieval Spain for 780 years starting from 711 until Granada fell in 1492 with the surrender of Sultan Muhammad XII of the Nasrid dynasty (1248–1492) to *Los Reyes Católicos* Ferdinand II of Aragón and Isabella of Castilla. The fall of Granada had no immediate negative impact on the resident Muslim community. In late 1494, large numbers of Muslims could still gather for Friday prayers at any one of many mosques in the Albaicín quarter. The grandeur of the gardens and the houses of the Muslim nobility remained evident. In 1493, Hernando de Talavera was appointed as the first archbishop of Granada. He was respectful of Muslims and encouraged priests to learn Arabic and use persuasion rather than force to attract Muslims to the Christian faith.[2]

However, the situation in Granada started to deteriorate in 1499. Cardinal Francisco Jiménez de Cisneros, archbishop of Toledo, endorsed a hard-line approach towards the Muslims in Granada. In 1501, he ordered mosques to be remade into churches, Qur'ans and Islamic books

---

1. Framiñán de Miguel, "Martín Pérez de Ayala," 209.
2. Frederiks, "Introduction," 2–3.

to be burned, and Muslims to get baptized. There were Muslim protests such as the first revolt of the Alpujarras (December 1499–April 1501). Muslims also started to seek refuge in North Africa, but harsh restrictions and taxation prevented mass emigration. Most Muslims yielded to the pressure and received baptism. They became known by the pejorative term "Moriscos" ("little Moors").[3]

In 1525, cordial relations in Aragón on the north of Granada began to disintegrate. Charles I of Spain (r. 1516–56)—also known as Charles V, Holy Roman Emperor (r. 1519–56)—proscribed all expressions of Morisco culture and compelled all Muslims in Aragón to convert or leave. The writings of Moriscos reveal the trauma of the Muslim converts and their efforts to retain their beliefs. There was a lull in the 1530s and 1540s when Charles had to focus on fighting the Ottomans for supremacy in central Europe and the Mediterranean while also resisting the rise of Protestantism. In 1556, the respite in Spain was broken when Philip II became king and had to tackle two problems—the persistent loyalty of the Moriscos in his native Spain to Islam and the increasing support for Protestantism from other parts of his domains. In his determination to uphold Catholic orthodoxy and eradicate all forms of heresy, Philip II intensified the Inquisition targeting not only the Lutherans and the Huguenots, but also Moriscos. Ottoman victories in major confrontations against the forces of Charles (Tripoli in 1551 and Bejaïa, Morocco in 1555) and Philip II (Balearic Islands and Algeria in 1558 and the Battle of Djerba in 1560) and the successful raids of Barbary corsairs on Spanish ships and costal towns led to suspicions that the Morisco community was fraternizing with Spain's enemies. Philip II responded by issuing a royal decree on 7 November 1566—the *pragmática*—to put into effect his father's edict in 1526 that disallowed all expressions of Morisco culture in Granada. The strong opposition of the Moriscos to this royal decree resulted in a second revolt known as the War of the Alpujarras (December 1568–March 1571). Philip II ordered the deportation of all Moriscos from Granada to Castilla. In September 1609, Philip III (1578–1621) expelled all Moriscos from the Iberian Peninsula, beginning with Valencia. It is estimated that 350,000 Moriscos were deported to North Africa between 1609 and 1614.[4]

Pérez de Ayala died on 1 August 1566 in Valencia before the *pragmática* became a royal decree. He earned a Bachelor of Arts in logic and theology (University of Alcalá, 1525), a Master of Arts (University of Salamanca, 1532), and a doctoral degree in theology (University of Alcalá, 1538). In

---

3. Frederiks, "Introduction," 4.
4. Frederiks, "Introduction," 5–7.

1545, Charles sent him to attend the Diet of Worms as a theologian. The king also appointed him to be his chaplain and traveled with him to the Diet of Regensburg. In 1548, Charles nominated Pérez de Ayala to be the bishop of Guadix, where he remained until 1560, when Philip II offered him the bishopric of Segovia. In 1564, the king made him archbishop of Valencia, where he remained until his death. Pérez de Ayala was actively involved in the Council of Trent as a theologian. His *De divinis apostolicis atque ecclesiasticus traditionibus*—on the role of the church in formulating church doctrine—was influential throughout Europe. His legacy as theologian and pastor can be assessed today through his written works.[5]

Pérez de Ayala is the only author of the eleven authors studied in the present book to have kept a journal. It is possible that he had not intended for it to be published, but wrote it as a personal reminder of God's goodness in his life. It is also possible that the journal was discovered after his death then published as his "autobiography." Whether what he wrote was a journal or an autobiography, there is an endearing warmth in the way he wrote that does not come through were one to read about him in a small footnote or an encyclopedia entry. Pérez de Ayala takes us from his early days as a young and diligent student learning Latin to his final years when he was afflicted with gout and kidney pain. He tells us what he did, where he went, whom he met, and even what he ate during his time as bishop and archbishop of the Catholic Church during the reigns of Charles and Philip II.

Martín Pérez de Ayala

This chapter highlights some of the noteworthy events in the life of Martín Pérez de Ayala as he recorded them in his journal. It is probable that the handwriting in the journal belongs to an anonymous editor who added notes on the margins to clarify or explain certain events recorded in the journal. The handwriting is unlikely to be Pérez de Ayala's. The last section of the journal (given the number "144" by the editor) begins with "He continued as best as he could to Valencia . . . ." All the preceding sections (1–143) are written in the first person singular, but Section 144 is in the third person singular. The first sentence of this journal is "Vida de D. Martin Perez de Ayala, del orden de Santiago, Arzobispo de Valencia, para gloria de Dios y confianza de pobres desvalidos." (Life of D. Martín Pérez de Ayala, of the Order of James, archbishop of Valencia, for the glory of God and confidence of the helpless poor.) The journal is referred to as *Vida* from hereon. It would have been necessary for Ribera to have known Pérez de Ayala as

---

5. Framiñán de Miguel, "Martín Pérez de Ayala," 207–12.

best as he could. Ribera's decision to print the *Catecismo* thirty-three years after Pérez de Ayala's death would not only be based on the quality of the *Catecismo*'s content, but also on the character of its author. If Ribera had read *Vida*, he would have noticed the following words on page 1:

> In the name of God Most Simple, Almighty, Father, Son, and Holy Spirit: *qui vocat ea quæ sunt, qui suscitat de pulvere egenum, ut sedeat cum principibus et solium gloriæ teneat.*[6] What is about to be said is said so that only he is praised and that people do not lose the trust they ought to have in his sublime mercies, which we have understood, believed in, almost touched, and experienced while living in this world . . . not to brag or to be praised because we understand that if there has been some good in our actions, it is because of the will of God; and if there has been bad (of which there is much), it is the harvest of our imperfections, weaknesses and miseries.

Early Years

Pérez de Ayala was born in Segura de la Sierra on November 1504 (or 1503).[7] "I was born of honest parents. Their marriage was legal, but not well-known because my father did not have much." Pérez de Ayala's mother almost died from being in labor that lasted two-and-a-half days or from the time when the sun "was in the first grades of Sagittarius until it was in the third grade of Sagittarius." The position of the sun during his birth—which he referred to as "an accident"—and his mother's difficult labor explained his physique and interests. The bottom half of his body was hairy and he liked the outdoors and doing things that were difficult. He believed in God yet thought about the influence of the stars. "If astrologers were correct in thinking that a difficult birth was a forecast of an arduous life ahead, the way my life turned out proved them right."[8]

Pérez de Ayala was a first-born child. He was named in honor of Saint Martin, bishop of Tours[9] whose feast was celebrated each year on November 11.[10] His father owned nothing when he got married except for

---

6. "He calls for the things which are not and raises the poor from the dust to make them sit with princes and inherit the throne of glory."

7. His mother was unsure of the exact year. He chose the latter one. Gutiérrez, *Españoles en Trento*, 775–76.

8. Pérez de Ayala, *Vida*, 1–3.

9. Gutiérrez, *Españoles en Trento*, 776.

10. Clugnet, "St. Martin of Tours," www.newadvent.org/cathen/09732b.htm.

a cape and a sword, but managed to earn a decent living from the sawmill he bought with the dowry. Unfortunately, the business burned down after four years. That mishap was the beginning and the cause of his parents getting into financial difficulties.[11] He was eleven years old when his father left home because of mounting debts from having mismanaged the family's assets. "We do not know what God did with him."[12]

Education

Pérez de Ayala began to learn Latin at the age of five before learning Romance. This was unusual because children in those days learned Romance first. He was an outstanding reader and classmates challenged him to see who could read the fastest. He made the most of everything put in front of him and did not eat lunch so that his studies would not be interrupted because he was afraid that others would wonder what plans God had for him. At fourteen, he went to the University of Alcalá to study arts. His mother wanted him to study canons and to prepare himself for ordination, which at that time was a common wish of widows who loved their sons. "But, I left the path that she was guiding me towards. This was the only time that I disobeyed her."[13]

Pérez de Ayala graduated in 1525 with a bachelor of arts in logic and theology. He also earned a master of arts from the University of Alcalá (1532) and a doctorate in theology from the University of Granada (1538). Charles founded the *Estudio* and *Colegio* in the city of Granada with help and support from Pedro de Alba—prior of Saint Jerome and author of one of the catechisms examined in the present book—and Gaspar de Ávalos, his successor. It was common practice to welcome graduates from Alcalá to teach at the university. Gaspar de Ávalos—*moderador* of the university and archbishop of Granada by appointment in 1529—hired Pérez de Ayala to teach arts for a stipend and food. He accepted and started to teach on November 6.[14]

Pérez de Ayala chose a career in religion because he had become tired of struggling financially. As a student in Alcalá, he did not have enough to eat, wear or even a place to sleep. His plan to join the Order of Saint Jerome was unsuccessful, but he did not explain why. If he had pursued ordination, it would have meant becoming a beggar or saying Mass for alms. He also abandoned the idea of becoming a monk because his

---

11. Pérez de Ayala, *Vida*, 3–4.
12. Pérez de Ayala, *Vida*, 8.
13. Pérez de Ayala, *Vida*, 9.
14. Serrano y Sanz, *Autobiografías y memorias*, 215.

mother would have been in financial need and he felt that he had a duty to take care of her. He was also thinking about getting married, but this was also against her wishes because she had made sacrifices for him to be a priest. If he had gotten married, it would not have helped her "because those who are married love their wives and their children more than their parents...."[15]

Pastoral Career

Bishopric of Guadix

In 1548, Charles appointed Pérez de Ayala to the bishopric of Guadix in Granada, but Pérez de Ayala hesitated to accept because it had never crossed his mind to be a bishop. "God is my witness." The main drawback was the bishopric's low income. Someone from Charles's inner circle informed Pérez de Ayala privately that the king was aware of his family's difficult financial situation. Pérez de Ayala then met Charles. "I kissed his hand for considering me and for his confidence in me, which was more than I deserved." He thought that Charles had nominated him because he was a preacher who knew the language and the customs of the Moriscos. He informed the king that he was not used to preaching and did not know the language and the customs of the Moriscos even though he had studied in Granada. If he had been nominated because of these reasons, he had to disabuse him and first prove that he could carry out the task with a clear conscience before accepting. Charles replied that he believed that Pérez de Ayala was well-qualified to preach at a moment's notice. He had not chosen him because of his knowledge of the language and the customs of the Moriscos, "but my trust in you that you will carry out your duties with a clear conscience." Pérez de Ayala accepted after deliberating for two days. If he had declined, "the Emperor was known to be the type of person who would not remember you for anything else."[16]

During his tenure as bishop of Guadix, Pérez de Ayala secluded himself for about three years (1554–57) to study Hebrew and translate the Hebrew Bible under the supervision of two Jewish tutors who had converted to the Catholic faith. He also studied Arabic, identified

15. Pérez de Ayala, *Vida*, 10–11.
16. Pérez de Ayala, *Vida*, 33–35.

errors and contradictions in the Qur'an, and wrote them in a manuscript titled "Errors and Contradictions of the Qur'an extracted by M. Pérez de Ayala and sent by him to Bartolomé Dorador of Santiago in Guadix for the latter's revision . . . ."[17] Pérez de Ayala collected his Greek codices during his stay at Trent from 1562 to 1563. The entire library is a valuable source of information on the holy fathers and the councils of the primitive and Spanish church.[18]

Bishopric of Segovia

Charles nominated Pérez de Ayala in July 1560 to the bishopric of Segovia in Castilla and León, but Pérez de Ayala was surprised because he had not asked for it and no one as far as he knew had asked on his behalf. Later that year, Charles invited him to preach in Toledo. The king and his soldiers were present. Pérez de Ayala let hem know what he thought about the daily raids of the Moors along the coast. He took the opportunity to unburden his conscience even though there were certain individuals who would later accuse him of having gone too far. (The journal is silent about what he said exactly.) The farewell from Guadix was not what he had expected. Some of the priests were "somewhat ruffled." He had reprimanded many of those in his church in Guadix for living badly. Some friars went to him "like apostates" and told him that he was "harsh and terrible." However, he was hopeful that certain decisions of the Council of Trent would help him deal with the bad apples in his diocese in Segovia. He had a hunch that preparations for the Council were underway and that Charles would send him (and he did). So Pérez de Ayala finished visiting all the churches in Segovia. He had trouble with a few in the Cathedral for pretending to be good examples and had to put them in prison. But, he knew that the Council was about to start and would put an end to their abuses so he did nothing further with them because it would have ended in appeals and litigation.[19]

Pérez de Ayala did not specify the nature of the abuses. We venture a possibility. The last period of the Council of Trent dealt with a number of issues of which the obligation of residence could have been connected to the abuses that Pérez de Ayala had in mind. The papal court was in the habit of giving dispensations from the canons that required bishops to reside in their dioceses and pastors in the parishes, and stipulated one bishop per

17. The manuscript is archived at the Instituto de Valencia de Don Juan in Valencia, Spain.
18. Andrés, "La biblioteca de un teólogo renacentista," 29–44.
19. Pérez de Ayala, *Vida*, 76–86.

diocese, one pastor per parish.[20] The dispensations lead to widespread abuse of non-residence and the holding of multiple benefices; for example, Milan, the largest and richest diocese in Italy, did not have a resident bishop for eighty years. Only half of the pastors in the diocese of Grenoble resided in their parishes. In Geneva, it was only 20 percent. Absentee bishops and pastors kept for themselves the revenue from the benefices and spent the rest of their time in unspiritual pursuits. Those who held multiple bishoprics collected funds from all of them. Albert of Brandenburg—Luther's nemesis—was the best-known offender. He simultaneously held the archbishoprics of Mainz, Magdeburg, and Halberstadt. Jean de Lorraine—the uncle of Cardinal Charles de Guise—held three archbishoprics and nine bishoprics.[21] Session XXIII of the Council of Trent—celebrated on 15 July 1563[22]—dealt with the obligation of residence. The decree reads in part as follows:

> ... the sacred and holy Synod ... declares, that all persons who are—under whatsoever name and title, even though they be cardinals of the holy Roman Church—set over any patriarchal, primatial, metropolitan, and cathedral churches whatsoever, are obliged to personal residence in their own church, or diocese, where they shall be bound to discharge the office enjoined them; and may not be absent thence, save for the causes and in the manner subjoined.[23]

The obligation of residence was the council's lightning-rod and critical factor in its pastoral reform plan.[24]

Synods

Synods provide first-hand information about a church and details of the community where it is located—demography, economy, geography, religious practices and more. However, the picture that emerges might be limited to the perspective of those who attended the synod or the bishop who presided it. The picture is also fragmented because a synod was focused on addressing shortcomings instead of commending virtuous behavior. Twenty three synods were convened in Segovia between 1216 and 1911.

---

20. O'Malley, *Trent*, 22.
21. O'Malley, *Trent*, 16.
22. Waterworth, *The Canons and Decrees*, cxcvi.
23. Waterworth, *The Canons and Decrees*, 175–76. Cited in O'Malley, *Trent*, 217.
24. O'Malley, *Trent*, 100.

Pérez de Ayala was in charge of two of them—one met in Turégano and the other at the Iglesia de San Andrés de Segovia.[25]

Turégano

The synod held at this city took place in 1561 or 1562. The records of this synod have not been found yet, but there is a manuscript in the Cathedral of Segovia with this note: "A synod was convened in Turégano without a *cabildo,* which is unheard of and never seen. The Royal Provisor (Philip II) requests the bishop of Segovia to accept the appeal made by the Dean and the *cabildo* and orders that the original proceedings and the *autos* of the aforementioned be submitted within fifteen days. Madrid, 13 March 1562." This notice is the only evidence so far that this synod took place.[26]

Iglesia de San Andrés de Segovia

The synod met at this church on 27 August 1564. Its objective was probably to develop a plan to apply the decrees of the Council of Trent. The records of this synod have also not been found. However, the city hall has proof that the mayor and four council men attended the synod.[27]

Archbishopric of Valencia

In 1564, on the eve of the Most Holy Trinity, while Pérez de Ayala was in Segovia, a letter arrived at his home from Philip II announcing his appointment to the archbishopric of Valencia. Pérez de Ayala's response was similar to the one he thought of giving after learning that Charles had nominated him to be the bishop of Guadix. He wrote in his journal that it had not crossed his mind to have such a post and that he spent three days thinking about it and entrusting himself to God. This time the reasons for declining would be different. He was leaning towards not accepting because he would be living with what he described as "new people and not all from our nation and kingdom where there is a city like a Babylon and the rest are infidels." The second reason was the cost of papal bulls. He would have to bear the cost of papal bulls sent to him from Rome by people who persecuted him and would cause him much vexation. The cost was so burdensome that he

---

25. García y García-Estévez, "Sínodo diocesano," 123–80.
26. García y García-Estévez, "Sínodo diocesano," 132–33.
27. García y García-Estévez, "Sínodo diocesano," 133.

would not have been able to move to another bishopric for at least three years. The third reason was his attachment to his current bishopric because the people of Segovia had a deep affection for him. In the end, Pérez de Ayala accepted the appointment because he did not want to come across as having no regard for the king's mercy towards him. He also did not want to be the first one to fail at executing a decree issued by the Council of Trent. The weather in Valencia was also a factor. It would be good for his health to live in a place with temperate weather where he could work better. He took up his post as archbishop of Valencia "with much applause on the Day of Saint Stephen, which was the twenty six of December." As Pérez de Ayala prepared to bid farewell to Segovia, Philip II visited him on the eve of the Day of All Saints. Pérez de Ayala kissed his hand and asked for his authorization to go to Valencia, but the king told him that he wanted him to go to Madrid first. Pérez de Ayala left Segovia on the eve of Our Lady's Conception and arrived on Saturday 9 December.[28]

Philip II and Pérez de Ayala deliberated three critical issues: the convocation of provincial councils, the instruction of Moriscos living in the Kingdom of Valencia, and holding *juntas* at the residence of the archbishop of Sevilla to deliberate on the requirement that prelates themselves should be instructing Moriscos using good catechisms. The editor wrote a "note (a)" on the margin of page 101 indicating that the archbishop was Fernando de Valdés.[29] Pérez de Ayala offered to bear the costs of those catechisms. The editor wrote a "note (b)" on the margin of page 102 of the journal with these words: "Catechism: prepared two in Arabic and Castilian and his successor V. D. Juan de Ribera, friend of S. Carlos Borromeo, had the catechism printed in Castilla year 1599." Borromeo (1538–84) was archbishop of Milan (1564–84) and prominent figure in the Tridentine Reform.[30] The second critical issue was the Inquisition and the Moriscos. The Inquisition would not do anything with them except those who sinned. The third critical issue was indulgences. Whoever was the Inquisitor would grant indulgences for everything the newly converted did in the past. Pérez de Ayala left Madrid after his meetings finished and returned to Valencia by 23 April 1565.[31] He became occupied immediately and wasted no time as a reformer along the pattern set by the Council of Trent. He gathered those from the church and

---

28. Pérez de Ayala, *Vida*, 98–100.

29. Fernando de Valdés (1483–1568) also served as bishop of Helia, Orense, León, and Sigüenza; archbishop of Sevilla; president of the Royal Chancellery of Valladolid; president of the State Council; and Grand Inquisitor. Novalín, *El inquisidor general Fernando de Valdés*, 1.

30. Mols, "Borromeo, Charles, St.," 2:539–41.

31. Pérez de Ayala, *Vida*, 101–2.

spoke to them about the discharge of his conscience and admonished the lords that they had the duty to ensure the salvation and good instruction of new Christians. He visited all the churches from May until the end of September. Many things were rectified and excesses were penalized when previously they were not even penalized albeit with clemency.[32]

Provincial Council of Valencia

Pérez de Ayala then made another significant step in response to the Council of Trent as he and Philip II had discussed in Madrid. After Pérez de Ayala finished visiting the churches in his diocese, he convened a provincial council for 7 October 1565. The first session was held on the Day of Saint Martin and dealt with doctrine. The second session took place during Advent; the third session on the Day of the Apostle Saint Thomas; and the fourth session on the Day of the Apostle Saint Mathias. There were no discrepancies or contradictions at the council because of "the mercy and gift of the Holy Spirit" and more so given that Pérez de Ayala was experiencing discomfort in his legs. "God be blessed because work never stopped." The provincial council concluded four months later in 1566, which was Pérez de Ayala's second year as the archbishop of Valencia. He was sixty two years old.[33] The journal provides no further details about this important council.[34]

Significance of the Provincial Council

This provincial council was the most important and extensive of Pérez de Ayala's works and the broadest and most complete of all the councils held in Spain. It was a significant council because it was the first council to be convened according to the decrees of the Council of Trent and a true application of its decrees in Valencia.[35] Pérez de Ayala intended for representation at this council to be as wide as possible. His convocation on 18 August 1565 included bishops, *cabildos* (chapters), men of Valencia, and "anyone irrespective of their dignity, office or authority and could attend councils held in Valencia by right, custom or privilege."[36] His appeal to them revealed his

---

32. Pérez de Ayala, *Vida*, 102.
33. Pérez de Ayala, *Vida*, 102.
34. The original text in Latin with its Spanish translation is available in Tejada y Ramiro, *Colección de cánones y de todos los Concilios de la Iglesia Española*. Cited in Plans, "La obra reformadora de Martín Pérez de Ayala," 211–17.
35. Plans, "La obra reformadora de Martín Pérez de Ayala," 216.
36. Tejada y Ramiro, *Colección de cánones*, 263.

commitment and urgency: "The sacred and ecumenical Tridentine council ... stipulated that provincial synods be convened within one year of its conclusion.... Although we were transferred from the church in Segovia to this one in Valencia after our return from Trent, we have ardently desired not only to carry out the other Tridentine decrees, but to convene this synod as soon as possible. Moreover, now that these obstacles (Pérez de Ayala mentioned in this same appeal that he had been ill) have disappeared with God's help and not wanting to pass up the opportunity to carry out something so useful and necessary ... we exhort and admonish in the Lord the most reverend bishops and each and everyone ... to come to this city to initiate and pursue this council with us."[37]

Highlights of the Provincial Council

The council convened from 7 October 1565 to 24 February 1566. Four topics were discussed over five sessions: Doctrine and its ministers (Session 1); the sacraments and their administration (Session 2); the government of churches and church personnel (Sessions 3 and 4); and the government of people (Session 5).[38] The outcome of these five sessions—written as 116 chapters—shows that this council had developed a comprehensive plan to reform the church in Valencia according to the decrees of the Council of Trent.

Doctrine and its ministers (Session 1). Cathedrals, metropolitan churches, collegiate churches, monasteries and convents had to establish a chair of sacred Scripture; priests had to explain the Scriptures and teach people what they need to do to be saved; and men who wanted to serve as priests had to be mature in age, have good habits, be literate, and be able to teach others what is necessary for salvation.[39]

The sacraments and their administration (Session 2). Ministers had to administer the sacraments "with utmost sincerity of heart and purity of soul"; adults had to be taught the fundamentals of the faith before they could be baptized; teachers of the followers of the sect of Muhammad were not allowed to visit women who had just given birth or the sick who were near death; and recent converts in Valencia were forbidden from observing the fasts, feasts or any of the rites of the sect of Muhammad.[40]

The government of churches and church personnel (Sessions 3 and 4). Bishops "by the integrity of their lives and their luminous doctrine"

37. Tejada y Ramiro, *Colección de cánones*, 264.
38. Plans, "La obra reformadora de Martín Pérez de Ayala," 215–16.
39. Tejada y Ramiro, *Colección de cánones*, 267–69.
40. Tejada y Ramiro, *Colección de cánones*, 270–81.

were to shine as lights placed on a candlestick so that men could see their good works and everyone would glorify God; no one could be promoted to the position of archbishop of Valencia unless he was a teacher, doctor or graduate in theology or canon law; celebration of new religious festivals was forbidden; people were not allowed to wander around the church during the Mass or the sermon; and all signs of the pagan world such as banners, helmets and shields had to disappear from the church.[41]

The government of people (Session 5). The number of religious festivals was limited to thirty-eight; everyone had to attend Mass; obstacles had to be removed so that people could attend Mass (for example, no games or dancing, establishments where food was sold, and stores had to be closed); music and dancing in front the altar were not allowed; beggars could beg at the door of temples or chapels during the Mass, but were not permitted to beg inside; a newly converted could not have as a servant an old Christian who was less than eighteen years old; tithes had to be paid in full; and usury was forbidden.[42]

Pérez de Ayala's Pastoral

On 24 February 1566, the decrees of this provincial council were read before priests and the public then signed by three officials besides Pérez de Ayala—the bishop of Mallorca, the procurator of Orihuela, and the council's secretary and notary.[43] Afterwards, Pérez de Ayala issued a pastoral to "all the faithful Christians" with the following three key points:[44]

1. A note of thanks. "With divine assistance we have reached the desired outcome to see the conclusion of this provincial council convened in my church by the decrees of the holy fathers and the sacred and ecumenical Tridentine."

2. A reminder. "A thousand years ago in the reign of Theodoric, a council of six bishops was convened in Valencia. . . . But, it must be noted with sadness, from then until the incursion of the Muhammadans, and from the *Reconquista* of this kingdom by James of Aragón to our days, no council has been convened except for a very few diocesan synods."

---

41. Tejada y Ramiro, *Colección de cánones*, 284–99.
42. Tejada y Ramiro, *Colección de cánones*, 304–11.
43. Tejada y Ramiro, *Colección de cánones*, 313.
44. Tejada y Ramiro, *Colección de cánones*, 263.

3. A word of encouragement. "And now for the sake of God and the sacred Council of Trent, these councils have been reestablished, we have to promise ourselves to improve in the future. Above all, we certainly hope that our council will be a useful beginning to cure the long-standing wounds of this province and be a good example for future ones to renew often the application of this medicine."

The Council of Trent

Royal Appointments

Charles appointed Pérez de Ayala to attend the Diets of Worms (1521), Speyer (1526), Augsburg (1530), and Regensburg (1546) and the Council of Trent. Pérez de Ayala wrote in his journal that he attended the Diet of Speyer as a theologian and observed that "the schismatics were far away from the truth in many things."[45] Besides this detail, he did not comment on the deliberations or the decisions of either this Diet or the other Diets that he attended. By comparison, the titles of six of the twenty one chapters of his journal indicate that he attended the Council of Trent.[46]

The Council of Trent was attended by 245 Spaniards.[47] Pérez de Ayala was one of only five Spaniards to participate in all three periods.[48] The first period (13 December 1545–17 September 1549), the second period (1 May 1551–23 April 1552), and the third period (18 January–4 December 1563) were convened by Pope Paul III, Pope Julius III, and Pope Pius IV, respectively. Pérez de Ayala attended the first period as a theologian;[49] the second period as bishop of Guadix;[50] and the third period as bishop of Segovia.[51] He participated in three conciliar deputations—the deputation that redacted the canons of the Eucharist, which he wrote with the bishop of Modena;[52] the

---

45. Pérez de Ayala, *Vida*, 23–24.

46. The First Trip to the Council of Trent (Chapter 5); The Second Trip to the Council of Trent (Chapter 7); Fifth Trip to Trent (Chapter 10); What Happened in Some of the Sessions of the Council (Chapter 11); Trip to the Council of Trent and The Last Trip of My Life (Chapter 17); and Some of the Things that Happened at the Council (Chapter 18).

47. Gutiérrez, *Españoles en Trento*, x.

48. Gutiérrez, *Españoles en Trento*, 1047.

49. Gutiérrez, *Españoles en Trento*, 9.

50. Gutiérrez, *Españoles en Trento*, 13.

51. Gutiérrez, *Españoles en Trento*, 19.

52. Pérez de Ayala, *Vida*, 53.

deputation that systematized the doctrine of penitence and extreme unction; and the deputation that formed the canon of this same doctrine.[53]

First and Short Trip to Trent

The main outcome of Pérez de Ayala's first trip[54] to Trent was the suspension of the council. In the beginning of the year 1543, Charles decided to go to Italy and Flanders to fight the Duke of Cleves and the captains of the King of France and take the duchy and state of Guelders. William Duke of Cleves was supporting the "Lutheran heresy" brewing in Charles's empire. King Francis I of France was an ally of the Ottoman Turks and had helped them win Nice. In 1541, Charles had fought Muslim pirates on the Mediterranean who were harassing Spanish ships from a base in Argel. Francis was also giving subsidies to a Dutch rebel who had joined forces with the Duke of Cleves to fight against Charles. Besides Pérez de Ayala, Charles selected three other prelates to go with him to Trent—Francisco Mendoza, bishop of Jaén, Don Gaspar de Ávalos, archbishop of Santiago, and Don Martín de Urrea, bishop of Huéscar.[55] Charles met the Pope in Cremona and was received in Trent by Cardinal Giovanni Morone.[56] After the council was postponed until 1545 because of the war, Charles and his armies fought the Duke of Cleves and Francis while Pérez de Ayala went to Louvain at the end of 1543 and spent two years at the Colegio de Lilio reading heretical works and improving his Greek and Hebrew—which he started to learn in Alcalá.[57]

The First Period of The Council of Trent

Pérez de Ayala wrote in his journal,

> War had started. There was no place for me to feel safe. Since clerics have no business fighting wars, I asked His Majesty for permission to go to the council. It had been meeting for nine months since 13 December 1545. It was at the end of August of 1546 and he granted me permission. I did not have a lot

---

53. Gutiérrez, *Españoles en Trento*, 782.
54. Pérez de Ayala, *Vida*, 20–22.
55. Kleinschmidt, *Charles V: The World Emperor*, Kindle edition location 2393/5018.
56. Cardinal Morone (1509–80) was president of the Council of Trent and one of the most prominent figures of the post-Tridentine Curia. Lutz, "Morone, Giovanni," 9:899–900.
57. Pérez de Ayala, *Vida*, 20–22.

of spending money so Don Diego de Mendoza, His Majesty's ambassador in Venice, entreated me to stay with him.... The council had been discussing the matter *de justificatione* for four months. It is the most important matter that can be addressed during these times because the heretics disputed a lot with the Catholics. This was a very important article because concord between both parties depended on it together with *de communione sub utraque specie*,[58] which the Lutherans derided and despised and thought that they were winning over the Catholics. His Majesty was hopeful that Germany would abide by the council and that everything would turn out well resulting in religious concord and peace.[59]

De justificatione

Deliberations on *de justificatione* began on 21 June 1546 during the sixth session of the first period of the council. The council believed that Luther's doctrine of justification by faith alone was at the root of most of his errors on the sacraments, the power of the keys, the indulgences, and purgatory. Given that no preceding council had been called upon to state fully the church's doctrine on *de justificatione*, four key questions were addressed.[60]

1. What is the meaning and the essence of justification? What does the expression "a man is justified" mean? The council defined "justification" as "the passage from the state of enmity with God, to that of friendship, and adoption as the child of God." The "essence of justification" is concerned with "the formal cause of justification," which is "charity or grace infused into the soul."

2. What are the causes of justification; that is, what does God effect and what is required on the part of man? The council agreed that people have been given free will by God to be used passively—not actively—together with him in the work of justification.

3. How are the words of the apostle Paul—"a man is justified by faith"—to be understood? The council concluded that man is said to be "justified by faith" because without faith it is impossible to please God.

---

58. *sub utraque* or "under each." Waterworth, *Canons and Decrees*, 78 (footnote b). *de communione sub utraque specie* or "communion under both species"; that is, bread and wine. Doeswyck, *The Ever Changing Church*, 93.

59. Pérez de Ayala, *Vida*, 28–29.

60. Waterworth, *Canons and Decrees*, ci–ciii.

Faith is "the first remote disposition" and "the root of justification," but not its "proximate and efficient cause, which is faith accompanied by baptism and penance." The "formal cause of justification" is "faith animated by charity and sanctifying grace." In brief, faith means "faith working by charity."

4. Do works precede or result from justification? The council concurred that "works antecedent to justification are only meritorious thereof to justification by a certain fitness or congruity. Works performed after justification and in the state of grace—being done in Christ—whose living member the just man is, and being made available by His merits, preserve and augment necessarily and essentially as an effect due to their performance, through the merits of Christ, and as the result of his gratuitous promises."

The results of months of deliberations were written as sixteen chapters-or decrees-and thirty-three canons. The decrees state the Catholic doctrine of justification in consecutive order.[61] Chapter 7 dealt directly with Luther's errors, especially on the formal cause of justification, the actual remission and cancellation of sins, and his favorite doctrine of justice,[62] and the canons condemned the errors of the heretics with the accustomed anathema.[63] These forty-nine chapters form the dogmatical position of the sixth session, which surpasses the other sessions of the council. The council itself has not been surpassed by any other council.[64]

De communione sub utraque specie

Discussions on *de communione sub utraque specie* were held on 11 October 1551 during the thirteenth session of the second period of the council. The final wording of the decree—in Chapter III under the heading "On the excellency of the most holy Eucharist over the rest of the Sacraments"—reads in part as follows:

> . . . the apostles had not as yet received the Eucharist from the hand of the Lord, when nevertheless Himself affirmed with truth that to be His own body which He presented (to them). And this faith has ever been in the Church of God, that, immediately after the consecration, the veritable Body of our Lord,

---

61. Waterworth, *Canons and Decrees*, 31.
62. Waterworth, *Canons and Decrees*, cvii, 34–36.
63. Waterworth, *Canons and Decrees*, cv, 45.
64. Waterworth, *Canons and Decrees*, cxi.

and His veritable Blood, together with His soul and divinity, are under the species of bread and wine; but the Body indeed under the species of bread, and the Blood under the species of wine, by the force of the words; but the body itself under the species of wine, and the blood under the species of bread, and the soul under both, (*sub utraque,* under each) by the force of that natural connexion and concomitancy whereby the parts of Christ our Lord, who hath now risen from the dead, to die no more, (I Corinthians vi. 9) are united together; and the divinity, furthermore, on account of the admirable hypostatical union thereof with His body and soul. Wherefore it is most true, that as much is contained under either species as under both; for Christ whole and entire is under the species of bread, and under any part whatsoever of that species; likewise the whole (Christ) is under the species of wine, and under the parts thereof.[65]

The Second Period of The Council of Trent

Pérez de Ayala experienced a life-threatening situation on his journey to attend the second period of the Council of Trent. Pope Pius III reconvened the council in 1551 because of "the pestering of His Majesty, the Emperor." Charles appointed Pérez de Ayala to attend the council, but the bishop tried to excuse himself because he was in debt from paying for papal bulls, settling disputes, and having a house. But the Emperor insisted. So Pérez de Ayala bid farewell to his church and left Guadix on March 7 "with 1,000 ducats borrowed from the churches that had a lot." He stopped at Baza to preach and gather supplies and went to Volteruela to see his mother and receive her blessing. His next stop—Barcelona—provided him with a much needed three-day rest. After leaving Barcelona for Trent, French spies started to shadow him. He was eventually intercepted by a group of "about fourteen or fifteen men" armed with arquebuses, crossbows, and lances who pretended to want to protect him from bandits. They detained him and interrogated him repeatedly regarding his former whereabouts, the purpose of his journey, and his relationship with the Emperor. He was released twenty nine days later without any explanation from the French after the Emperor made an appeal to the King of France. Fearful that his captors would still want to kill him, Pérez de Ayala disguised himself because he was "heavy from not being in the habit of exercising." He stopped at two cities—Alejandría de la Palla to visit its governor (a personal friend)

---

65. Waterworth, *Canons and Decrees*, 77–78.

and Milan to recover from some bleeding—before finally arriving at Trent on the Saturday of Pentecost, 15 of May of 1551.[66]

The Third Period of The Council of Trent

Pérez de Ayala was in Turégano in September of 1561 recovering from a third gout attack when he received orders from Charles to attend the Council of Trent. However, he informed the Emperor that it would be difficult for him to return to Trent. His poor health would limit whatever good would come out of the council. He was worn out and his funds were depleted. There were certain individuals in Trent who disliked his preference for speaking freely what was in his mind. (Pérez de Ayala did not name them.) Charles replied and said, "You must go even if you have to crawl. If you do not take advantage to do good, you will avoid at least some evil with more experience and doctrine . . . and the liberty that God gave you." Pérez de Ayala complied, readied his bishopric for leasing, and left Turégano for Trent on 9 March 1562.[67]

Reflections on Trent

Pérez de Ayala noted that the church had become self-indulgent, but ran into a wall of resistance at Trent coming from "sycophants and corrupt men . . . deserving to be banished from the church" such as authoritarian bishops who went to Trent to uphold everything that Rome wanted. He took action "for the common good of the universal church" and resisted those who fought against reform and others who wanted dogma out of the articles of faith based on their personal opinions. There was acrimony over issues such as the residence of the bishops; bishops who did not want to lose their authority; the Pope's authority over the church (some were against the proposal of granting any authority to the council); and clandestine marriages. Those who favored maintaining the *status quo* demanded assurances that everything would remain the way it was and that there should be no other authority except that of the Pope.[68]

Pérez de Ayala's journal only mentions but offers no details about these thorny issues—the obligation of residence; bishops who did not want to lose their authority; clandestine marriages; and who is the vicar of Christ. The

---

66. Pérez de Ayala, *Vida*, 45–53.
67. Pérez de Ayala, *Vida*, 80–85.
68. Pérez de Ayala, *Vida*, 85–92.

record of these issues in the journal can be viewed as evidence of Pérez de Ayala's commitment to see the Catholic Church reformed, its priests living up to their responsibilities to meet the spiritual needs of their communities, and the people being instructed properly in the doctrines of the Catholic Church. Pérez de Ayala had this commitment even before there would be a council that would become known as the Council of Trent. What the council did was to fortify his zeal to pursue boldly what he believed was the right thing to do in spite of internal opposition from the church and challenging external circumstances. As Archbishop Ribera pondered about printing a catechism that would suit his situation, he would not have been able to overlook Pérez de Ayala's pre- and post-Tridentine zeal and commitment. Therefore, it is important for the following section to highlight the seriousness of the issues that Pérez de Ayala had to solve.

The Obligation of Residence and Bishops

The section "Bishopric of Segovia" discusses the obligation of residence. The intent behind the requirement of one bishop per diocese and one pastor per parish was for them to focus on their job of spiritual shepherds. If this policy were to succeed, the papal practice of giving dispensations had to stop. However, this meant that the council had to deal with the delicate issue of the authority of the Apostolic See.[69] The overwhelming majority of bishops at the third period of the council were from Italy. Many of them were indebted to the favor of Pope Pius IV and were not keen to support any reform that would impinge upon papal prerogatives.[70] So, two of the four issues—the obligation of residence and bishops who wanted to maintain their authority—were connected. The bishops—chosen by the Pope—and the Pope were supporting each other and attempting to slow the progress towards reform.

Clandestine Marriages

Clandestine marriages were marriages entered into without witnesses. This created a terrible problem. It was easy for one of the partners—usually the husband—to deny that an exchange of vows had taken place then marry someone else. Abuse was rampant. The Lateran Council IV of 1215 forbade clandestine marriages, but they continued to take place and the

---

69. O'Malley, *Trent*, 22.
70. O'Malley, *Trent*, 173.

church still recognized them as true marriages. The core theological issue was: if the sacrament of marriage centered on the consent of the spouses, how could the church legitimately declare this union invalid? Did the church have the power and the authority to impose a condition on the validity of marriage that intruded on the partners' exchange of vows, which is what made marriage a sacrament? How could the church declare future marriages to be invalid when in the past it recognized them as valid even though they were forbidden?[71]

The council discussed the problem as two questions: (1) Should clandestine marriages be declared null and void? (2) What conditions are to be declared essential, for a marriage not to be regarded as clandestine, but as lawfully contracted in the face of the church? Deliberations began on 14 May 1562 (Session XIX of the third period of the council).[72] The answers became available later that year on 11 November in the form of "The Decree on the Reformation on Marriage."[73] The decree was the council's great innovation. No single provision of the entire council affected the Catholic laity more directly than this decree. The church would only recognize marriages witnessed by a priest; marriages between minors would also be valid because the presence of a priest was required; and parental consent was not required for marriages between minors to be declared valid. The decree strongly reinforced the church's claim of having authority over marriage and was decisive in placing the institution of marriage under the protection of the church. The decree reaffirmed that matrimony was sacred and indissoluble; shielded both parties against the abuses of clandestine marriages; and protected matrimony as never before.[74]

The Vicar of Christ

Pérez de Ayala wrote in his journal,

> It should be mentioned for the glory of God what happened to me at the council on the sixth of November of that year[75] on the matter of *Ordine* and how it affected bishops. Were they *Deo non mediante Papa* (God without the mediation of the Pope)? ... the Roman bishops and their minions held the view that they were from the Pope whom they viewed as the vicar of God. Some of

---

71. O'Malley, *Trent*, 224–25.
72. Waterworth, *Canons and Decrees*, clxxi.
73. Waterworth, *Canons and Decrees*, 196–99.
74. O'Malley, *Trent*, 226–27; 256–57.
75. The year was 1562 according to *note b* on the margin of page 87 of the journal.

the prelates—the archbishop of Granada,[76] myself, the French and the Germans—opposed this dogma. But, all the resistance came from me and the archbishop of Granada.[77]

The council had spent ten bitter, complicated, and frustrating months debating holy orders (September 1562–July 1563).[78] Pérez de Ayala and the archbishop believed that bishops, as successors of the apostles, received their institution from Christ, and not from Peter.[79] But, the Italians—who wanted to protect the Pope's authority—interpreted their opposition as an attempt to subvert papal authority. The Italians argued that Christ only made Peter a bishop, after which Peter then passed the episcopal authority to the other apostles.[80] Pérez de Ayala and the archbishop believed that although bishops are subject to the Pope by the law of God and bound canonically to obey him, all the privileges conferred on the episcopacy—the highest order of the hierarchy—should be proclaimed to be theirs by divine right. They regarded bishops as the vicars of Christ—not of the Pope.[81] The goal of Pérez de Ayala and the archbishop was to enhance episcopal authority because they regarded the bishop as the linchpin to the success in reforming the church. They argued that Christ instituted the office of bishop and that his apostles were the first ones to hold it. Thus, the bishops had the full authority of that office—not by delegation from the Pope—but by divine ordinance.[82] The Italians wanted to declare bishops by *divine ordination,* but Pérez de Ayala and the archbishop found the wording unsatisfactory and preferred *by institution of Christ*[83] because "divine ordination" meant the ordinary providence of God by which all things are ordained or permitted by him.[84] The final wording—in the form of Canon VII—was made public on 15 July 1563 at Session XXIII.[85]

---

76. Pedro Guerrero was the archbishop of Granada according to *note c* on the margin of page 88 of the journal.

77. Pérez de Ayala, *Vida,* 85–92.

78. O'Malley, *Trent,* 195–196.

79. Waterworth, *Canons and Decrees,* ccii.

80. O'Malley, *Trent,* 197.

81. Waterworth, *Canons and Decrees,* ccvi.

82. O'Malley, *Trent,* 196–97.

83. Waterworth, *Canons and Decrees,* ccxviii.

84. Waterworth, *Canons and Decrees,* ccxix.

85. Waterworth, *Canons and Decrees,* 170–74.

Final Months

After spending one entire night overcome with kidney pain, Pérez de Ayala wrote in his journal, "I live beneath the powerful hand of God . . . living for what God wants to do with me. Today Friday twenty eight of June of 1566 I am ready. I am waiting for God's mercy on the eight day of our illness not afraid of the end. *Sed sive morimur, sive vivamus, Domini sumus.*"[86] Twenty years earlier Pérez de Ayala was in Amberes, the city where he began to write *De divinis, apostolicis atque ecclesiasticis traditionibus*. He had been writing well into the night when he asked his servant to bring him some bread and wine. Informed that the cupboard was bare, Pérez de Ayala retired for the evening. "I knelt beside the bed and cried when I started to think about God and my hardship. . . . I went to sleep that night . . . very sad and melancholic." He then had a dream. A beautiful maiden took him by the hand and led him into a house made of gold and filled with ornaments of gold. She said to him, "Do not be sad. Your hardships are over."[87] Pérez de Ayala entered that house on 5 August 1566 at the age of sixty-two.

Fernando de Loaces became the next archbishop of Valencia, but died seven months later. Juan de Ribera took over on 21 March 1569 and remained at his post for forty-two years until he passed away on 6 January 1611 or twenty-one months after Philip III issued the decree on 9 April 1609 to expel the Moriscos from the Iberian Peninsula.

Juan de Ribera

Ribera and Spanish Kings

The life and ministry of Archbishop Juan de Ribera (1532–1611) overlapped the reigns of three kings—Charles (1517–56), Philip II (1556–98) and Philip III (1598–1621)—and coincided with the rise of the Spanish Empire, the convening of the Council of Trent, the maximum extension of Spanish global dominance, and the implementation of the reforms of the Council of Trent.[88]

---

86. Pérez de Ayala, *Vida*, 105.
87. Pérez de Ayala, *Vida*, 24–25.
88. Robres Lluch, *San Juan de Ribera*, 6.

Ribera, the Man

Ribera was born in Sevilla sometime in December of 1532. His father's ancestry included members of the Spanish royalty—Queen Isabella the Catholic, Kings Alfonso X, Alfonso XI, Charles and Philip II of Castilla and King Ferdinand V the Catholic of Aragón.[89] On 22 May 1543, Ribera received his clerical tonsure at the Iglesia de San Esteban in Sevilla from the bishop of Morocco, Sebastián de Obregón.[90] Ribera entered the University of Salamanca in the summer of 1544 to study canon law (but four years later changed to arts) and in 1551 enrolled in the bachelor of arts program in theology.

Comfort to Asceticism

Unlike Pérez de Ayala who suffered financial hardship during his years as a university student, Ribera lived comfortably in the house that his father provided for him with a butler. Although[91] Ribera came from a privileged family, he was known for his generosity to the poor, admiration for the ecclesiastical life, devotion to the Eucharist, and passion for Christ.[92]

Ribera often gave the proceeds from the sales of his books and jewelry as alms then retired to a hermitage. During Lent, he fasted for three days and only ate bread and drank water. The most vivid picture that Ribera's university classmates had of him was seeing him either going to or coming from classes. He maintained this same discipline even after he became the archbishop of Valencia. In the summer, he went to a convent of the barefoot to experience the same ascetic life as the rest of the residents. At other times, he went to more remote convents with three servants to prepare and serve food. Ribera led such an exemplary life that students engaged in unwholesome conversation would desist as soon they saw him coming towards them. Ribera was easily displeased with the slightest sign of dishonesty. One of the professors made the regular comment that the Lord had sent Ribera to Salamanca to reform its university. Faculty motivated students who performed below par by pointing them to Ribera as a student who did not rest on the laurels of his family name, but one who worked hard.[93]

---

89. Robres Lluch, *San Juan de Ribera*, 5.
90. Robres Lluch, *San Juan de Ribera*, 15.
91. Robres Lluch, *San Juan de Ribera*, 25.
92. Robres Lluch, *San Juan de Ribera*, 15.
93. Robres Lluch, *San Juan de Ribera*, 27–28.

Pérez de Ayala and Ribera

Both Ribera and Pérez de Ayala occupy a place of honor among those who studied or taught at the University of Salamanca. Ribera was highly regarded in the fields of theology, canon law, and sacred scripture.[94] His appetite for learning continued after he finished his studies. By the time he passed away in 1611, his library consisted of 2,651 volumes, eighteen incunables, and works of theology, canon, law, liturgy, church fathers, humanism, hagiography, sermons, and languages.[95]

Pérez de Ayala also collected books and manuscripts. Some of them—eighteen Latin manuscripts and fifty Latin books—were bequeathed to the library of Philip II at El Escorial. The manuscripts—such as the *Comentario al Apocalipsis* written by the Beato de Liébana in the middle of the tenth century, a Bible of the Visigoth period, the works of Pedro Pascual against the sect of Muhammad, and the tenth-century *Códice Hispalense* on the councils of Toledo—were of exceptional quality. Another part of the collection—forty nine Hebrew, Latin and Spanish codices—became the property of the convent of Santiago in Uclés.[96] More information about Ribera is available in Chapter 11 of the present book.

---

94. Robres Lluch, *San Juan de Ribera*, 46.
95. Robres Lluch, *San Juan de Ribera*, 40.
96. Andrés, "La biblioteca de un teólogo renacentista," 99–111.

Chapter 3

Overview of the *Catecismo*

Introduction

THIS CHAPTER—AN OVERVIEW OF the *Catecismo* and thirteen other catechisms and polemical treatises published over a period of 103 years—highlights the features of the *Catecismo* that could have lead archbishop Juan de Ribera to publish it. We begin this overview by either imagining ourselves flying high on a hot air balloon to get a broad yet clear picture of the land below or picturing Ribera in Valencia trying to decide which catechism or polemical treatise could help his efforts to evangelize the Moriscos in Spain. All fourteen works are spread out on a table in front of him or pinned to a wall of his spacious office. He might have asked six questions: (1) What was the year of publication? (2) What was happening historically in Spain at the time publication? (3) To whom was the catechism or polemical treatise written? (4) What was the overall content of these works? (5) What portion of the overall content did each work emphasize? (6) How was the content disseminated?

Year of Publication[1]

> 1496. *Breve doctrina y enseñanza que ha de saber y poner en obra todo cristiano y cristiana. En la cual deben ser enseñados, los mozuelos primero que en otra cosa.*[2] Hernando de Talavera (b. 1428/1430-d. 1507).

---

1. Unless otherwise indicated, dates of publication are from Thomas, David, and John Chesworth, eds. *Christian-Muslim Relations: A Bibliographical History*.

2. Brief doctrine and teaching that every Christian must know and practice. Children ought to be taught first and what should they learn above everything else.

1500. *Instrucción de la vida cristiana compuesta para los Moriscos nuevamente convertidos.*[3] Antonio García de Villalpando (b. before 1475–d. 1513).

1515. *Confusión o confutación de la secta mahomética y del Alcorán.*[4] Juan Andrés (b. ca. 1450–d. after 1515).

1527. *Doctrina Cristiana.* Pedro Ramiro de Alba (b. ca. 1480–d. 1528).

1532. *Libro llamado Antialcorano.*[5] Bernardo Pérez de Chinchón (b. 1488/1493–d. 1552 or before).

1535. *Diálogos Christianos contra la secta mahomética y contra la pertinacia de los judíos.*[6] Bernardo Pérez de Chinchón.

1555. *Confutación del alcorán y secta mahometana, sacado de sus propios libros, y de la vida del mismo Mahoma.*[7] Lope Obregón (b. ca. the last decade of the fifteenth century/first third of the sixteenth century–d. second half of the sixteenth century).

1566. *Doctrina Cristiana en lengua arábiga y castellana para la instrucción de los moriscos del Ilustrísimo Sr. D. Martín de Ayala, Arzobispo de Valencia.*[8] Martín Pérez de Ayala (b. 1503/1504–d. 1566).

1568. *Catecismo provechoso.* Alonso de Orozco (b. 1500–d. 1591).

1586. *Catecheses mystagogicae pro aduenis ex secta Mahometana. Ad parochos & potentates.*[9] Pedro Guerra de Lorca (b. early sixteenth century–d. 1597).

1588. *Catecismo del Sacromonte.* Anonymous.

1591. *Doctrina Cristiana.* Jerónimo de Ripalda (b. 1536–d. 1618).

Before 1592.[10] *Doctrina cristiana.* Gaspar Astete (b. 1537–d. 1601).

1599. *Catecismo.* Martín Pérez de Ayala.

3. Instruction on the Christian life written for newly converted Moriscos.
4. Confusion or confutation of the sect of Muhammad and the Qur'an.
5. The book known as against the Qur'an.
6. Christian dialogues against the sect of Muhammad and against the obstinacy of the Jews.
7. Refutation of the Qur'an and the sect of Muhammad taken from their own books and the life of Muhammad.
8. Christian doctrine in Arabic and Castilian for the instruction of the Moriscos.
9. Catechisms of instruction for those coming from the sect of Muhammad. To pastors and authorities.
10. Resines, "Lectura crítica de los catecismos de Astete y Ripalda. Primera parte," 73–131.

OVERVIEW OF THE *CATECISMO*

The year of publication positions each catechism and polemical treatise within the framework of key events between Christians and Moriscos in sixteenth-century Spain. Some seventy-seven years had passed from the time the soldiers of Queen Isabella and King Ferdinand conquered Muslim Granada in 1492 until Ribera became archbishop of Valencia in 1569—barely three years after Pérez de Ayala had passed away while holding that same office. Hernando de Talavera became Granada's first archbishop in 1493 after his appointment by Queen Isabella and King Ferdinand. There were high hopes when Talavera began his mission. He encouraged his priests to learn Arabic. Muslims reciprocated his respect for them and held him in high regard. Some were beginning to embrace the Catholic faith, but Queen Isabella and King Ferdinand felt that Talavera's gentle approach was not up to their expectations. In 1499, they turned to Francisco Jiménez Cisneros, archbishop of Toledo. However, his aggressiveness alienated Muslims.[11]

Key Historical Events

The information below aligns the catechisms and polemical treatises with some of the key events in the history between Christians and Moriscos after Cisneros took over Talavera's job. This alignment offers a glimpse of Spain's history during the time when these works were published and helps identify additional distinctive features of the *Catecismo*.

1496. Talavera publishes *Breve doctrina y enseñanza*.

1499.** Cisneros arrives in Granada and launches his campaign to evangelize Moriscos.[12]

1500–1502.*[13] Mudéjars in Castilla convert.

1500. Villalpando publishes *Instruction de la vida cristiana*. Muslims in Albaicín rebel against policies directed at them.

1501.** A *pragmática* orders Moriscos in Granada to receive baptism.

1502.** A *pragmática* orders the conversion or expulsion of mudéjares living in the Kingdom of Castilla.

1515. Juan Andrés publishes *Confusión o confutación*.

---

11. Fredericks, "Introduction," 3–4.
12. Years with two asterisks are from Bernabé Pons, *Los moriscos*, 185–87.
13. Years with an asterisk are from Domínguez Ortiz and Vincent, *Historia de los moriscos*, 17.

1516.** Cisneros issues a decree requesting Moriscos to refrain from their cultural practices, but it is suspended.

1521.** War of the Germanías in Valencia. Mudéjares in Valencia are threatened to receive baptism.

1524.** Pope Clement VII agrees that Muslims who have not been baptized can be expelled. His bull *Idcirco nostris* frees Charles from the commitments to respect the custom and traditions of Muslim living in Aragón.

1525.** A junta of theologians and jurists in Madrid rules that the baptism of Moriscos are valid because it is uncertain that violence was exerted on them. Charles issues a charter ordering Muslims in Valencia to convert or go into exile.

1526.** Mudéjares from Valencia rebel in Benaguacil and Espadán. An edict prohibits Granadan Moriscos from speaking their language and following their customs and practices. Moriscos of the Crown of Aragón convert. Charles' stay in Granada.[14]

1527. Pedro Ramiro de Alba publishes *Doctrina Christiana*.

1528.** Cortes de Monzón lays the foundation for the preaching to Moriscos in churches.

1532. Bernardo Pérez de Chinchón publishes *Antialcorano*.

1535. Chinchón publishes *Diálogos Christianos*.

1554.** The Synod of Guadix launches a series of measures to remove any cultural sign that distinguishes Moriscos from Christians.

1555–56.* Muslims show renewed interest in the Western Mediterranean. Charles abdicates.

1555. Lope Obregón publishes *Confutación del alcorán y secta mahometana*.

1566. Pérez de Ayala publishes *Doctrina Cristiana*.

1567.** A *pragmática* permanently forbids Moriscos from following any customs or traditions that could be perceived as Islamic.

1568. Alonso de Orozco publishes *Catecismo provechoso*. Armed uprisings in numerous villages in the Alpujarras region of Granada. War of Granada erupts.

---

14. Domínguez Ortiz and Vincent, *Historia de los moriscos*, 17.

1570.** Uprisings in the region of the Alpujarras crushed. Moriscos from Granada are deported to different territories of Castilla. Moriscos in Valencia are ordered to relinquish their weapons.

1582.** *Junta* in Lisboa makes an official request to Philip II to expel the Moriscos from Spain.

1586. Pedro Guerra de Lorca publishes *Catecheses mystagogicae*.

1588. Publication of the anonymous *Catecismo del Sacromonte*.

1591. Jerónimo de Ripalda publishes *Doctrina Cristiana*.

1592. Gaspar Astete publishes *Doctrina cristiana* before 1592.

1595.** Philip II rejects the idea of setting up a Chair of Arabic at the University of Valencia.

1598.** Peace between Spain and France. Death of Philip II.[15] Philip III becomes King of Spain.

1599. Archbishop Ribera publishes Pérez de Ayala's *Catecismo*.

1609-14.* General expulsion of the Moriscos from Spain.

These fourteen catechisms and polemical treatises were published over a period of 103 years characterized by tension and fights between Moriscos and royal and church authorities. There might have been short periods of tranquility, but overall this was a time when all parties were at odds with each other. Even so, the process of evangelizing Moriscos and teaching them Catholic doctrine continued. Some Moriscos did embrace the Catholic faith against all odds. However, by the time Ribera became the archbishop of Valencia the fruit was not commensurate to the efforts poured into the task of attracting Moriscos to move away from the religion of their ancestors and assimilating them into the rest of Spanish society.

Sometime towards the end of the reign of Philip II and the beginning of Philip III's reign, debate had already begun regarding how to deal with the Moriscos' fierce allegiance to their religious beliefs and practices. One group advocated giving them more time and continuing the evangelistic mission towards them. Another group proposed a more dramatic alternative; that is, expulsion from the peninsula. Ribera belonged to the latter group. However, there is the possibility that he might have had a change of heart as evidenced by his decision to publish the *Catecismo*. It is beyond the scope of the present book to explore his direct or indirect involvement in the program of expulsion.

---

15. Domínguez Ortiz and Vincent, *Historia de los moriscos*, 17.

The catechisms and polemical treatises were not written in a historical vacuum, but in an era characterized by discord and warfare that might have heightened the value of the *Catecismo* in Ribera's estimation. If relationships between Christians and Moriscos were already strained during the time when Pérez de Ayala was alive, they were worse towards the end of the sixteenth century. If Ribera was committed to the task of bringing new sheep into his fold, he would need a resource such as a catechism, a polemical treatise or a combination of both that would repair instead of widen the gap between those who wanted their neighbors to adopt the Catholic faith and those who resisted.

The year of publication and historical context raise four questions that help uncover other features that might have made the Catecismo attractive for Ribera to publish it.

Addressee. Who is the audience, the recipient or the user of the catechism or polemical treatise? If the catechism or polemical treatise is a dialogue, to whom is the priest talking?

Content. What is the content of the catechisms and polemical treatises? Is it apologetics, polemics, knowledge or *praxis*? These four terms can be defined as follows:

Apologetics: The defense of Christ and his religion.

Polemics: The critique of Muḥammad and his religion.

Knowledge: What everyone—not just one baptized into the Catholic faith—should know about the religion of Christ.

Praxis: How converts to the religion of Christ should behave to show that they are good Catholics.

Area of Focus. On which of the four types of content—apologetics, polemics, knowledge or *praxis*—does the catechism or polemical treatise focus? The answer depends on who is addressee.

Method. The authors used one of two methods to present the content of their work. One, a dialogue between the author, the Moor or the recently baptized Morisco. Second, a presentation resembling a lecture or a sermon where interaction between the author and the audience is nonexistent or minimal.

The answers to the four questions are:

Content Arranged by Addressee

Breve doctrina y enseñanza. Recently baptized residents of the Kingdom of Granada who previously followed the sect of Muhammad. (Some of the catechisms and polemical treatises use "the sect of Muhammad" or

OVERVIEW OF THE *CATECISMO* 37

"the religion of Muhammad" instead of "Islam." They also use the term "Moor" or "followers of the sect of Muhammad" instead of "Muslim.")

Confusión o confutación. Followers of the sect of Muhammad who are indifferent, hostile or resistant to the religion of Christ. (Some of the catechisms and polemical treatises use "the religion of Christ," "the Christian religion" or "the evangelical religion" instead of "Christianity." The expression "follower of the religion of Christ" is used instead of "Christian.")

Antialcorano. Canons, rectors, vicars, and all church leaders responsible for overseeing newly baptized in the Kingdoms of Aragón, Granada, and Valencia.

Diálogos Christianos. Joseph Zumilla, Pérez de Chinchón's Arabic teacher.

Confutación del alcorán y secta mahometana. Priests in Ávila in the Kingdom of Castilla and León responsible for instructing newly baptized Moriscos and individuals interested in understanding the sect of Muhammad.

Doctrina Cristiana (Pérez de Ayala). Newly baptized Moriscos.

Catecismo provechoso. All newly baptized, particularly those from the Kingdom of Aragón. A man by the name of "Felipe" who became a Christian after having followed the sect of Muhammad for thirty years.

Doctrina Christiana (Alba). Recently baptized and previously of the sect of Muhammad.

Catecheses mystagogicae. Presbyters and pastors responsible for the instruction of new converts in the Kingdom of Granada.

Catecismo del Sacromonte. A recently baptized Morisco being trained on how to present the religion of Christ to members of his family and acquaintances who are still followers of the sect of Muhammad.

Doctrina Cristiana (Ripalda). A child by the name of "Francisco" whose previous religious background is unknown.

Doctrina cristiana (Astete). All Christians.

Catecismo. A Moor who travelled from the Berber region to Spain in search of Pérez de Ayala to discuss becoming a Christian.

Content Arranged by Area of Focus

Breve doctrina y enseñanza. Knowledge and *praxis*.

Confusión o confutación. Polemics.

Antialcorano. Apologetics and polemics.

Diálogos Christianos. Apologetics.

Confutación del alcorán y secta mahometana. Polemics.

Doctrina Cristiana (Pérez de Ayala). Knowledge and *praxis*.

Catecismo provechoso. Knowledge, *praxis*, and brief apologetics and polemics.

Doctrina Christiana (Alba). Knowledge, *praxis*, and brief polemics.

Catecheses mystagogicae. Polemics.

Catecismo del Sacromonte. Knowledge, *praxis*, apologetics, and polemics.

Doctrina Cristiana (Ripalda). Knowledge and *praxis*.

Doctrina cristiana (Astete). Knowledge and *praxis*.

Catecismo. Pre-apologetics, apologetics, polemics, knowledge, and *praxis*.

Content Arranged by Method

Breve doctrina y enseñanza. Lectures or sermons.

Confusión o confutación. Lectures. Andrés asks questions, but the Moor is not given the opportunity to respond.

Antialcorano. Sermons.

Diálogos Christianos. Dialogues.

Confutación del alcorán y secta mahometana. Lectures or sermons.

Doctrina Cristiana (Pérez de Ayala). Lectures or sermons.

Catecismo provechoso. Dialogues.

Doctrina Christiana (Alba). Lectures or sermons.

Catecheses mystagogicae. Sermons.

Catecismo del Sacromonte. Dialogues.

Doctrina Cristiana (Ripalda). Presentation in the form of questions and answers as if the Christian were taking an exam.

Doctrina cristiana (Astete). Presentation in the form of very short questions requiring the respondent to provide short answers.

Catecismo. Dialogues.

Preliminary Observations

In terms of Addressee, the *Catecismo* and Juan Andrés' *Confusión o Confutación* are the only ones whose Addressee is a Muslim who has yet to be baptized. But, there is a difference between these two Muslims for no two Muslims are alike. (Chapter 5 discusses further.) The Addressee determines the Type of Content covered in the catechism or polemical treatise. Not only is the *Catecismo* the only catechism and polemical treatise that covers all four types of content—apologetics, polemics, knowledge, and *praxis*—but it also has content that can be classified as "pre-apologetics." (Chapter 4 discusses further.) The scope of the content in the *Catecismo* is considerable relative to the other works. It is not surprising that Ribera wrote in his cover letter to the *Catecismo* that the catechism "has everything needed to instruct an infidel on the faith of the gospel, particularly one who has followed the sect of Muhammad." In terms of Method, the *Catecismo*, *Confusión o confutación*, and Chinchón's *Diálogos Christianos* are the only ones that use dialogues. Ribera wrote in his cover letter to the *Catecismo* that a dialogue is "the clearest and most distinct way to teach when the disciple has questions and the teacher has answers. This is how many do it today as it was done in ancient times by doctors to teach truth and confute lies." Although the *Catecismo*, *Confusión o confutación*, and *Diálogos Christianos* use this same method, there is a difference among them. (Chapter 5 discusses further.) The *Catecismo* can be viewed as an actual conversation between a Moor and a teacher. The former asks a wide range of probing questions—even challenging ones—which the latter seems pleased to answer (and in excruciating detail on more than one occasion). Juan Andrés also asks questions in *Confusión o confutación*, but rarely gives the other side an opportunity to answer.

The following inspection of the Content (apologetics, polemics, knowledge or *praxis*) and the Area of Focus is like guiding our imaginary hot air balloon down closer to the ground to find other qualities in the *Catecismo* that might have lead Ribera to publish it. This inspection neither compares the *Catecismo* with the other works nor compares the works amongst themselves. (Chapter 5 discusses further.) A comparison at this stage would get us lost walking around the trees without first knowing how big is the forest. The section below includes brief biographical details of the authors (except Pérez de Ayala).

Martín Pérez de Ayala

The *Catecismo* (1599) is a dialogue between a Moor who travelled from the Berber region of North Africa to Spain in search of Pérez de Ayala to discuss becoming a Christian. The content of the *Catecismo*—Book One (twenty-five dialogues) and Book Two (forty-six dialogues in five parts)—can be organized as follows:

Book One. Pre-Apologetics

Who is God and how is he one (Dialogue III). He rules the universe (Dialogue IV).

What is man and the perfection and immortality of his soul (Dialogue V). Man's final destination is God and the true religion is the path to God (Dialogue VI). Natural light cannot guide man to the path of true religion (Dialogue VII). Original sin and the corruption of man's nature (Dialogue VIII). The corruption of man's nature and the cause and effects of sin (Dialogue IX). There is only one path to God (Dialogue X).

Philosophy (Dialogue XI) and Jewish law (Dialogue XII) cannot be the paths to God.

Book One. Apologetics

The Christian religion is the only path to God (Dialogue XX).

The gospel is true and excellent because of its preaching, its Scriptures, and its effects (Dialogue XXI); the dignity of Christ (Dialogue XXII); Christ who is the promised Messiah and true God (Dialogue XXIII); the miracles of Christ (Dialogue XXIV); and the virtues in those who obey the gospel (Dialogue XXV).

Book One. Polemics

The life of Muhammad (Dialogue XIII). Mistakes, lies, and fables in the Qur'an (Dialogue XV). Contradictions in the Qur'an (Dialogue XVI). The sect of Muhammad cannot be the path to God (Dialogue XIII) because its final destination for man is false (Dialogue XIV) and its doctrine is bad (Dialogue XVII). The sect of Muhammad is false because its followers can mask their true religious convictions (Dialogue XVIII) and because of the way it is preached (Dialogue XIX).

Book Two. Knowledge and *praxis*

Faith (Dialogues I–IX). Hope and its Annexes (Dialogues I–VI). Charity and Works (Dialogues I–IX). The Sacraments and Their Use (Dialogues I–X). Obedience (Dialogues I–XII).

Hernando de Talavera

Hernando de Talavera was born in Talavera de la Reina between 1428 and 1430. He studied calligraphy in Barcelona (ca. 1442) and arts and theology at the University of Salamanca (ca. 1444). In 1460, he was ordained a priest. He taught moral theology at Salamanca between 1463 and 1466 and entered the Order of Saint Jerome in 1466. In the early 1470s, he became confessor and counsellor to Queen Isabella of Castilla and, for a time, to King Ferdinand of Aragón. In 1492, they appointed Talavera to be the first archbishop of Granada. Under Talavera's leadership, Granada became a "laboratory" for new approaches to attracting new converts, teaching them the tenets of the Catholic faith, and acculturating them to live together with Christians. Talavera encouraged his priests to learn Arabic and translated catechisms into Arabic to help people understand them. However, the wish of Queen Isabella and King Ferdinand for more tangible results from Talavera's soft strategy led to their decision in 1499 to send the archbishop of Toledo—Francisco Jiménez de Cisneros—to Granada who then proceeded to implement a campaign of forced conversions.[16]

The content of *Breve doctrina y enseñanza* (1496) can be divided into:

Knowledge

The Apostles' Creed, the Lord's Prayer, Hail Mary, Hail Holy Queen, and the Ten Commandments.

---

16. Iannuzi, "Hernando de Talavera," 60–66.

Praxis

The Sign of the Cross, the Mass, Easter, Communion, the Sacrament of Confirmation, Deeds of Mercy, Lent, Tithes, Vows, Sacred Objects, and Confession.

Antonio García de Villalpando

Antonio García de Villalpando was born sometime before 1475. He has been described as the "humblest among the chaplains of the great [royal] chapels." In 1498, the archbishop of Toledo—Francisco Jiménez de Cisneros—appointed Villalpando to be his vicar general and representative in the archdiocese. Villalpando wrote *Instrucción de la vida cristiana* (1500) when Cisneros was implementing a campaign to evangelize Muslims in Granada. No extant copies of the catechism are known. However, Francisco Méndez would have seen a copy because he noted in *Tipografía española* that the title of *Instrucción* revealed its intention: "*Instrucción de la vida cristiana*, composed for the newly converted Moriscos by order of the Cardinal Archbishop Jiménez, by his visitor general and canon of Toledo, Dr Antonio García de Villalpando, printed there by Pedro Hagenbach, German, on 25 February 1500. Book in 4° of 57 pages." *Instrucción* was written at a crucial time in Queen Isabella and King Ferdinand's efforts to draw Muslims into the Catholic faith. They had set aside Talavera's soft policy in favor of Cisnero's more aggressive methods. However, this led to violent Muslim uprisings in Albaicín (1499) and Alpujarras (1500). As a way forward, Cisneros commissioned Villalpando to write *Instrucción* and had it printed with the intention of distributing it widely.[17]

Juan Andrés

In the Prologue of *Confusión o confutación* (1515), Andrés introduces himself as "*quondam alfaquí* of Játiva, now a Christian and a priest because of divine goodness"[18] and a "Catholic and faithful Christian."[19] He describes what happened in 1487 when he was at the Cathedral of Valencia on the day of "Our Lady of August" listening to the preaching of Juan Marqués, the preacher and confessor of King Ferdinand: "Suddenly the

---

17. Carrasco Manchado, "Antonio García de Villalpando," 49–53.
18. Ruiz García, *Juan Andrés*, 87.
19. Ruiz García, *Juan Andrés*, 93.

resplendent rays of divine light and the end[20] that I mentioned previously, removed and cleared the darkness of my understanding and opened the eyes of my soul. And because I understood that the Muhammadan sect was perverse and bad, it was clear to me that salvation, the end for which man was created, is obtained only through the holy law of Christ."[21] Andrés spoke of his days prior to leaving Islam as a "lengthy time of being lost and astray from the truth."[22]

After Andrés became a Christian, he received baptism and changed his name from Ibn 'Abd Allah to Juan Andrés in honor of the Galilean fishermen who became followers of Christ. He also resigned his post as the village *alfaquí*, which he assumed after his father passed away. Andrés began his ministry to Muslims in Valencia then moved to Granada and Aragón at the behest of King Ferdinand and Queen Isabella. While in Aragón he translated the Qur'an and the six books of the *sunna* from Arabic to Aragonese at the request of Martín García, bishop of Barcelona and Inquisitor of Aragón. Andrés wrote *Confusión o confutación* to collect "some of the fabulous fictions, plain lies, willful deceptions, senseless words, stupidities, mad words, blasphemies, tactless words, absurdities, fabrications, and contradictions"[23] in the Qur'an. *Confusión o confutación* had three objectives: to show that there is no basis for believing that the law of Muhammad is true; to help "ignorant Moors" see that no wise person believes in Muhammad; and to lead everyone to "the holy law and true end" they were created for.[24]

The content of the twelve chapters of *Confusión o confutación* can be ordered as follows:

Polemics

The foundation of the sect of Muhammad: Muhammad (Chapter 1). The Qur'an (Chapter 2). The *sunna* (Chapter 3).

The Qur'an: It is not the word of God (Chapter 4). Absurdities and falsehoods (Chapter 5). Contradictions (Chapter 10).

Muhammad: Scandals (Chapter 6). Wives (Chapter 7). Al-Buraq (Chapter 8).

The final destination of those who follow the sect of Muhammad: The promised paradise (Chapter 9).

20. Ruiz García, *Juan Andrés*, 88.
21. Ruiz García, *Juan Andrés*, 89–90.
22. Ruiz García, *Juan Andrés*, 90.
23. Ruiz García, *Juan Andrés*, 91.
24. Ruiz García, *Juan Andrés*, 92.

The foundation of the sect of Muhammad attests to the superiority of the Christian faith: Jesus Christ according to the Qur'an and the *sunna* (Chapter 11). The growth of the sect of Muhammad (Chapter 12).

Pedro Ramiro de Alba

Pedro Ramiro de Alba was born around 1480 in Alba de Tormes in Salamanca. He studied under Hernando de Talavera in Granada (c. 1492–95); became Granada's fifth archbishop in 1526 after Charles heard him preach and nominated him to the post; and wrote *Doctrina Christiana* in 1527 after Charles put him in charge of instructing Muslims in the Catholic faith. That same year, Ramiro de Alba established courses of study that laid the foundation for the establishment of the University of Granada and founded the College of San Miguel for *morisquillos* (Morisco children).[25]

The content of the four parts of *Doctrina Christiana* can be arranged as follows:

Polemics

New converts must not believe in Muhammad and the Qur'an (Part 4). What new converts must not do (Part 4).

Knowledge and *praxis*

The Creed (Part 1). What Christians must know (Part 2). The Ten Commandments (Part 3).

Part 4 is the most original of the four parts. There is no sign of contempt for Islam, but a warm-hearted appeal to Muslims to change their beliefs and practices.[26]

Bernardo Pérez de Chinchón

Bernardo Pérez—whose parents were Jewish converts—was born in Chinchón, Castilla at the end of the fifteenth century. He studied at the University of Alcalá de Henares and became involved in evangelizing

---

25. Resines, *El Catecismo de Pedro Ramiro de Alba*, 21–22.
26. Thomas and Chesworth, "Pedro Ramírez de Alba," 94.

Moriscos in the Kingdom of Valencia after publishing *Antialcorano* (1532) and *Diálogos Christianos* (1534).²⁷

The content of the twenty-six chapters in *Antialcorano* can be classified as follows:

Apologetics

The sonship of Christ (Sermon 18). The humanity and divinity of Christ (Sermon 21). The Holy Spirit (Sermon 19). The Trinity (Sermon 18). The gospel is perfect (Sermon 13), good (Sermon 23), and agrees with natural and divine reason (Sermon 26).

Polemics

Muhammad: Compared with Christ (Sermon 15). His false revelation (Sermon 16). Liar, sinner, false prophet (Sermon 14).

The teachings of the law of Muhammad: Lack what is required for a law to be good (Sermon 8). Paradise consists of bodily delights (Sermon 9). Circumcision is still valid (Sermons 10 and 11). Polygamy, fornication, and ownership of female slaves condoned (Sermon 20). War is justified (Sermon 24). Mistakes on the sonship of Christ and the Trinity (Sermon 18). The humanity and divinity of Christ denied (Sermon 21).

The Qur'an and the *sunna*: Consist of Muhammad's lies (Sermons 17 and 22).

The content of the seven dialogues in *Diálogos Christianos* can be categorized as follows:

Apologetics

The Christian Scriptures: Manifest the truth of the Christian law (Dialogue 2). Divine and natural reason show that the law of the prophets were true and complete when Christ came (Dialogue 4). Christians neither falsified nor corrupted the law of the prophets (Dialogue 5). Prove the Christian law (Dialogues 6, 7). Testimonies from Christians verify the truth of the Christian law (Dialogue 3).

---

27. Pons Fuster, "Bernardo Pérez de Chinchón," 119–24.

Polemics

Why the Moor is wrong to reject the following Christian beliefs (Dialogue 1): God is one in essence and three in persons; Christ's death, resurrection, and ascension; circumcision is invalid; the apostles and evangelists wrote the truth about Christ; and Muhammad was not a prophet sent by God to give a law (the Qur'an) to the world.

The Christian Scriptures: Demonstrate that the law of Muhammad is deceptive and false (Dialogue 2) and disprove the law of Muhammad (Dialogues 6 and 7).

Lope Obregón

Little is known about Lope Obregón. He was born probably between the last decade of the fifteenth century and first third of the sixteenth century. As priest of the Basílica of San Vicente in Ávila in Castilla and Aragón, he worked under bishop Diego de Álava y Esquivel, who, after returning from the first period of the Council of Trent (1545-49), urged his priests to evangelize and instruct the Moriscos. Obregón followed Juan Andrés by also considering the Qur'an to be divided into four books: the second division starting with Book 7, the third at Book 19, and the last one at Book 38. However, Obregón took some *suras* out of order and claimed that the fourth division consisted of 175 chapters or five fewer than Andrés' division. Obregón also followed Andrés' practice of providing the Arabic of his Qur'anic citations in phonetic translation into Latin letters—an uncommon practice in polemical works of the sixteenth century except for Juan Martín Figuerola's *Lumbre de la fé contra la secta mahometana*[28] (1518-21). Obregón—like Andrés—also believed that quoting the Qur'an in Arabic could convince his audience that evidence of Christian truth can be found in the Qur'an.[29] The content of the fifteen chapters of *Confutación del alcorán y secta mahometama* can be ordered as follows:

Polemics

Muhammad: Birth, ancestry, and profession (Chapter 1). Overpowered by the devil (Chapter 4). Death (Chapter 1).

---

28. *The light of faith against the Muhammadan sect.*
29. Szpiech, "Lope Obregón," 169-75.

Muhammad's reaction to his critics: Escaped Mecca (Chapter 5); quarreled with the Jews of Medina (Chapter 6); claimed to have travelled to heaven (Chapter 7); condemned his critics to hell (Chapter 8); promised paradise to his followers (Chapter 7); raised an army to attack the Medinans (Chapter 8); falsified a miracle (Chapter 8); killed his critics (Chapter 8); betrayed the Jews of Medina and killed them (Chapter 9); and attacked the Persians and Jerusalem (Chapter 10).

After Muhammad died: Internecine wars among his successors (Chapter 11).

The Qur'an: Contradictions (Chapter 5). Lies and more contradictions (Chapter 13). Contradictions between the Qur'an and the law of Muhammad (Chapter 14). Fabulous utterances, lies, prophecies, and revelations (Chapter 15). Compilation of the Qur'an (Chapter 11). Muhammad's Jewish secretaries Sergius (Chapter 5) and Abdia (Chapter 9).

The *sunna*: What is the *sunna* and how it was compiled (Chapter 12).

The Sect of Muhammad: Heaven and earth's reaction (Chapter 1).

Martín Pérez de Ayala

The content of *Doctrina Cristiana* (1566) is entirely knowledge and *praxis* and can be grouped as follows:

The prayers that every Christian must know (while making the Sign of the Cross, the Lord's Prayer, Hail Mary, the Creed, Hail Holy Queen, and the Confession); the Ten Commandments; the six commandments of the church; the seven mortal sins; the seven works of mercy for the body; the seven works of mercy for the soul; the seven sacraments of the church; the three theological and the four cardinal virtues; the prayers offered during Mass; and a summary of the ceremonies and positions of the body during Mass.

Pérez de Ayala in his introduction to the *Doctrina Cristiana* describes it as "esta breve Summa de la doctrina Christiana" (or "this summary of the Christian doctrine"). It is short—2,753 words—compared to the *Catecismo*, which has at least 96,776 words.[30] The shortest section of *Doctrina Cristiana*—"los pecados mortales son siete" (or "the seven mortal sins")—has twelve words. The longest section—"las oraciones que se han de dezir en la yglesia y en la missa" (or "the prayers that ought to be said in church and in the mass")—has 538 words.

---

30. This number is less than the actual total number of words because Dialogues III, V and IX in Part Five of Book Two of the digitized copy of the *Catecismo* are incomplete.

The introduction of *Doctrina Cristiana* sets the tone for new converts to receive the teaching of the Catholic faith. Pérez de Ayala addresses them as "hijos muy amados en Christo" ("beloved children in Christ") and refers to himself as "vuestro pastor y padre espiritual" ("your pastor and spiritual father"). His statement "que de todas entrañas dessea vuestra salvacion" ("I wish for your salvation with all my heart . . .") reveals his tender heart towards his spiritual children.

Pérez de Ayala had *Doctrina Cristiana* translated into "the vulgar Arabic of this Kingdom" so that new converts who did not understand Spanish could still benefit from being instructed "in the faith and the Christian religion." They were to "learn with diligence and humility, charming understanding to faith, in the service of God." He mentions that he is preparing another catechism—or "mayor instruction"—to inform the faith of new converts and settle their doubts. This other catechism is written in Spanish, but he will send catechists and preachers who knew Arabic so well that new converts would not miss anything from their instruction. The introduction concludes with a blessing: "God enlighten your understanding so that you may benefit from *La Doctrina*, believing and practicing what it teaches you, and grow roots in the church like new plants grafted in Jesus Christ our Lord. He will give you his grace. Amen."[31]

Alonso de Orozco

Alonso de Orozco was born on 17 August 1500 in Oropesa, Toledo. He studied law at the University of Salamanca when the city was the meeting place for Castilian nobility and the university was the cultural center and oracle of Europe. He was the royal preacher in the courts of Charles and Philip II and confessor to Doña Juana, infanta of Spain, sister of Philip II, and governor of Portugal when her father Charles was absent.[32] Orozco was responsible for the foundation of Augustinian monasteries for both friars and nuns. Although always welcome at royal events, he chose to live in austere poverty (eating only one daily meal at midday and sleeping no more than three hours a day) and spent his time serving those who suffered the most.[33] Pope John Paul II canonized him on 19 May 2002.[34] The

---

31. Pérez de Ayala, *Doctrina Cristiana*, 2–3.
32. Aparicio López, "Alonzo de Orozco," 528.
33. "Alonso de Orozco: Biography (1500–1591)."
34. Aparicio López, "Alonzo de Orozco," 530.

content of *Catecismo provechoso* (1568)—twenty-three chapters and the Lord's Prayer—can be catalogued as follows:[35]

Apologetics

The Christian law is true (Chapter II). The excellence of faith (Chapter IV).

Polemics

All sects are false (Chapter II). The Catholic faith condemns the sect of Muhammad (Chapter III).

Knowledge and *praxis*

Hope (Chapter V). Charity (Chapter VI). The Creed (Chapters VII-XVIII). The Ten Commandments (Chapters XIX-XX). The Five Commandments of the Church and The Seven Sacraments (Chapters XXI). The Seven Deadly Sins (Chapter XXIII). The Seven Works of Mercy (Chapter XXII). The Lord's Prayer (no chapter numbers are assigned after Chapter XXII).

Pedro Guerra de Lorca

Pedro Guerra de Lorca was born in Granada in the early sixteenth century. He was among the first to write about the ancient Christian identity of Granada. His excellent preaching abilities lead to his appointment as canon in the cathedral (1588). The violent uprising of Moriscos in the War of the Alpujarras (1568–71), prompted Philip II to order them to move to Castilla. While a group of ecclesiastical authorities favored their complete removal from the peninsula, another group advocated for the continuation of evangelistic efforts towards the Moriscos. *Catecheses mystagogicae* (1586) was written in this environment of tense debate between the two groups. Lorca felt that the church leaders in Castilla were ill-prepared to receive Moriscos and wrote the catechism to equip them. After the third and final session of the Council of Trent concluded in late 1563, the Catholic Church renewed its efforts to teach Moriscos. Lorca remained committed to the task of integrating Moriscos into Spanish society. His catechism did not just repeat the themes of other

---

35. The digital version of *Catecismo provechoso*—archived at www.hispana.mcu.es—is missing Chapters XVIII to XIX (pages 73–82).

catechisms of his era, but was innovative in combining the critique of Islam with the need to evangelize the Moriscos. He was a doctor of theology with an impressive grasp of theological, polemical, and legal works. He mastered Latin and could cite the Complutense Bible in Greek.[36]

Catecheses mystagogicae consists of sixteen catechisms of entirely polemical material written in Latin. The content of the catechisms—each one using one of the apostle Paul's epistles to address a specific custom of the Moors—can[37] be structured as follows:

The sect of Muhammad (Gal 4. 1st Catechism). Dress and language (Eph 4. 2nd Catechism). Invoking the devil (Col 2. 3rd Catechism). Circumcision (Gal 5. 4th Catechism). Fornication (Eph 5. 5th Catechism). Other rites (Rom 6. 6th Catechism). Superstition concerning foods (Rom 14. 7th Catechism). Communion with the Saracens (Gal 1. 8th Catechism). Making a proselyte from the sect of Muhammad (2 Cor 6. 9th Catechism). Teaching children (1 Cor 3. 10th Catechism). Catechizing the unlearned (2 Tim 4. 11th Catechism). Caring for the dead (1 Cor 15. 12th Catechism). Existing laws and laws to be promulgated (1 Tim 1. 13th Catechism). Punishing heretics (Titus 3. 14th Catechism). Spiritual government of proselytes (Titus 3. 15th Catechism). Temporal government of proselytes (Rom 13. 16th Catechism).

Catecismo del Sacromonte

It is impossible to know who wrote *Catecismo del Sacromonte*. The manuscript provides no hints. The author might have written it for his personal use, which could explain why he had not felt the need to add his name. It can be deduced that he was a Jesuit priest because the catechism uses Latin and cultured expressions, religious technical terms, and mode or argumentation, which are signs of someone who has received a scholastic clerical education.[38]

The paltry title *Catecismo del Sacromonte* is followed by a paragraph—too long to be a title—yet too short to be an introduction: "This catechism is useful for all faithful Christians because it is an all-encompassing and substantive declaration of Christian doctrine. It is especially very beneficial for Morisco new Christians, and for converting Moors because its style is a dispute in defense of our holy catholic faith against the sect of Muhammad. It is written as a dialogue between a priest and a Morisco he addresses as

---

36. Busic, "Pedro Guerra de Lorca," 250–58.
37. The present book uses the English translation in Busic, "Saving the Lost Sheep."
38. Resines, *Catecismo del Sacromonte*, 44.

novice."[39] The content of this catechism—written in Granada for Christians, Moors, and Moriscos[40]—can be assembled as follows:

Apologetics

The excellence of the Catholic Church (Chapters 11, 12 and 17). The mysteries of faith (Chapter 16, 18 and 19). The effects of faith (Chapter 17). The integrity of the Scriptures (Chapter 15).

Polemics

Eight reasons why Moors have no faith to live by (Chapter 2). Moors follow the sect of their ancestors (Chapter 3). The bad condition of the Moors (Chapter 4). The law of Muhammad is not the law of God (Chapter 5). Moors are condemned (Chapter 6). Moors have fought against Christians throughout history (Chapter 26). The greatness of the Catholic Church against Muhammad (Chapter 27). Muhammad violated all Ten Commandments (Chapters 31–41).

Knowledge

Original sin (Chapter 14). The law of sin (Chapter 29). Evil brought by sin (Chapter 30). Remedies against sin (Chapter 31). The Creation (Chapter 21). The Fall of Man (Chapter 21). The remedy for man's sin (Chapter 22).

Praxis

The Sacraments (Chapters 23–25).

The author of *Catecismo del Sacromonte* used all his knowledge for the single purpose of teaching and converting Moors because he was aware of how difficult it was for them to renounce their beliefs and embrace the Catholic doctrine. Although his dialogue is a dispute, his tone is respectful.[41]

---

39. Resines, *Catecismo del Sacromonte*, 44.
40. Resines, *Catecismo del Sacromonte*, 47–48.
41. Resines, *Catecismo del Sacromonte*, 48.

Jerónimo de Ripalda

Jerónimo de Ripalda was born in Teruel in 1536 and studied at the University of Alcalá de Henares. His ministry as a Jesuit priest and a skilled orator and preacher lasted sixty years.[42] The content of *Doctrina Cristiana* (1591) can be aligned around the following main themes and topics:

Knowledge and *praxis*

The Beginning of Christian Doctrine (The Obligations of a Christian and The Creed). The Fourteen Articles of Faith. Prayers (the Lord's Prayer, Hail Mary, and Hail Holy Queen). The Ten Commandments. The Commandments of the Church. The Sacraments. Indulgences (Works of Mercy and The Enemies of the Soul). Mortal Sins (Virtues to Combat Mortal Sins and The Three Theological Virtues). The Four Cardinal Virtues (The Powers of the Soul and The Five Senses). The Gifts and Fruits of the Holy Spirit. The Eight Beatitudes. The Order to Follow During the Mass. The Mysteries to Meditate on While Praying the Rosary. What Christians Must Do Every Morning.

Gaspar Astete

Gaspar Astete was born in Salamanca in 1537. He entered the Order of Jesuits in 1555 and taught humanities and philosophy at the University of Salamanca and the Seminary of Burgos. The content of his *Doctrina cristiana*—published sometime before 1592[43]—can be divided as follows:

Knowledge and *praxis*

Introduction to Christian Doctrine: The Creed. The Fourteen Articles of Faith. The Lord's Prayer. Hail Mary. Hail Holy Queen. The Ten Commandments. The Confession. Act of Contrition. Short Morning Prayer.

Declaration of Christian Doctrine: The Sign of the Cross. The Christian Condition of The Catechumen.

---

42. Resines, "Lectura crítica de los catecismos de Astete y Ripalda. Segunda Parte," 72–287.

43. This book uses the edition of the *Catecismo de la Doctrina* that includes material from Gabriel Menéndez de Luarca (d. 1812). This later edition was published in Valladolid in 1787. Astete's edition (published before 1592) was written for instructing children. Menéndez de Luarca's additional material made Astete's catechism suitable for adults. In the later edition, Astete´s material is in italics so that it is possible to arrive at the original text of *Catecismo de la Doctrina*. Resines, "Lectura crítica de los catecismos de Astete y Ripalda. Primera Parte," 77–79.

Division of Christian Doctrine:[44] Part One—The Creed and The Fourteen Articles of Faith. Part Two-What to Ask For and The Prayers of the Holy Mother Church.[45] Part Three—The Ten Commandments. Part Four—The Sacraments.

Capital Sins. Virtues to Combat Capital Sins. The Enemies of the Soul. The Theological Virtues. The Cardinal Virtues. The Five Senses. The Power of the Soul. The Gifts of The Holy Spirit. The Fruits of The Holy Spirit. The Eight Beatitudes. The End of Life. Twelve Means for Anyone Who Wishes to be Saved and Live a True Christian Life.[46]

Table 1. Type of Content

	Pre-Apologetics	Polemics	Apologetics	Knowledge	praxis
Breve doctrina y enseñanza				✓	✓
Confusión o confutación		✓			
Doctrina Cristiana (Alba)	✓	(brief)		✓	✓
Antialcorano		✓	✓		
Diálogos Christianos			✓		
Confutación del alcorán y secta mahometana		✓			
Doctrina Cristiana (Ayala)				✓	✓
Catecismo provechoso	✓	(brief)	✓		
Catecheses mystagogicae		✓			
Sacromonte		✓	✓	✓	✓

44. Explains the division of Christian doctrine into four parts, which form the main body of *Catecismo de la Doctrina*. Resines, "Lectura crítica de los catecismos de Astete y Ripalda. Primera Parte," 88.

45. This part provides the traditional explanation of the Lord's Prayer, Hail Mary, Hail Holy Queen, and angels. Resines, "Lectura crítica de los catecismos de Astete y Ripalda. Primera Parte," 88.

46. Astete, *Catecismo de la doctrina cristiana*, 187–225.

	Pre-Apologetics	Polemics	Apologetics	Knowledge	*praxis*
Doctrina Cristiana (Ripalda)				✔	✔
Doctrina cristiana (Astete)				✔	✔
Catecismo	✔	✔	✔	✔	✔

Summary

The relationship between Moriscos and the authorities was already frayed by the time Pérez de Ayala began to write the *Catecismo* sometime during his tenure as bishop of Guadix (1548–60). The armed revolt of the Moriscos known as the War of the Alpujarras (1568–71) exploded barely two years after Pérez de Ayala had passed away, but the volatile ingredients of that violent conflict were not far beneath the surface when he was the archbishop of Valencia (1564–66). The next chapter shows that the rebellion caused a fracture that was near impossible to repair. Pérez de Ayala and Ribera lived in troubled times, but those times were worse in Ribera's case. Ribera needed the right tool to instruct the Moriscos of his archdiocese.

In terms of content, the *Catecismo* is more than a catechism like Ripalda's *Doctrina Cristiana* and Astete's *Doctrina cristiana*. The *Catecismo* is also more than a polemical treatise like *Confusión o confutación, Antialcorano*, and *Confutación del alcorán y secta mahometana*. Alba's *Doctrina Christiana* and *Catecismo provechoso* critique Muhammad and his sect, but that is not their primary focus. The *Catecismo* is the only catechism and polemical treatise that covers all four areas—apologetics, polemics, knowledge and *praxis*—and an additional section that can be categorized as "pre-apologetics."

In terms of disseminating the content, only three of the works besides *Catecismo* use the format of a dialogue—*Diálogos Christianos, Catecismo provechoso,* and *Catecismo del Sacromonte*. Ribera in his cover letter to the *Catecismo* noted that the use of dialogues was "the clearest way to teach when the disciple has questions and the teacher has answers." Furthermore, the *Catecismo* and *Diálogos Christianos* are the only ones of the four dialogues to involve a Moor who has yet to be baptized.

Chapter 4

The Religious Context of the *Catecismo*

THIS CHAPTER, WHICH IS an overview of the religious context in which the *Catecismo* and the other catechisms and polemical treatises were written, presents what can be referred to as "The Triple Challenge," reviews key decisions that royal and ecclesiastical authorities promulgated that affected how Moriscos practiced their religion, and examines how Moriscos responded to those proclamations. The Triple Challenge refers to the Moriscos' confession (what they held in their heart), their beliefs (what they held in their mind), and their behavior (the rules and regulations they followed). The religious context accentuates the potential of the *Catecismo* as an evangelistic tool addressed to Moriscos and the reasons why Ribera decided to print it. If the *Catecismo* and the other catechisms and polemical treatises were not aware of the Triple Challenge, it would have been difficult for Moriscos to stop practicing their religion to accept Catholic doctrine.

The Triple Challenge: Heart, Mind, and Behavior

The following presentation of the three sections of the Triple Challenge is not concerned with how Muslims today practice Islam, but focuses on Moriscos who lived in Spain during the sixteenth century until the beginning of their expulsion in 1609.[1] These Moriscos followed the Maliki school[2] and used *aljamía* (Spanish written with Arabic characters) to record what they believed, what they obeyed, and what they confessed.[3] The first section

   1. Longás, *Vida religiosa de los moriscos*, xxvii.
   2. Longás, *Vida religiosa de los moriscos*, xxiv.
   3. In the early 1900s, these manuscripts in *aljamía* were archived in the library of the Centro de Estudios Históricos, a collection belonging to Pascual de Gayangos, and the Real Academia de la Historia. Longás, *Vida religiosa de los moriscos*, xxi.

on what Moriscos confessed deals with what was in their hearts (confession); the second section on what they believed considers what was in their mind (beliefs); and the third section on what they obeyed covers their behavior (rules and regulations). A full picture emerges from these three sections showing how Islam permeated the life of a Morisco. No area of his or her life was left untouched by Islam. The monarchy and civil and religious authorities faced a daunting challenge to persuade Moriscos to move from only being baptized to abandoning their confession, their beliefs, and their commandments for those of the Catholic Church.

Questions for Pérez de Ayala et al.: How aware were the authors of the catechisms and polemical treatises of this triple challenge? How do their works demonstrate such awareness? How do they attempt to address the mind, the actions, and the heart of the Moriscos? Or do these works appear as if their authors were talking past the Moriscos? Chapter 9 answers these questions.

The First Challenge. The Profession of Faith of the Moriscos (Heart)

Besides the obligatory confession "There is no God but Allah, and Muhammad is his prophet," Moriscos also recited another prayer (though supererogatory) which contained the confession and included the divine attributes of Allah. The words of that prayer were as follows:[4]

Allah is the Creator

> Know this (Allah protect us and our prophet): Everyone is obligated to know that Allah (honored and noble is he) is one in his kingdom. He created everything that exists in the world, what is high and what is low, the throne and the footstool, the heavens and the earth, what is in them and what exists between them. All creatures have been formed by his power; nothing moves without his permission; no one superior to him is above all the creatures. He has no partner in his kingdom.[5]

---

4. Longás, *Vida religiosa de los moriscos*, 13–15.

5. Longás does not provide Qur'anic references. The prayer that Allah has no partner is likely referring to Q. 6:163, 9:31, 17:111, and 25:2.

Allah Sustains His Creation

"He always provides what life needs. He does not slumber or become careless in his watch."

Allah is Omniscient

"He knows what is absent and what is present; the things in the heavens and nothing on earth is hidden from him. He knows what exists on the earth and the seas. No leaf falls without him noticing it. There is no grain hidden on the earth—green or dry—whose existence he does not know about."

Allah is Omnipotent

"He encompasses everything. He knows and grasps the number of everything. He does what he pleases because his power reaches everywhere. Kingdom, riches, honor and eternal duration belong to him."

Allah is the Judge

"Judgment rests with him. Praise belongs to him. Beautiful are his names. No one can resist his judgment. No one can forbid what he orders in his kingdom. He judges creatures as he pleases."

Allah is Perfect and Just

"He does not have the hope of satisfaction. He fears no penalty. In him there exists no obligation or greed because all of his grace is virtue and all of his revenge is justice."

Allah is Transcendent

"In relation to him there is no before or after, no above or below, right hand or left hand, before or behind, universal or particular."

Allah is Self-Existent

"He cannot be spoken of as when was he, where was he or how was he. He existed, but not in a place. He was master of space and ordered time. But he did not acquire the properties of time or space."

Allah is Incomprehensible

> Imagination cannot conceive him. Intelligence cannot grasp him. Reason cannot explain him. He is not discernible to the senses or intelligible to the soul. He is not the object of the either imagination or reason. Unlike every other thing, he cannot be perceived by imagination and thought. At every moment he hears the one who entreats him. He is the first and the last. The one who manifests and the one who hides. He knows everything that exists.

Is this divine being whom the Moriscos believed in, worshiped, and obeyed the same as the one taught in the Catholic Church? What do the catechisms and polemical treatises mean when they speak of God? Chapter 5 answers these questions.

The Second Challenge. The Religious Beliefs of the Moriscos (Mind)

Moriscos were to have full confidence in the following thirteen core articles worded precisely to remind them daily what they must believe while protecting themselves from foreign beliefs:[6]

Allah

(1) Allah is only one, creator, and ruler of everything. There is no Lord except him. He created everything from nothing. There is no one or nothing like him. He did not begat nor was he begotten. He was not a son or had a son. Nothing can compare with him.

---

6. Longás, *Vida religiosa de los Moriscos*, 2–6.

Death

(2) All creatures will die except Allah who always was and will always be. Two angels—one on the right and one on the left—will give a public account on the Day of Judgment of a person's good deeds; (3) Two angels will ask the dead who was his Lord, his prophet, and his law; (4) The last one to die will the Angel of Death who is in charge of receiving all the souls.

Hell and Paradise

(5) Allah will hear Muhammad when he asks him to pull out from Hell and send to Paradise those who believed in the oneness of Allah; (6) If a person's good deeds outweigh his bad deeds, they will be saved. Otherwise, they will be condemned. If their good deeds and their bad deeds weigh the same, they will be in a place between Paradise and Hell. Muhammad will pray for them and they will be taken to Paradise; (7) Everyone must go through As-Sirat (the bridge to heaven). Believers will go through speedily as lightning, but unbelievers will fall into Hell; (8) Believers will enjoy eternal glory in the company of Muhammad; (9) Hell is for law breakers and those cursed by Allah. It would have been better for them not to have been born. Hell—a frozen place of cold fire—is stench, poison, boils, serpents, worms, and wild beasts. Demons will torment the evil ones with unending punishment.

The Day of Judgment

(10) Allah and his prophet will judge everyone. The good ones will see the face of Allah. Everyone will be shown their good and bad deeds. The good ones will be on the right. The bad ones will be on the left. There will be pain, wailing, and tribulations; (11) The first ones to belong to Muhammad's flock will give an account of their good deeds to Allah.

The Qur'an and Muhammad

(12) Allah sent the Qur'an through Muhammad to revoke all other laws and lead people from error to everlasting good. Muslims must follow Muhammad. Deeds are evidence of faith and must conform to the law for Allah to accept them.

The Resurrection

(13) Souls will return to their bodies. The good ones will be worthy of eternal glory.

These precise beliefs would have been a challenge to the monarchy and civil and religious authorities as they attempted to attract Moriscos to the Catholic faith. Chapter 5 examines how the catechisms and polemical treatises dealt with this set of beliefs.

The Third Challenge. The Religious Commandments of the Moriscos (Behavior)

Thirty seven commandments—brief precepts written in prose as well as in verses to facilitate learning—specified what to do and what not to do.[7]

Allah

(1) Do not swear using the name of Allah; (2) Only worship Allah. Do not use images to represent him. Honor his prophet.

Entertainment

(3) Do not play dice or meaningless games.

Food and Wine

(4) Do not drink wine or anything that inebriates; (5) Do not eat bacon, blood or pork. Do not eat meat slaughtered improperly.

Good People, Infidels, and Christians

(6) Do not live in the land of the infidels or where injustice exists. Do not live with bad neighbors. Do not befriend bad Muslims; (7) Do not use the language, follow the traditions or wear the clothing of Christians and sinners; (8) Live with good people. Spend at least one-third of your assets when you can without regrets.

---

7. Longás, *Vida religiosa de los Moriscos*, 7–13.

Islamic Rituals

(9) Fast during Ramadan; (10) Honor every Friday and especially religious holidays; (11) Pay *zakat*; (12) Perform the *hajj*.

Muhammad, the Law, and The Day of Judgment

(13) Defend the Law even if it costs you your life and your property; (14) Honor and obey everything the prophet said, did, and taught. On the Day of Judgment you will enter Paradise without being tested; (15) Learn and teach the Law to the whole world or you will be in Hell.

Ritual Cleanliness

(16) Be clean always through ablutions, purifications, and the five daily prayers.

Sexual Relations

(17) Do not be intimate with your wife unless both of you are in a state of legal purity.

Sin, the World, and Repentance

(18) Abhor the world; (19) Do not sin or condone sin; (20) Repent truthfully.

Speech

(21) Speak good always. Speaking bad is impermissible.

Treatment of Others

(22) Do not be two-faced. Help people to be at peace with each other. Advise those who are in error. Settle down the irate; (23) Do not delight in what is forbidden. Do not lay your eyes on what belongs to someone else. Guard against the enemy. Forgive those who harm you. Ask for forgiveness from people you have injured. Don't be proud. Obey your superiors. Have mercy on those younger than you. Be a brother to your equals; (24) Do not steal or

kill. Do not commit adultery; (25) Greet Muslims. Help them as a service to Allah. If they are sick, visit them. If they die, bury them; (26) Honor the wise; (27) Honor your neighbors whether they are relatives, strangers or unbelievers; (28) Obey your father and your mother even when they are unbelievers; (29) Oppose Muslims who try to break a Qur'anic precept or the *sunna*; (30) Prevent the work of those who disobey the Law; (31) Redeem the captive. Advise orphans and widows; (32) Shelter the sojourner and the poor; (33) Judge fairly. Do not be greedy. Be sincere with your masters even when they are not Muslims. Pay them what is theirs by right. Honor the rich. Do not despise the poor. Guard from envy and anger. Do not be carried away by sorcerers, soothsayers, augurs or fortune-tellers. Listen only to Allah; (34) Wish your neighbor what you wish for yourself.

Vows and Integrity

(35) Do not buy anything you suspect is the proceeds of a robbery; (36) Do not break your vows unless they are against the Law. If you break them, make restitution; and (37) Do not use false weights. Do not take advantage of lies and betrayals. Do not be an usurer.

The comprehensiveness of these commandments would have posed a challenge to the authorities as they sought to persuade Moriscos to embrace the Catholic Church. Were the authors of the catechisms and polemical treatises aware of this Triple Challenge? Did they address the mind, the actions, and the heart of the Moriscos? There were significant differences between Catholic doctrine and Islamic teaching; for example, Moriscos believed that Allah does not have a son. How did the catechisms and polemical treatises address this and other differences? A Morisco might have asked, "The commandments that I need to obey teach me to be good to everyone. Are they not sufficient? What is wrong with them? Why should I replace them with the rituals of your church? If they are not good enough, what is good enough? Why are your rituals better than the commandments of my religion?" Chapter 5 answers these questions and examines how the catechisms and polemical treatises attempted to help the Catholic Church face this Triple Challenge.

The Problem. Teaching New Converts

Nominal Christianity

Was the Catholic Church prepared to meet the Triple Challenge? There was religious ignorance in Spain during the sixteenth century. Clergy zealous in their catechetical mission despaired at the sight of the bleak landscape. The problem started in the Middle Ages (c. 1000–1453). Christians, Jews, and Muslims living together created a phenomenon whereby they could maintain cordial relations without crossing into each other's religious territory. This separation resulted in Christians—the largest of the three groups in terms of population—having a poor understanding of what they believed. They were born into the religion of Christ, but remained inside their communities until they defected, got married or converted to another religion. In the meantime, their religious practices—revolving around the cycle of birth, marriage, food, social customs, and death—did not demand of them to have or express deep Christian convictions.[8]

Religious Ignorance

The first bishop of Mexico—Juan de Zumárraga (1468–1548)—wrote that Christians in Spain had to be reprimanded for boasting about being a Christian yet not knowing what it meant. "What excuse do they have for not knowing the Creed, the commandments, and the Lord's Prayer?" People walked around blind, but did not miss the light or tried to find it. Religious ignorance was institutionalized and well-protected. Opportunities for spiritual formation through preaching and printed materials were squandered. Luis de León (1527–91)—an Augustinian friar—pointed out that the common folk had two problems: ignorance and arrogance, but arrogance was the more serious issue.[9]

Idolatry and Superstition

The Council of Sevilla in 1512—the first council in Spain—discovered that many congregants did not even know the basic prayers. In 1528, people living in the mountains of Navarra and Vizcaya worshiped the devil in the form of a goat. In mid-sixteenth century, many in the church hierarchy commented that there was no need to go to the Americas to evangelize

---

8. Resines, *La Catequesis en España*, 178–79.
9. Resines, *La Catequesis en España*, 179–80.

because Spain had pockets of "The Indies" in areas such as Asturias, Andalucía, Cataluña and Galicia with unbridled religious ignorance and practice of pre-Christian rites.[10]

Incompetent Clergy

In the Alpujarras, people had not heard a sermon in more than twenty years. In 1568, the canon of Asturias wrote that there were few monasteries in the country, priests were "idiots," and the need for good workers was urgent. The word of God was rarely preached because of the lack of preachers. In Valencia, many candidates to the presbytery were only interested in securing a stable income. Few priests knew how to preach. Their superiors neglected their spiritual formation because they were satisfied as long as the priests knew the sacraments and how to read, write, and pronounce Latin. Concubinage, quarrels, corruption and misery were widespread. Clerical absenteeism was rampant. Many canons were not priests yet collected benefices without fulfilling any duties. They lived ostentatious secular lifestyles and frequented frivolous social gatherings instead of taking care of souls. In Barcelona, there were 4,502 ordinations between 1546 and 1570, but only six percent were assigned to be priests of a diocese while the rest entered the clergy for the benefices. The quality of the priests was low, concubinage was widespread as in Valencia, and spirituality was negligible. In Cuenca, in the 1560s, absenteeism among those who took advantage of benefices was high. Priests failed to administer the sacraments, stopped studying after their ordination, and never explained Christian doctrine. They preferred to speculate on the grains given as tithes and go hunting. The laity barely celebrated the holidays.[11]

Church Reform

The church outside of Spain also needed to be reformed. Rome was the hub of moral corruption between 1497 and 1537. But, laity-led attempts at church reform were made. The Brethren of the Common Life in Holland and the Ursulines in Italy were launched by laypeople who pursued daily prayer, personal sanctification, and doing charity. The humanists were another group of laity promoting reform grounded on learning. They believed that learning increased a person's personal piety, which in turn made them

---

10. Morgado García, "El clero en la España de los siglos XVI y XVII," 81–82.
11. Morgado García, "El clero en la España de los siglos XVI y XVII," 80–81.

better Christians. Although their leader Desiderius Erasmus (ca. 1469–1536) was critical of the spiritual rot in the Catholic Church, he never joined the Protestants and remained a Catholic until the end of his life. He emphasized studying the Bible and the church fathers as the foundation for a critical and historical theology with strong Catholic characteristics. In 1521, Thomas More (1478–1535)—one of Erasmus' greatest friends—responded to the Protestant movement in Europe by helping King Henry VIII write his book *Defense of the Seven Sacraments* against Luther's teachings.[12]

Despite these attempts at reform, the Catholic Church remained corrupt from its highest levels (popes, cardinals, bishops, and abbots) to its lowest levels (monks). The Concordat of Vienna in 1448 gave popes control over church appointments, which led to simony. The European nobility took advantage of this practice to monopolize high church offices. Secular rulers had one or more of their younger sons appointed to a bishopric even though they were unsuitable. Royal sons became bishops in their childhood without being ordained. Many of them grew up to live in open concubinage and father children. Pluralism was also a serious problem. A bishop could guarantee his income to sustain a regal standard of living by overseeing several dioceses simultaneously. However, pluralism led to absenteeism as some bishops never visited their flock. Many monks also did not live according to their vocation. They were poorly trained, lived in concubinage, and sought multiple benefices. Monastic vows became meaningless as personal possessions replaced common property, community prayers were rare, and community life was nonexistent.[13]

The Solution. A Catechism from the Council of Trent

It was not a surprise that meeting the spiritual needs of the people, getting rid of the incompetence and moral turpitude of the clergy, and reforming the inner life of the church were at the top of the agenda when the first period of the Council of Trent convened on 13 December 1545.[14] The completion in July 1568 of the revision of the breviary—which bishops, priests,

---

12. Spiteri, *A History of the Roman Catholic Church Until the Council of Trent (At Your Fingertips)*, Kindle edition location 2651/3620.

13. Spiteri, *A History of the Roman Catholic Church Until the Council of Trent (At Your Fingertips)*, Kindle edition location 2661/3620.

14. Spiteri, *The Catholic Counter-Reformation (At Your Fingertips)*, Kindle location 339/4613.

deacons, and sub-deacons—were required to recite daily—aided the reform of the spiritual life of clergy and congregants.[15]

On 17 June 1546, a decree on reform issued at the fifth session of the council stipulated that all bishops, archbishops, and prelates were obligated to preach the gospel. Everyone in charge of a church was required on Sundays and festivals to teach the congregants everything they needed to know about how to enter heaven, vices to avoid, and virtues to cultivate.[16]

On 11 November 1563, a decree on reform issued at the twenty-fourth session instructed bishops and priests to explain the efficacy of the sacraments in the vernacular tongue of the congregants according to a catechism that the council was to prescribe for the bishops to translate into the common language of the people.[17]

On 4 December 1563, the twenty-fifth session issued a decree commissioning a group of fathers to put together a catechism.[18] Pope Pius V appointed Archbishop of Milan Carlo Borromeo (1538–84) to head a committee responsible for ensuring that every statement of the catechism was doctrinally correct. It was ready by July 1566 and published in Latin and Italian at the end of that year. (Pérez de Ayala died on 5 August 1566.) The original title of the catechism was *The Catechism of the Council of Trent for Parish Priests*, but it is better known as *The Roman Catechism*.[19]

The Roman Catechism: Model and Yardstick

This catechism would have been the model for Pérez de Ayala's *Catecismo*, Orozco's *Catecismo provechoso*, *Catecismo del Sacromonte*, Ripalda's *Doctrina Cristiana*, and Astete's *Doctrina cristiana*. Talavera's *Breve doctrina y enseñanza*, Alba's *Doctrina Christiana* and Pérez de Ayala's *Doctrina Cristiana* were published before *The Roman Catechism* was published. Lorca's *Catecheses mystagogicae* stands apart from the rest as noted below. Ribera could have used *The Roman Catechism* as the yardstick to help him select one of these catechisms for his own evangelistic program.

15. Spiteri, *The Catholic Counter-Reformation (At Your Fingertips)*, Kindle location 758/4613.
16. Schroeder, *The Canons and Decrees of the Council of Trent*, Kindle location 977/6821.
17. Schroeder, *The Canons and Decrees of the Council of Trent*, Kindle location 4428/6821.
18. Schroeder, *The Canons and Decrees of the Council of Trent*, Kindle location 5481/6821.
19. Spiteri, *The Catholic Counter-Reformation (At Your Fingertips)*, Kindle location 745/4613.

Priests and The Roman Catechism

The preface of *The Roman Catechism* answers thirteen questions on issues relevant to pastors involved in the catechesis of new converts and old Christians. This catechism was not only doctrine for the faithful to live by, but also instruction for the priests. The core of the thirteen answers is as follows:[20]

(1) The chief end of man is eternal salvation, but he cannot find it by relying on his mind. He needs faith; (2) Faith comes from listening to the prophets sent by God; (3) In these last days, God has spoken through Christ who appointed apostles, prophets, pastors and teachers to preach and teach his message; (4) The words of a pastor are not the words of a man, but of Christ; (5) Pastors must preach and teach sound doctrine to the faithful because there are false prophets everywhere; (6) Heretics have tried to use their catechisms to overthrow the Catholic faith and deceive the faithful; (7) The fathers of this Synod of Trent are determined to oppose these heretics with the rudiments of the faith delivered in a fixed form to the faithful; (8) There have been many treatises on Christian doctrine, but now it is necessary to put forward a new catechism sanctioned by an ecumenical council and the Pope. Since there is one Lord and faith, there should also be one common rule and prescribed form of delivering the faith to the faithful; (9) This catechism does not elaborate on all the dogmas of the Catholic faith, but only what is necessary for pastors to understand before they instruct the faithful; (10) The pastor's paramount duty is to love, but he has two obligations before he loves: First, understand that eternal life means to know God and Jesus Christ. Second, keep Christ's commandments so that the faithful also walk as Christ walked; (11) Pastors should adapt their preaching and teaching to the age, capacity, manners, and condition of their audience; (12) Pastors should study the Word of God—which consists of Scripture and tradition—because it perfects the faithful and equips them for every good work. Christian doctrine has been distilled into the Apostle's Creed, the Sacraments, the Decalogue, and the Lord's Prayer; and (13) Pastors should connect their explanations of the gospel and the catechism to the Creed, the Sacraments, the Decalogue or the Lord's Prayer.

---

20. Buckley, *The Catechism of the Council of Trent (Illustrated)*, 2–10.

What Christians Should Believe and The Roman Catechism

Priests were obligated to teach new and old Christians what to believe (the Creed, the Sacraments, the Decalogue, and the Lord's Prayer) according to *The Roman Catechism* and parts one to four of the catechism.[21]

The Creed (or the Twelve Articles of Faith). (1) "I believe in God, the Father Almighty, Creator of Heaven and Earth"; (2) "And in Jesus Christ, His only Son, our Lord"; (3) "Who was conceived of the Holy Ghost, born of the Virgin Mary"; (4) "Suffered under Pontius Pilate, was crucified, dead, and buried"; (5) "He descended into Hell, the third day He arose again from the dead"; (6) "He ascended into Heaven, sitteth at the right hand of God, the Father Almighty"; (7) "From Whence He shall come to judge the living and the dead"; (8) "I believe in the Holy Ghost"; (9) "I believe in the Holy Catholic Church"; (10) "The forgiveness of sins"; (11) "The resurrection of the flesh"; and (12) "Life everlasting."[22]

The Sacraments. Baptism, Confirmation, the Eucharist, Penance, Extreme Unction, Order, and Matrimony.[23]

The Decalogue. (1) "Thou shall not have strange gods before Me"; (2) "Thou shall not take the name of the Lord thy God in vain"; (3) "Remember that thou keep holy the sabbath day. Six days shalt thou labour, and shalt do all thy works; but on the seventh day is the sabbath of the Lord thy God: on it thou shalt do no work . . . "; (4) "Honor thy father and thy mother, that thy days may be long upon the land, which the Lord thy God giveth thee"; (5) "Thou shall not kill"; (6) "Thou shall not commit adultery"; (7) "Thou shall not steal"; (8) "Thou shall not bear false witness against thy neighbor"; and (9) and (10) "Thou shalt not covet thy neighbor's house; thou shalt not covet thy neighbor's wife, nor his man-servant, nor his maid-servant, nor his ox, nor his ass, nor anything that is his."[24]

The Lord's Prayer. "Hallowed by Thy name. Thy kingdom come. They will be done. Give us this day our daily bread. And forgive us our debts, as we also forgive our debtors. And lead us not into temptation. But deliver us from evil. Amen."[25]

The catechism used 852 questions to explain the Creed (161 questions), the Sacraments (330), the Decalogue (223), and the Lord's Prayer (138); for example, on the sacrament of baptism—*what* is the meaning of baptism (Questions III and V), *why* should a person be baptized (Question XXX), *how* should a person be baptized (Question VII), *when* should

---

21. Buckley, *The Catechism of the Council of Trent (Illustrated)*, 11–530.
22. Buckley, *The Catechism of the Council of Trent (Illustrated)*, 15–120.
23. Buckley, *The Catechism of the Council of Trent (Illustrated)*, 140–307.
24. Buckley, *The Catechism of the Council of Trent (Illustrated)*, 317–419.
25. Buckley, *The Catechism of the Council of Trent (Illustrated)*, 460–527.

a person be baptized (Question XXXI), and *who* can be baptized (Questions XXIII).²⁶

The catechism's comprehensiveness was an indication that priests were woefully unprepared to take care of their flock. They first needed to learn what the council expected them to teach. There are three possibilities for this level of specificity: The council was (1) validating its commitment to stamp out nominal Christianity and clergy incompetence (see "The Problem: Teaching New Converts" above); (2) admonishing priests to take their calling seriously while equipping them to teach the right doctrine the correct way; and (3) conveying its high expectations of the priests and intention to hold them accountable.

Implementing the Solution

Catecismo

Book Two of Pérez de Ayala's *Catecismo*—consisting of forty-six dialogues divided into five parts—discusses the four sections of *The Roman Catechism*: The Creed (Part 1, Dialogue IX), the Lord's Prayer (Part 2, Dialogue III), the Decalogue (Part 3, Dialogue II), and the Sacraments (Part 4, Dialogues I to X). As the Teacher and the Moor approach the end of their twenty-fifth dialogue, the Moor says:

> I am greatly comforted by the many reasons you have given, my father, to condemn the false sects in the world and confirm the holy evangelical law of Jesus Christ. I am very convinced and persuaded to receive your holy faith. I give endless thanks to God for enlightening my understanding and bringing me to the knowledge of the truth—and I also thank you very much, my father, for the work that you have done to warn me so particularly about the lies of the false sects and to tell me about the excellencies and fundamentals of the Christian religion. You have certainly removed many doubts that afflicted my understanding. May God reward your work. Now that you have by the grace of God brought me to the door of health and general knowledge of the true path to heaven and have been the instrument of my conversion, be also the teacher of my instruction and teach me specifically what I ought to know, believe and do, and what the Christian religion teaches about walking this path well.
>
> (Book One, Dialogue XXV, 252–53).

---

26. Buckley, *The Catechism of the Council of Trent (Illustrated)*, 141–151.

By the time the Moor makes the above confession, the Teacher had spent the previous twenty-four dialogues making a case for the religion of Christ.

> Now that I see that you want to receive the faith of Jesus Christ and be a Christian, I will continue to instruct you on what a Christian needs to know and believe. This is my responsibility because you—a man with a free will—cannot receive baptism unless first there is instruction on what you have to believe as a Christian. You need to know the law that you are receiving so that later you cannot say that you got baptized out of ignorance but instead make an open confession when you are required to do so....
>
> (Book One, Dialogue XXV, 253).

The Teacher's response seems to indicate that instruction had to precede baptism. If this was the correct sequence, the baptism of the Moor's co-religionists as ordered by the Catholic Church and the monarchy was not the result of genuine conversions because Moors were being baptized against their will and without prior instruction.

Book Two of the *Catecismo* is an extensive explanation of the Creed, the Sacraments, the Decalogue, and the Lord's Prayer to satisfy the Moor's quest to know what he should believe and do as a Christian. The Teacher does not start immediately with the Creed, but first uses eight dialogues to answer the Moor's question "What is a Christian?" and others related to it. Each answer prompts the Moor to ask more questions. When their discussion moves to the Creed, the Moor has asked twenty eight questions; for example: "What is a Christian?" (First Dialogue, 254–57); "Why should I make the Sign of the Cross on my forehead, on my mouth, and across my chest?" and "Why do I need to make the Sign of the Cross three times?" (Dialogue III, 260–62); "What is faith?"; "What is the holy Scripture?"; "What is the gospel?"; and "Did the gospels preach the same gospel as the one the church now has?" (Dialogue VI, 264–68).

Pérez de Ayala's *Doctrina Cristiana*

Pérez de Ayala's *Catecismo* and *Doctrina Cristiana* present the Creed, the Sacraments, the Decalogue, and the Lord's Prayer differently; for example, *Doctrina Cristiana* introduces the Creed without a dialogue. The Creed is preceded by the Ave Maria and followed by La Salve Regina. In the *Catecismo*, the Moor asks twenty eight questions just on the Creed (Book Two,

Dialogue IX); for example, "Why do we call him Father saying 'I believe in God, the Father?'" (275); "What is the meaning of Christ?" (280); "Why is he called Lord?" (281); and "Could God have redeemed us in some other way without sending his Son as man?" (282). The short *Doctrina Cristiana* would have been more suitable for a quick review, memorization, and reading out loud in church while the *Catecismo* would have been more adequate for private reading and reflection.

Catecismo provechoso

Orozco phrased the Creed as fourteen articles: (1) Believe in an omnipotent God; (2) Believe that he is Father; (3) Believe that he is Son; (4) Believe that he is Holy Spirit; (5) Believe that he is Creator; (6) Believe that he is Savior; (7) Believe that he is the one who glorifies; (8) Believe that Jesus Christ was conceived of the Holy Spirit; (9) Believe that Christ was born of the Virgin Mary who was a virgin before she conceived and remained a virgin during her pregnancy and after giving birth; (10) Believe that he suffered and died for us sinners; (11) Believe that he descended to Hell to rescue the souls of the saints who were waiting for his coming; (12) Believe that he resurrected on the third day; (13) Believe that he ascended to heaven and is seated at the right of the Father; and (14) Believe that he will return to judge the living and the dead; glorify those who obeyed his holy commandments; and punish forever those who did not obey them. Orozco wrote that it is still the same Creed because to believe in the fourteen articles is to believe in the twelve articles.[27]

The *Catecismo* and *Catecismo provechoso* also differ in how they discuss the Creed, the Sacraments, the Decalogue, and the Lord's Prayer. We will limit the comparison to the first article of the Creed, which Orozco phrased as "I believe in God, the Father Almighty, Creator of heaven and earth." Unlike the Mooor in the *Catecismo*, Felipe (a Christian who had followed the religion of Muḥammad for thirty years) did not ask a single question. All he said after the priest (Orozco) explained the article was "Blessed are those who worship, serve and love such a powerful and good God with all their hearts. How unfortunate of the idolaters, Moors, heretics, and Hebrews who do not say, 'I believe in God, the Father Almighty, Creator of Heaven and Earth.'"[28] Felipe's reaction to the remainder of Orozco's explanations is the same; that is, he agrees with what he just heard without asking questions.

27. Orozco, *Catecismo provechoso*, 27 [r]–28 [r].
28. Orozco, *Catecismo provechoso*, 31 [l]–31 [r].

Catecismo del Sacromonte

This catechism has forty nine chapters.[29] While one of the parties in the *Catecismo* is a Moor interested in becoming a follower of the religion of Christ, the other conversant in *Catecismo del Sacromonte* is a novice—a recently baptized Morisco being trained on how to present the religion of Christ to family members and acquaintances who continue to follow the sect of Muhammad. The novice—like the Moor but unlike Felipe—participates in the dialogue by asking questions. The Creed is discussed in Chapters 14 to 19.[30] After the priest presents the fundamentals of the Christian faith in Chapters 14 to 15, the novice asks for a summary. Chapter 16 provides it in the form of fourteen articles just like in *Catecismo provechoso*. The first seven articles speak of the divinity of Christ and the remaining seven of his humanity. The novice asks, "If someone believes something contrary to what you just said about what the Catholic faith teaches, would he be considered an infidel?"; "In how many ways can one sin against the faith?"; "Would I be doubting the faith when thoughts contrary to the faith come to me against my will and I cannot get rid of them?"; and "How does faith grow?"[31]

The Sacraments are discussed in Chapter 23 and Chapter 24. The novice asks questions and makes comments; for example, "How should I respond to the Moors who tell me that their sacraments consist of their ablutions, prayers, circumcision and other ceremonies?"; "Why did Christ put in place the sacraments?"; "How many sacraments are there?"; and "What I find most admirable in the holy sacraments is in the Eucharist because we confess that the true body and blood of Christ is in it."[32]

Prayer is discussed in Chapter 25. The novice asks, "What is prayer?"; "What effects does prayer have?"; and "How many times is it good to pray every day?" The novice also requests, "Give me some good words that I can carry in my heart." The priest tells him to pray and say, "My Lord Jesus Christ, you shed your blood for me, have mercy on me because I am a great sinner."[33] This is a surprising answer. The priest does not take the opportunity to teach the Lord's Prayer at this point or anywhere else in his dialogue with the novice.

---

29. The original edition had fifty chapters, but the numbering of Chapter 31 was duplicated by mistake. Resines' transcription of the catechism numbers those chapters as 31 and 31 bis. Resines, *Catecismo del Sacromonte*, 50.

30. Resines, *Catecismo del Sacromonte*, 53.

31. Resines, *Catecismo del Sacromonte*, 208–9.

32. Resines, *Catecismo del Sacromonte*, 234–37.

33. Resines, *Catecismo del Sacromonte*, 241–44.

The Decalogue is discussed from Chapters 31 to 47. Instruction begins after the novice asks the priest to show how Muḥammad broke the Ten Commandments "so that the falsehood of Muḥammad and his law can be brought out by comparing it with God and his law." After the priest explains each commandment, the novice asks how Muḥammad broke it, interjects a comment or asks another question; for example, after explaining the fifth commandment, the novice says, "I beg of you to tell me how has the Lord God taught us to love our neighbors, which is something that pleases him much"; "I see that we have an infinite obligation to love and help our neighbors"; "In what ways is this commandment broken?"; and "Now I beg of you to tell me how does Muḥammad and his law break this holy and just commandment." After the priest finishes his explanation of the tenth commandment, the novice asks him to say something about Muḥammad. The priest obliges and says, "We would not want to walk in such a dirty swamp." He adds that pestilence is in the heart that produces evil and wants the novice to know what one must do so that God may live in their hearts. Upon hearing this, the novice shouts, "Oh, what a beautiful conclusion to the ten commandments! I am willing to listen."[34]

Alba's *Doctrina Christiana*

This catechism has four parts. (1) Part One introduces the Creed and explains all twelve Articles of Faith to tackle the errors and heresies of the Moors; (2) Part Two presents the Lord's Prayer whose seven petitions encompass everything to honor God and keep a person physically and spiritually healthy. Part Two also has the seven Sacraments, which bestow grace upon the one who receives them piously; (3) Part Three discusses the Ten Commandments. When a man asked Jesus what he should do to inherit eternal life, Jesus told him to keep the commandments (Mark 10:17–19); and (4) Part Four teaches what new Christians must not believe and must not do.[35]

Alba wrote this catechism for "new Christians who used to be Moors."[36] He confronts the sect of Muḥammad; for example, the Moors reject the fourth article of faith ("Jesus Christ was crucified, he died and

---

34. Resines, *Catecismo del Sacromonte*, 266–316.
35. Resines, *El Catecismo de Pedro Ramiro de Alba*, 133–80.
36. Resines, *El Catecismo de Pedro Ramiro de Alba*, 133.

was buried") because of a single verse Qur'an (Sura An-Nisa 4:157), which says, "but they killed him not, nor crucified him . . . ." Alba states that this passage is contradicted by Sura Al-Maidah 5:117, which he renders as "[Jesus says] I have not told them more than what You have told me: 'Serve God, my Lord and your Lord.' I was their witness while I was with them, but after You called me, You were the one who watched over them.'"[37] But, Alba does not explain where is the contradiction. A more complete reading of this verse says, "I only said to them what You commanded me: 'Serve God, my Lord and your Lord!' And I was a witness over them as long as I was among them. But when You took me, You became the Watcher over them. You are a Witness over everything."[38] Sura Al-Maidah 5:117 can be compared with Sura Al-Imran 3:55—"(Remember) when God said, 'Jesus! Surely I am going to take you and raise you to myself . . . .'"[39] The phrases "took me" and "take you" refer to "in death."[40] Both verses can be compared with Jesus' own words in Sura Maryam 19:33—"Peace (be) upon me the day I was born, and the day I die, and the day I am raised up alive."[41]

Catecheses mystagogicae

Lorca's work—a polemical treatise—does not teach the four parts of *The Roman Catechism*. It is only mentioned briefly in the Eleventh Catechism of *Catecheses mystagogicae* ("On Catechizing the Unlearned, Paul's Second Letter to Timothy 4, is recalled, 'Preach the Word, insist opportunely and inopportunely, etc.'"). The right-hand side margin of *Catecheses mystagogicae* has this exhortation: "The Catechism published by the mandate of Pius V should be read over by the pastors."[42] After explaining ecclesiastical ceremonies such as the Mass, priests are strongly encouraged "to give account and instruction of even the minute [details] of the Church's rite to their proselytes, now advanced in doctrine, demanded according that excellent catechetical work published for those very pastors by order of Pius V, the High Pontiff." Lorca does not mention *The Roman Catechism* by name, but it is obvious that he is referring to it. He describes it as a "plain presentation" of all matters instituted by the apostles and the Roman Church in the sacraments and other rites of

37. Resines, *El Catecismo de Pedro Ramiro de Alba*, 139.
38. Droge, *The Qurʾān: A New Annotated Translation*, 75.
39. Droge, *The Qurʾān: A New Annotated Translation*, 36.
40. Droge, *The Qurʾān: A New Annotated Translation*, 75, 36.
41. Droge, *The Qurʾān: A New Annotated Translation*, 195.
42. Busic, "Saving the Lost Sheep," 237, 502–23.

the Church. Therefore, pastors—this catechism's intended audience—should read it "over in hand night and day."[43]

The objective of the Eleventh Catechism is to instruct pastors on how they should carry out their duties; for example, the preaching of the word should be done with arguments, supplication and reproofs; pastors who do not work at catechesis shall be dragged to hell with their people, but pastors who labor will receive an eternal prize from God; the catechesis of adults who retain their dress and Algarabia should begin at the vespertine hour of feast days; proselytes should not have two names; the observance of baptism should be proposed often so that proselytes renounce their false names and Muhammad; every article of the Catholic faith should be taught to those who have received baptism; pastors must be diligent in catechesis for they are sewers of the word of God; they should remove "the perverse dogmas of the Muhammadan sect" by the roots from their proselytes so that their seed might bear fruit; ensure that proselytes memorize what they are learning; and be hopeful that their proselytes become disciples who can teach others and "attack" the sect.[44]

Key Decisions

Treaty of Capitulation

After Granada fell, Boabdil, Sultan of Granada, and Queen Isabella and King Ferdinand signed a capitulation treaty on 25 November 1491. There were sixty-seven articles in the treaty; for example, Moors were allowed to continue living where they had been living and under their own laws; mosques, minarets, and muezzins were not to be taken away; Christians were not permitted to enter a mosque; Moors should not be forced to become a Christian; and Christians who had converted to Islam were not to be mistreated or forced to become a Christian.[45]

Talavera: Gentle Approach

Hernando de Talavera—the first archbishop of Granada—did not force the Moors to leave their religion. His goal was their sincere conversions and to adhere to the capitulation treaty that allowed Muslims to continue practicing

---

43. Busic, "Saving the Lost Sheep," 511–12.
44. Busic, "Saving the Lost Sheep," 519–21.
45. Cowans, *Early Modern Spain*, 16–19.

their religion unhindered. He learned Arabic and edited a grammar and a dictionary of Arabic to better understand the Moors. His innovative methods of progressive inculturation of the Catholic faith into Islamic customs and traditions included the use of Arabic in the liturgy and Islamic dances and musical instruments. Muslims addressed him as "Santo *alfaquí*."[46]

Cisneros: New Approach

Queen Isabella and King Ferdinand preferred a different approach and sent Cardinal Jiménez Cisneros to Granada in 1499. Cisneros worked with Talavera. As a result, three thousand Moors converted in one day. In his efforts to see more conversions, Cisneros gathered a large number of Arabic works and shipped them to the University of Alcalá believing that these encouraged Moors to remain Moors. Despite this large number of conversions in one day, the bulk of the population resisted all the means used to convert them. They complained to the Sultan of Egypt informing him that they were being forced to convert in violation of the capitulation treaty. The Sultan then threatened to force all the Christians in Egypt to convert to Islam. The monarchy responded by giving the Moors the option to become Christians or emigrate to Barbary. Bloody fights ensued even as conversions continued. In 1500, there were revolts in Granada in Alpujarras, Almería, Baza and Guadix. In 1501, new revolts erupted that were calmed down only after Charles went to Granada. He allowed those who did not want to become Christians to go to Barbary. Those who converted were followed by conversions of those who lived in Castilla.[47]

Juana I of Castilla and mother of Charles granted the Moriscos six years to stop wearing Islamic clothing, which was extended to another ten years. This ruling was suspended in 1518 after the Moriscos petitioned Charles. In April 1525, Charles made arrangements for the instruction of the Moriscos—those who had already been baptized as well as those who had not been. He declared on the basis of the opinion of the Royal Council that Moors who had been baptized were Christians because they received baptism while in full use of their judgment and not mad or drunk.[48]

---

46. García-Ferrer, *Fray Hernando de Talavera y Granada*, 39–40.
47. Longás, *Vida religiosa de los moriscos*, xxxix.
48. Longás, *Vida religiosa de los moriscos*, xl.

New Prohibitions

Five months later, an edict was published with these resolutions: Moriscos were not allowed to leave their place of residence or they would become the slave of whomever caught them; they were forbidden from selling gold, silver, jewelry, silk, cattle, or any merchandise; they were to place a half moon made of cloth onto their hats; they were not allowed to work on church-sanctioned holidays; they should remove their head coverings and genuflect when the Holiest passed by or when time for prayers was announced; and the lords and governors of Morisco towns were to close mosques and do their part to implement these resolutions.[49]

Charles continued to exhaust all possible means to keep instructing the true faith to the Moriscos because he was convinced that conversions were insincere. Those who kept committing the same offenses were punished. If previous measures were ineffective, he was prepared to resort to expulsion.[50]

Edict of Expulsion

Pope Clement VII issued an edict that threatened with major excommunication anyone who opposed the Emperor. All Moors were to hear the gospel without rejoinder or excuse and be baptized by 8 December or leave Spain. Shortly after, a general edict was published whereby Charles ordered all the Moriscos in Valencia to leave on 31 December 1525 and those in the rest of Spain were to leave by 31 January 1526. The Moriscos protested at the severity of the measures. Many of them in Valencia chose baptism, but first petitioned Charles to order the Inquisition not to harass them or their property for a period of forty years. During that time they would not be required to change the way they dressed or their language; new Christians were to have their own cemeteries; marriage between family members to the second degree be allowed for forty years; those who used to work as *alfaquí* should continue to live off the lands given to them as alms; and Moriscos be able to carry arms. However, Charles did not agree to their requests.[51]

---

49. Longás, *Vida religiosa de los moriscos*, xl.
50. Longás, *Vida religiosa de los moriscos*, xli.
51. Longás, *Vida religiosa de los moriscos*, xlii.

New Resolutions

In 1526, a junta of theologians consisting of archbishops and bishops announced new resolutions requesting Moriscos to stop using Arabic, the baths, and their traditional garb; to keep the doors of their houses open on Fridays, Saturdays, and religious holidays; and not use nicknames or aliases. Charles suspended them at the request of the Moriscos.[52]

These resolutions were reiterated again in 1530, but their execution was put on hold. In 1566, when the forty years of pause came to an end, a junta in Madrid reiterated the resolutions of 1526: Moriscos were required to speak Castilian within the following three years; speaking, reading and writing in Arabic in public and in private was forbidden; contracts written in Arabic were invalid; books in Arabic were to be surrendered; the making of Morisco garb was forbidden and those made of silk or cloth could only be worn for another year and two years, respectively; women were required to leave their faces uncovered and not permitted to dress as a *morisca*; Muslim ceremonies at weddings were forbidden; the doors of Morisco houses were to be left open on Fridays and wedding days; the use of Moorish names was to stop; and the use of baths was forbidden.[53]

These resolutions were announced publicly in Granada on 1 January 1567. The demolition of baths began. Officials announced to the Moriscos that time had come for them to stop wearing their Morisco garb. Moriscos were also required to register their children between the ages of three and fifteen and enroll them in school to learn Castilian and Christian doctrine. Moriscos who had moved to the city of Granada from farmsteads protested that they were too poor to learn a new trade to support their families. Nevertheless, the carrying out of the resolutions proceeded.[54] Given these key decisions, did Moriscos follow the Catholic Church? How did other Moriscos practice their religion?

Some Cases of Assimilation

The number of Moriscos who replaced their Islamic beliefs and practices with the doctrine and rituals of the Catholic faith was not as high as the monarchy and the church authorities had hoped for. However, some Moriscos did assimilate during the first years of conversion (between 1500 and 1526) and before the War of Granada (1568–1570). Some who lived

---

52. Longás, *Vida religiosa de los moriscos*, xliv.
53. Longás, *Vida religiosa de los moriscos*, xlvi.
54. Longás, *Vida religiosa de los moriscos*, xlvii–xlviii.

in the most Islamized parts of the country revered Mary, defended her, believed in her virginity, and regarded her as "Mother of our Savior to whom all Christians call upon as advocate in our tribulations and needs." Other Moriscos joined religious confraternities (*cofradías*) located in churches and convents for members to display their religiosity. Talavera encouraged Moriscos to join these *cofradías* to help them through life and face death. There were at least two in Granada—one for men (La Resurrección) and one for women (Concepción de Nuestra Señora). Moriscos financed La Resurrección and requested its members to attend their burial. Some Moriscos belonged to more than one *cofradía*.[55]

Religious Practice under Duress

Fatwa from Oran

In early sixteenth century, Moriscos living in Granada who had been forced to convert wanted to know how to live as Sunni Muslims under Catholic rule. They asked Ubaydallah Ahmad Ben Bu Jumua al-Magrawi al-Wahrani—a *mufti* in Oran, North Africa—which of their religious beliefs could they deny publicly and which of their ritual obligations could they break. His reply in early December 1504 came as a *fatwa* addressed to them, but not to Moriscos living in Aragón and Valencia because they were not forced to convert until the end of the 1520s.[56]

Fifteen of the nineteen recommendations in the *fatwa* covered religious practices: Moriscos should educate their children in their religion unless the enemy discovers them; idols and images have no power; ritual prayers can be offered with covert gestures; *zakat* can be paid by pretending that it is a gift for a beggar; ablutions for major defilements can be discharged with bathing in the ocean; if prevented during the prescribed hours, ritual prayers can be completed at night; *masḥ* (purification by rubbing on a clean substance like wood or earth) can replace *ṭahārā* (ritual purification by water); prayers at Christian altars are permissible when instead traditional Muslim prayers are prayed (these prayers are valid even when they are not directed towards Mecca); if there is no intent to use the wine, drinking it when forced is permitted; if unavoidable, eating pork and forbidden food is allowed when it is believed they are still unclean; daughters marrying Christians is permitted when there is no other option and

---

55. Pedraza, "El otro Morisco," 230–34.

56. Harvey, "Crypto-Islam in Sixteenth Century Islam," 164–67. Cited in Bernabé Pons, "Taqiyya, niyya y el islam de los Moriscos," 491–527.

provided Moriscos still believe that it is forbidden; marrying a Christian woman is acceptable because Christians have a scripture; if forced to take usury, keep the capital and give all the interest to the poor; if forced to deny their beliefs, Moriscos should be evasive or deny inwardly what they are forced to believe; and if told to curse Muhammad, pronounce his name as Mamad because that is how Christians pronounce it.[57]

The remaining four rulings focused on what Moriscos should do when forced to agree with Catholic doctrine. If coerced to say that Jesus is the son of God, they were to suppress the word governing the genitive; that is, "Jesus is the son of (the worshipper) the God of Mary, who is righty adored." If told that Mary was God's wife, they were to recognize that the pronoun refers to the cousin whom Mary married during the time of the children of Israel and then separated from her before they had children or that God married her to him by his power. If compelled to say that Jesus passed away on the cross, Moriscos should understand that "passed away" meant that it was done to perpetuate his memory and that God had him "pass away" to take him to heaven.[58] Although the Moriscos had not asked the *mufti* about *taqiyya* nor had he used that word in his reply,[59] he was in effect instructing them to practice *taqiyya* or "The prudent disguise of the true nature of one's belief because of fear or for precaution."[60]

Taqiyya

The concept of *taqiyya* expressed as "legitimate dissimulation" can be seen in the following *aljamiado* text in one of the works of the *Mancebo de Arévalo*,[61] a Morisco who travelled throughout Spain in the sixteenth century collecting Islamic doctrines:

> Speaking of the afflictions which we are suffering, one of the [Islamic] scholars of this kingdom [of Aragón] said: "I know very well that we are passing through a terrible period, but Allah will not for that reason refrain from visiting punishments on us, should we fail to do such good as is in our power. In so far as the obligations of the law are concerned, [hiding our true belief as a] precaution is something to which we may all have recourse,

---

57. Harvey, "Crypto-Islam in Sixteenth-Century Islam," 168–69.
58. Harvey, "Crypto-Islam in Sixteenth Century Islam," 169.
59. Bernabé Pons, "Taqiyya, niyya y el islam de los moriscos," 500.
60. Harvey, "Una referencia explícita de la legalidad de la práctica de la taqiyya por los moriscos," 561.
61. Chesworth and Bernabé Pons, "The Young Man of Arévalo," 159–68.

for we have special exemption so to do, and thus we may fulfill those obligations during the alien canticles whereby the Christians seek their salvation. It all may be classified as *legitimate dissimulation,* for true doctrine may not be forbidden by any law, however cruel."[62]

The Moors believed that their doctrine was the truth and that it was legitimate to conceal their true beliefs when required to obey the teachings of the Catholic Church.

Christians were aware that Moriscos practiced *taqiyya*. Martín de Salvatierra—bishop of Segorbe—wrote to Philip II on 30 July 1587 and mentioned "that it is plain and absolutely certain" that the "traditions, doctrines and teachings" of the Moors allowed them to receive baptism, confess Christ or perform a Christian deed, but would not be offending their prophet on the condition that they still "believed, loved, and worshipped him in their hearts." In 1606, Pedro de Valencia—chronicler of Philip III— wrote in his *Tratado acerca de los moriscos de España* that Muḥammad commanded his people "to love each other and to treat each other well, but to hate and mistreat" those who did not belonged to his sect. He "invented a diabolical machine" so that his people would know what to do when it was risky to practice their religion. They were permitted to deny it, eat anything forbidden, use any external sign to show their denial, and still not be disloyal. The *Catecismo* and *Catecismo del Sacromonte* were also cognizant that Moriscos practiced *taqiyya*.[63]

Niyya

The term *taqiyya* is not found in the *fatwa* of the *mufti* of Oran, but the word *niyya* (intent) does appear. *Niyya*—a core concept familiar to Moriscos—is "the rational decision or the believer's intent that the act he is about to perform is to be taken as that act of *ibada* and not as something different." When he expresses *niyya* (either aloud or silently) prior to performing his *salat*, he is expressing his decision that the act he is about to perform should be taken as *salat* and not *dua* or another prayer. When he expresses his *niyya* to perform *zakat,* he is expressing his intent that this act should be valid as *zakat* and not as *sadaqa* or another donation. *Niyya* validates the ritual that is about to be performed. What the *fatwa* did was not only to instruct the Moriscos on how to remain steadfast in

---

62. Harvey, "An Explicit Reference to the Lawfulness of the Exercise of Taqīya by Moriscos," 42.

63. Rubio, "La taqiyya en las fuentes cristianas, 533–36.

their beliefs while living under duress, but to emphasize the significance of intent. The *fatwa* stated, "Allah only receives the good intent and does not consider the exterior." Church authorities had a copy of the *fatwa* and drew two conclusions. One, Islam allowed Moriscos to lie under any circumstance about their religion. Second, any of their cultural displays were part of their Islamic ritual and the one who performed them was a Muslim. Thus, Moriscos were irremediably full Muslims.[64]

The monarchy and the civil and church authorities might have made a mistake in considering Moriscos as "newly baptized" or "new converts." If they were in fact Muslims, the catechisms and polemical treatises would have been written with that in mind. Chapter 5 explores how these works address Christian doctrines that Moriscos found most objectionable such as the divinity of Christ and the Trinity.

The Social Context of the *Catecismo*

Conversion and Rebellion

Three pivotal events impacted the relationship between Moriscos and Christians: (1) The conversion of the *mudéjares* in Castilla (1500–1502) ruptured the *convivencia* of medieval times; (2) the War of the Alpujarras in Granada (1568–71) wiped out any possibility of mutual understanding; and (3) the general expulsion (1609–14), which was a victory for the Catholic Church. However, the following events need to be considered to avoid the impression that Moriscos and Christians were in a constant state of conflict: the conversion of the Moriscos of the Crown of Aragón and Charles' stay in Granada (1526); the renewed Muslim interest in the western Mediterranean and Charles' abdication (1555–56); the decision of the Junta of Lisboa to expel the Moriscos (1582); and the peace between Spain and France and the death of Philip II (1598).[65]

The ministry of Pérez de Ayala fit into the above events as follows: Bishop of Guadix in Granada (16 May 1548–17 July 1560), bishop of Segovia in Castilla and León (17 July 1560–6 September 1564), and archbishop of Valencia (6 September 1564–5 August 1566). He had already passed away when the rebellion of the Moriscos in Granada broke out on 24 December 1568. Ribera's time as archbishop of Valencia (3 December 1568–6 January 1611) overlapped the period leading up to the general expulsion in 1609 and two years afterwards. Ribera wrote in his cover letter to the *Catecismo*

---

64. Bernabé Pons, "Taqiyya, niyya y el islam de los moriscos," 504–11.
65. Domínguez Ortiz and Vincent, *Historia de los moriscos*, 17.

that he chose to make it known because Pérez de Ayala was familiar with "the newly converted from the Moors." Ribera also mentioned that there were many Moriscos in Guadix when Pérez de Ayala began to write the *Catecismo*, but stopped writing after his transfer to Segovia for it had few Moriscos. Ribera explained that Pérez de Ayala continued to write the *Catecismo* after moving to Valencia because of the similarities between Valencia and Granada. Although Pérez de Ayala had already passed away when the rebellion took place, its aftermath caused irreparable damage that spread to Valencia and affected Ribera's work to such an extent that he had to consider using the *Catecismo* for his own evangelistic work.

General Picture

The future looked promising for the Moors after Queen Isabella, King Ferdinand and Sultan Boabdil signed the capitulations treaty in late 1491 in Granada. However, despite his promises, Charles asked the Pope repeatedly for permission to order the Moriscos to get baptized or expel them. It came on 12 March 1524. Those who refused baptism were to leave or face permanent servitude. Mosques were converted into churches. The constant vigilance and restrictive measures of the inquisitors reached such levels that the deputies of Aragón, Cataluña and Valencia complained to Charles at the courts convened in Monzón in 1528. They petitioned that nothing further should be done against the Moriscos irrespective of how much they adhered to their religion until sufficient time had been granted to them to embrace the Catholic faith. Shortly after, the inquisitors came up with the idea of asking the Moriscos to abandon their *morerías* (special neighborhoods assigned just for Moriscos to live in) and move to old Christian neighborhoods. The purpose was to spy on the Moriscos and catch them performing any religious ritual. In 1526 and 1549, a new ruling stipulated that only Moriscos who had record of their grandparent's baptism before the fall of Granada would qualify as old Christians.[66]

Polemics and Hostility

The mistrust between Moriscos and Christians was intense. Both accused each other of practicing *taqiyya*. Moriscos argued that the old Christians "were not stupid" yet believed in mysterious Catholic doctrine just to avoid

---

66. Janer, *Condición social de los moriscos de España*, 51–52.

facing the Inquisition.⁶⁷ Moriscos, on the other hand, were not always successful in diverting the social pressure when they tried to mask their beliefs. A certain Morisco was having a meal at the home of his Christian neighbors. He excused himself when bacon was served and informed his hosts that he was following a family tradition of not eating bacon because his parents never ate it. However, his neighbors and the authorities knew well that he was observing an Islamic prohibition. This was not an isolated case of a clash between a Christian and Morisco who tried to cover up his true beliefs. Moriscos being accused of hypocrisy led to a common impression of them. In 1531, the bishop of Túy had just been nominated to the presidency of Granada when he received a letter from a friar introducing the Moriscos of Granada as "cunning, opinionated and sneaky." In 1560, the Inquisition said that all the Moriscos were "secret Muslims." In 1568, this same Inquisition stated: "We are in the midst of our heathen enemies."⁶⁸

In the late sixteenth century, the Inquisitor of Aragón commented that he had never found a new convert who was likely to be a Christian. In Cataluña, a priest was tasked with writing certificates that would have kept some of the Moriscos under his charge from being expelled from the country. He wrote that the works he saw the Moriscos "do outwardly seem to show that they were good Christians." They stayed in the country, but were later discovered to be "as Moors as those who were expelled." The Moriscos of Castilla were also regarded as Muslims. One witness claimed that all of them could have been sent to the Inquisition.⁶⁹

Aftermath of the War of the Alpujarras

In 1552, Moriscos were mandated to turn in their arms. If they were to use them without a license, the penalty was six years in the galleys. In 1566, they were forbidden from wearing Morisco garb and using Arabic. In late 1568, they rebelled against both measures and on Christmas Eve of that year started what became known as the War of the Alpujarras.⁷⁰ The total population of Granada was slightly above 150,000. The rebellion lasted until November 1570. Thirty thousand Moriscos (including four thousand Turks and Berbers)⁷¹ and twenty thousand men from the Christian side fought

---

67. Cardaillac, "Un aspecto de las relaciones entre Moriscos y cristianos," 121.
68. Cardaillac, "Un aspecto de las relaciones entre Moriscos y cristianos," 115–16.
69. Cardaillac, "Un aspecto de las relaciones entre Moriscos y cristianos," 116–17.
70. Janer, *Condición social de los moriscos de España*, 52.
71. Domínguez Ortiz and Vincent, *Historia de los moriscos*, 39.

each other during the critical phase (December 1569–January 1570)[72] of this ruthless all-out war[73] of "brothers against brothers."[74] The rebellion was essentially a rural uprising. A minority desperate to preserve its identity dug the ditch that decidedly kept both sides apart.[75]

The rebellion led to the start of the expulsion of Moriscos in 1569 from Granada to different parts of the Crown of Castilla. This continued after the rebellion was crushed in November 1570. Eventually, a conservative estimate of eighty thousand Moriscos were expelled.[76] On the eve of the rebellion in 1568, there were approximately 155,000 Christians and 120,000 Moriscos (43 percent of the total population of Granada—a significant percentage for a minority and the highest percent of Moriscos in the country).[77] Moriscos in Granada did not live in cities except in Guadix (where Pérez de Ayala was bishop), Baza, Almería, Motril where they represented from 30 to 40 percent of the residents[78] and Granada where they represent almost half.[79]

The year 1570 created the sharpest cut in the history of the Moriscos. Although help for the Moriscos in Granada from other Moriscos in the country did not play a significant role throughout the rebellion, they became a sword of Damocles hanging over the heads of the Christians. Every Morisco was a suspect. Every Christian was a potential informer. The time for using persuasive means to win the Moriscos was over.[80] After the rebellion was crushed, restrictions on the Moriscos increased. In 1582, Moriscos in Valencia were forbidden from going near the coast or be in maritime villages. In 1586, Moriscos who had gone to Valencia were expelled from Valencia. In 1592, the Courts of Madrid proposed to Philip II that Moriscos should be spread out by provinces; not be permitted to go beyond five leagues from their villages under penalty of death; not allowed to hold public office; and be assigned to work in the most dangerous war-related ministries. In 1595, the Moriscos of Aragón had to give up their arms. By this time a range of measures had been put in place to force Moriscos to

---

72. Domínguez Ortiz and Vincent, *Historia de los moriscos*, 36.
73. Domínguez Ortiz and Vincent, *Historia de los moriscos*, 37, 41.
74. Bernabé Pons, "Una visión propicia del mundo," 105.
75. Domínguez Ortiz and Vincent, *Historia de los moriscos*, 47.
76. Domínguez Ortiz and Vincent, *Historia de los moriscos*, 80.
77. Domínguez Ortiz and Vincent, *Historia de los moriscos*, 78.
78. This 30 to 40 percent range bears out what Ribera wrote in his cover letter to the *Catecismo* that there were many Moriscos in Guadix when Pérez de Ayala began to write his catechism.
79. Domínguez Ortiz and Vincent, *Historia de los moriscos*, 80.
80. Domínguez Ortiz and Vincent, *Historia de los moriscos*, 57.

join the Catholic Church or face the galleys or death.[81] The impact of the rebellion was severe and felt throughout the entire country. The defeat and the expulsion in 1570 would culminate in the general expulsion of 1609.[82] The time leading up to that expulsion coincided with the time Ribera was in Valencia. He became its archbishop on 3 December 1568. The War of the Alpujarras exploded twenty-one days later.

The Moriscos of Granada

The previous section presented a general picture of the social condition of the Moriscos prior to and after the War of the Alpujarras. This section looks more closely at the Moriscos from Pérez de Ayala's perspective while he was bishop of Guadix (1548–60) where he began to write the *Catecismo*. Its opening pages mention that it is a dialogue between a Moor who travelled from the Berber region to Spain looking for him to discuss becoming a Christian. But, was it an actual dialogue? The section above mentions that 30 to 40 percent of the population of Guadix were Moriscos. This means that Pérez de Ayala had a significant number of people to instruct in the Catholic faith. His pastoral experience with them would have informed his writing. The *Catecismo* could be his detailed record of a dialogue with one Muslim or a record of several conversations with several Muslims over a period of time. This possibility would not have escaped Ribera's attention.

The Moriscos of Granada were different from those living in the rest of Spain. As the *Reconquista* advanced, Muslims were pushed further into a corner in Granada. There was no time for them and Christians to develop the kind of harmonious relationships that existed between Muslims and Christians in Aragón and Valencia. The failure of the authorities to abide by the capitulation treaty lead to rebellion. The geographical proximity of the Moriscos of Granada to Muslims in North Africa facilitated regular contacts. Furthermore, Spain's foreign policy had shifted its focus away from that area to the newly discovered Americas. All this gave hope to the Moriscos of Granada that North African Muslims could help them recover their kingdom. Granada became "the heart and head" of a potential Islamic restoration. Its Moriscos were the most politically-minded and could launch a reverse *Reconquista*. Their mindset was different from the one in the Moriscos in other parts of the Peninsula. In the eyes of the authorities, the Moriscos of Granada were a grave threat to the state.[83] This was the

---

81. Janer, *Condición social de los Moriscos de España*, 52.
82. Bernabé Pons, "Una Visión Propicia del Mundo," 105.
83. Gallego y Burín and Sandoval, *Los Moriscos del Reino de Granada*, 13–14.

volatile political atmosphere that Pérez de Ayala had to work in when he became the bishop of Guadix in May 1548. To make matters worse, Guadix, Alpujarras and Baza were the most dangerous places and ideal bases for launching a revolt. They were almost isolated due to the weather, ruggedness of the terrain, long borders, and poor communication. The size of the Morisco population was significant.[84] As noted above, a rebellion did start in Alpujarras. Pérez de Ayala also faced internal issues in his diocese. The bishopric was in serious disarray when he took over. It had been vacant for two years because the previous appointee had not accepted it. A dispute—started when the bishopric of Guadix was created in 1492—whether Guadix or Toledo had jurisdiction over the diocese of Baza was still unresolved. As a result, churches lacked support and the poorly trained clergy were ineffective and unmotivated.[85] Pérez de Ayala wrote that the honesty, humility, and modesty of the priests had been damaged; their zeal had disappeared; and their charity and vigilance had become cold.[86]

Synod of Guadix

Pérez de Ayala set out to work in the spirit of the Council of Trent by convening a synod. The bulk of its measures were directed at the Moriscos. After sixty-five years of Catholic rule, they had managed to preserve their language, ceremonies, customs, and traditions through clandestine practice. It was evident that the campaign of evangelization coupled with harsh penalties—had not only failed, but deepened the Moriscos' hatred towards their rulers and increased their yearning for fellow Muslims in North Africa to rescue them. Other measures of the synod were directed at shaping old Christians and particularly the clergy into good role models. The Moriscos would then see that one discipline and one justice applied to both groups. This would prevent a bloody clash that would end up destroying one of them. The outcome of the synod—held from 22 January to 10 February 1554 at a critical point in the life of the Moriscos—was 254 constitutions organized into eight areas: preaching; administration of the sacraments; worship; priests and their emoluments; integrity and discipline of priests; doctrine and discipline of the people; tithes and first fruits; and stewards, prosecutors, and notaries.[87]

---

84. Gallego y Burín and Sandoval, *Los Moriscos del Reino de Granada*, 25.
85. Gallego y Burín and Sandoval, *Los Moriscos del Reino de Granada*, 29.
86. Gallego y Burín and Sandoval, *Los Moriscos del Reino de Granada*, 260.
87. Gallego y Burín and Sandoval, *Los Moriscos del Reino de Granada*, 29–31.

Zeal for Reform

The breadth of these constitutions and the speed in which they were written into final form demonstrate Pérez de Ayala's zeal to reform the churches in his diocese and instruct Moriscos according to the Council of Trent. He put the house in order in just twenty days. This would not have been an easy feat. The clergy must have grown accustomed to working without supervision for two years and would have preferred the status quo. He wrote in his journal and admitted that it was a difficult task. Some came to the synod with bad intentions. One of them preached "without grace or fruit."[88] There was resistance, but he recorded that he did what he had to do. The synod concluded "in twenty days and with unspeakable heaviness."[89]

Jesus Christ and The Trinity

The synod viewed Moriscos as "not good Christians" yet its constitutions were merciful, forgiving, and welcome anyone who was ready to follow the path laid out by the church for them.[90] The theology underpinning the synod's proceedings showed awareness of the doctrines that Moriscos found impossible to accept; for example, the divinity of Jesus Christ and the Trinity.

Jesus Christ

The proceedings stated, "It is necessary to present and explain by way of preaching that every person because of sin needs a redeemer who is both God and man at the same time."[91] There are multiple references in the proceedings concerning the salvific and redemptive work of Christ, the merits of his death and its universal application, the sinner's adoption, his entry into heaven, and freedom from sin and hell. There are also references to the divinity of Christ and exhortations to priests to preach this fundamental pillar.[92] Pérez de Ayala insisted on the regular preaching of these doctrines because they are the ones Moriscos "struggled most with and believed in less and have the greatest need

---

88. Pérez de Ayala, *Catecismo*, 67.
89. Pérez de Ayala, *Catecismo*, 66.
90. Guardia Guardia, "Doctrina teológica del Sínodo de Guadix de 1554," 13.
91. Guardia Guardia, "Doctrina teológica del Sínodo de Guadix de 1554," 14.
92. Guardia Guardia, "Doctrina teológica del Sínodo de Guadix de 1554," 14–15.

to be informed."[93] Moriscos rejected the divinity of Christ because it is irrational for God to be a man and for a man to be God. During Mass, they showed their rejection by talking loudly, hiding in corners or behind columns, and looking away as the host was raised.[94]

The Trinity

Moriscos argued that belief in the Trinity is belief in three gods. This associating partners with God is an unforgivable sin and the worst sin of the Christians. References to the Trinity in the proceedings are presented in the context of the celebration of the Mass. Upon entering a church, a person was to make the Sign of the Cross and say, "In the Name of the Father, the Son, and the Holy Spirit." The Sanctus of the Mass declared God to be "one and triune." References to the Trinity found in Pérez de Ayala's *Doctrina Cristiana* were included in the proceedings. The faithful made three signs of the cross—the one in the forehead pointed to the Father, the one on the chest pointed to the Son, and the one across the shoulders pointed to the Holy Spirit. The final references to the Trinity in the proceedings were in the symbols of faith—the Confession and the Creed.[95]

The common formula in a catechism like Ripalda's *Doctrina Cristiana* was "In the name of the Father, and the Son, and the Holy Spirit. Amen Jesus." However, the formula was different when instructing Moriscos. Pérez de Ayala's *Catecismo* declared, "In the name of the Father, and the Son, and the Holy Spirit, one God. Amen." Ribera liked this Trinitarian wording, but expanded it to meet the needs of the Moriscos of his diocese—"In the name of the Most Holy Trinity, Father, Son, and Holy Spirit, three persons and only one true God."[96] (Chapter 5 examines how the catechisms and polemical treatises address the doctrines of Jesus Christ and the Trinity.)

The Literary Context of the *Catecismo*

The Catechisms

There was a marked difference between the way Catholic doctrine was taught in the Middle Ages and the sixteenth century. Doctrinal teaching in

---

93. Guardia Guardia, "Doctrina teológica del Sínodo de Guadix de 1554," 18.
94. Guardia Guardia, "Doctrina teológica del Sínodo de Guadix de 1554," 17.
95. Guardia Guardia, "Doctrina teológica del Sínodo de Guadix de 1554," 21–22.
96. Guardia Guardia, "Doctrina teológica del Sínodo de Guadix de 1554," 22.

the Middle Ages was characterized by the influence of scholastic theology on language and analysis, moralism, subjective interpretation of the liturgy, and a gap between liturgy and catechesis. The catechisms of this period evolved into nothing more than *cartillas* or primers for learning how to read. Attempts were made to remedy the deficiency. In 1050, the Council of Coyanza made the Creed and the Lord's Prayer the foundation of the catechism. In the beginning of the second half of the Middle Ages, the Hail Mary and the Decalogue were added. In 1322, the Council of Valladolid made moral catechesis a priority and added the sacraments and a list of vices and virtues. The proceedings of this council were reaffirmed at the Council of Toledo (1323) and the synods of Tortosa (1429) and Aranda (1473). Cisneros and Talavera showed the same concern as these councils for the proper instruction of their flock. In 1470, Cisneros published a *sacramental* explaining the symbol and the commandments to adults. In 1497, he convened a synod in Alcalá and the following year Talavera also convened a synod. The outcome of these synods was the catechism *Constituciones del arçobispado de Toledo. E la tabla de lo que ha de enseñar a los niños.*[97] As the fifteenth century came to a close, a series of simple yet important *doctrinas* were published, including Talavera's *Breve y muy provechosa doctrina de lo que debe saber todo Cristiano con otros tratados muy provechosos*[98] (1498). In 1512, the Council of Sevilla not only stipulated that all clergy should know how to explain Catholic doctrine, but also required instruction to follow the strict order of the Articles of Faith, the Sacraments and the Commandments.[99]

Apologetic Literature

Literature published in the first quarter of the sixteenth century (ca. 1500–1525) was apologetic and defensive in nature. This was not a novelty. Literature critiquing Islam was available during the previous two centuries. The task of catechesis was also defensive. The church had to explain its doctrines as part of its efforts to attract Moriscos to the Catholic faith. Catechisms published from 1525 to ca. 1559 responded to Luther's ideas, humanism, and Erasmianism.[100] The University of Alcalá played an

---

97. Constitutions of the Archbishopric of Toledo. A table on what children ought to be taught.

98. Brief and useful doctrine that every Christian must know.

99. Ramón Guerrero, "Catecismos de autores españoles en la primera mitad del siglo XVI (1500–1559)," 2:225–26.

100. Ramón Guerrero, "Catecismos de autores españoles en la primera mitad del siglo XVI (1500–1559)," 2:229.

important role in the catechetical work done in the sixteenth century. The output from the close collaboration between theologians and humanists was rich in theology and capable of renewing faith and enlightening the soul. This teaching was unlike the one from the Middle Ages, which led to a legalistic Christianity.[101] Pérez de Ayala, Chinchón, and Ripalda graduated from the University of Alcalá.

The Availability of Catechisms

Prior to the sixteenth century, the Catholic Church used the above-mentioned councils and synods to demonstrate its keen intention to disseminate its teachings through the use of catechisms (Cisneros and Talavera). In the sixteenth century, the printing press, the Reformation, and the Council of Trent were crucial in the increase in the number of catechisms published. Luther published his *Small Catechism* in 1527. Calvin published his *Catechism of the Church* in 1541. Protestant catechisms such as Urbanus Regius's *Novae Doctrinae ad Veterem Collatio* and W. Perkins's *Cathólico Reformado* were translated into Spanish. In 1566, the Council of Trent responded to the rise of Protestant catechisms with its own catechism, but it was written in Latin for the clergy instead of the general public. (The section "Teaching of New Converts" in Chapter 5 will look again at this catechism.) Luther's catechism taught the Apostle's Creed, the Lord's Prayer, and the Ten Commandments. By comparison, the catechisms of the Catholic Church had four basic formulations—the Creed, the Lord's Prayer, the Ten Commandments, and the Sacraments.[102]

Questions and Answers

Some of the Catholic catechisms which used the format of questions and answers included Juan de Valdes' *Diálogo de doctrina cristiana* (1529), Constantino Ponce de la Fuente's *Suma de doctrina cristiana* (1543), Pedro de Soto's *Compendium doctrinae catholicae* (1549), Diego Jiménez Arias's *Enchiridión* (1552), Andrés Flórez's *Doctrina cristiana del Ermitaño y Niño* (1552), Domingo de Soto's *Summa de la doctrina cristiana* (1554), Ripalda's

---

101. Ramón Guerrero, "Catecismos de autores españoles en la primera mitad del siglo XVI (1500-1559)," 2:227–28.
102. Gómez, "Catecismos dialogados españoles (siglo XVI)," 121.

Doctrina Cristiana (1591), Astete's Doctrina cristiana (before 1592), Santiago Ledesma's Doctrina cristiana (1598), and Pérez de Ayala's Catecismo.[103]

There was no official catechism for the general public prior to the Council of Trent. The church in Spain began to fill the gap by publishing three different Spanish translations of *A Small Catechism for Catholics* by Dutch Jesuit Peter Canisius (1566, 1576, and 1595). Canisius' catechism followed the order of the four basic formulations—the Creed, the Lord's Prayer, the Ten Commandments, and the Sacraments.[104]

In 1549, Pedro de Soto—a Dominican priest—translated his *Compendium doctrinae catholicae* into Spanish. In it he defended among other things the need for works to justify faith and the advantages of not translating the Bible. The *Enchridión* was a warning against the publication of catechisms in Romance. It also follows the order—the Creed, the Lord's Prayer, the Ten Commandments, and the Sacraments. In 1554, Domingo de Soto changed the order—which the Roman Catechism would later follow—to the Creed, the Sacraments, the Ten Commandments, and the Lord's Prayer. He added the Commandments of the church to the basic formulations because failure to obey these commandments was a mortal sin. Flórez's *Doctrina cristiana del Ermitaño y Niño* and Ayala's *Catecismo* also followed Canisius' order of the formulations.[105]

The Creed

The Creed is found in Book Two, Part 1, Dialogue VIII of the *Catecismo*. This dialogue begins after the Moor (now a Christian and addressed as "Disciple") asks the Teacher, "Is there something shorter than the gospel, which summarizes what Christians must believe?" The Teacher answers in the affirmative saying that it is called "The Creed" and uses the following dialogue to explain it.

The Lord's Prayer

The Lord's Prayer is found in Book Two, Part 2, Dialogue III. In the previous dialogue, the Teacher answers the Disciples's question about the meaning of prayer. The Disciple follows that explanation by asking "What things should we ordinarily and mainly ask God for?" thus opening Dialogue III.

---

103. Gómez, "Catecismos dialogados españoles (siglo XVI)," 117.
104. Gómez, "Catecismos dialogados españoles (siglo XVI)," 122.
105. Gómez, "Catecismos dialogados españoles (siglo XVI)," 123.

The Ten Commandments

The Ten Commandments are recorded in Book Two, Part 3, Dialogue II. This dialogue begins near the end of the previous dialogue when the Disciple asks, "How many commandments of the Law of God are there?"

The Sacraments

The sacraments are found in Book Two, Part 4, Dialogues I to IX. The discussion begins after the Disciple asks, "Did God provide another remedy against sin that is necessary or helpful for one to walk in the path of heaven while on earth?" The Teacher uses Dialogues II to VI and IX to X to explain the sacraments—Baptism, Confirmation, Eucharist, Penitence, Confession, Extreme Unction, Order, and Matrimony.

Formats

Catechisms were written in one of two formats. Those presented in the format of a dialogue were aimed at comprehension and memorization. Those written in an expository format were meant to be read from a pulpit or for private reflection.[106] Examples of the former would be the works of Talavera, Andrés, Alba, Chinchón (*Antialcorano*), Pérez de Ayala (*Doctrina Cristiana*), Lorca, Ripalda, and Astete. Examples of the latter would be Chinchón (*Diálogos Christianos*), Orozco, *Catecismo del Sacromonte*, and Pérez de Ayala (*Catecismo*). Domingo de Soto's *Summa de la doctrina cristiana* used both formats simultaneously to take advantage of the strengths that each format offered. But, Juan de Valdes' *Diálogo de doctrina cristiana* and Constantino Ponce de la Fuente's *Suma de doctrina cristiana* avoided the monotonous succession of questions and answers by being three-person conversations. Andrés Flórez's *Doctrina cristiana del Ermitaño y Niño* and Pérez de Ayala's *Catecismo* are dialogues between two people only.[107]

Dialogues were lengthy and sometimes even wearisome. As noted previously, the Teacher in the *Catecismo* was in the habit of answering even the shortest questions in excruciating detail. Ribera in his cover letter to the *Catecismo* exhorted his priests to memorize it, but did anyone take his advice? Book One has 57,050 words and Book Two has 39,779 words (Book Two, Part Five, Dialogues III, V and IX are incomplete in the digital

---

106. Gómez, "Catecismos dialogados españoles (siglo XVI)," 124–25.
107. Gómez, "Catecismos dialogados españoles (siglo XVI)," 126.

copy) for a total of 96,829 words. The longest dialogue—Book Two, Part One, Dialogue IX—has 11,340 words.

Canisius popularized a third format—short questions followed by short answers. It is uncertain whether he came up with this format in response to the ponderous dialogues. Ripalda and Astete seemed to have mastered Canisius's format by reducing the length of the questions and answers to the barest minimum.[108] The Creed occupies the first fourteen pages of Astete's *Doctrina cristiana*. The questions and answers begin on page 15:

Q: Are you a Christian?

A: Yes, by the grace of God.

Q: From whom does the name Christian come from?

A: From Christ our Lord.

Q: What is the meaning of Christian?

A: Man of Christ.

A succinct presentation on the beginnings of Christian doctrine occupies the first two pages of Ripalda's *Doctrina Cristiana*. The questions and answers begin on page 2:

Q: Tell me, child, what is your name?

A: Pedro, Juan or Francisco.

Q: Are you a Christian?

A: Yes, by the grace of our Lord Jesus Christ.

Q: What is the meaning of Christian?

A: A man who has faith in Christ and professed it at baptism.

Astete's and Ripalda's ability to be concise explains in large part why their catechisms were the most famous ones.[109] However, as shown below, there was a problem with some of these short answers. Astete's and Ripalda's catechisms reveal nothing about the identity of the questioner or the respondent. They are mere abstractions.[110] In the *Catecismo*, we know

---

108. Gómez, "Catecismos dialogados españoles (siglo XVI)," 127.
109. Resines, "Los catecismos del siglo XVI y su modo de presentar la fe," 201.
110. Gómez, "Catecismos dialogados españoles (siglo XVI)," 127.

that one party is the Teacher who teaches on behalf of Pérez de Ayala and a Moor from Barbary.

Some of the catechisms such as Andrés Flórez's *Doctrina cristiana del Ermitaño y Niño* were written in verse to be sung to aid memorization. Some catechisms were translated such as Juan Pérez de Betolaza's *Doctrina cristiana en Romance y Basquence* (into Castillian and Basque) and Jerónimo Juttlar's *Doctrina cristiana* (into Catalan) in accordance with the proceedings of the Council of Trent that people should be instructed in their language. Pérez de Ayala's *Doctrina Cristiana* was translated into Arabic. This catechism also included guidelines on body posture during the Mass;[111] for example, kneel at the beginning (for confession) and at the end of the Mass (to receive the blessing) and in between, stand (for certain types of prayers) or sit (during the offertory).

Short Catechisms

The need of the Catholic Church to respond vigorously to the advance of what it regarded as the heresies of Protestantism meant that catechisms had to be doctrinally precise and communicate clearly. Unfortunately, the short catechisms of the sixteenth century were unable to strike a balance between accuracy and clarity. Astete's catechism asked, "What is prayer?" and answered, "To lift the heart to God and ask him for mercy." It defines *what* is prayer, but not *who* should pray. The reader would have known, but the answer was still too imprecise. Ripalda's catechism asked, "What is grace?" and answered, "A divine being that makes us sons of God, heirs of his glory." The term "a divine being" is an abstract philosophical construct. The answer should have been clear, but it wasn't.[112]

Catechisms written in expository format, on the other hand, were not constrained by space. Some explanations to a doctrinal point consumed several pages. Authors infused their answers with as much of their knowledge as they could—including, but not limited to biblical and patristic sources and conciliar proceedings. The possibility of misunderstanding was limited. Unfortunately, many of these catechisms did not go outside of the libraries of the curious and the intellectuals. When the choice had to be made, shorter catechisms were preferred.[113]

---

111. Gómez, "Catecismos dialogados españoles (siglo XVI)," 199.
112. Resines, "Los catecismos del XVI y su modo de presentar la fe," 202.
113. Resines, "Los catecismos del XVI y su modo de presentar la fe," 203.

Polemical Literature

The following overview of the literary context of the polemical treatises starts from about a century earlier to events that led to a renewed interest in Spain and Europe in polemical literature against Islam and highlights the significance of the representative works that preceded Juan Andres' *Confusión o confutación* (1515), Chinchón's *Antialcorano* (1532), Obregón's *Confutación del alcorán y secta mahometana* (1555), and Pérez de Ayala's *Catecismo* (1599).

In the fifteenth century, armies of the Ottoman Empire seemed invincible. Sultan Murad II (1404–51) captured Salonika in northern Greece (1430), defeated the Christian armies at the Battle of Varna (1444), and defeated the Hungarians at the Second Battle of Kosovo (1448). In 1453, his son Sultan Mehmed the Conqueror (1432–81) captured Constantinople. These victories had consequences. First, Pope Nicholas V (1447–55) and his successors Calixtus III (1455–58), Pius II (1458–64), Paul II (1464–71), Sixtus IV (1471–84), Innocent VIII (1484–92), and Alexander VI (1492–1503) made it their official policy to defeat the Turks on the battlefield. Second, there was a renewed interest in Europe for the anti-Islamic literature written by Petrus Alfonsi, Peter of Cluny, and Nicholas of Cusa.[114]

Petrus Alfonsi

Petrus Alfonsi (second half of the eleventh century—after 1116) wrote *Dialogi contra Iudeos* ("Dialogues against the Jews") in 1110 to defend himself against Jews who accused him of having abandoned his former faith. One of the twelve dialogues—Dialogue V—attacked Islam saying that Muhammad was a false prophet, Muslim rituals such as ablutions, fasting and pilgrimage were remnants of pagan worship to Venus, the Qur'an was a false revelation, and Islam was a heretical doctrine. *Dialogues* not only became the most widely read and used medieval anti-Jewish text, but was also popular among those interested in Islam. Scribes only recopied Dialogue V. The Dominicans stipulated that reading this dialogue together with the Latin translation of the Qur'an was required to understand Islam. Throughout the Middle Ages, many writers and readers considered *Dialogues* to be an important source of polemics against Islam.[115]

---

114. Cantarino, "Notas para la polémica contra el Islam en España," 133.
115. Tolan, "Petrus Alfonsi," 3:356–62.

Peter of Cluny

Peter of Cluny or Peter the Venerable (1092–1156) travelled to Spain from his monastery in Cluny and commissioned the translation of works related to Muhammad and Islam and the first full Latin translation of the Qur'an by Robert of Ketton. He wanted to provide Christendom with a "bookshelf" or "arsenal" of intellectual firepower to fight the "Saracen heresy" and wrote *Summa totius haeresis Saracenorum* ("Sum of the entire heresy of the Saracens") and *Contra sectam Saracenorum* ("Against the sect of the Saracens"). *Summa totius haeresis Saracenorum*—published sometime in 1143–44—presented Muhammad as a shrewd exploiter of ignorant Arabs; condemned Muhammad's picture of paradise as a place of eternal lust; and showed that Islam is the sum of all the heresies previously known to Christendom. *Contra sectam Saracenorum*—published sometime in 1155–56—was the first attempt of a leading authority of the Latin church to debunk Islam by saying that Muhammad was not a prophet and the Qur'an shows nothing extraordinary about him. Peter wrote this tract in Latin—which Muslims could not understand—because he was hoping that it would be translated into Arabic. But, he was also aiming at Christians who secretly admired Islam. *Contra sectam Saracenorum* was both apologetic and polemical.[116]

Nicholas of Cusa

Nicholas of Cusa (1401–64) attended the Council of Basel in 1433 where he met Juan de Segovia (q.v.) and obtained a copy of Robert of Ketton's translation of the Qur'an. In 1453, he published *De pace fidei* ("On the peace of faith") in Latin in the aftermath of the fall of Constantinople. This work pictures a heavenly vision of seventeen sages of different religions discussing unity of belief in the midst of diversity of rites. During the heady early days in Basel, conciliarists like Nicholas dreamt of a time when divisions in the Catholic Church would end, the Pope and the Holy Roman Emperor would be reconciled, and the Greek Orthodox and Rome would be allies. *De pace fidei* took that dream to the next level; that is, unity of creed with diversity of practice. In 1461, Nicholas published *Cribatio Alchorani* ("Sifting the Qur'an") in Latin, which was the product of extensive reading of Robert of Ketton's translation of the Qur'an and other anti-Muslim polemics and numerous conversations with scholars interested in Qur'an such as Juan de Segovia. This work stands out because of its irenic tone in an era when polemics against Islam was vitriolic and

---

116. Iogna-Prat and Tolan, "Peter of Cluny," 3:604–9.

Turks were caricatured as Scythian barbarians. In 1454, Nicholas wrote *Epistola ad Ioannem de Segovia* ("Letter to Juan de Segovia"). After Constantinople fell, Juan de Segovia wrote to Nicholas in 1454 and invited him to help organize a conference between Christians and Muslims "to pierce the heart of the Saracens with the sword of the Divine Spirit." Nicholas expressed support when he wrote back stating that Christianity is the religion of peace and should use peace to win over the Turks who spread their religion with the sword. He had in mind a gathering of lay people from different Christian groups living under Muslim rule. This conference would have put into practice the irenic spirit envisioned in *De pace fidei*. This letter is significant in that it shows two friends working to bring together the Catholic Church in Europe and the Turks to engage in peaceful dialogue. However, their ideas faded for lack of support.[117]

Europe on the Defensive

Sultans Murad II and Mehmed the Conqueror put Christian Europe on the defensive. The latter saw war as its best option to deal decisively with the military threat of Islam. However, the situation in the Iberian Peninsula was different. The Moors were the ones on the defensive. They would have become increasingly aware that the fall of Granada in 1492 not only achieved the political unity that Catholic monarchs had been fighting for since the beginning of the Reconquista in 722, but that religious unity would be their rulers' next goal. Isabella and Ferdinand initiated a plan that would impact the Moors living in the peninsula. One historian described the queen and the king as "the most enlightened princes to have ruled the earth, . . . great custodians of the religion and the faith, of lofty and courageous heart." In the sixteenth century, renewed interest in the Iberian Peninsula in polemical literature was forged between two bookends. One, the military threat posed by Ottoman forces in Europe. Second, Moors in the peninsula lacked military power, but had the capacity to disrupt and even put an end to the country's Christian unity.[118]

Moors had been forced to receive baptism, but the Catholic Church had to implement measures to ensure that conversions were genuine. First, it had to train its clergy. Priests were woefully ill-equipped for the task of evangelization due to their ignorance of the Moriscos' religious beliefs. This led to the publication of Pedro de Alcalá's *Arte para ligeramente saber la lengua arábiga* (The Art of Gently Learning Arabic) and the companion

---

117. Tolan, "Nicholas of Cusa," 5:421–28.
118. Cantarino, "Notas para la polémica contra el Islam en España," 134.

Spanish-Arabic dictionary *Vocabulista arábigo en letra catellana* (Arabic Vocabulary in Castilian). Both were printed in Granada in 1505.[119] *Arte* and *Vocabulista arábigo* were written as part of Talavera's soft approach to the instruction of Moriscos whereby priests had to learn Arabic. *Vocabulista arábigo* was the first ever system devised for transliterating Arabic into Roman letters.[120] Second, the church had to instruct Moriscos in the rudiments of Catholic doctrine. This was done through catechisms such as those examined in the present book. Third, the church had to draw Moriscos away from their religion by showing them the errors in the Qur'an. This was accomplished through *antialcoranes* (against the Qur'an) such as those written by Andrés, Chinchón, and Obregón. The *antialcoranes* had a second role—to justify war against the Turks—by demonstrating that what Islam taught was morally suspect and unworthy to be followed because its founder was not who he claimed to be.[121]

There had been two main lines of thinking about Islam since the middle of the fifteenth century. One group of writers learned about Islam by reading its texts and interacting with Muslims. They were less polemical and more interested in using reason and logic. Chinchón belonged to this group. The second group of writers such as Jaime Bleda and Alfonso Espina produced work that was belligerent, irascible, and blunt. But, there were also writers such as Andrés who held to a midway position between these two groups.[122] An author's focus was influenced by circumstances. The Moriscos and the menace from the Turks were significant issues in the sixteenth century. During the first decades of the century, the Islamic question in Granada was secondary because the authorities were occupied with the expulsion of the Jews. Furthermore, Spain had been successful in sending troops to North Africa as part of the expansionist policy it adopted after the fall of Granada in 1492. Spain was the victor and Islam was perceived in less harsh terms. The Catholic Church was feeling optimistic. But, this favorable picture started to change in the middle of the sixteenth century. Corsairs from Argel kept threatening the Iberian coast; Spain lost control of some of its possessions in the Magreb; assimilation of the Moriscos was not progressing as envisioned; and the Turks were winning most of the battles in Central Europe. The War of the Alpujarras increased the sense of

---

119. de Bunes, "El enfrentamiento con el Islam en el Siglo de Oro: Los antialcoranes," 44.

120. Zwartjes, "Pedro de Alcalá," 6:73–78.

121. de Bunes, "El enfrentamiento con el Islam en el Siglo de Oro: Los antialcoranes," 45.

122. de Bunes, "El enfrentamiento con el Islam en el Siglo de Oro: Los antialcoranes," 46.

danger. Even the victory at the Battle of Lepanto in October 1571 failed to lift the gloom. Polemical literature of this time became hostile.[123] The focus of this literature shifted again due to a new set of factors—a truce signed with the Turks, French incursions into Argel, internal and external problems unrelated to Islam, failure of the monarchy's foreign policy in North Africa, and the end of the presence of Moriscos. As a result, there was a decrease in the number of polemical works published.[124] These historical realities are important to keep in mind when considering why archbishop Ribera chose to publish the *Catecismo*.

Polemical works besides being different in focus due to historical realities were also different in terms of how they presented their material and the sources they used. Moriscos occupied one of the lowest levels of society. This meant that critique of Islam was simple and without the complex reasoning typical of theological schools. Writers like Andrés who knew Arabic quoted from Islamic sources to strengthen their arguments. They also referenced medieval sources such as Peter of Cluny.[125] Cluny conceived of the framework that he used to present the theological grounds of his arguments—defense of the Christian religion, the life of Muhammad, presentation of Muhammad's doctrine, study of the Qur'an, letter from a Saracen who tries to convert a Christian to Islam, and the Christian's rebuttals to the Saracen. Subsequent writers such as Andrés used this framework as a reference and adapted it to their particular situation.[126] The warm reception of Andrés' *Confusión o confutación* is attested by the fact that it was published in three Castilian editions (1532, 1537, and 1560) and translated into German (1568 and 1598), French (1574), English (1652), Latin (1646) and Italian (1537, 1540, 1545, and 1597).[127]

Talavera and Andrés

Talavera and Andrés were some of the best examples of the first decade of the sixteenth century to use the power of ideas to respond to Islam. Both of them shared the view that all possible means should be used to instruct the

123. de Bunes, "El enfrentamiento con el Islam en el Siglo de Oro: Los antialcoranes," 47.

124. de Bunes, "El enfrentamiento con el Islam en el Siglo de Oro: Los antialcoranes," 48.

125. de Bunes, "El enfrentamiento con el Islam en el Siglo de Oro: Los antialcoranes," 49.

126. Andrés, *La teología española en el siglo XVI*, 345.

127. de Bunes, "El enfrentamiento con el Islam en el Siglo de Oro: Los Antialcoranes," 49.

Moriscos. Chinchón's *Antialcorano* was based in part on Andrés' *Confusión o confutación*. The polemics in *Antialcorano* was straightforward and easy to follow because it dealt with actual issues arising from living with Moriscos. Chinchón's approach was logical and not difficult to understand for anyone who wanted to know the truth about Islam. Once Chinchón became certain that his arguments were convincing, he did not hesitate to pronounce eternal damnation on those who still refused to believe. Afterwards, other writers also used and adopted this coercive line. Polemics turned to belligerence with Lope de Obregón's *Confutación del alcorán y secta mahometana* (1555). Previous works were nuanced, but *Confutación del alcorán y secta mahometana* started immediately to attack Muhammad. This approach was a precursor to works written when the Moriscos were being expelled. The shift towards belligerence was connected to the historical realities mentioned above. Furthermore, the monarchy was becoming absolutist. The Christianity born out of the Council of Trent was becoming less optimistic and more cohesive. The seeds of Catholic doctrine had been sown and it was time for the harvest. Polemic literature was abandoning its paternalism and starting to consider Moriscos as authentic Muslims.[128]

---

128. de Bunes, "El enfrentamiento con el Islam en el Siglo de Oro: Los Antialcoranes," 51–52.

Chapter 5

The Content of the *Catecismo*

The Need, Request, and Criteria
for a New Catechism

Meetings in Madrid and Valencia (1595–1600)

BY THE EARLY 1590s, the previous eighty-five to ninety years of catechetical work among Moriscos had borne so little fruit that the need for a new catechism was considered.[1] Between 12 March 1595 and 19 February 1600, a series of meetings were held in Madrid and Valencia with active participation of Philip II to discuss solutions. On 17 May 1595, he put forward the resolution that Moriscos be taught Castilian and Valencian, catechisms be written in both languages, and Ribera be notified that he should go through Pérez de Ayala's *Catecismo*— adding and deleting what was necessary then sending a copy to him before it went to the printer.[2] On 4 November 1595, Philip II conveyed his resolution by letter to Ribera and said, "Someone has told me[3] that Archbishop Martín de Ayala arranged a catechism for the instruction of the new converts of Valencia." Philip II added that the *Catecismo* could "possibly" be used in the new campaign to instruct Moriscos and requested Ribera to select and lead a team of "zealous and well-educated men with experience in Morisco ministry" to check the *Catecismo* and to publish it quickly after they had completed their editorial work.[4] On 24 July 1597, the assessor of the Holy Office of the Inquisition evaluated the *Catecismo* that Ribera and his team sent him. The assessor opined—and Philip II agreed—

---

1. Robres Lluch, *San Juan de Ribera*, 407.
2. Boronat y Barrachina, *Los moriscos españoles y su expulsión. Tomo I*, 656, 660.
3. The uncertainty as to how did Philip II learn about the existence of the *Catecismo* does not affect the purposes of this chapter and the present book.
4. Boronat y Barrachina, *Los moriscos españoles y su expulsión. Tomo I*, 360.

that Book One should be printed in Latin instead of Spanish to prevent fools and illiterate people from reading it.[5] (Polemical works against Islam and Muhammad were banned in 1559.[6]) The decision of Philip II to print Book One in Spanish despite the assessor's opinion remains a mystery. Perhaps the late date of the printing (1599) warranted a more direct action to evangelize the Moriscos. A Spanish translation of both books of the *Catecismo* suggests a desire to spread the work widely because not many pastors were skilled in Latin.[7] Almost two years later (10 May 1599) a resolution was passed to ask Ribera to proceed with the printing of the *Catecismo*.[8] Less than two weeks later (May 23) Philip II wrote to Ribera and said, "Go ahead and print the catechism that you went through for the instruction of the new converts in your and other dioceses."[9]

Ribera's Letters

On 16 July 1599, Ribera wrote a letter to the preachers of his archdiocese to draw their attention to four points of utmost importance: the goal of preaching, their attitude towards the Moriscos, their conversation with them, and how to teach doctrine. First, he reminded them that the goal of preaching is "to see the new Christians of the Moors of Valencia obey the gospel." Second, he exhorted them to be considerate of their Morisco flock even though the latter were hostile—"Your apostolic task among the Moriscos will be difficult because you are taking care of people who hate us. A long-standing gap separates us from them because we have not been charitable or friendly towards them." Third, he urged them to choose their words carefully—"it is always best not to inflame the emotions of the new converts during private and public conversations by saying something bad about their sect." Fourth, he advised them to teach to be understood— "doctrine should be simple and conveyed using common terms" and "the sense and meaning of words should also be easy to understand and acted upon." Ribera then informed his preachers that they would know more from a catechism he was printing, which was "adapted to the talents of (the

  5. Boronat y Barrachina, *Los moriscos españoles y su expulsión. Tomo I*, 667–68.
  6. García Cárcel, "Estudio crítico del catecismo de Ribera-Ayala," 166.
  7. Our explanation is an educated guess. It is beyond the scope of the present book to explore this mystery.
  8. Boronat y Barrachina, *Los moriscos españoles y su expulsión. Tomo I*, 669.
  9. Boronat y Barrachina, *Los moriscos españoles y su expulsión. Estudio histórico-crítico. Tomo II*, 8–10.

Moriscos)."[10] He did not reveal that it was the catechism that he and Philip II had been discussing. On 27 October 1599, copies of the *Catecismo* became available with a cover letter from Ribera pointing out to his rectors, preachers, and confessors why it had been printed.

Significance

First, the meetings in Madrid and Valencia show commitment and urgency on the part of the monarchy and the Catholic Church to the catechesis of the Moriscos even though the Junta of Lisboa had already decided in 1582 to expel them from the country. Second, these meetings only considered Pérez de Ayala's *Catecismo*. No deliberations were held on any of the other catechisms and polemical treatises examined in the present book—not even Pérez de Ayala's *Doctrina Cristiana* or the catechisms that had received permission from Philip II to be printed: Lope Obregón's *Confutación del alcoran y secta mahometana* (published in 1555), Orozco's *Catecismo provechoso* (published in 1566) and Lorca's *Catecheses mystagogicae* (published in 1586). Third, reading the cover letter to the *Catecismo* gives the impression that Ribera decided unilaterally to print the *Catecismo*. However, the decision appears to have been a collective one because Philip II and the Holy Office of the Inquisition were involved. It is even possible that it was Philip II who came up with the idea of printing the *Catecismo*. Fourth, the *Catecismo* might have remained as scattered sheets of paper in a dark corner except for these meetings that authorized Ribera to prepare them for better use.

What is the significance of Ribera's letter to his preachers and his cover letter to the *Catecismo*? First, the letter of 16 July 1599—like the meetings in Madrid and Valencia—demonstrate commitment to the instruction of the Moriscos even though it was written seventeen years after the Junta of Lisboa had made the decision to expel the Moriscos from the country. Second, the letter reveals Ribera's clear vision, pastoral attitude, and gentle approach to instructing the Moriscos despite the fact that at the beginning of that same letter he seems to show some disillusionment when he admits that few of them had left the sect of Muhammad. Third, the letter's four high priority points and the cover letter to the *Catecismo* provide some of the criteria for Part C of this chapter.

---

10. Ximenez, *Vida del Beato Juan de Ribera*, 450.

Criteria

The criteria for evaluating the new catechism come from the following four sources:

> **Source 1.** *San Juan de Ribera. Patriarca de Antioquía, Arzobispo y Virrey de Valencia. Un obispo según el ideal de Trento.*[11]
>
> **Source 2.** The letter dated 16 July 1599 from Ribera to the preachers of his archdiocese.
>
> **Source 3.** The cover letter that Ribera wrote for the *Catecismo*.
>
> **Source 4.** The Triple Challenge presented in Chapter 4 above.

The information in these four sources have been converted into the following questions that will be used as the criteria to assess the *Catecismo* and the twelve catechisms and polemical treatises introduced in Chapter 3. (From hereon this collection of twelve catechisms and polemical treatises will be referred to as "the Group of twelve.")

Source 1

Catechisms published before the early 1590s were commendable attempts at instructing the Moriscos, but the lack of results meant that a different catechism was needed. The new catechism was to have these characteristics: It would not be a catechism for children, but a handbook and a primer for rectors with apologetic material that responds to the usual objections raised by Islamic clerics and an exposition of the life and doctrines of Muhammad. Given that the catechesis of Moriscos had become stagnant, it was most urgent for the new catechism to discuss Christian theological concepts in such a way that Moriscos could understand.[12] The characteristics of that new catechism have been modified into the following questions to be used as criteria:

1. Is the catechism written for children? (The correct answer should be negative.)
2. Is the catechism or polemical treatise[13] written with rectors in mind?

---

11. Robres Lluch, *San Juan de Ribera*, 407.
12. Robres Lluch, *San Juan de Ribera*, 407.
13. The meetings in Madrid and Valencia discussed the printing of a catechism, but we have drawn a distinction between "catechism" and "polemical treatise" for the

3. Is the catechism or polemical treatise like a handbook and a primer?
4. Does the catechism or polemical treatise have apologetic material that addresses the usual objections raised by Islamic clerics?
5. Does the catechism or polemical treatise provide an exposition on the life and doctrines of Muhammad?
6. Most urgently, does the catechism or polemical treatise present Christian theological concepts adapted to the abilities and talents of the Moriscos?

Source 2

The second source—the four points underlined in Ribera's letter of 16 July 1599 to his preachers—have been turned into the following questions to be used as criteria:

1. Does the catechism or polemical treatise teach the gospel?
2. Is the tone of the catechism or polemical treatise "charitable and friendly"?
3. Could the catechism or polemical treatise inflame the emotions of the Moriscos?
4. Does the catechism or polemical treatise use "common and ordinary terms" to preach "intelligible" doctrine so that Moriscos know what they must believe and do?

Source 3

The third source—the cover letter that Ribera wrote where he gives six reasons[14] for printing the *Catecismo*—have been modified into the following questions to be used as criteria:

---

purposes of this book. We have adapted the information from the four sources and applied it to the catechisms and polemical treatises in the Group of twelve—not just the catechisms.

14. The *Catecismo* (1) shows that Pérez de Ayala had experience ministering to Moriscos; (2) presents the gospel to the Moor; uses "natural and moral reasons and facts" to show (3) "the purity and beauty" of the religion of Christ and (4) "the clumsiness and blunders" of the sect of Muhammad; (5) communicates in a way that is suited to the abilities and talents of the Moriscos; and (6) uses the format of a dialogue, "which is the clearest and most distinct way to teach when the one being instructed has questions and the teacher has answers"?

1. Does the author of the catechism or polemical treatise have experience talking with and instructing Moriscos?
2. Does the catechism or polemical treatise discuss all the material needed to teach the gospel to an unbeliever—especially someone who comes from the sect of Muhammad? This question is similar to Question 1 in *Source 2*.
3. Does the catechism or polemical treatise use "natural and moral reasons and facts" to show the "purity and beauty" of the religion of Christ?
4. Does the catechism or polemical treatise use "natural and moral reasons and facts" to show the "clumsiness and blunders" of the sect of Muhammad?
5. Does the catechism or polemical treatise communicate in a style tailored to the abilities and talents of the one being instructed? This question is similar to Question 4 in *Source 2*.
6. Does the catechism or polemical treatise use the format of a dialogue, "which is the clearest and most distinct way to teach when the one being instructed has questions and the teacher has answers"?

Source 4

The fourth and final source comes from Chapter 4 of the present book. The questions at the end of the section titled "Heart, Mind, Actions—A Triple Challenge" have been transformed into the following two questions to be used as criteria:[15]

1. Is the catechism or polemical treatise aware of the Triple Challenge; that is, the confession, the beliefs, and the commandments that control the heart, the mind, and the behavior of the Moriscos?
2. Does the catechism or polemical treatise grapple with the Triple Challenge?

---

15. Questions 1 and 2 are inseparable. Both of them have to be asked. Given that it cannot be assumed that all catechisms and polemical treatises are aware of the Triple Challenge, Question 1 exists to differentiate them. Given that it is also not enough to know which ones are aware of the challenge, Question 2 is needed to see *how* they grapple with the challenge. In other words, *who* (Question 1) and *how* (Question 2).

A Bird's-Eye View of All the Criteria Used for Evaluating the New Catechism[16]

Source 1

1. Is the catechism written for children?
2. Is the catechism or polemical treatise written with rectors in mind?
3. Is the catechism or polemical treatise like a handbook and a primer?
4. Does the catechism or polemical treatise have apologetic material that addresses the usual objections raised by Islamic clerics?
5. Does the catechism or polemical treatise provide an exposition on the life and doctrines of Muhammad?
6. Most urgently, does the catechism or polemical treatise present Christian theological concepts adapted to the abilities and talents of the Moriscos?

Source 2

1. Does the catechism or polemical treatise discuss all the material needed to teach the gospel to an unbeliever—especially someone who comes from the sect of Muhammad? This question combines Question 1 from Source 2 and Question 2 from Source 3.
2. Is the tone of the catechism or polemical treatise "charitable and friendly"?
3. Could the catechism or polemical treatise inflame the emotions of the Moriscos?
4. Does the catechism or polemical treatise use "common and ordinary terms" to preach "intelligible" doctrine so that Moriscos know what they must believe and do? This question combines Question 2 from Source 2 and Question 5 from Source 3.

Source 3

1. Does the author of the catechism or polemical treatise have experience talking with and instructing Moriscos?

16. If sources have similar questions, the latter ones have been combined into one question.

2. Does the catechism or polemical treatise use "natural and moral reasons and facts" to show the "purity and beauty" of the religion of Christ?
3. Does the catechism or polemical treatise use "natural and moral reasons and facts" to show the "clumsiness and blunders" of the sect of Muhammad?
4. Does the catechism or polemical treatise use the format of a dialogue, "which is the clearest and most distinct way to teach when the one being instructed has questions and the teacher has answers"?

Source 4

1. Is the catechism or polemical treatise aware of the Triple Challenge; that is, the confession, the beliefs, and the commandments that control the heart, the mind, and the behavior of the Moriscos?
2. Does the catechism or polemical treatise grapple with the Triple Challenge?

Steps

The process of evaluating the new catechism uses the analogy of competitive sports and follows three steps. Each of the four sources represents a "Round." Each question in a Source represents an "Event." The *Catecismo* and the catechisms and polemical treatises in the Group of twelve are the "Competitors." There are thirteen Competitors, four Rounds and sixteen Events.

Table 2. The Competition

Thirteen Competitors

Round 1	Round 2	Round 3	Round 4
Six Events	Four Events	Four Events	Two Events

Sixteen Events

Step 1

This step applies the sixteen criteria to assess the *Catecismo* and the Group of twelve. Competitors start from Round 1. Those who "win" the events—that is, meet the criteria—progress to the next round until Round 4. Each round reduces the number of competitors reaching the final round. This step consists of:

    Chapter 6 (The New *Catecismo*: Audience and Format).

    Chapter 7 (The New *Catecismo*: The Gospel and Reaction).

    Chapter 8 (The New *Catecismo*: Experience and Evidence).

    Chapter 9 (The New *Catecismo*: Heart, Mind, and Behavior).

Step 2

This step analyzes the results from Step 1—the competitors who reach Round 4—according to their content in two areas: apologetics and polemics. This step consists of:

    Chapter 10 (The Content of the *Catecismo*: Apologetics and Polemics).

Step 3

This step uses the results from Step 2 to offer preliminary answers to the present book's two central questions: (1) What was the potential of the *Catecismo* as an evangelistic tool addressed to Moriscos? and (2) Why was the *Catecismo* chosen in late 1599 to bolster Ribera's evangelistic task? This step consists of:

    Chapter 11 (Juan de Ribera's Catecismo: The Legacy of Martín Pérez de Ayala).

An Original Approach

The approach described in this chapter adapts an activity that is familiar to a modern audience (competitive sports) to understand how a decision could have been made in sixteenth-century Spain (the selection of the *Catecismo* for publication). The information in the four sources were converted into sixteen questions (events) to act as criteria to assess thirteen competitors. Philip II, Ribera, and other high-level ecclesiastical decision-makers had these same four sources. What is clear: Philip II made an official request for a new catechism; the need for such a catechism was urgent; and Ribera's letters reveal what he believed a new catechism might look like. What is unclear because of a lack of records of that time (correspondence and decrees) is an indication of which of the four sources were used and how many were used. This methodology—a deliberate and systematic process of using the objective criteria extracted from all four sources to evaluate the attempts of all thirteen competitors to persuade the Moors and the Moriscos to abandon their religious beliefs and traditions in favor of Catholic doctrine and practices—leads to an outcome (the selection of the *Catecismo* for publication) that can be understood and explained.

Chapter 6

The New *Catecismo*: Audience and Format

Step 1

Round One, Six Events

STEP 1 CONSISTS OF Chapter 6 to 9. There is one round with six events in Chapter 6.

Round One, Event 1. Is the catechism written for children?

The correct answer should be negative. Ripalda's *Doctrina Cristiana* is the only catechism in the Group of twelve written for children. The presence of an adult protagonist in a catechism or polemical treatise means that the work was written for adults. Three different types of adult protagonists are present: Moors (*Confusión o confutación, Diálogos Christianos,* and *Catecismo*), Moriscos (*Breve doctrina y enseñanza,* Ripalda's *Doctrina Cristiana, Antialcorano,* Pérez de Ayala's *Doctrina Cristiana, Catecismo provechoso, Catecheses mystagogicae,* and *Catecismo del Sacromonte*), and Christians (Astete's *Doctrina cristiana*).

Results

All of the above catechisms and polemical treatises advance to Event 2 except Ripalda's *Doctrina Cristiana*.

Round One, Event 2. Is the catechism or polemical treatise written with rectors in mind?

Many priests at the time were ill-equipped and incompetent. A catechism or polemical treatise addressed to rectors would have facilitated and even sped up the transmission of the doctrines of the religion of Christ from the top levels of the Catholic Church down to the level of the priests who had the most direct contact with and responsibility to instruct Moriscos. The following five works specified that they were dedicated to rectors or other church leaders in mind:

> *Antialcorano.* Dedicated to Ehrard de Lamark—archbishop-at-large of Valencia (1520–39)—and Guillén Desprats and Juan Gay, the two general vicars who governed the diocese on his behalf.
>
> *Diálogos Christianos.* Dedicated to Juan Gay, the general vicar who governed the diocese of Valencia during the absence of its archbishop Ehrard de Lamark.
>
> *Confutación del alcorán y secta mahometana.* Dedicated to Diego de Álava y Esquivel, bishop of Ávila, president of the Real Audiencia of Granada, and the emperor's council. The work was approved by the Holy Inquisition.[1]
>
> *Catecheses mystagogicae.* Dedicated to pastors and authorities.[2]
>
> *Catecismo.* Addressed to rectors, preachers, and confessors.[3]

The following seven works did not identify rectors or other church leaders, but mentioned who commissioned their works or granted license for them to be printed. This seal of approval would have communicated a sense of urgency to the priests to take seriously their responsibility to instruct new converts:

> *Breve doctrina y enseñanza.* The digital copy of this catechism archived at the Biblioteca Digital Hispánica does not indicate who commissioned this work.[4] We assume that it was commissioned by or dedicated to Queen Isabella and King Ferdinand for they appointed Talavera to be Granada's first archbishop.
>
> *Confusión o confutación.* Andrés wrote at the request of Martín García, bishop of Barcelona and inquisitor of Aragón. Five ecclesiastical

---

1. First page beneath the title *Confusión o confutación de la secta mahomética.*
2. Busic, "Saving the Lost Sheep," 230.
3. Cover letter to the *Catecismo.*
4. This information was printed at the beginning of a catechism.

leaders approved the printing. Although Andrés did not specify which rector(s) he had in mind, it is evident that his polemical work was written for adults who were his co-religionists.

Alba's *Doctrina Christiana*. Commissioned by Charles at the Junta de la Capilla Real de Granada held on 7 December 1526.[5]

Pérez de Ayala's *Doctrina Cristiana*. The digital copy of this catechism archived at the Biblioteca Nacional de España does not indicate who commissioned this work or to whom it was dedicated. According to page 3 of this digital copy, Pérez de Ayala wrote *Doctrina Cristiana* for new converts whom he addresses as "children most beloved in Christ" and refers to himself as their "pastor and spiritual father." This catechism was written for clergy in the style of a school primer.[6]

Catecismo provechoso. Three licenses were granted to this work. One from the bishop of Utica and general vicar of the archbishop of Zaragoza; one from the Holy Office of the Inquisition of the Kingdom of Aragón; and one from Philip II. The *Catecismo provechoso* must have been a substantial work to have received such close attention from the highest levels of the Catholic Church and the king himself. All of them agreed that this catechism did not contain anything offensive to the Catholic Church, but instead was "useful and beneficial"[7] for the instruction of new converts.

Catecismo del Sacromonte. The transcription of this catechism[8] provides no information about to whom it was dedicated or who commissioned or licensed it for printing. Given that the name of the author—a Jesuit priest—is unknown, it seems likely that this catechism was intended for personal use.[9]

Astete's *Doctrina cristiana*. The digital version of this catechism does not reveal to whom was this catechism dedicated or who commissioned or licensed it for publication.[10]

---

5. Resines, *El Catecismo de Pedro Ramiro de Alba*, 132.
6. Framiñán de Miguel, "Martín Pérez de Ayala," 6:212.
7. Digital copy of *Catecismo provechoso*, 9.
8. Resines, *Catecismo del Sacromonte*, 160–321.
9. Resines, *Catecismo del Sacromonte*, 44.
10. The present book uses the edition of the *Catecismo de la doctrina cristiana* with questions and answers added by Gabriel Menéndez de Luarca (1742–1812) and printed in 1787. Menéndez de Luarca was professor of philosophy and theology at the University of Salamanca and prison canon of the Cathedral of Segovia.

Results

Antialcorano, Diálogos Christianos, Confutación del alcorán y secta mahometana, Catecheses mystagogicae, and *Catecismo* proceed to Event 3. Although *Breve doctrina y enseñanza, Confusión o confutación,* Alba's *Doctrina Christiana,* Pérez de Ayala's *Doctrina Cristiana, Catecismo provechoso, Catecismo del Sacromonte,* and Astete's *Doctrina cristiana* do not specify that they were written with rectors or other church leaders in mind, they will also move to the next event for two reasons. First, it is evident that they were written for individuals responsible for the instruction of new converts. Second, the missing information could be in yet to be discovered secondary sources. Thus, the *Catecismo* and the following eleven works in the Group of twelve proceed to the next event:

Antialcorano, Diálogos Christianos, Confutación del alcorán y secta mahometana, Catecheses mystagogicae, Catecismo, Breve doctrina y enseñanza, Confusión o confutación, Doctrina Christiana (Alba), *Doctrina Cristiana* (Ayala), *Catecismo provechoso, Catecismo del Sacromonte,* and *Doctrina cristiana* (Astete).

Round One, Event 3. Is the catechism or polemical treatise like a handbook and a primer?

This question can be answered by dividing "handbook and primer" into three categories.

Category 1. Handbook and primer only on Catholic doctrine. *Breve doctrina y enseñanza, Doctrina Cristiana* (Ayala), and *Doctrina cristiana* (Astete).

Category 2. Handbook and primer only on Muhammad, his doctrine, and his sect. *Confusión o confutación, Antialcorano, Diálogos Christianos, Confutación del alcorán y secta mahometana,* and *Catecheses mystagogicae.*

Category 3. Handbook and primer on both Catholic doctrine and Muhammad, his doctrine, and his sect. *Catecismo Provechoso, Doctrina cristiana* (Alba), *Catecismo del Sacromonte,* and *Catecismo.*

Results

The *Catecismo* and eleven works in the Group of twelve mentioned above proceed to Event 4.

Round One, Event 4. Does the catechism or polemical treatise have apologetic material that addresses the usual objections raised by Islamic clerics?

Breve doctrina y enseñanza, *Doctrina Cristiana* (Ayala), and *Doctrina cristiana* (Astete) are not works of apologetics.[11] *Catecheses mystagogicae* leans more toward polemics.[12] Furthermore, it was written in Latin, which made it incomprehensible to the Moriscos. Philip II wanted catechisms written in Castilian and Valencian.

Results

The original group of thirteen competitors (*Catecismo* and the Group of twelve) has now been reduced to eight. *Confusión o confutación*, *Doctrina Cristiana* (Alba), *Antialcorano*, *Diálogos Christianos*, *Confutación del alcorán y secta mahometana*, *Catecismo provechoso*, and *Catecismo del Sacromonte*, and *Catecismo* progress to Event 5.

Round One, Event 5. Does the catechism or polemical treatise give an exposition on the life and doctrines of Muhammad?

Doctrina Christiana (Alba) does not go beyond this event. Alba mentions the doctrines of Muhammad, but does not give an exposition on his life such as those found in the works that will move to the next event. Andrés, Pérez de Chinchón, Obregón, and Pérez de Ayala discuss Muhammad at length. The first three of these four authors provide a full frontal assault on Muhammad. Such an exposition would not have been one of the goals of *Doctrina Christiana*. Alba stated that his catechism was a "brief art and instruction" (with an emphasis on "brief") for new Christians converted to the Catholic faith, but mainly those who used to be Moors. He does not focus on Muhammad except when mentioning him in reference to a specific religious custom that new Christians should avoid. However, this somewhat indirect approach

---

11. Apologetics at this stage is defined as "The defense of Christ and his religion." See above "The Content of the Catechisms and Polemical Treatises. 2. Type of Content" in Chapter 3. A comprehensive definition is available in Chapter 10.

12. Polemics at this stage is defined as "The critique of Muhammad and his religion." See above "The Content of the Catechisms and Polemical Treatises. 2. Type of Content" in Chapter 3. A comprehensive definition is available in Chapter 10.

would have been sufficient to discourage new Christians from continuing to follow Muhammad and obey his doctrine.

Alba's "brief art and instruction" has four parts of which the last part—Part Four—is the most important one. It is noteworthy that this part is not placed at the beginning of the catechism. Alba prepares the groundwork—the first three parts of the catechism—before using the last part of the catechism to critique Muhammad and his doctrine. Part One focuses on what new Christians *must believe,* which is everything that the Catholic Church believes or the Creed. Part Two instructs new Christians on what they *must know:* the Sign of the Cross, prayers (the Lord's Prayer, Ave Maria, and Salve Regina), the seven sacraments, the powers of the soul (memory, understanding, and the will), the enemies of the soul (the devil, the world, and the flesh), the three states (married, widowed, and never married), three ways to sin (thought, word, and deed), virtues, deeds of mercy, and the seven mortal sins (pride, greed, lust, gluttony, wrath, envy, and acedia).[13] Part Three pays attention to what new Christians *must do* according to Christian law—The Ten Commandments.

Part One of *Doctrina Christiana* makes occasional contrasts between Christian teachings and teachings in the Qur'an, but Muhammad is not mentioned. Although a discussion of how a Qur'anic teaching is contrary to Christian teaching can be viewed as an indirect reference or critique of Muhammad because he claimed to be the prophet of Allah who brought the final message to mankind. Part One makes at least three contrasts. One, the Catholic Church teaches that all sins can be forgiven while the Qur'an teaches that grievous sins cannot be forgiven.[14] Two, everyone will be resurrected on the day of judgment to be rewarded contrasted with the unlimited sensual pleasures in paradise that await Moors. Third, the Qur'an teaches that angels and demons will die then resurrect.[15] Part Two makes no mention at all about Muhammad or what he taught. Part Three mentions Muhammad twice—one time as having violated the Fifth Commandment and the second time for transgressing the Sixth Commandment.[16]

Part Four of *Doctrina Christiana* is the most important part because it gives two types of instructions to new Christians—what they *must stop believing* and what they *must stop practicing.* Alba uses the groundwork that he laid with the first three chapters to critique Muhammad. *Doctrina Christiana's* first type of instruction admonishes new Christians to stop

---

13. Resines, *El Catecismo de Pedro Ramiro de Alba,* 133–15.
14. Q. 4:48.
15. Resines, *El Catecismo de Pedro Ramiro de Alba,* 142–43.
16. Resines, *El Catecismo de Pedro Ramiro de Alba,* 159–60.

believing that Muhammad was a man of God and his prophet. He was a "very bad man," "liar," "lewd," "demon-possessed," "ignorant," "unable to read or write," "idolater," "sorcerer," "tyrant," "killer," "stole the wives of other men," "heretical" and "blasphemous."[17] Muhammad is connected to a doctrine or practice associated with him. New Christians must stop believing what he taught about God, angels, demons, man's soul, the stars, Mecca, paradise, wine, those who die in battle, and disputes about his law. Second, they must stop practicing all their religious customs such as Ramadan, *salat,* and *zakat.* New Christians should also stop being superstitious. Men can have only one wife.[18]

Results

The *Catecismo* and six works from the Group of twelve (*Confusión o confutación, Antialcorano, Diálogos Christianos, Confutación del alcorán y secta mahometana, Catecismo Provechoso,* and *Catecismo del Sacromonte*) proceed to Event 6.

Round One, Event 6. Most urgently, do the catechisms or polemical treatise present Christian theological concepts adapted to the abilities and talents of the Moriscos?

"Christian theological concepts"

There were two types of "Christian theological concepts." The first type pertains to concepts that Moriscos traditionally had disagreements with the followers of Christ; for example, his divinity and crucifixion, man's sin and need for redemption, and the Trinity. However, Moriscos were expected to agree with these concepts after receiving proper instruction. The second type of concepts refers to beliefs and habits that Moriscos were required to adopt to demonstrate that they agree with the first type of concepts. In terms of beliefs, Moriscos were to believe in the twelve Articles of Faith in the Creed. In terms of habits, they were to keep the Ten Commandments, observe the seven Sacraments, pray (the Lord's Prayer, Ave Maria, and Salve Regina), and do good deeds. Both types of concepts can be differentiated as follows: The first type emphasizes what Moriscos should *confess* while the second type concentrates on what they should *do* to prove that they had confessed; for example, if they had confessed that Christ is divine (first type), they would pray according to the pattern

---

17. Resines, *El Catecismo de Pedro Ramiro de Alba,* 168.
18. Resines, *El Catecismo de Pedro Ramiro de Alba,* 177–80.

he outlined in the Lord's Prayer (second type). As we shall see shortly, the seven competitors participating in this sixth event discuss either both types of concepts or just one of them.

"adapted to the abilities and talents of the Moriscos"

The second phrase—"adapted to the abilities and talents of the Moriscos"—shows awareness of a reality and a hurdle. The reality is that Muhammad and his teachings have been the sole influences on the worldview of the Moriscos. The hurdle is for the remaining seven competitors in the Group of twelve to bridge the gap between that reality and Christian theological concepts; for example, Jesus was only a prophet (the worldview of the Moriscos) vs. Jesus was God (Christian theological concept). The analysis of each competitor's awareness of the reality and the hurdle is found under "Bridging the Gap" below.

"most urgently"

The third phrase—"most urgently"—shows urgency like Event 2 (Is the catechism and polemical treatise written with rectors in mind?). However, the sense of urgency in both events is not the same. The stress in Event 2 is on *who* teaches while the primary issue in Event 6 is *what* is taught. The combination of both events evinces concern for having *the right instructors* (priests) teaching *the right things* (Christian theological concepts).

Christian Theological Concepts: Summary

Confusión o confutación	Jesus Christ, the Christian Scriptures
Antialcorano	Jesus Christ, the Christian Scriptures, the Holy Spirit, the Trinity
Diálogos Christianos	Jesus Christ, the Christian Scriptures, the Trinity
Confutación del alcorán y secta mahometana	
Catecismo provechoso	Jesus Christ, the Holy Spirit
Catecismo del Sacromonte	The Creation, the Christian Scriptures, the Fall of Man, Sin
Catecismo	God, Jesus Christ, the Christian Scriptures, Sin

The answer to Round One, Event 6 focuses on three theological concepts—Jesus Christ, the Trinity, and the Christian Scriptures—for three reasons. First, these concepts are considerable obstacles that keep Moors and Moriscos from leaving their religion to embrace Christianity. They believe that the Christian Scriptures have been corrupted, Jesus was a prophet and not God, and hell is the destiny of Christians who believe in the Trinity.[19] Second, more authors have written about these concepts (five of the seven). Third, it is possible to analyze what these five authors wrote. By comparison, analysis about what these authors and the remaining two wrote on the creation is not possible because only *Catecismo del Sacromonte* discusses this concept.

Jesus Christ: Bridging the Gap

Each work had its distinctive way of helping Moriscos understand who is Jesus Christ.

Confusión o confutación	The Qur'an, Jesus, Muhammad
Antialcorano	The Qur'an, the *sunna*
Diálogos Christianos	Logic
Catecismo provechoso	A simile (the sun and a ray of sunlight), the Christian Scriptures
Catecismo del Sacromonte	Similes (flowers, sunlight, streams of water), images (God, ourselves)
Catecismo	Jesus' words, Jesus' followers, kings and prophets, Old Testament prophecies, John the Baptist

Confusión o confutación

Moriscos were familiar with—and perhaps even memorized—passages in the Qur'an that mention Jesus Christ. Andrés bridges the gap by referring to those same passages to underscore certain truths he believes are embedded in them about the birth, ministry, and "excellences" of Christ. He uses Sahih al-Bukhari, Sahih Muslim, and seven passages in the Qur'an to

---

19. The belief that Christians will go to hell and stay there forever for believing in the Trinity is pointed out in Dialogue 2 of *Diálogos Christianos* in Pons Fuster, *Antialcorano. Diálogos Christianos*, 419.

stimulate Moriscos to be open to the possibility that there could be something more to the Jesus they esteem.

The Birth of Jesus

Two passages in the Qur'an suggest that Jesus is superior to any prophet or saint in the world. First, Q. 19:16–34.[20] The Spirit of God in the form of a human being announces to Mary the birth of Jesus whom he refers to as "a boy (who is) pure" and "a sign to the people and a mercy" from God. Even though Jesus is still in the cradle, he can talk like an adult. Second, Q. 19:23–25. The pains of childbirth drove Mary to the trunk of a date palm. She shouted, "I wish I had died before (this) and was completely forgotten!" Jesus could not have been more than a few minutes old when he was able to tell her to shake the trunk of the date palm to get its ripe dates: "Eat and drink and be comforted."

The Ministry of Jesus

Two passages in the Qur'an—Q. 3:49–55 and Q. 5:110–115—mention Jesus' ability to perform signs. He created a bird from clay, healed the lepers and the blind, raised the dead, and brought down a table from the sky with food for his hungry disciples. Andrés points out that the Qur'an does not mention any other prophet—not even Muhammad—as having the ability to do miracles.[21]

The Excellences of Jesus

The Qur'an speaks of what Andrés refers to as "three excellences" of Jesus, which are not attributed to any other prophet—not even Muhammad.[22] First excellence: Jesus not only ascended to heaven, but will return one day. The ascension could be implied in Q. 3:45–46, which speaks of "Jesus, son of Mary, eminent in this world and the Hereafter." Andrés does not give the source for the return of Jesus, but could be referring to Q. 43:61,[23] Sahih al-Bukhari Volume 3, Book 43, Number 656, and Sahih Muslim

---

20. Ruiz García, *Juan Andrés*, 213.
21. Ruiz García, *Juan Andrés*, 213–14.
22. Ruiz García, *Juan Andrés*, 217.
23. If the passage is read continuously, the pronoun "it" could refer to Jesus. Droge, *The Qur'ān*, 332.

41:7023. Second excellence: Jesus is "a word from God," Q. 4:171. Third excellence: Jesus is "a spirit from Him," Q. 4:171. Andrés uses authoritative sources familiar to Moriscos to bridge the gap and show that Jesus is both man and true God.

Jesus and Muhammad

Andrés also bridges the gap by making three comparisons between Jesus and Muhammad.[24] First, their ancestors. Muhammad's forefathers were "idolaters, coarse, brutal and foolish." Jesus' predecessors included prophets, saints, messengers, and people who were "perfect and saints." Second, their places of worship. Muhammad and his relatives went to the "temple of idols and demons." Jesus and his family worshiped at a temple sanctified by God and served by "prophets, saints and priests." Third, their parents. There was nothing extraordinary about Muhammad's father and mother. As for Jesus, even the Qur'an declares that he did not have a human father but was conceived by the Holy Spirit. Andrés bridges the gap further by helping Moriscos note the logical implication in Jesus's miraculous birth. If Moors take Mary to be the mother of Jesus, they should take his father to be the Holy Spirit who is fully God because everything that proceeds from God is God.[25] Given that the Holy Spirit proceeds from the Father to the Son, Moors should conclude and believe that Jesus Christ is the Son of God.

Antialcorano

The Qur'an and the *sunna*

Pérez de Chinchón bridges the gap with the Qur'an and the *sunna*. He is fond of using the phrase "You would agree with me that according to your Qur'an . . ." in his arguments. He doesn't just say "the Qur'an," but "*your* Qur'an" for two possible reasons. First, to force the Moriscos to focus on their religion's sacred text and prevent any premature attempt to debunk the Christian theological concept under discussion. Second, to inform the Moriscos that he is as familiar as they are with what they believe. They cannot accuse him of misrepresenting their beliefs. Another phrase that Pérez de Chinchón uses is "You would agree with me . . . ." The audience has to agree because he is referring to something in their belief system. The third phrase that Pérez

---

24. Ruiz García, *Juan Andrés*, 102–3.

25. Q. 2:87 and 253, Q. 5:110, and Q. 16:102 identify the Holy Spirit as the angel Gabriel. McAuliffe, "Holy Spirit," Two, 442.

de Chinchón uses is "You cannot deny that you believe . . . ." If they were to deny, they would find themselves in a predicament. All these phrases and their permutations are tactics to ensure that the Moriscos agree not because of what is said in the Christian Scriptures, but what is declared in the only teachings that they consider to be sound—the Qur'an and the *sunna*. Pérez de Chinchón uses the Moriscos' worldview in two ways that place him in a winning position: to argue in favor of the Christian theological concept while simultaneously critiquing that worldview. Moriscos are left with no option except to agree with him.

Jesus Christ, The Word of God

Pérez de Chinchón mentions—almost *verbatim*—the same three excellences of Jesus found in Andrés' *Confusión o confutación*.[26] However, there is a difference. Pérez de Chinchón—unlike Andrés—does not limit himself to quoting passages from the Qur'an, but goes a step further by asking his Morisco audience to think deeply. Pérez de Chinchón is not having a dialogue with an individual Morisco or a group of Moriscos, but preaching a series of sermons to them. This particular sermon is titled "Sermon 12. Our gospel is true and is the one that Jesus Christ and his apostles preached. The Moors are obligated to say so and believe."[27] Pérez de Chinchón asks, "What is your understanding of Jesus being 'the word of God'?" If Jesus is "the word of God" because he preached the word of God, Moses and all the prophets should also be called "word of God" because they preached the word of God.

Pérez de Chinchón presses his case.

> Even *your own* Muhammad should be called "word of God" because *you* (not I) say that he preached the Qur'an, which *you* (not I) say that it is God's law. It is *your own* Qur'an that refers to Jesus—not Muhammad—as "word of God." Now *you have to tell me* why Jesus is called "word of God" and not the other prophets, including Muhammad.

Given that the Qur'an refers to Jesus as "the word of God," the implication is clear.[28]

> If *you say* that it is because the message that Jesus preached comes from the mouth of God and that Jesus is holy and one

---

26. Pons Fuster, *Antialcorano. Diálogos Christianos*, 198–99.
27. Pons Fuster, *Antialcorano. Diálogos Christianos*, 197–207.
28. Pons Fuster, *Antialcorano. Diálogos Christianos*, 199.

of God's greatest messengers, you would be obligated as a minimum to agree with what *your mouth* has just proven; that is, the law of Jesus Christ is good and his gospel is holy for *your own* Qur'an declares that they are "guidance and light" for everyone (Q. 5:44).

Given that the Qur'an asserts that Jesus is the word of God (Q. 3:39 and 3:45) and that God desires to use his word to verify that something is true (Q. 8), Moriscos are obligated to believe both assertions. Otherwise, they would be going against the law of Christ, which their own Qur'an praises. They would also be opposing the Qur'an itself for it expects the law of Christ to be taken seriously since it speaks so highly of it. However, if Moriscos respond by saying that other parts of their own Qur'an state that the gospel of Christ is bad, they are digging a bigger hole to fall into because the Qur'an would be contradicting itself. It is lying that the gospel is true or lying that it is false. Such contradiction shows that it is not impossible for a law not to contain lies and falsehoods.[29] Pérez de Chinchón uses the Morisco's highest religious authority—the Qur'an—to help Moriscos understand and even agree to a Christian theological concept that they reject; that is, the correct connection between Jesus Christ and "the word of God." (The potential risks in Pérez de Chinchón's approach is discussed at the end of this chapter.)

Diálogos Christianos

Logic

Pérez de Chinchón turns to the Qur'an and the *sunna* in *Antialcorano* to bridge the gap. In *Diálogos Christianos* he calls on logic, which he defines as "the science that discovers the truth."[30] Moors and Christians pray a similar prayer asking God regularly to guide them to his truth. Afterwards, they are convinced and satisfied that he has answered their prayers. However, they contradict each other in significant ways; for example, Christians believe that Jesus was (and is) the Son of God, but Moors disagree. A person with "a mind 'very free' of passion and 'very grounded' on reason"[31] (one who thinks logically) would say that one of them—the Moor or the Christian—is not telling the truth. A person cannot "be" and "not be" at the same time. It is

---

29. Pons Fuster, *Antialcorano. Diálogos Christianos*, 199.

30. "Dispute written in the form of a dialogue between the teacher Bernardo Pérez de Chinchón, canon of Gandía, and his teacher Joseph Arávigo on certain articles of our holy catholic faith, which the Moors and Jews deny." Pons Fuster, *Antialcorano. Diálogos Christianos*, 407.

31. Pons Fuster, *Antialcorano. Diálogos Christianos*, 413–14.

not possible for one person to say "Joseph is a man" at the same time another person is saying "Joseph is not a man" when Joseph is in fact a man. One of them is lying. It stands to reason that the one who is lying cannot have the law of God because God does not give lies as law. Furthermore, he is one. It is impossible for him to issue two sets of contradictory laws.[32]

God is good, just, wise, kind and powerful. He has given us reason, free will, and his law to show that he wants everyone to be saved. What father who is a physician would not save his dying son who asks him for help? There is no greater father and wiser physician than God who not only knows our need for salvation, but also has the medicine—guidance—to save us. If after asking God for guidance, we are still sick—we believe that we are saved when in fact we are not—the fault is not God's, but ours. We did not use the capacity to reason and the free will he gave us.[33] Joseph—Pérez de Chinchón's Arabic teacher and a Moor who has become a Christian—says that some Moors do not believe that people have a free will. "People sin because God has willed it." Pérez de Chinchón explains why they are mistaken.[34]

Logic can be used to bridge the gap in all the other contradictions between what the Christians and the Moors believe. Some of the contradictions include the Trinity, the divinity and crucifixion of Jesus, Muhammad, and the Qur'an.[35] Two observations can be made about using logic. First, Pérez de Chinchón still uses the Qur'an in *Diálogos Christianos* to bridge the gap. For example, he points out that Jesus is referred to as "the word of God,"[36] but does not go into details because he has already done so in *Antialcorano*.[37] Second, Andrés, the *Catecismo del Sacromonte*, and Pérez de Ayala's *Catecismo* also use reason to argue for the superiority of the religion of Christ over the sect of Muhammad, but *Diálogos Christianos* first defines "logic" then launches it to soften the Moors' resistance; that is, make them think logically before bringing in the Qur'an and the *sunna*.

---

32. Pons Fuster, *Antialcorano. Diálogos Christianos*, 407–9.
33. Pons Fuster, *Antialcorano. Diálogos Christianos*, 409–14.
34. Pons Fuster, *Antialcorano. Diálogos Christianos*, 410–12.
35. Pons Fuster, *Antialcorano. Diálogos Christianos*, 407–9.
36. Pons Fuster, *Antialcorano. Diálogos Christianos*, 449.
37. See above "Jesus Christ, The Word of God."

Catecismo Provechoso

A Simile

Orozco bridges the gap by first recognizing the difficulty in explaining "the mystery of the eternal generation of the Son." Philosophers opine that divine matters are clear, but the problem is that our understanding is like the eyes of the owl. The sun is the most visible body in the sky yet the eyes of the owl cannot look at it directly. The wisest sages have drawn similes, but most of them fall short of representing this mystery. One simile that seems to succeed notes the relationship between the sun and the rays of light that emanate from the sun. The sun and the rays are not two suns, but one and the same essence. God the Father—the eternal light—in eternity "generated" or "begat" the Word who is described as "the radiance of (the Father's) glory" (Heb 1:2).[38]

Orozco decides wisely not to explain the *process* of "generation" or "begetting"; that is, *how* it happened, but bridges the gap by referring to the Scriptures. God the Father declared, "You are My Son, today I have begotten You" (Ps 2:7) and "This is My beloved Son, with whom I am well-pleased; listen to Him!" (Matt 17:1–8). The name of this Son is "Jesus" who refers to God as "My Father who is in heaven" (Matt 10:32–33) and the one who sent him (Matt 10:40). His name is "Christ" for he was anointed like the priests of the Old Testament (Ps 45:7). However, the latter were fallible humans, but Christ is "King of kings and Lord of Lords" (Rev 19:16).[39]

Catecismo del Sacromonte

Similes

This catechism is also a training manual for the novice who is learning how to answer the Moors. Two of those queries are pertinent to this section. Moors say, "If God has a son, this means that God is married and has a wife" and "It is inconvenient for God to have a son because the son would fight the father."[40] The novice does not want the simplistic answer "The Bible says so." The priest bridges the first gap as follows: God having a son does not mean that he is married. Flowers come from trees that are

---

38. Orozco, *Catecismo provechoso*, 31 [l].
39. Orozco, *Catecismo provechoso*, 32 [r].
40. Resines, *Catecismo del Sacromonte*, 216.

not married. Rays of sunlight are generated from a sun without a spouse. Streams flow from a head water without a wife.

Images

The second gap is bridged as follows: First, when do flowers battle their trees? When do rays of sunlight fight against the sun? When do streams exchange blows with their head water? Second, there are images in our mind. The sun is an image in our mind. Our self is also an image in our mind. When we say that we know ourselves, it means that what we know is the image of ourselves in our mind. When we say that God knows himself, we are saying that he knows the image that he has of himself in his mind. This image is the Son of God. In other words, the Son of God is the image of God that God has of himself in his mind. However, the image of ourselves in our mind we cannot call our son because we are not "as one" as God for he embodies or defines oneness. The image of God that God has of himself in his mind is the Son of God because the nature and the substance of the image are divine. The image is not a portion or a fraction of that oneness, but fully God. There cannot be two substances because God is the consummate oneness. Thus, the image—the Son of God—is of the same substance as the Father who generates the image. God defines oneness. His infinity is so perfect that everything that he has, everything that is in him, and everything that he generates is also fully God.[41]

Catecismo

The followers of Muhammad make three charges against the divinity of Christ.[42] First, there would be too many gods fighting each other. Second, God would need a wife to have a son. Third, Jesus never said that he was God. The *Catecismo del Sacromonte* already countered the first two charges. Pérez de Ayala responds differently. First, conflict among the gods is impossible because the Christian religion has never taught the existence of many gods, but only one divine being revealed in three persons with one will and one mind. Second, God who can see and hear without physical eyes and ears (Ps 92:11) has his "perfect and ineffable way" to engender without needing a physical body. As for the third charge, Pérez de Ayala bridges the gap in five ways. First, he quotes the words of Jesus as recorded by his disciples.

---

41. Resines, *Catecismo del Sacromonte*, 217.
42. Pérez de Ayala, *Catecismo*, 222.

Second, the followers of Jesus believed that he was God. Third, kings and prophets in the Old Testament wrote about the Messiah. Fourth, prophecies about the Messiah in the Old Testament. Fifth, John the Baptist's declarations. The five ways are summarized below.

The Words of Jesus Recorded by His Disciples[43]

Jesus was a godly man and could not have lied about being the Son of God. If he had been lying, he would not have been able to perform miracles, which are signs of God's approval.[44] The disciples could not have lied about what they wrote because even Muhammad acknowledged that they were "clean and saintly."[45] John wrote that Jesus had said that he is the first and the last (Rev 22:13); God is his Father and both of them are working together (John 5:17); he is in the Father and the Father is in him (John 10:38); he and the Father are one (John 10:30); his teachings are from the Father (John 7:16); everything the Father has belongs to him (John 16:15); and to honor him is tantamount to honoring the Father (John 5:23). Matthew recorded Jesus stating that baptism should be in his and the name of the Father (Matt 28:19). Luke documented Jesus saying that the Father had handed everything to him and that only he knows the Father (Luke 10:22).

Jesus' Followers Believed That He Was God[46]

Peter looked at Jesus and declared, "You are the Christ, the Son of the living God" (Matt 16:13–17). The Apostle Paul spoke of Christ as "over all, God blessed forever. Amen" (Rom 9:5). On another occasion, he referred to the church as "the church of God which He purchased with His own blood" (Acts 20:28).

---

43. Pérez de Ayala, *Catecismo*, 223–25.
44. Pérez de Ayala, *Catecismo*, 227–28.
45. Pérez de Ayala, *Catecismo*, 224. Pérez de Ayala does not indicate where in the Qur'an, the *hadith* or *sira* did Muhammad acknowledge that the disciples were "clean and saintly." When the disciples are mentioned in the Qur'an, they say, "We believe in Allah, and bear witness that we are Muslims," Q. 3:52; "We believe. And bear witness that we are Muslims," Q. 5:111; and "We are Allah's helpers," Q. 61:14. Sahih Muslim 1:81–82: "It is narrated on the authority Abdullah b. Mas'ud that the Messenger of Allah observed: Never a Prophet had been sent before me by Allah towards his nation who had not among his people (his) disciples and companions who followed his ways and obeyed his command."
46. Pérez de Ayala, *Catecismo*, 225.

Kings and Prophets in the Old Testament

Pérez de Ayala has to bridge two gaps in the Moor's understanding of the identity of the Messiah; specifically, that the Messiah is God and Christ is the Messiah. The first gap is bridged by reviewing what kings and prophets in the Old Testament announced about the Messiah. King David: God said to the Messiah, "You are My Son" (Ps 2:7) and asked him to sit at his right hand (Ps 110:1). The throne of the Messiah will last forever (Ps 45:6) and homage should be rendered to him (Ps 2:12). Solomon: the Messiah will endure as long as the sun and the moon (Ps 72:5). Isaiah: God anointed the Messiah to bring good news to the afflicted (Isa 61:1) and to comfort (Isa 51:3) and save Israel (Isa 46:13). His name will be "Mighty God" (Isa 9:6–7) Jeremiah: the Messiah will also be called "The LORD our righteousness." He will do justice and be a wise king (Jer 23:5–6).

Prophecies in the Old Testament

The *Catecismo* bridges the second gap—Christ is the Messiah—by noting that prophecies about the Messiah in the Old Testament converge in Jesus; for example, the Messiah would be a descendant of King David (Ps 131) and be a prophet like Moses from among the Israelites (Deut 18:15–22). He would be born of a virgin (Isa 7:14) in Bethlehem (Mic 5). He would preach openly (Isa 40 and 61); enter Jerusalem riding on a donkey (Zcc 9); go to his death in silence; and die among criminals (Isa 53 and Pss 21 and 68). He would resurrect and ascend to heaven (Dan 7).

John the Baptist

The fifth way that the *Catecismo* bridges the gap is to mention John the Baptist whom the Moors revere. He pointed to the Messiah and said, "Behold, the Lamb of God who takes away the sin of the world!" (John 1:29). He was older than Jesus yet said that Jesus existed before him (John 1:30) and that he was unworthy to untie the thong of his sandals (John 1:27). John the Baptist recognized the humanity and divinity of Jesus.

The Trinity: Bridging the Gap

It is not a surprise that Pérez de Chinchón, Orozco, *Catecismo del Sacromonte,* and Pérez de Ayala share the same understanding of what is the Trinity, but express that understanding in their own way. Pérez de Chinchón's *Antialcorano* and *Catecismo del Sacromonte* are equally succinct yet accurate: "God is triune in persons and one in essence"[47] and "God is omnipotent—Father, Son, and Holy Spirit—three persons and one true God."[48] But, *Catecismo del Sacromonte* goes further: "The Father is God and wholly God. So is the Son and the Holy Spirit. All three are neither more than God nor more perfect than one of them. One of them is not less than all three. This divine unity who is God cannot be more than one and cannot be God without being triune. It is as natural for God to be triune as it is for him to be one. God cannot be God without being triune and one."[49]

In *Diálogos Christianos*, Joseph (Pérez de Chinchón's Arabic teacher playing the role of a Moor) repeats Pérez de Chinchón's definition found in *Antialcorano*.[50] In Orozco's *Catecismo Provechoso*, "God is one absolutely perfect essence, one majesty, and one eternity. God is also triune in persons: Father, Son, and Holy Spirit. Not three lords, but one lord. Not three Gods, but only one God."[51] When Christians pray, they should address him as "Thou are the One who is triune yet one; the one only alone yet has had fellowship throughout eternity. Being one in essence—in knowledge, power, and goodness—Thou are Father, Son, and Holy Spirit triune and one."[52] Pérez de Ayala's *Catecismo* lacks a short statement like *Antialcorano*'s and *Catecismo del Sacromonte*'s and an expansive one like *Catecismo del Sacromonte*'s and *Catecismo Provechoso*'s. The statements "the Trinity of persons"[53] and "one true God"[54] in *Catecismo* are separated by a distance of 80 pages. However, the context of these two statements indicate that Pérez de Ayala agrees with everything that the above authors wrote about The Trinity.

47. Pons Fuster, *Antialcorano. Diálogos Christianos*, 295.
48. Resines, *Catecismo del Sacromonte*, 214.
49. Resines, *Catecismo del Sacromonte*, 217.
50. Pons Fuster, *Antialcorano. Diálogos Christianos*, 429.
51. Orozco, *Catecismo provechoso*, 57 [r].
52. Orozco, *Catecismo provechoso*, 117 [r].
53. Pérez de Ayala, *Catecismo*, 181.
54. Pérez de Ayala, *Catecismo*, 261.

Bridging the Gap: Summary

Antialcorano	Reason, religious authorities (the Bible, the Qur'an, Muhammad), witnesses (Peter, demons, Jews, Thomas, God)
Diálogos Christianos	Natural reason, divine law
Catecismo provechoso	Reason, the Creed (first, second, and third articles), metaphors (water, fire, a dove)
Catecismo del Sacromonte	Simile (a headwater, a river, a lake)
Catecismo	Muhammad, Jesus Christ, the Creed (first, third, and tenth articles)

Antialcorano

Pérez de Chinchón appeals to reason, religious authorities, and witnesses to bridge the gap in the Moors' understanding of the Trinity. Religious authorities refer to the sources that govern the thinking and behavior of Christians and Moriscos. The Bible for the former and the Qur'an or Muhammad for the latter.[55]

Reason

Reason can help explain three concepts: God generating God, how Jesus was with God in the beginning, and how the Son is equal to the Father.

God Generates God

Q. 38:72 states that Allah fashioned Adam and breathed into his soul, but does does not reveal what Adam's soul is made of. Gen 1 declares that God created the heavens and the earth without identifying the materials he used in the creation. Both cases show that the divine being creates according to his will and not according to what materials he has on hand. Pérez de Chinchón notices two truths. First, x brings out or generates something as good as and equal to itself; for example, fire from fire or a son from his father. Second, x generates something better than itself; for example, the flint that is struck to generate a fire. These two truths can help explain God generating God and

---

55. Pons Fuster, *Antialcorano. Diálogos Christianos*, 295.

the mystery of the Trinity. Fire generates fire or a son comes from his father so it should not be strange to consider God generating God.[56]

Jesus was with God in the Beginning

Pérez de Chinchón asks four questions to explain the rationale behind the thought of God generating God. First, is the world as good as God? If the answer were affirmative, the answer would be wrong because the created cannot be as good as the creator. Second, if the answer were negative, can God not generate another being equal to him? If the answer is yes, that being equal to him is his Son. If the answer were no, God is less capable than his creation; in other words, fire can generate fire while God cannot generate God. Third, is it good or bad for God to generate a son? If it is good, it stands to reason that there is no imperfection in God in whom all goodness dwells. If it is bad, it would also be bad for fire to generate fire and for a father to engender a son. Fourth, was God all alone before he created everything? There is no greater evil than aloneness. A soul that is alone can neither sing nor cry.[57] It is more in line with reason for God to have had fellowship ("company" or "companionship"); that is, someone who was with him, to love him, and to comprehend him before he created everything. This fellowship was with his one and only eternal Son who is also equal to him. Jesus has always been with God. Otherwise, Jesus would have had a beginning.[58]

The Son is equal to the Father

Pérez de Chinchón explains the equality of the Son and the Father by making four points about Jesus not having a beginning. First, what never had a beginning has always been with God. Second, what never had a beginning is eternal. What is eternal is equal to God. The fellowship that God had since the beginning is equal to him. Third, God is infinite. The one who comprehends him fully must have infinite comprehension. The fellowship has infinite comprehension because he is equal to God. Fourth, God is "very infinite." The one who is to love him comprehensively ought to have infinite

---

56. Pons Fuster, *Antialcorano. Diálogos Christianos*, 288–89.
57. Pons Fuster, *Antialcorano. Diálogos Christianos*, 290.
58. Pons Fuster, *Antialcorano. Diálogos Christianos*, 290–91.

love. The fellowship who has loved God eternally is infinite love and is equal with God who is also infinite love.[59]

Objections

Moors and Moriscos would raise two objections to everything said above. First, how can God who is a spirit generate something equal to him and without the participation of male and female? The answer has two parts: First, fire can generate fire without male and female so God can also engender without both genders. Second, God does not require materials to create.[60] The second objection: If God had that eternal fellowship from the beginning, there would be two gods. This is against natural reason, which argues for the existence of not more than one God. Answer: God can make a person appear and be seen simultaneously in many places. That person would need God's help for this to happen. However, God would not need such help. His very nature enables him to be in the heavens, on the earth, and everywhere else simultaneously while still remaining as one being instead of two or more gods.[61]

Religious Authorities

If the reasons above are not strong enough to persuade the Moors, the second way to bridge the gap is to hear from witnesses who knew about the Trinity more than anyone else. The religious authority of the Moors and the Moriscos—the Qur'an—states that they are obligated to believe everything that Jesus said because Muhammad considered him to be the word of God, the spirit of God, and a messenger of God. If Muhammad is correct, Jesus could not have lied about being the Son of God and Moors have to believe that Jesus is God. The religious authority of the Christians—their Scriptures—records what witnesses said about the divinity of Jesus.

Witnesses

Pérez de Chinchón calls on the following witnesses among the many who are available. Peter confessed, "You are the Christ, the Son of the living God"

---

59. Pons Fuster, *Antialcorano. Diálogos Christianos*, 290–91.

60. Pons Fuster, *Antialcorano. Diálogos Christianos*, 291–92. See also "God Generates God" above.

61. Pons Fuster, *Antialcorano. Diálogos Christianos*, 292.

(Matt 16:13–16). Demons addressed him as "Son of the Most High God" (Mark 5:1–7). The Jews accused him of making himself to be "the Son of God" (John 19:1–7). Thomas saw him risen from the dead and shouted, "My Lord and my God!" (John 20:26–28). After Jesus got baptized, a voice from heaven announced, "This is my Beloved Son, in whom I am well-pleased" (Matt 3:13–17). The high priest asked him, "Are You the Christ, the Son of the Blessed One?" He replied, "I am" (Mark 14:60–64).

Pérez de Chinchón's approach to bridging the gap—an appeal to reason, religious authorities, and witnesses—can help Moors see that understanding the uniqueness of Jesus—the fellowship that God had in the beginning before he began the creation—can be a first step in understanding the Trinity.

Diálogos Christianos

Reason as Methodology

According to the Moors, Christians who believe in the Trinity and the divinity of Jesus Christ will go to hell and remain there forever. Moors who do not believe in the Trinity and the divinity of Jesus Christ will be able to leave hell and go to paradise even if they had committed the most horrific sins. The way to bridge the gap between a Christian's and a Moor's understanding of the Trinity is to let reason be the judge.[62] Although Pérez de Chinchón has already discussed using reason[63] and logic,[64] there is a difference here in *Diálogos Christianos* in the conversation about the Trinity. The first difference is that reason is developed as a *methodology* for discerning truth from falsehood while the *application* of logic and reason is seen in the dialogue on the Trinity in *Antialcorano* and Jesus Christ in *Dialogos Christianos*.

The second difference is that Joseph's[65] musings give birth to the methodology. This is significant because Joseph used to be a Moor, but has been baptized into the Catholic Church. Here in *Diálogos Christianos* he plays the role of a Moor and thinks like one. If his musings were typical of Moors, there is hope that they can think themselves out of their religion and embrace the Catholic faith. In other dialogues, Pérez de Chinchón devised how to bridge the gaps, but in this dialogue he only provides the initial spark.

---

62. Pons Fuster, *Antialcorano. Diálogos Christianos*, 419.
63. See above "*Antialcorano*" in "The Trinity: Bridging the Gap."
64. See above "*Diálogos Christianos*" in "Jesus Christ: Bridging the Gap."
65. Pérez de Chinchón's Arabic teacher Joseph Zumilla.

The next section is a brief description of how the methodology developed; that is, what Joseph did with the initial spark.

Who Is the Heretic?

On the Trinity, Christians and Moors are convinced that it is the other party who is the heretic destined to eternal hell. How to determine who is correct? Pérez de Chinchón favors using reason as the guide.[66] Truth is like the *vihuela*[67]. If one cord is out of tune, the rest of the cords will also sound out of tune. If one truth is denied, other truths will also be denied. Truth also resembles the links in a chain. If one link breaks, the entire chain breaks. Lies are like a pile of stones. If a wall is to be built with them, mortar is needed to bind the stones together. If lies are to be believed, inject some truths into them and the lies will become truths.[68] What is the solution when Christians and Moors do not agree on the same issue? How to tell who is lying? Who's the heretic?

Divine Law: The Musings of a Moor

Joseph agrees with Pérez de Chinchón that our natural reason should be used as the judge of natural things,[69] but adds the following: First, the divine law revealed by God to his prophets should be the judge of the supernatural things of God. Two, our natural reason can also make inferences about supernatural things because nothing supernatural is isolated from reason. What is supernatural to us is natural to God. So, disagreements can be settled through our natural reason and God's divine law. However, even if we do not have a divine law, we could still separate truth from falsehood unless malice has blinded us because there is "divine splendor"[70] in our intellect or understanding.

If the Christian says that his law is divine, but the Moor says that it is not, we decide who is right by also using our intellect or understanding with its "divine splendor." If this were insufficient, we pay attention to witnesses. If the Christian and the Moor do not trust each other's witnesses, we look

---

66. Pons Fuster, *Antialcorano. Diálogos Christianos*, 419.

67. An ancient musical instrument like the guitar. It was popular during the Middle Ages and the Renaissance.

68. Pons Fuster, *Antialcorano. Diálogos Christianos*, 420.

69. Pons Fuster, *Antialcorano. Diálogos Christianos*, 423.

70. Pons Fuster, *Antialcorano. Diálogos Christianos*, 422.

to third parties; for example, prophets and philosophers who were neither Christian nor Moor and history written by both Jews and Gentiles.[71]

A Difficult Question

What if the Christian were to quote a certain prophet, but the Moor says that he is not mentioned in the Qur'an? According to the law of Muhammad, Joseph would be a heretic for agreeing with the Christian. But, he would be an infidel for disagreeing with the Christian because Christians say that doubters are infidels. Joseph is in a dilemma.[72]

The Answer

The dilemma engages Joseph and Pérez de Chinchón in a cordial exchange that generates three key points that encapsulate Pérez de Chinchón's answer. One, God is absolute truth and cannot issue contradictory statements such as "Joseph is a man" and "Joseph is not a man." Even if he were to do so, the true statement—the one that is the least contradictory to good judgment, natural reason, philosophy, and metaphysics—is the one that should be believed.[73] Two, it is impossible for the Qur'an not to be lying for it disagrees with the gospel in everything. The Moor needs to abandon the Qur'an and use natural reason and "divine inspiration." But, if the Moor counters and says that it is the Christian who should abandon the gospel and use natural reason and "divine inspiration," the Christian will first pray then sit down with the Moor to cross-check reason with reason, law with law, and prophets with prophets to evaluate which is nearest to natural reason and "divine virtue and majesty."[74] Three, if the reason or understanding of the Christian is unable to answer the Moor's tough questions, the Moor should keep in mind that God's divine law can defend itself. Furthermore, the Christian can secure the help of learned doctors.[75] In sum, Pérez de Chinchón and Joseph agree that God and reason will lead them to the truth.

---

71. Pérez de Chinchón does not provide specific names of either prophets and philosophers or Jewish and Gentile historians.
   72. Pons Fuster, *Antialcorano. Diálogos Christianos*, 423.
   73. Pons Fuster, *Antialcorano. Diálogos Christianos*, 423.
   74. Pons Fuster, *Antialcorano. Diálogos Christianos*, 423–24.
   75. Pons Fuster, *Antialcorano. Diálogos Christianos*, 425.

Catecismo provechoso

The following examples do not prove the concept of the Trinity, but show that God deals with human beings in terms of oneness: one ark saved eight people; one lamb as sin sacrifice came through one of Israel's tribes; and one dove descended on Jesus after he was baptized.[76] Orozco does not spend time trying to explain the Trinity for two reasons. First, not even the angels in heaven can comprehend all there is to know about the Trinity. Second, the Trinity is "high theology" that the command is not "See!" or "Understand!" but "Hear, O Israel! The Lord is our God, the Lord is one!" (Deut 6:4).[77] Orozco's strategy is to present God, Jesus Christ, and the Holy Spirit separately across three chapters of his catecismo where each chapter discusses one of the fourteen articles of the Creed. The remainder of this section summarizes Orozco's understanding of the Trinity.

God

The First Article of the Creed is "Believe in one powerful God."[78] There cannot be more than one God because a kingdom should not have more than one king. The human body has only one soul and one heart.[79] There is no gap to bridge because Moors agree that there is only God.[80]

Jesus Christ

The Second Article of the Creed is "I believe in Jesus Christ his Son."[81] Please refer to "Jesus Christ: Bridging the Gap" above in *Catecismo Provechoso* for how Orozco's bridges this gap.

---

76. Orozco, *Catecismo provechoso*, 62 [r].
77. Orozco, *Catecismo provechoso*, 57 [r]–62 [l].
78. Orozco, *Catecismo provechoso*, 27 [r].
79. Orozco, *Catecismo provechoso*, 30 [r].
80. Orozco does not discuss whether or not Christians and Moors believe in the same God.
81. Orozco, *Catecismo provechoso*, 31 [r].

The Holy Spirit

The Eight Article of the Creed is "I believe in the Holy Spirit."[82] Orozco uses the metaphors of water, fire, and a dove to bridge the gap. He quotes from the Old and New Testaments and offers his own interpretation.

Water[83]

Orozco uses Rev 22:1[84] ("Then he showed me a river of the water of life, clear as crystal, coming from the throne of God and of the Lamb") as his primary biblical text and interprets it as follows: The "river of the water of life" is the Holy Spirit. The "throne of God and of the Lamb" represents the will of the Father and the Son. Their will "produces"[85] the river of the water of life; that is, the Holy Spirit. The water of this river is "life" because the Father and the Son are eternal life. The water is "clear as crystal." A crystal is a durable and transparent stone. So is the Holy Spirit being God "did not have, does not have, and will not have an ending."[86]

Orozco points to one instance in the Old Testament where the Holy Spirit is promised and two instances in the New Testament where the power of this promise is experienced. Isaiah foretold that the Holy Spirit would rest on Jesus (Isa 11:1–2). Jesus spoke of this Spirit as water that can quench the thirst of everyone—not just the Samaritan woman (John 4:14). This water is also the Holy Spirit who guides the followers of Jesus into all the truth (John 16:13).[87]

---

82. Orozco, *Catecismo provechoso*, 57 [r].

83. Orozco, *Catecismo provechoso*, 58 [r]–60 [r].

84. The biblical reference given in *Catecismo provechoso* is Rev 20 instead of Rev 22. Orozco, *Catecismo provechoso*, 59 [l].

85. Orozco does not explain the "production" of the Holy Spirit by the will of the Father and the Son because the Trinity is "high theology." If he were to give an explanation, he would say that the Father and the Son "breathe out" or "exhale" the Holy Spirit. See "The Eight Article, which says I believe in the Holy Spirit," 58 [r] and 62 [r]. If his explanation were deemed inadequate, Rev 22:1 cannot imply that the Holy Spirit is inferior to the Father and the Son.

86. Orozco, *Catecismo provechoso*, 59 [r].

87. The biblical reference given in *Catecismo provechoso* is John 10 instead of John 16:13. Orozco, *Catecismo provechoso*, 59 [r]

FIRE

Orozco uses Acts 2:1–3 as his main passage. The evil of the world rises from the fires of hell. The tongue of the serpent ruined Adam and Eve. Tongues of fire descending from heaven is a suitable metaphor for the Holy Spirit. The tongue of the teacher teaches his students. The followers of Jesus are empowered to speak on his behalf. Other Old Testament events depict the Holy Spirit as fire. The fire that consumed the offerings of Abel, Noah, Abraham and Solomon.[88] The chariot of fire that took Elijah to heaven (2 Kgs 2:11). The throne of God, its wheels, and the river flowing from it (Dan 7:9–10).

A DOVE[89]

The Holy Spirit descended as a dove on Jesus after he got baptized in the Jordan River (Matt 3:16–17). Orozco interprets the dove in two ways.[90] First, it is a clear sign that Jesus is holy and our Redeemer. Second, the gentleness of the dove "is sweeter than honey" and "makes us meek" and able to forgive others.

Catecismo del Sacromonte

CAN ONE BE THREE?

The novice asks, "How is it possible that one can be three?"[91] The Jesuit priest's answer given above (The Trinity: Bridging the Gap. Overview) in a nutshell: The Father, the Son, and the Holy Spirit are wholly God. This unity or wholeness is not more than God and one of them—Father, Son, or Holy Spirit—is not less than the unity. It is as natural for God to be one as it is for him to be triune. God cannot be God without being one and triune simultaneously.[92]

---

88. Orozco does not provide biblical references. They are Gen 4:3–5 (Abel), Gen 8:20–21 (Noah), Gen 22 (Abraham), and Solomon (2 Chr 7:1). Solomon is the only instance of these four where fire comes from heaven and consumes an offering. Orozco is probably thinking that three other instances of consumption by fire from heaven—Lev 9:24 (Moses), 1 Chr 21:26 (David), and 1 Kgs 18:38 (Elijah)—also happened with the sacrifices of Abel, Noah, and Abraham.
89. Orozco, *Catecismo provechoso*, 60 [r]–61 [l].
90. Orozco, *Catecismo provechoso*, 61 [r].
91. Resines, *Catecismo del Sacromonte*, 200.
92. Resines, *Catecismo del Sacromonte*, 217.

Is the Holy Spirit the Son of God?

The novice's next question is, "Why is the Holy Spirit not called the Son of God and is not the Son of God even though he has the same nature as the Father?" The priest's answer focuses on *how* the Spirit came about. The Holy Spirit was not begotten as the Son was begotten yet is identical to the Father and the Son. The Holy Spirit is identical to the Father in terms of divinity because of the divine unity. Thus, the Holy Spirit is neither the Son nor the grandson of the Father. The Holy Spirit is also neither the son nor the brother of Christ.

A Simile

The novice responds with "I adore him (God) even though I do not understand him"[93] and asks for "another comparison."[94] The priest replies with this simile: Imagine a headwater from which a river flows and this river runs into a lake. The water in the headwater comes from nowhere. The water in the river comes from the headwater and the water in the lake comes from the river. The water in the headwater, the river, and the lake is the same water and yet the headwater is neither the river nor the lake. The Father is eternal for he is "the headwater of deity." His being does not come from another besides himself. The divinity of the Son—"the infinite river"—is from the headwater. The divinity of the Holy Spirit—"the immense lake"—is from the Father and the Son. Now imagine a bridge built just on the river—not at the headwater or the lake. Water from the headwater and the lake go by the bridge even though it is only the river that has a bridge. The fullness of divinity is in the Son and it was only the Son who became incarnate—not the Father or the Holy Spirit. The fullness of divinity is also in the Father and the Holy Spirit. Thus, all three—Father, Son, and Holy Spirit—are one true God and each of them is fully God for neither God can be partly God nor a portion or fraction of God be God.[95]

---

93. Resines, *Catecismo del Sacromonte*, 217. The novice could be saying that he does not understand the Trinity or the priest's answer to the question "How is it possible that one can be three?" or "Why is the Holy Spirit not called the Son of God and is not the Son of God even though he has the same nature as the Father?" The simile—"another comparison"—that the priest is about to provide seems to indicate that the novice is likely saying that he does not understand the Trinity.

94. Resines, *Catecismo del Sacromonte*, 218.

95. Resines, *Catecismo del Sacromonte*, 218.

Catecismo

Pérez de Ayala uses three different bridges to narrow the gap: Muhammad, Jesus Christ, and three articles of the Creed.

Muhammad

Muhammad not only acknowledged the divinity of Christ, but also the Trinity in Q. 4:171. First, this verse refers to Christ as the word of God. Second, "the trinity of persons" is noted in the references to God, Jesus as his word, and the Spirit point to what Pérez de Ayala refers to as "the trinity of persons."[96]

Jesus Christ

Pérez de Ayala's use of Christ as one of the bridges is similar to the approach that Pérez de Chinchón adopted in *Antialcorano*.[97] Christ was a man of "great holiness and truth" and would not have lied. Moors, therefore, must believe everything he revealed even though they are hard to believe such as the Trinity. Christ revealed the Trinity without saying so directly; for example, he did not say, "What I'm about to reveal is connected to the Trinity" or "What I just revealed is another truth about the Trinity."[98]

Articles in the Creed

First Article

Pérez de Ayala like Orozco explicates each person of the Trinity with a respective article in the Creed. In the first article of the Creed,[99] Orozco focuses on the *power* of God[100] while Pérez de Ayala pays attention to the *fatherhood* of God. The Moor in Pérez de Ayala's *Catecismo* wants to know why God is called "Father." God is called "Father" because he is to be understood as the Father in "the Trinity of Persons" who through an "ineffable and eternal

---

96. Pérez de Ayala, *Catecismo*, 181.

97. See above "*Antialcorano*. Religious Authorities" in "The Trinity: Bridging the Gap."

98. Pérez de Ayala, *Catecismo*, 227.

99. "I believe in God Father Omnipotent, Creator of the heavens and the earth." Pérez de Ayala, *Catecismo*, 271.

100. See above "*Catecismo provechoso*. God" in "The Trinity: Bridging the Gap."

generation" engenders the Son. This Son has the same substance as the Father and is equal in perfection and coeternal with the Father.[101]

Third Article

Orozco and Pérez de Ayala address two different articles. Orozco concentrates on the second article ("I believe in Jesus Christ his Son"[102]) while Pérez de Ayala devotes his time to the third article, which states that Jesus Christ was conceived by the work of the Holy Spirit.[103] Pérez de Ayala interprets this article to mean that the Son of God came at the right time predetermined by the Trinity. There are two aspects to this interpretation. First, Jesus Christ took on a human body conceived in Mary via the Holy Spirit (Luke 1:35). Second, Jesus Christ came according to the will of the Father (John 6:38). As a result of having chosen two different articles, Orozco discusses the *identity* of the second person of the Trinity while Pérez de Ayala considers the *decision* of the Trinity to send the second person of the Trinity.

Tenth Article

This article declares, "I believe in the Holy Spirit." Orozco labels this article as article eight.[104] He uses similes to bridge the gap while Pérez de Ayala refers to the Christian Scriptures. The Holy Spirit is the third person of the Trinity; has the same being and perfection as the Father; and is equal and coeternal with the Father (Isa 48 and Jer 23). The Holy Spirit is also the spirit of truth and the Spirit of Christ (John 15).

The Integrity of the Christian Scriptures: Bridging the Gap

Pérez de Chinchón's *Antialcorano* and *Diálogos Christianos* use the Qur'an and natural and divine reasons, respectively. The *Catecismo del Sacromonte* uses the Scriptures. Pérez de Ayala relies on history. The only instance that the *Catecismo del Sacromonte* points to the Qur'an is to allude to three passages (Q. 3:69–71 and 100 and Q. 2:109) that criticize the Jews and the

---

101. Pérez de Ayala, *Catecismo*, 276.

102. See above "*Catecismo provechoso*. Jesus Christ" in "The Trinity: Bridging the Gap."

103. Pérez de Ayala, *Catecismo*, 281.

104. See above "*Catecismo provechoso*. The Holy Spirit" in "The Trinity: Bridging the Gap."

Christians for corrupting the Scriptures. However, a close examination of these passages does not support their accusation. The People of the Book are charged with mixing truth with falsehood and concealing the truth (Q. 3:69–71). But, there are three problems with these passages. First, neither the passages nor their context specify the falsehoods. Second, "concealing the truth" does not mean "corrupting the truth." Third, "concealing the truth" also does not mean "the truth was concealed because of corruption." The People of the Book are denounced for turning believers (Moors) into disbelievers (Q. 3:100). However, there is no mention of what method is used for this turning to happen. The corruption of the Scriptures as the method cannot be inferred. The People of the Book are blamed for turning believers into disbelievers because of jealousy (Q. 2:109). But, this passage fails to address two issues. First, it is silent about what the People of the Book are jealous about. Second, even if they had been jealous, no evidence is given for concluding that their jealousy lead them to corrupt the Scriptures.

Bridging the Gap: Summary

Antialcorano	The Qur'an.
Diálogos Christianos	Natural and divine reasons.
Catecismo del Sacromonte	The Scriptures.
Catecismo	History.

Antialcorano

The Qur'an

Pérez de Chinchón's opening gambit is his statement "You do not even know that you are deceived." Water and fire represent what is good and what is bad, respectively. If the law of Muhammad is bad, but the Moriscos believe that it is good, their hand is in the fire. They cannot even feel that their capacity to reason has burnt out. If they say that their law is good; that is, that their hand is in the water, old Christians and Moriscos should reason together to verify the claim. If the Moriscos refuse to reason, they are fools. Truth can withstand all lies and attacks. If the gospel of Christ is good, Moriscos are obligated to believe it.[105]

---

105. Pons Fuster, *Antialcorano. Diálogos Christianos*, 198.

Pérez de Chinchón draws on the Moriscos' authorities. He wants Moriscos "to remember well everything that *your own* Qur'an and *sunna* say about Jesus Christ because I want you to witness what I am about to say." Pérez de Chinchón presses his argument:

> If Jesus is "the word of God" because he preached the word of God, then Moses and all the prophets should also be called "word of God" because they preached the word of God. Even *your own* Muhammad should be called "word of God" because you (not I) say that he preached the Qur'an, which you (not I) say that it is God's law. It is *your own* Qur'an that refers to Jesus—not Muhammad—as "word of God." Now *you have to tell me* why Jesus is called "word of God" and not the other prophets, including Muhammad. If *you say* that it is because the message that Jesus preached comes from the mouth of God and that Jesus is holy and one of God's greatest messengers, you would be obligated as a minimum to agree with what *your mouth* has just proven; that is, the law of Jesus Christ is good and his gospel is holy for *your own*[106] Qur'an declares that they are "guidance and light" for everyone (Q. 5:44; 3:3; Q. 28:43). Given that the Qur'an asserts that Jesus is the word of God (Q. 3:39, 45) and that God desires to use his word to verify that something is true (Q. 8), Moriscos are obligated to believe both assertions. Otherwise, they would be going against the law of Christ, which their own Qur'an praises. They would also be opposing the Qur'an itself for it expects the law of Christ to be taken seriously since it speaks so highly of it. However, if Moriscos respond by saying that other parts of their own Qur'an state that the gospel of Christ is bad, they are digging a bigger hole to fall into because the Qur'an would be contradicting itself. It is lying that the gospel is true or lying that it is false. Such contradiction shows that it is not impossible for a law not to contain lies and falsehoods.[107] Pérez de Chinchón uses the Qur'an—the Moriscos' highest religious authority—to help them understand the Christian theological concept of Christ as "the word of God."[108]

The *Antialcorano* gives five reasons why the gospel could not have been corrupted as the Moriscos claim.[109] First, the four Gospels were not

---

106. Italics here and above added for emphasis.

107. Pons Fuster, *Antialcorano. Diálogos Christianos*, 199.

108. The end of this chapter discusses the potential risks in Pérez de Chinchón's approach.

109. Pons Fuster, *Antialcorano. Diálogos Christianos*, 201–2.

written at the same time, but in this order: Matthew, Mark, Luke, and John. Second, they did not write from the same place. Matthew and Mark wrote from Judea and Rome, respectively. (Pérez de Chinchón does not mention where Luke and John were when they wrote their accounts.) Third, some of the authors were eyewitnesses (Jesus chose Matthew and John to be his disciples) or followers of one of the disciples (Mark was Peter's disciple) or the apostle Paul (Luke travelled with him). Fourth, they concur on all the essentials of the law of Christ. Fifth, there was no motive for Matthew, Mark, Luke and John to corrupt the gospel. They did not preach for money and only wanted to preach what Christ told them. They died destitute even though they could have become wealthy if they had served emperors and worshiped their gods.

Diálogos Christianos

Natural and Divine Reasons

Four possible culprits could have corrupted or falsified the Scriptures. One, the author of the Scriptures; that is, God himself. Second, the prophets who broadcast the Scriptures. Third, the recipients of the Scriptures. Fourth, disasters such as war and captivity. Pérez de Chinchón uses "natural and divine reasons" to bridge the gap and declare that these culprits are innocent.

Culprit Number 1: God[110]

If God gave the Scriptures to guide people to choose good over evil and lead them to him, it is against reason to think that God himself would be the same one to corrupt his own Scriptures. A king would not print coins with his image and coat of arms then proceed to counterfeit them. God is "the utmost goodness, truth and wisdom." The psalmist declared, "The precepts of the LORD are right ... the commandment of the LORD is pure ... the judgments of the LORD are true ..." (Ps 19:8–10).[111]

---

110. Pons Fuster, *Antialcorano. Diálogos Christianos*, 433–34.
111. The psalm mentioned in page 434 of *Antialcorano. Diálogos Christianos* is Ps 18.

Culprit Number 2: The Prophets[112]

God—the author of the prophecies recorded in the Scriptures—personally selected the prophets. He spoke to Moses face-to-face as one speaks to a friend (Exod 33:11). He referred to David as "a man after My heart, who will do all my will" (1 Sam 13:14; Acts 13:22). He sent his seraphim to touch the mouth of Isaiah with a burning coal, removed his iniquity and forgave his sin (Isa 6:1–7). He chose Jeremiah and said to him, "Before you were born I consecrated you; I have appointed you a prophet to the nations" (Jer 1:5) and "Behold, I have put My words in your mouth" (Jer 1:9). When Jeremiah said that he could not speak because of his youth, God touched his mouth and declared, "I have put my words in your mouth" (Jer 1:6–9). God spoke and his Spirit entered Ezekiel who then said, "I heard him speaking to me" (Ezek 2:2). God put his words in a scroll, told Ezekiel to eat it and go to Israel to "speak my words" (Ezek 3:1–2). God also told Ezekiel, "Take into your heart all My words which I will speak to you and listen carefully" (Ezek 3:10). If these prophets and the rest of the Old Testament prophets not mentioned here had deleted from or added to the prophecies, God would not have chosen them in the first place to be his prophets.

Culprit Number 3: The Recipients[113]

The Israelites in the Old Testament disobeyed God frequently in a myriad of ways. They complained that the water of Marah was bitter (Exod 15:22–25). They grumbled all the way to the Promised Land and even wanted to return to Egypt (Exod 16). They whined about the lack of water in the desert (Exod 17). They built and worshiped a golden calf while waiting for Moses to come down from Mount Sinai (Exod 32). They bewailed at the prospect of having to fight their enemies (Num 12). They criticized Moses's leadership and accused him of taking them into the wilderness to die (Num 16). God rebuked and punished the Israelites for these and other sins, but never had to chastise them for altering the Scriptures. In fact, he took measures to preserve the Scriptures. First, fathers were duty-bound to teach the Scriptures to their sons so that they would not forget how God delivered Israel from captivity in Egypt (Exod 13:8–10). Second, after the Israelites promised that they would obey all of God's commandments, Moses read the Book of the Covenant and sprinkled the blood of sacrificed young bulls on an altar and on the Israelites to symbolize that they were serious about fulfilling

---

112. Pons Fuster, *Antialcorano. Diálogos Christianos*, 434–48.
113. Pons Fuster, *Antialcorano. Diálogos Christianos*, 438–42.

their promise to follow God's commandments (Exod 24:4–8). Third, God reminded the Israelites of the deadly consequences of taking away or adding to his words (Deut 4:2). Fourth, God warned that curses—pestilence, disease, drought, famine, military defeats, madness, blindness, and exile—would devastate all of Israel for failure to obey his commandments. The severity of the penalty for transgressing God's commandments—the curses—did not result in anyone modifying those commandments. Fifth, Moses' final exhortation before he died was to command every Israelite and even foreigners to assemble before God every seven years to read God's law so that they would be careful to obey it (Deut 31:10–13).

Culprit Number 4: Disasters

It is against reason to believe that war and captivity led to the corruption or falsification of the Scriptures. First, not every Israelite was captured. Those who escaped hid and preserved God's law. Second, priests and elders knew God's words by heart just like Moors who have memorized the Qur'an. Third, captivity did not last more than seventy years. During that time prophets like Ezekiel and Jeremiah lived among the exiles and kept God's words fresh in the minds of the people.[114]

The constant disobedience of the Israelites did not involve tampering with the Scriptures. If distortion had occurred, Jesus cannot be referred as "the promised Messiah." Even the Qur'an speaks of him as "the Messiah, Jesus Son of Mary."[115] Moriscos and Christians can agree that the Scriptures had not been corrupted prior to the arrival of the promised Messiah. If both sides make assertions about the Scriptures, they are referring to the same prophets and the same Scriptures. What remains to be seen is whose assertions are grounded in truth.[116]

---

114. Pons Fuster, *Antialcorano. Diálogos Christianos*, 442–44.
115. Q. 3:35; Q. 4:157, 172; Q. 5:17, 72, 75; Q. 9:31.
116. Pons Fuster, *Antialcorano. Diálogos Christianos*, 444.

Catecismo del Sacromonte

THE SCRIPTURES[117]

The novice asks, "If the followers of Muhammad say that Christians have falsified their Scriptures, how should I reply?"[118] The priest gives five reasons why it was impossible for Jews and Christians to have falsified their Scriptures. First, the same God who gave the Scriptures is the same one who preserves it. In the Old Testament, the prophet Isaiah declared that "The word of our God stands forever" even though the grass withers and the flower fades (Isa 40:8). In the New Testament, Peter quoted those same words in his epistle to believers living in Asia (1 Pet 1:25). If God could not prevent the Scriptures from corruption, why would he give them in the first place? Second, God rebuked the Jews for committing all kinds of sins, but he never reproached them for corrupting the Scriptures. Third, Jews did not get along with the Christians and it would have demanded an extraordinary effort on both parties to agree to change the Scriptures. If such collusion had occurred, there would be records. However, there are none. Fourth, the New Testament agrees with the Old Testament in that the New Testament records the Old Testament prophecies that Christ fulfilled. Fifth, God is the ultimate author of the Scriptures. He proclaimed "I will put my law within them and on their heart I will write it" (Jer 31:33). Christ promised his disciples that the Holy Spirit would guide his disciples "into all the truth" and disclose to them "what is to come" (John 16:13).

Catecismo

HISTORY

The Moor asks the Teacher, "When you speak of the 'gospel,' are you referring to the same one that Christ preached? I have heard that it is in the Qur'an, but that it is not the same one that Christ preached because it has been falsified." The Teacher gives six reasons grounded in history to explain why the gospel could not have been falsified.[119] First, those who claim that the Scriptures have been falsified must first ask five questions: Have all or only parts of the Scriptures been falsified? Where are the falsifications? Who falsified the Scriptures? When were the Scriptures falsified?

---

117. Resines, *Catecismo del Sacromonte*, 202–6.
118. Resines, *Catecismo del Sacromonte*, 204.
119. Pérez de Ayala, *Catecismo*, 202–5.

Why were they falsified? However, Muḥammad and his followers neither asked nor answered these questions. They professed that if the Gospels do not concur with the Qur'an, the Gospels have been falsified. Second, at least two hundred years before the time of Muḥammad, the church fathers and learned men[120] quoted the same Scriptures and in the same way when writing about the same matters. Third, the Catholic Church has kept the Scriptures "pure and uncontaminated." Fourth, even the most callous community would do its utmost to protect the doctrines of its religion. Fifth, it would have been impossible for all the codices of the Christian Scriptures kept in locations spread across wide distances to be falsified and not one single codex to have escaped falsification. Sixth, it would have also been impossible for the Catholic Church guided by the Holy Spirit to have failed to notice the falsifications or allowed itself to be tricked or lied to about the falsifications. The table below summarizes how Pérez de Chinchón, *Catecismo del Sacromonte,* and Pérez de Ayala bridge the gap.

Results

This event asks, "Most urgently, does the catechism or polemical treatise present Christian theological concepts adapted to the abilities and talents of the Moriscos?" Of the seven works that participated in this event, Obregón's *Confutación del alcorán y secta mahometana* is the only one that does not meet the criteria. The following ones move to Round Two: Andrés's *Confusión o confutación,* Pérez de Chinchón's *Antialcorano* and *Diálogos Christianos,* Orozco's *Catecismo Provechoso, Catecismo del Sacromonte,* and Pérez de Ayala's *Catecismo.*

---

120. Pérez de Ayala mentioned (year of death in parenthesis) Tertullian (c. 240), Ambrosius (c. 250), Origen of Alexandria (254), Cyprian (c. 258), Athanasius (373), Basil the Great (379), Gregorian of Nazianzus (389), Gregory of Nyssa (394), Hieronymus (420), Augustine (430), and Theodoret of Cyrus (457). Pérez de Ayala, *Catecismo,* 204.

Table 3. Results of Round One, All Six Events

	1[121]	2[122]	3[123]	4[124]	5[125]	6[126]
Breve doctrina y enseñanza		✔	✔			
Confusión o confutación		✔	✔	✔	✔	✔
Doctrina Christiana (Alba)		✔	✔	✔		
Antialcorano		✔	✔	✔	✔	✔
Diálogos Christianos		✔	✔	✔	✔	✔
Confutación del Alcorán y secta Mahometana		✔	✔	✔	✔	
Doctrina Cristiana (Ayala)		✔	✔			
Catecismo provechoso		✔	✔	✔	✔	✔
Catecheses mystagogicae		✔	✔			
Catecismo del Sacromonte		✔	✔	✔	✔	✔
Doctrina Cristiana (Ripalda)	✔					
Doctrina cristiana (Astete)		✔	✔			
Catecismo		✔	✔	✔	✔	✔

121. Event 1. Is the catechism written for children?

122. Event 2. Is the catechism or polemical treatise written with rectors in mind?

123. Event 3. Is the catechism or polemical treatise like a handbook and a primer?

124. Event 4. Does the catechism or polemical treatise have apologetic material that addresses the usual objections raised by Islamic clerics?

125. Event 5. Does the catechism or polemical treatise provide an exposition on the life and doctrines of Muhammad?

126. Event 6. Most urgently, does the catechism or polemical treatise present Christian theological concepts adapted to the abilities and talents of the Moriscos?

Chapter 7

The New *Catecismo*: The Gospel and Reaction

Step 1

Round Two, Four Events

Round Two, Event 1. Does the catechism or polemical treatise discuss all the material needed to teach the gospel to an unbeliever, especially someone who comes from the sect of Muhammad?

"the gospel"

THREE TERMS OR PHRASES in this question need to be clarified or defined before it can be answered. First, the "gospel" refers to the *content of the gospel* that Jesus Christ died for the sins of humanity, was buried, raised from the dead on the third day, and appeared to his disciples and more than five hundred eyewitnesses at one time "according to the Scriptures," 1 Cor 15.1–8.

"all the material"

Second, "all the material" can refer to five *core elements of the gospel*: humanity's sinfulness and Jesus Christ's crucifixion, burial, appearances, and ascension. If any of these core elements is missing, the message to the Moor or Morisco is lacking.

"especially someone who comes from the sect of Muhammad"

Third, the phrase "especially someone who comes from the sect of Muhammad" is emphasized because followers of Muhammad question *the integrity of the gospel.* The gospel is not concerned with what an imaginary good man did according to hearsay, fairy tales or legends, but what Jesus Christ accomplished "according to the Scriptures."

Round One, Event 6 (Most urgently, does the catechism or polemical treatise present Christian theological concepts adapted to the abilities and talenst of the Moriscos?) bridges significant gaps that followers of the sect of Muhammad have about two core elements in the gospel: the identity of Jesus Christ and the integrity of the Christian Scriptures. It would have been difficult for any of the six authors examined in this question to make much progress in their conversations with a Moor or Morisco without first bridging these two gaps. These authors would agree with everything said about the gospel in 1 Cor 15:1–8 even though their presentation is not identical to the apostle Paul's. The material they present to the followers of the sect of Muhammad is summarized below.

Confusión o confutación

What does Andrés say about the gospel? He mentions briefly three of its key elements. The title of chapter 11 announces: "How the Qur'an testifies about Jesus Christ . . . how he died and resurrected and ascended to heaven." Andrés adds, "All the above I will prove with the very Qur'an and the *sunna*."[1] However, three points should be noted. First, although Andrés stated that he would use the Qur'an and the *sunna* to prove Christ's death, resurrection, and ascension, he only touched on the ascension. Second, he does not even raise the sinful human condition much less discuss it. Third, a Morisco would know that Andrés believes that Christ *did die, resurrect, and ascend to heaven,* but would not know *why* he died. These flaws are compensated by Andrés ability to use the Qur'an to undermine Muhammad's credibility and the Qur'an's claims to be Allah's perfect revelation to humanity.

Diálogos Christianos

Given that Christ's mission is "according to the Scriptures," Pérez de Chinchón points out Scriptures such as Deut 28:66–67, Ps 22:17–23, Isa

---

1. Ruiz García, *Juan Andrés,* 210.

55:2, Jer 11:19, and Zech 12:10. Isa 40:2 announces the coming salvation; Matt 1:19–21 declares its arrival;[2] and Peter speaks as one of its witnesses (1 Pet 3:18). In John 3:14–15, Jesus refers to his crucifixion as the lifting up foreshadowed in Num 21:4–9[3] in the Old Testament. Christ's resurrection is connected to Jonah's experience (Jonah 2:17–3.10) of having been in the belly of a whale (Matt 12:40; Luke 11:29–30).[4] Hos 6:2 and Exod 19:10–12 also allude to Christ's resurrection.[5] Pérez de Chinchón also refers to Dan 7:13–14, Isa 23:10–14, Rev 1:17–19, and Ps 109:11.[6]

Catecismo

What is the gospel?

The Moor asks, "What is the gospel?"[7] The Teacher says that the gospel is the good news or glad tidings that the Son of God became a man to pay for our sins and reconcile us to God by taking us away from darkness and the power of sin to the light of the kingdom of God.[8]

Where is this gospel recorded?

This gospel—"the sacred doctrine of the New Testament"—is recorded in the four Gospels, which are the same ones that the apostles preached and the church uses today.[9]

What does the gospel teach?

Some of the gospel's teachings include The Beatitudes[10] and loving our neighbor by doing deeds of mercy, which include physical ones (feed the hungry; give a drink to the thirsty; clothe the naked; shelter the pilgrim;

---

2. Pons Fuster, *Antialcorano. Diálogos Christianos*, 489.
3. Pons Fuster, *Antialcorano. Diálogos Christianos*, 504. Pérez de Chinchón refers to this passage as "Numbers XXIII" instead of "Numbers XXI."
4. Pons Fuster, *Antialcorano. Diálogos Christianos*, 506.
5. Pons Fuster, *Antialcorano. Diálogos Christianos*, 504.
6. Pons Fuster, *Antialcorano. Diálogos Christianos*, 507.
7. Pérez de Ayala, *Catecismo*, 265.
8. Pérez de Ayala, *Catecismo*, 265–66.
9. Pérez de Ayala, *Catecismo*, 267.
10. Pérez de Ayala, *Catecismo*, 414–17.

visit the sick; redeem the captive; and bury the dead) and spiritual ones. (comfort the sorrowful; teach the ignorant; give counsel; forgive insults; bear the shortcomings of our neighbor; pray for them; and rebuke in a brotherly way).[11]

What is the effect of the gospel?

The Teacher gives three examples of people changed by the gospel: the apostle Paul (Acts 9:1–9), an Ethiopian court official (Acts 8:26–40), and the Roman centurion Cornelius (Acts 10). Experience shows that the more a person orders his or her life according to the gospel, they become more "virtuous and spiritual" and "respect, revere and obey" God more.[12]

Round Two, Event 2. Is the tone of the catechism or polemical treatise "charitable and friendly"?

The section below explains briefly why the answer is "yes" for all six catechisms and polemical treatises except Andrés' *Confusión o confutación* and Pérez de Chinchón's *Antialcorano*.

Confusión o confutación

Starting from as early as the prologue of *Confusión o confutación*, the tone of Juan Andrés towards the Qur'an, Muhammad, the Moors, the sect of Muhammad, and the law of Muhammad seems "uncharitable and unfriendly."[13] The Qur'an is a collection of "fictions, clear lies, willful lies, senseless words, stupidities, mad words, blasphemies, tactless words, absurdities, falsehood, and contradictions." Muhammad was a "false prophet" and "wicked and evil." Moors are "ignorant." The sect of Muhammad is "false and brutal." The wise will not accept it while ordinary people laugh at its "stupidities" and lament "the blindness and damnation" of its followers. There is no basis or rationale for the law of Muhammad to be true law.[14]

---

11. Pérez de Ayala, *Catecismo*, 356–58.
12. Pérez de Ayala, *Catecismo*, 248–49.
13. Ruiz García, *Juan Andrés*, 87.
14. Ruiz García, *Juan Andrés*, 91–92.

Antialcorano

The tone towards Muhammad, the Qur'an, and the law of Muhammad can be detected from reading the titles of some of the twenty-six sermons in *Antialcorano*; for example, "The law or sect of Muhammad does not have the truth";[15] "The law of Muhammad cannot be the law of God because of the one who gave it is bad, a liar, a big sinner, and a false and lying prophet";[16] "The lies in the false revelation of Muhammad";[17] "The many big lies that the false prophet Muhammad put in the Qur'an, which the Moors believe against natural and divine reason";[18] and "The many other lies in the law of Muhammad, the *sunna*, and his other books, which the Moors believe and do not deny."[19]

The titles of three sermons indicate that there is something wrong with the revelation that Moors claim to have received from Allah: "How our gospel is true and is the one that Jesus Christ and his apostles preached, and how the Moors are obligated to believe it and say so";[20] "Circumcision is bad and the Moors have to believe the gospel and our faith more than their own, and other matters about this";[21] and "The Moor is more obligated to believe the gospel than the Qur'an and the perfection of the gospel."[22]

Diálogos Christianos

Pérez de Chinchón wrote *Antialcorano* and *Diálogos Christianos* yet there is almost no similarity in their tones. *Diálogos Christianos* is "charitable and friendly" for two reasons. First, Pérez de Chinchón and his Arabic teacher Joseph are in the country side, which is probably the most cordial environment possible for a Christian and a Moor or Morisco to discuss something as contentious as the differences between Jesus Christ and Muhammad and their religions. Second, they defer to each other. Pérez de Chinchón begins with a polite request. "Joseph, now that we are alone in this garden and free from our daily cares shall we chat about certain things that I have been thinking about?" Joseph answers, "I'd be happy to hear everything

---

15. Pons Fuster, *Antialcorano. Diálogos Christianos*, 157.
16. Pons Fuster, *Antialcorano. Diálogos Christianos*, 233.
17. Pons Fuster, *Antialcorano. Diálogos Christianos*, 261.
18. Pons Fuster, *Antialcorano. Diálogos Christianos*, 277.
19. Pons Fuster, *Antialcorano. Diálogos Christianos*, 319.
20. Pons Fuster, *Antialcorano. Diálogos Christianos*, 197.
21. Pons Fuster, *Antialcorano. Diálogos Christianos*, 187.
22. Pons Fuster, *Antialcorano. Diálogos Christianos*, 209.

that you have to say because I know that your goodwill towards me is such that I would not fall into error when talking with you. I also know that you would not despise me when I am mistaken because your love will cover up all my faults if there are any." Pérez de Chinchón calls Joseph "my teacher and Mister Joseph." Joseph believes that their dialogues will be a great gain and promises to give his full attention. Pérez de Chinchón shudders at the mere thought that one of them would die believing that he is right when in reality he is in grave error. Their friendship prevents them from harming or mistrusting each other. Acting contrary to understanding ("a friend of the truth") is to behave like an animal. Joseph says that he is not one those who do not want to reason about what they believe or talk to those who do not have the same beliefs as he does.[23]

Catecismo provechoso

The tone of *Catecismo provechoso*—like Pérez de Chinchón's *Antialcorano*—can also be discerned from some of the chapter titles; specifically, Chapters II ("All sects are false and the only true one is the Christian law.")[24] and III ("How our holy faith condemns the sect of Muhammad.").[25] Chapter II makes the charge that the sect of Muhammad consists of "lies sown by Satan, the father of lies."[26] Chapter III describes Muhammad as "a deceiver" and "a wicked man" whose "crazy things and dreams were devised by the devil."[27] It would seem that the tone of *Catecismo provechoso* is "uncharitable and unfriendly" like *Confusión o confutación* and *Antialcorano*. However, that is not the case as we shall see in the third question of this round—"Could the catechism or polemical treatise inflame the emotions of the Moriscos?"

Catecismo del Sacromonte

The tone of this catechism[28] is apparent from its eight charges against Moriscos as to why they are not the Christians they claim to be: (1) Every year the Inquisition adjudicates that many Moriscos are still members of the sect of Muhammad; (2) They move to Barbary as soon as they can; (3) They

23. Pons Fuster, *Antialcorano. Diálogos Christianos*, 403–4.
24. Orozco, *Catecismo provechoso*, 10 [l].
25. Orozco, *Catecismo provechoso*, 13 [l].
26. Orozco, *Catecismo provechoso*, 10 [r].
27. Orozco, *Catecismo provechoso*, 14 [l]–14 [r].
28. Resines, *Catecismo del Sacromonte*, 162–63.

are unwilling to give up their customs; (4) They have destroyed churches and killed priests; (5) They do not attend Mass, but disrespectful when they do attend; (6) They never marry Old Christians; (7) They have little regard for Old Christians; and (8) If they understood Christianity, they would pay more attention to their salvation.

These charges give the impression that the *Catecismo del Sacromonte* is as "uncharitable and unfriendly" as *Confusión o confutación* and *Antialcorano*. However, the third question of this round will reveal whether this impression is correct or not.

Catecismo

The tone of Pérez de Ayala's *Catecismo*—like Pérez de Chinchón's *Antialcorano* and Orozco's *Catecismo provechoso*—can also be detected from the titles of its chapters; specifically, the titles of seven of the twenty-five dialogues in Book One of the *Catecismo*. Three charges are made against the sect of Muhammad. First, it cannot be the path to God because Muhammad lived a life of debauchery.[29] Second, it is weak because it permits its followers to pretend that they are not Moors.[30] Third, it is false because of the way it was preached.[31]

The *Catecismo* also censures Muhammad, his law, his doctrine, and the Qur'an. Muhammad contradicts himself in the Qur'an.[32] The law of Muhammad is false because the final destination it promises to humanity is false.[33] The doctrine of Muhammad is bad because its content is bad.[34] The Qur'an contains errors, lies, and fables.[35] The third event of this round will address the apparent "uncharitable and unfriendly" tone of the *Catecismo*.

Results

According to Event 2 ("Is the tone of the catechism or polemical treatise 'charitable and friendly'?") none of the works below can proceed to Event 3 ("Could the catechism or polemical treatise inflame the emotions of

29. Pérez de Ayala, *Catecismo*, 81.
30. Pérez de Ayala, *Catecismo*, 132.
31. Pérez de Ayala, *Catecismo*, 139.
32. Pérez de Ayala, *Catecismo*, 120.
33. Pérez de Ayala, *Catecismo*, 95.
34. Pérez de Ayala, *Catecismo*, 125.
35. Pérez de Ayala, Catecismo, 106.

the Moriscos?") except *Diálogos Christianos*. But, they are permitted to advance because—as will be seen shortly—Events 2 and 3 are connected. The criteria set up by Event 3 will help make the final decision as to which of the following six works may be regarded as "charitable and friendly:" *Confusión o confutación, Antialcorano, Diálogos Christianos, Catecismo provechoso, Catecismo del Sacromonte,* and *Catecismo*.

Round Two, Event 3. Could the catechism or polemical treatise inflame the emotions of the Moriscos?

Events 2 and 3 are connected. If the tone of the catechism or polemical treatise is "uncharitable and unfriendly," the critique against the Qur'an, the Moors, Muhammad, and his sect and his law is expected[36] to inflame the feelings of the Moor or the Morisco. The tone of *Catecismo provechoso, Catecismo del Sacromonte,* and *Catecismo* seems "uncharitable and unfriendly." These three works are in the format of a dialogue between a representative of the Catholic Church and a Morisco. The response of the latter provides an approximate idea of whether the feelings of the Moriscos would be inflamed or not. Otherwise, the answer to the question in this round would be speculative.

Catecismo provechoso

Felipe embraced the Catholic faith after being a Moor for thirty years. The priest calls him "baptized and washed in the blessed blood of our Savior Jesus Christ."[37] There are six reasons why the tone of *Catecismo provechoso* is not "uncharitable and unfriendly."

1. Thanksgiving. Felipe says to the priest, "I give thanks to my Savior Jesus Christ. He illuminated my former blindness in the hellish and insane sect of Muhammad."[38] On another occasion, Felipe gives "thousands of praises and thanks" because God's "secret judgment" condemned his parents and grandparents, but rescued him without him deserving it.[39]

---

36. The phrasing of Event 3 shows awareness that Moors are known to become emotional when Muhammad and their religion is exposed.
37. Orozco, *Catecismo provechoso*, 8 [r].
38. Orozco, *Catecismo provechoso*, 8 [r].
39. Orozco, *Catecismo provechoso*, 13 [r].

2. New Identity. Felipe views himself as "the adopted son of God" and no longer a member of the sect of Muhammad, but a member of "the Holy Roman Church."[40]

3. Regret. Felipe laments, "My heart hurts greatly for having wasted so much time and misused thirty years being lost in those wrong-headed errors."[41] Felipe's thanksgiving, new identity, and regret indicate that he has experienced a genuine conversion resulting in him having a new resilience, a new perspective, and a new mission.

4. New Resilience. Prior to his conversion, Felipe—like many if not all Moors and Moriscos—could become incensed when facing any criticism against Muhammad and his teachings. The priest recalls that Muhammad robbed, killed, and lied about being a prophet of God. Felipe reacts calmly and says that if Moors knew the truth about Muhammad being "a thug who lived a degenerate life," they would curse him and embrace Jesus Christ as "King and Lord of all creation."[42]

5. New Perspective. Felipe's genuine conversion also enables him to assess his former religion. The sect of Muhammad is a "hellish and insane" sect of "wrong-headed errors."[43] Muhammad had "dreams full of vanities that deceived many souls."[44]

6. New Mission. Felipe now wants to talk to his kin in Arabic about the religion of Christ.[45] This self-appointed mission shows that Felipe can absorb criticisms against his former religion *and* simultaneously denounce it due in large part to his genuine conversion.

These six reasons remove the initial impression that the tone of Orozco's *Catecismo provechoso* is "uncharitable and unfriendly." However, a caveat is needed. Criticism from the priest does not inflame Felipe for three reasons: (1) Felipe had become convinced that Muhammad and his sect were false *before* being "baptized and washed in the blood of Jesus Christ";[46] (2) Now

---

40. Orozco, *Catecismo provechoso*, 13 [r].
41. Orozco, *Catecismo provechoso*, 8 [r].
42. Orozco, *Catecismo provechoso*, 14 [l]–14 [r].
43. Orozco, *Catecismo provechoso*, 8 [r].
44. Orozco, *Catecismo provechoso*, 12 [r].
45. Orozco, *Catecismo provechoso*, 13 [r].
46. If the biblical definition of "baptism" is "to be baptized and washed in the blood of Jesus Christ" and if this baptism (1) occurs at the moment of "conversion"; (2) is not the same as "to be baptized with water"; and (3) is invisible compared with water baptism, a Moor should have been converted first ("baptized and washed in the blood of Jesus Christ") before receiving water baptism. It is beyond the scope of this book

that he has been "baptized and washed" he is even more convinced that Muhammad and his sect are false; and (3) Strictly speaking, Felipe should not be regarded as a Morisco because he does not fit the definition; that is, a recently baptized Moor whose "baptism with water" raises suspicions because he has not abandoned his non-fundamental secular customs.[47]

It would be more accurate to regard Felipe as "a Moor who has become an adopted son of God." This caveat means that it should not be assumed that Moriscos who read or listen to *Catecismo provechoso* would not become inflamed. The tone of *Catecismo provechoso* will be discussed further in "Final Observations" after the review below on the tone of Pérez de Ayala's *Catecismo*.

Catecismo del Sacromonte

The priest makes eight charges against the Moriscos,[48] but the novice replies calmly, "Many (Moriscos) are mistaken, but not all of them." Furthermore, he agrees with two of the priest's assertions: (1) The law of Christ loves God more, is more just, and better than the law of Muhammad and (2) The law of Muhammad is unjust, bad, and contrary to the law of Christ.[49]

The novice also agrees with four implications that the priest draws out from these two assertions: (1) A law that is unjust, bad, and contrary to the law of Christ cannot be from God; (2) The law of Muhammad cannot be the law of God; (3) Muhammad lied about his law being the law of God; and (4) Muhammad is not a prophet of God.[50]

Three reasons why the novice is not flustered: (1) The *relationship* between him and the priest is similar to the one between Pérez de Chinchón and Joseph; that is, friendly and respectful. The dialogue starts with the priest blessing the novice—"The eternal God who made you in his image grant you eternal life." The novice replies, "May he do likewise to you."[51] The priest is like a shepherd who protects his sheep. The priest loves the novice and wishes for the followers of the sect of Muhammad to follow the

to discuss the biblical basis for the sequence "first baptized and washed in the blood of Jesus Christ (conversion) then baptized with water." If this assertion is correct, the Catholic Church, the Inquisition, and the Spanish monarchy were faced with the problem of converting Moors after they had been baptized with water. Moriscos were Moors who had been baptized with water before they had converted.

47. Resines, *Catecismo del Sacromonte*, 47–48.
48. See above "Catecismo del Sacromonte" in Round 2, Event 2.
49. Resines, *Catecismo del Sacromonte*, 162.
50. Resines, *Catecismo del Sacromonte*, 170–71.
51. Resines, *Catecismo del Sacromonte*, 160.

true path;[52] (2) The novice—like Felipe in *Catecismo provechoso*—has a *new identity*. The priest does not deem the novice to be one of the Moriscos whom eight charges have been lobbied against, but as "a brother"[53] and "a good Christian."[54] The novice—like Felipe—should not be regarded as a Morisco (he probably was never one); and (3) The novice—like Felipe—has a *mission*. He is eager for the priest to train him to always seek the glory of God and the salvation of souls.[55]

These three reasons remove the initial impression that *Catecismo del Sacromonte* is "uncharitable and unfriendly." A similar caveat has to be made as in the case of Felipe. Although the novice is self-controlled, this does not mean that Moriscos listening to or reading *Catecismo del Sacromonte* would not be inflamed by the priest's criticisms. The tone of *Catecismo del Sacromonte* will be discussed further in "Final Observations" after the review below on the tone of Pérez de Ayala's *Catecismo*.

Catecismo

The tone of this catechism seems "uncharitable and unfriendly." However, this is not the case for five reasons: (1) The Moor wants to become a Christian. This is the main reason why he left his home in the Berber region of North Africa and travelled to Spain to look for Pérez de Ayala;[56] (2) The Moor admits that he is not satisfied with the religion of his forefathers;[57] (3) The Moor's desire to become a Christian is genuine. The Teacher is suspicious of his true intentions because Moors are known for pretending to be Christians so they can be spies or become rich. But, the Moor says, "I do not want to waste my time. I want to be saved and find the path to salvation";[58] (4) The conversation between the Moor and the Teacher is friendly and respectful from the outset even though they just met. There is no prior or existing relationship such as the one between Pérez de Chinchón and Joseph in *Diálogos Christianos* and between the priest and the novice in *Catecismo del Sacromonte*. The first dialogue in *Catecismo* begins with the Moor's polite greeting that addresses the Teacher as "my

---

52. Resines, *Catecismo del Sacromonte*, 162.
53. Resines, *Catecismo del Sacromonte*, 161.
54. Resines, *Catecismo del Sacromonte*, 163.
55. Resines, *Catecismo del Sacromonte*, 161.
56. Pérez de Ayala, *Catecismo*, 1.
57. Pérez de Ayala, *Catecismo*, 2.
58. Pérez de Ayala, *Catecismo*, 2.

father"—"May God save you, my father."[59] The Teacher's reciprocation refers to the Moor as "brother"—"May he also be with you, brother";[60] and (5) The Teacher does not critique Muhammad until Dialogue XIII.[61] The first twelve dialogues predisposes the Moor towards a more favorable impression of Christ without being offended.[62]

A similar caveat has to be made as in the case of Felipe in *Catecismo provechoso* and the novice in *Catecismo del Sacromonte*. The ability of the Moor in the *Catecismo* to remain impassive cannot be extrapolated to other Moors.

Table 4. Summary of Round Two, Events 2 and 3

Event 2. Is the tone of the catechism or polemical treatise "charitable and friendly"?

Event 3. Could the catechism or polemical treatise inflame the emotions of the Moriscos?

	Event 2	Event 3
Confusión o confutación	No	Yes
Antialcorano	No	Yes
Diálogos Christianos	Yes	No
Catecismo provechoso	No	No
Catecismo del Sacromonte	No	No
Catecismo	No	No

Conclusion

It cannot be stated with absolute certainty how Moriscos reacted to the material in these six catechisms and polemical treatises unless there are historical records indicating a link between the content in these works and some

---

59. Pérez de Ayala, *Catecismo*, 1.

60. Pérez de Ayala, *Catecismo*, 1.

61. Pérez de Ayala, *Catecismo*, 81.

62. See above "Martín Pérez de Ayala. *Catecismo para instrucción de los nuevamente convertidos de Moros*. Book One. Pre-Apologetics" in "Chapter 3. Overview of the *Catecismo* and Other Catechisms and Polemical Treatises in Sixteenth-Century Spain" for an overview of the content of these first twelve dialogues.

form of public backlash. By comparison, there is a correlation between the decree and execution of royal and ecclesiastical policies and the rebellion in Albaicín (1500), the War of Germanías (1521), and the uprisings in Benaguacil and Espadán (1526) and Alpujarras (1568).[63]

Despite the lack of certainty, an attempt is made to understand the following, which brings Events 2 and 3 to a close: All six catechisms and polemical treatises judge the same material that is sensitive to Moors and Moriscos; that is, the Qur'an, Muhammad, his law, and his sect. The tone of all six works except Pérez de Chinchón's *Diálogos Christianos* is "uncharitable and unfriendly." Why might *Confusión o Confutación* and *Antialcorano* inflame the emotions of the Moriscos, but not *Catecismo provechoso*, *Catecismo del Sacromonte*, and *Catecismo*?

There are two reasons. First, *Confusión o confutación* and *Antialcorano* are not dialogues.[64] A catechism or a polemical treatise written in the format of a dialogue can provide an approximate idea of how a Moor or a Morisco is responding to criticism. The phrase "Tell me, Moor"[65] appears 37 times in *Confusión o confutación* and gives the impression that Andrés is talking with someone; for example, "Tell me, Moor, what sin did the angels commit that condemned them to death like Adam?"[66] and "Tell me, Moor, which command permits a married man to take away a married woman he falls in love with?"[67] If Andrés is asking an actual Moor, he does not give him an opportunity to rebut but proceeds immediately to answer the question himself. By comparison, Pérez de Chinchón invites Joseph to dialogue with him by saying, "But, tell me Joseph, my friend."[68] Second, the limited information about this Moor is a sign that there is no connection between him and Andrés. He does not have a name, but four deductions can be made about him on the basis of what Andrés reveals about him:

(1) He is a devout follower of the sect of Muhammad for we are told that he reads the Qur'an daily;[69] (2) He is well-educated. Andrés calls him wise and an astrologer, a philosopher and a theologian;[70] (3) He seems to have an open-mind. *Confusión o Confutación* discloses that he has good

63. See "Key Historical Events" above in Chapter 3.

64. This reason also answers Round 3, Event 4. Does the catechism or polemical treatise use the format of a dialogue, "which is the clearest and most distinct way to teach when the one being instructed has questions and the teacher has answers"?

65. "Dime tú, moro." Sometimes, "Well, tell me, Moor." ("Pues dime tú, moro.")

66. Ruiz García, *Juan Andrés*, 136.

67. Ruiz García, *Juan Andrés*, 166.

68. Pons Fuster, *Antialcorano. Diálogos Christianos*, 418.

69. Ruiz García, *Juan Andrés*, 142, 169.

70. Ruiz García, *Juan Andrés*, 144. Andrés calls him "astrologer" twice: 155 and 202.

judgment and uses reason;[71] (4) If he has an avocation, it might have something to do with camels for we learn that there are many of these animals at his native place.[72] It is possible that this Moor is working simultaneously as an astrologer, a philosopher, and a theologian. However, it is also plausible that Andrés is disputing not with a single anonymous Moor, but a composite of at least three Moors whereby each is an expert in one area (astrology, philosophy or theology). Irrespective of whether Andrés is having a dispute with one Moor or more than one, the following is what is relevant: these four deductions not only reveal something about the Moor *himself,* but also something much more important—there is no chemistry whatsoever between Andrés and the Moor. Absent is the cordiality and respect that characterize the exchanges between Pérez de Chinchón and Joseph (*Diálogos Christianos*), the priest and the novice (*Catecismo del Sacromonte*), and the Moor and the teacher in Pérez de Ayala's *Catecismo*.

Antialcorano—like *Confusión o confutación*—is also not structured as dialogues, but as a series of twenty-six sermons. Three features of these sermons show their potential to inflame the emotions of the Moriscos:

(1) The *objectives* of these sermons: to instruct these new converts and confute the sect of Muhammad.[73] Even if both objectives share equal time, the manner in which the "confute" objective is carried out seems problematic; (2) The *delivery* of these sermons: either listened to in public during Mass or read privately at another time.[74] If these sermons were meant to be delivered during Mass, it is difficult to see how a Moor or Morisco could be persuaded to attend church to hear his prophet and his religion censured; and (3) The *intended audience* of these sermons: not Moors, but canons, rectors, vicars, and everyone with spiritual oversight over "Moors who have recently converted to the Christian faith."[75] In the same way that it is difficult to see how a Moor or Morisco could be convinced to attend Mass to be reproached, it is also difficult to imagine one of them picking up a copy of *Antialcorano* to read given that the title itself is also a dead giveaway. While personal information about the Moor in *Confusión o confutación* is sparse, absolutely nothing is known about the Moors in *Antialcorano* except that they are from Valencia, Aragón, and Granada.[76]

71. Ruiz García, *Juan Andrés*, 147, 157.
72. Ruiz García, *Juan Andrés*, 201.
73. Pons Fuster, *Antialcorano. Diálogos Christianos*, 79.
74. *Antialcorano* has a preface written to readers, which seems to indicate that these sermons were also meant to be read. Pons Fuster, *Antialcorano. Diálogos Christianos*, 87.
75. Pons Fuster, *Antialcorano. Diálogos Christianos*, 75.
76. Pons Fuster, *Antialcorano. Diálogos Christianos*, 75.

The objectives "to instruct" and "to confute" would be difficult—if not impossible—to achieve due to the lack of a relationship between the instructor and the recipient of the instruction. This assertion is not without basis given the observed responses of Joseph in *Diálogos Christianos*, Felipe in *Catecismo provechoso*, the novice in *Catecismo del Sacromonte*, and the Moor in Pérez de Ayala's *Catecismo*.

Results

Diálogos Christianos, Catecismo provechoso, Catecismo del Sacromonte, and *Catecismo* proceed to Event 4.

Round Two, Event 4. Does the catechism or polemical treatise use "common and ordinary terms" to preach "intelligible doctrine" so that Moriscos know what they must believe and do?

Yes. This can be noted in how *Diálogos Christianos, Catecismo provechoso, Catecismo del Sacromonte,* and *Catecismo* bridge the gap when discussing the integrity of the Scriptures, Jesus Christ, and the Trinity.[77]

Results

Diálogos Christianos, Catecismo provechoso, Catecismo del Sacromonte, and *Catecismo* proceed to Round Three.

---

77. See above Round 1, Event 6. Most urgently, does the catechism or polemical treatise present Christian theological concepts adapted to the abilities and talents of the Moriscos?

Table 5. Results of Round Two, All Four Events

	1[78]	2[79]	3[80]	4[81]
Confusión o confutación	✔		✔	
Antialcorano	✔		✔	
Diálogos Christianos	✔	✔		✔
Catecismo provechoso	✔			✔
Catecheses mystagogicae	✔			
Catecismo del Sacromonte	✔			✔
Catecismo	✔			✔

78. Event 1. Does the catechism or polemical treatise discuss all the material needed to teach the gospel to an unbeliever—especially someone who comes from the sect of Muhammad?

79. Event 2. Is the tone of the catechism or polemical treatise "charitable and friendly"?

80. Event 3. Could the catechism or polemical inflame the emotions of the Moriscos?

81. Event 4. Does the catechism or polemical treatise use "common and ordinary terms" to preach "intelligible" doctrine so that Moriscos know what they must believe and do?

Chapter 8

The New *Catecismo*: Experience and Evidence

Step 1

Round Three, Four Events

Round Three, Event 1. Does the author of the catechism or polemical treatise have experience talking with and instructing Moriscos?

A BRIEF EXAMINATION OF each work shows that all four authors have experience.

Catecismo

Five pieces of evidence demonstrate that Pérez de Ayala has experience talking with and instructing Moriscos. First, although Charles knows that Pérez de Ayala is a neophyte in Morisco ministry, he still nominates him to be the bishop of Guadix because of his *potential* to become a good pastor to the Moriscos.[1] Second, the Moor took the initiative to travel the long distance from his home in Barbary to Guadix. He would like for Pérez de Ayala to teach him personally because he has heard that the bishop is instructing Moriscos with "great zeal and skill" and believes that Pérez de Ayala "has the doctrines" that can help him become a Christian.[2] Third, according to the Teacher, Pérez de Ayala has been occupied during the past two years

---

1. See "Martín Pérez de Ayala. Pastoral Career. Bishopric of Guadix" above in Chapter 2.
2. Pérez de Ayala, *Catecismo*, 4.

preaching and teaching Moriscos thus regrettably is unable to personally instruct the Moor. The spread of Pérez de Ayala's good reputation to attract a Moor from Northern Africa vindicates Charles' decision. Fourth, Philip II—another king—also has a high regard for Pérez de Ayala's Morisco ministry. Both of them discuss the need for prelates to instruct Moriscos using good catechisms. The bishop offers to bear the costs of printing.[3] Fifth, Ribera in his cover letter to the *Catecismo* acknowledges Pérez de Ayala's experience by noting that the writing of the catechism coincided with the three periods of Pérez de Ayala's ministry. He began to write the *Catecismo* while serving as bishop of Guadix where many Moriscos resided; took a break from writing when he was bishop of Segovia because not many Moriscos lived there; and resumed writing after becoming the archbishop of Valencia due to its sizable population of Moriscos. It is not inconceivable for Pérez de Ayala to have incorporated into the *Catecismo* the experience he gained in Guadix and Valencia.

Diálogos Christianos

Observations

The following three observations made on the basis of what Pérez de Chinchón wrote to his readers in the prologue of *Diálogos Christianos* show his experience interacting with Moors and Moriscos. First, he not only has had many disputes with *moriscados*,[4] but has made friends with them—including Joseph.[5] Pérez de Chinchón does not refer to his encounters with *moriscados* as "conversations," "exchanges" or "pleasantries," but "disputes." According to him, "there is no greater evil in the world today than the nefarious sect of Muhammad." The way to confront it is through "dispute," which he defines as "to use human and divine reasons to prove the falsity of the sect of Muhammad and the truth of the Christian faith."[6] It is remarkable that Pérez de Chinchón can still befriend *moriscados* after their disputes, which would have been intense encounters given that one of his objectives is to prove that the sect of Muhammad is false. Second, Pérez de Chinchón refers to Joseph as "my Arabic teacher."[7] However, the breadth and depth of

---

3. See "Martín Pérez de Ayala. Pastoral Career. Archbishopric of Valencia" above in Chapter 2.
4. Moors who are able to read Arabic and/or Castilian, but not Latin.
5. Pons Fuster, *Antialcorano. Diálogos Christianos*, 401.
6. Pons Fuster, *Antialcorano. Diálogos Christianos*, 399.
7. Pons Fuster, *Antialcorano. Diálogos Christianos*, 401.

the subject matter covered in *Diálogos Christianos*[8] indicates that he learned more than just Arabic from Joseph. In fact, they learned from each other. Joseph is already a Christian, but is pleased to play the role of a Moor involved in a dispute that he may be better informed of the truth of the Christian faith.[9] Third, *Diálogos Christianos* is a faithful record of Pérez de Chinchón's experience. That is why he had his work printed as dialogues so that it reflects the actual dialogues between him and Joseph.[10]

Sense of Urgency

Given that *Diálogos Christianos* are real dialogues, they create a sense of urgency. First, the clergy shares a collective blame—and Pérez de Chinchón includes himself—for allowing "true religion to be crushed" while falsehood is being dispensed. Second, he decides to do what every prelate should do; that is, to be zealous about the salvation of souls.[11] Third, it is vital to prove that the sect of Muhammad is false and the Christian faith is true. Thus, Chinchón exhorts his fellow prelates to be active missionaries to the Moriscos and forsake "non-spiritual pursuits"[12] (*andar en cortes*) and the accumulation of "spiritually unfruitful wealth" (*atesorar ducados que son tierra amarilla*).[13] Fourth, he is not bothered by those who criticize *Diálogos Christianos* as "somewhat poor in style or doctrine."[14] It is better to clothe the poor in sackcloth than to let them go naked for not wanting to dress them in brocade.[15] He is also not bothered by those who also criticize him for not writing in Latin. The *moriscados* who might want to read *Diálogos Christianos* do not know Latin. The Christians who would like to read it to learn how to dispute also do not know Latin. His intention is to write for both clergy and laity.[16] He is more concerned with getting the message out to the widest audience as quickly as possible.

8. See "Bernardo Pérez de Chinchón" above in Chapter 3.
9. Pons Fuster, *Antialcorano. Diálogos Christianos*, 401.
10. Pons Fuster, *Antialcorano. Diálogos Christianos*, 401.
11. Pons Fuster, *Antialcorano. Diálogos Christianos*, 399.
12. Pons Fuster, *Antialcorano. Diálogos Christianos*, 399.
13. Pons Fuster, *Antialcorano. Diálogos Christianos*, 399.
14. Pons Fuster, *Antialcorano. Diálogos Christianos*, 401.
15. Pons Fuster, *Antialcorano. Diálogos Christianos*, 401.
16. Pons Fuster, *Antialcorano. Diálogos Christianos*, 402.

Catecismo provechoso

Vanities and Lies

Orozco might have had substantial experience, but if the content of a catechism or polemical treatise were a yardstick of its author's experience, the material in *Catecismo provechoso* classified as polemics is not as extensive as *Catecismo* or *Diálogos Christianos*. Only two of the twenty-three chapters of *Catecismo provechoso* can be categorized as polemics against Muhammad and his sect:[17] Chapter II ("How all the sects are false and the Christian law is the true one.")[18] and Chapter III ("How our holy faith condemns the sect of Muhammad.").[19]

When discussing the sect of Muhammad in Chapter II,[20] Orozco limits himself to making the assertion that the sect of the Moors consists of "vanities and lies sown by Satan—the father of lies—to confuse souls who end up condemned to eternal torment in hell."[21] Orozco elaborates his assertion in Chapter III in two ways. He writes about *the author* of the "vanities and lies" and *why* the sect of the Moors consists of vanities and lies. First, although Orozco—unlike Pérez de Ayala—does not provide a summary of the life of Muḥammad, he presents enough details that lead him to conclude that Muhammad was as a robber, a murderer, an unlettered idiot, a liar who deceived many by proclaiming himself to be the prophet of Allah, and "an enemy of the truth and a minister of the Antichrist."[22] Even Felipe admits that Muhammad lived a "horrendously vicious life."[23] Second, Orozco appraises five components of the sect of the Moors to support his assertion that it consists of "vanities and lies:" the source of the material found in the sect's religious text; the law of this sect; the miracles of this sect's founder; the teachings of this founder; and his blunders and contradictions.

(1) Sergius is the *source* of some of the material in the Qur'an. When Muhammad was a boy, he traveled to Syria with his uncle Abu Talib. Sergius—a Syrian Christian monk also known as Bahira—said that his scriptures prophesied the advent of Muhammad and warned Abu Talib to protect Muhammad.[24] According to Islamic sources, Bahira confirmed that

---

17. See "Alonso de Orozco" above in Chapter 3.
18. Orozco, *Catecismo provechoso*, 10 [l].
19. Orozco, *Catecismo provechoso*, 13 [l].
20. This chapter discusses four sects—the heretics, Jews, Gentiles, and Muhammad's.
21. Orozco, *Catecismo provechoso*, 10 [r].
22. Orozco, *Catecismo provechoso*, 17 [l].
23. Orozco, *Catecismo provechoso*, 14 [r].
24. Newby, "Baḥîrâ," *A Concise Encyclopedia of Islam*, 39–40.

Muhammad was a true prophet. However, a Christian source—the *Bahira Legend* in Syriac—indicates that the monk had not acknowledged Muhammad as a prophet. Furthermore, Sergius fabricated an entire theological system that led people of the time to believe that Muhammad was a prophet. The monk taught Muhammad during the evening. The following day, Muhammad recited what he had been told then claimed that it was a revelation from the angel Gabriel. Sergius codified what he taught Muhammad into what would be known as the Qur'an;[25] (2) The *law of Muhammad* is "tyrannical" for it forbids its followers to argue about its content and permits the killing of those who refuse to believe it; (3) The *miracles of Muhammad* are "false and laughable."[26] He claimed to have made a camel talk and to hide a part of the moon in his sleeve. (4) The *teachings of Muhammad*. Moors should take revenge into their own hands and cause as much pain as the enemy inflicted on them;[27] and (5) *Blunders and contradictions*. Muhammad said that he did not understand everything in the Qur'an. In the beginning, he claimed that his mission was to give the law to the Arabs only, but later said that he was to give it to the whole world.[28]

If a reader were pressed for time and could only use the Table of Contents of a catechism or polemical treatise to gauge its author's experience in polemics, a review of the Table of Contents of *Catecismo provechoso* and the *Catecismo* might lead to the conclusion that Orozco lacks Pérez de Ayala's experience.

A Comparison of the Polemical Material Listed in The Table of Contents of *Catecismo provechoso* and the *Catecismo*

Catecismo provechoso

"How all the sects are false and the Christian law is the true one" (Chapter II) and "How our holy faith condemns the sect of Muhammad" (Chapter III).

Catecismo

"The beginning of proofs that the sect of Muhammad cannot be the path to God and an account of the vicious life of its legislator" (Dialogue XIII); "The

---

25. Penn, *Envisioning Islam*, 111. See also Roggema, *The Legend of Sergius Baḥīrā*, and Guillaume, *The Life of Muhammad*, 79–81.

26. Orozco, *Catecismo provechoso*, 16 [l].

27. Orozco, *Catecismo provechoso*, 16 [l].

28. *Catecismo provechoso*, 17 [l].

false end and blessedness taught in the law of Muhammad proves that it is false" (Dialogue XIV); "The errors, lies, and fables that Muhammad put in the Qur'an" (Dialogue XV); "The many places in the Qur'an where Muhammad contradicts himself" (Dialogue XVI); "The content of the doctrine of Muhammad shows how bad is his doctrine" (Dialogue XVII); "The sect of Muhammad is weak and false because it permits Moors who for fear of danger are permitted to confess outwardly a different law from what they have internally" (Dialogue XVIII); and "The sect of Muhammad is false because of the way it was preached" (Dialogue XIX).

The seven chapters of polemical material in the *Catecismo* can be organized into eight areas: The life of Muhammad (Dialogue XIII, which resembles a short biography that borrows from traditional accounts); the path to God (Dialogue XIII); humanity's final destination (Dialogue XIV); the religious text of the sect of Muhammad (Dialogues XV and XVI); the doctrine of the sect (Dialogue XVII); *taqiyya* (Dialogue XVIII); and the manner in which the teachings of the sect were disseminated (Dialogue XV). These seven chapters argue that the sect of Muhammad is false because it is false in all these eight areas.

Orozco's limited discussion of these eight areas could have been more of a function of what Orozco wanted to accomplish in his dialogue with Felipe instead of what appears to be his limited experience talking with and instructing Moriscos. It is evident that Orozco wanted to focus on imparting Catholic doctrine. Of the twenty-three chapters in his catechism, he dedicates eleven chapters on the Articles of the Creed, two chapters on the Ten Commandments, one chapter on the Seven Sacraments, one chapter on Deeds of Mercy, and one chapter on virtues and mortal sins.

Orozco does not reveal what personal role he had in persuading Felipe to be "baptized and washed in the blood of Jesus Christ." Another priest might have lead Felipe to the point of making the decision to leave the sect of Muhammad. But, if it was Orozco instead of another priest, he must have had considerable experience to be able to convince Felipe—a follower of the sect of Muhammad for thirty years—to become "an adopted son of God" and "a member of the Roman Church." In conclusion, the fairest assessment is that Orozco has the experience even though it is not reflected in what he discusses in his catechism.

THE NEW *CATECISMO*: EXPERIENCE AND EVIDENCE

Catecismo del Sacromonte

Didactic Style

The priest's *didactic style* reveals his experience. He does not just lecture the novice. When the opportunity presents itself, he asks questions or answers a question with another question. This style forces the novice to think and process the wealth of information under discussion.[29] It is plausible that the priest refined and adopted this style as a result of many years of instructing Moriscos. The novice after being instructed in this style might have adopted it in his own ministry to Moriscos. The following are some examples of the priest's didactic style:

The priest asks the novice

"Tell me about Gentiles who worship demons and idols. Are they saved?"; "If a Gentile asks a Moor about what law will save him, what will the Moor say?";[30] "If the law of Christ and of Muhammad are all one, why are Christians and Moors not one?"[31]; and "But if the law of Christ loves God more than the law of Muhammad, why is it difficult for Moors to believe that the law of Christ is the law of God?"[32]

The priest answers the novice with another question

The novice asks, "If Moors say that their Qur'an is divine Scripture, how should I answer?" The priest responds with, "How would you answer?" The novice asks, "How should I answer those who say that Jews and Christians departed from the law of Moses?" The priests says, "You tell me."[33] The novice queries, "How should I respond to followers of Muhammad who say that Christians have corrupted their Scriptures?" The priest retorts, "Why are you surprised that those who follow one who testified falsely against God also do the same?"[34] The priest asserts that faith enables a person to see

---

29. See "Catecismo del Sacromonte" above in Chapter 3.
30. Resines, *Catecismo del Sacromonte*, 164.
31. Resines, *Catecismo del Sacromonte*, 168.
32. Resines, *Catecismo del Sacromonte*, 170.
33. Resines, *Catecismo del Sacromonte*, 191.
34. Resines, *Catecismo del Sacromonte*, 204.

things as if they are real. The novice asks, "How?" The priests replies with "What do the first articles (of the Creed) teach about faith?"[35]

Summary

This event asks, "Does the author of the catechism or polemical treatise have experience talking with and instructing Moriscos?"

> *Catecismo.* Charles saw Pérez de Ayala's *potential* ministry to Moriscos; Philip saw Pérez de Ayala's *actual* ministry to Moriscos; the Moor specifically requests Pérez de Ayala's help; the Teacher notes that Pérez de Ayala is a busy pastor of Moriscos; and Ribera in his cover letter recognizes Pérez de Ayala's experience.
>
> *Diálogos Christianos.* These dialogues are actual conversations between Pérez de Chinchón and Joseph.
>
> *Catecismo provechoso.* Orozco can substantiate his assertion that the sect of Muhammad consists of "vanities and lies."
>
> *Catecismo del Sacromonte.* The anonymous author uses a didactic style.

Conclusion

There is evidence that all four authors have experience as spiritual shepherds of Moriscos. The question "Which one of them is the most experienced?" is not one of the criteria, but arises naturally after surveying the table above. If it can be assumed that their Morisco ministry lasted until their year of death,[36] Pérez de Chinchón, Pérez de Ayala, and Orozco had twenty,[37] eighteen,[38] and twenty-three[39] years of experience, respectively.[40] Having an idea of their

---

35. Resines, *Catecismo del Sacromonte,* 211.

36. 1552 (Pérez de Chinchón), 1566 (Pérez de Ayala), and 1591 (Orozco). See Chapter 3 above.

37. Pérez de Chinchón's Morisco ministry began after he published *Antialcorano* in 1532. See "Bernardo Pérez de Chinchón" above in Chapter 3.

38. Pérez de Ayala's Morisco ministry began after he became bishop of Guadix in 1548. See "Martín Pérez de Ayala. Pastoral Career. Bishopric of Guadix" above in Chapter 2.

39. It is difficult to ascertain when Orozco began his Morisco ministry. If the year of publication is used as in the case of Pérez de Chinchón whose Morisco ministry began after he published *Antialcorano, Catecismo provechoso* was published in 1568. See Chapter 3 above.

40. It is impossible to determine the years of experience of the author of *Catecismo de Sacromonte* because he is unknown.

years of experience satisfies the curious mind. What is more important is whether or not their experience is reflected in their works regardless of how many years they ministered to Moriscos.

Results

Diálogos Christianos, Catecismo provechoso, Catecismo del Sacromonte, and *Catecismo* proceed to Event 2.

Round Three, Event 2. Does the catechism or polemical treatise use "natural and moral reasons and facts" to show the "purity and beauty" of the religion of Christ?

Yes. A brief examination of each work will justify this answer.

Catecismo provechoso

Natural and Moral Reasons

Orozco provides six "natural and moral reasons and facts." First, the religion of Christ is "pure and beautiful" because God is good. Although no person can merit eternal glory through his or her good moral deeds, the goodness of God is such that all good deeds will be rewarded. Even good deeds done without faith in God either at the national or personal level will be rewarded albeit only in this life. At the national level, the Roman Empire governed its colonies with justice and God allowed it to exist for five hundred years. At the personal level, God grants more wealth, domain, and honor to the person who does good moral deeds. Of course, he also rewards good moral deeds done with faith in him. The more such deeds are done, the more virtuous the person becomes to the point where God gives him or her the faith that procures eternal glory. The Ethiopian treasurer (Acts 8:26–40) and the Roman centurion Cornelius (Acts 10:1–43) are two examples. Second, God is just. His justice is such that no evil will be left unpunished. Third, the religion of Christ is like a "celestial school" and a "bottomless sea of perfections" that teaches about the power, majesty, and wisdom of God.[41]

The religion of Christ is "pure and beautiful" also because of what it teaches about *faith*; specifically, *where* it comes from and its *value* at both the human and angelic levels. First, faith is a gift—"a treasure"—from God

---

41. Orozco, *Catecismo provechoso*, 18 [r].

granted freely by him. Second, faith at the human level is critical for without faith it is impossible to please God or honor and serve him as king and redeemer.[42] God infuses "the soul of the baptized" with faith that they may believe the truth in all his revelations. Third, faith is of cardinal importance even at the angelic level. Angels without faith lost against God and became bad angels. Angels with faith received glory.[43]

Catecismo del Sacromonte

The Effects and Excellencies of Faith

The author of *Catecismo del Sacromonte*—like Orozco—also asserts that the religion of Christ is "pure and beautiful" because of *faith*. More specifically, Orozco speaks of the *value* of faith at the human level while *Catecismo del Sacromonte* looks at the *effects and excellencies*[44] of faith. Both authors are concerned with the same effect—the impact of faith on the person who has faith—but express themselves differently. Those who have faith—defined as people who believe in the invisible things needed for salvation[45]—are impacted in four ways for having faith. First, their souls are joined to God, "the eternal truth who dwells in unapproachable light." Second, they begin to experience on earth the eternal life that they will enjoy fully in the future. Third, they are guided to do right and avoid wrong. Fourth, they have victory over temptation.[46]

Catecismo

The Admirable Effects of Faith

Pérez de Ayala—like Orozco and the author of *Catecismo del Sacromonte*—also writes about the impact of faith. The religion of Christ[47] is "pure and beautiful" because of its *admirable effects*[48] on the world and individuals. First, the religion of Christ banishes idolatry and the cult of demons from

---

42. Orozco, *Catecismo provechoso*, 10 [r].
43. Orozco, *Catecismo provechoso*, 20 [r].
44. Resines, *Catecismo del Sacromonte*, 210.
45. Resines, *Catecismo del Sacromonte*, 180.
46. Resines, *Catecismo del Sacromonte*, 210.
47. Pérez de Ayala also refers to the religion of Christ as "the gospel."
48. Pérez de Ayala, *Catecismo*, 187–209.

everywhere it has spread in the world.[49] Second, God always leads people to the Christian religion[50] when they ask him for light. Three examples are given.[51] Two of them are mentioned in *Catecismo provechoso*—the Roman centurion[52] and the Ethiopian treasurer.[53] The third example is Saul of Tarsus (Acts 9:1–9).[54] Third, the Christian religion shapes virtue. Experience shows that the more people order their lives according to the "evangelical doctrine," the more virtuous and spiritual they are and the more they esteem, revere, and obey God. Fourth, the Christian religion thrives despite extreme opposition. History testifies that the more the religion of Christ is persecuted, the more it grows and strengthens and sets deeper roots.[55]

Diálogos Christianos

Cause and Impact

Orozco, *Catecismo del Sacromonte,* and Pérez de Ayala concur that the religion of Christ is "pure and beautiful" because of the *impact* that faith has on the people who have faith. Pérez de Chinchón's *Diálogos Christianos* enables us to approach the second event of this round from a different angle. The first three catechisms and polemical treatises discuss impact, but *Diálogos Christianos* direct our attention to *who caused the impact;* that is, Jesus Christ. It is he who makes his religion "pure and beautiful." However, "purity and beauty" are not subjective concepts because what is known about Christ is recorded in the Scriptures of the Christian religion. There are two possible ways to state Pérez de Chinchón's answer: the religion of Christ is "pure and beautiful" because of Jesus Christ *or* the religion of Christ is "pure and beautiful" because of what its Scriptures say about Jesus Christ.[56] A Moor or Morisco might be inclined to attack the integrity of the

---

49. Pérez de Ayala, *Catecismo,* 191.

50. Pérez de Ayala is fond of using the term "Christian religion" (*la Christiana religion*).

51. Pérez de Ayala, *Catecismo,* 245–53.

52. Pérez de Ayala, *Catecismo,* 245.

53. Pérez de Ayala, *Catecismo,* 246.

54. Pérez de Ayala, *Catecismo,* 247.

55. Pérez de Ayala, *Catecismo,* 248–49.

56. Orozco, *Catecismo del Sacromonte,* and Pérez de Ayala would agree with both answers.

Scriptures in an attempt to undermine the person of Christ, but Pérez de Chinchón has prepared a robust defense.[57]

Pérez de Chinchón's discussion of what the Scriptures say regarding Jesus Christ is contained in twenty-eight articles.[58] Each article is a specific prophecy in the Old Testament about the Messiah with the fulfillment in the New Testament. Each prophecy can be viewed as a "natural and moral reason and fact" that the religion of Christ is "pure and beautiful." These prophecies encompass three phases—the Messiah before time, his ministry on earth, and his return. Only ten of those twenty-three prophecies are mentioned here. First, the Messiah before time. The Old Testament prophesies his incarnation.[59] He would be born of a virgin[60] in the city of Bethlehem;[61] be a descendant of King David;[62] and bear the sins of humanity on the cross.[63] Second, the Messiah's time on earth. Darkness would cover the land on the day of his death.[64] He would rise from the dead on the third day.[65] Healing comes to those who put their faith in his crucifixion.[66] Third, the Messiah's return. He will judge the world.[67] His reign will last forever.[68]

Summary

Natural reasons and facts

Catecismo del Sacromonte. The impact of faith: Its effects and excellencies.

Catecismo provechoso. The impact of faith: Its value.

Catecismo. The impact of faith: Its admirable effects.

---

57. See "Diálogos Christianos" above in "The Integrity of the Scriptures: Bridging the Gap" in Chapter 6.
58. Pons Fuster, *Antialcorano. Diálogos Christianos*, 485–513.
59. Pons Fuster, *Antialcorano. Diálogos Christianos*, 487–88.
60. Pons Fuster, *Antialcorano. Diálogos Christianos*, 493–94.
61. Pons Fuster, *Antialcorano. Diálogos Christianos*, 496.
62. Pons Fuster, *Antialcorano. Diálogos Christianos*, 494–96.
63. Pons Fuster, *Antialcorano. Diálogos Christianos*, 496–97.
64. Pons Fuster, *Antialcorano. Diálogos Christianos*, 506.
65. Pons Fuster, *Antialcorano. Diálogos Christianos*, 506–7.
66. Pons Fuster, *Antialcorano. Diálogos Christianos*, 505.
67. Pons Fuster, *Antialcorano. Diálogos Christianos*, 509.
68. Pons Fuster, *Antialcorano. Diálogos Christianos*, 510–13.

Moral reasons and facts

Catecismo provechoso. God is good, just, powerful, majestic, and wise.

Diálogos Christianos. The author of the impact of faith: Jesus Christ.

Conclusion

Although Orozco and Pérez de Chinchón are the only authors who present "moral reasons and facts" for the "purity and beauty" of the Christian religion, *Catecismo del Sacromonte* and Pérez de Ayala would not disagree with them. They would not be able to discuss the "effects and excellencies" of faith (*Catecismo del Sacromonte*) and the "admirable effects" of faith (*Catecismo*) unless they also believe that God is good, just, powerful, majestic, and wise even though they did not express such belief in their writing.

Results

Diálogos Christianos, Catecismo provechoso, Catecismo del Sacromonte, and *Catecismo* proceed to Event 3.

Round Three, Event 3. Does the catechism or polemical treatise use "natural and moral reasons and facts" to show the "clumsiness and blunders" of the sect of Muhammad?

This question can also be understood as an investigation of the statement "The 'clumsiness and blunders' of the sect of Muhammad are attributable to Muhammad proclaiming himself to be the prophet of God." Pérez de Ayala wrote that inspecting the life of the person who introduces a law as religion is the first of four steps necessary "to examine and destroy" that religion.[69] If Muhammad is not the prophet of God, the ramification is that his sect would be "clumsy" and contain "blunders." Are there "natural and moral reasons and facts" to demonstrate that Muhammad was a prophet of God? Pérez de Chinchón, Orozco, *Catecismo del Sacromonte,* and Pérez de Ayala found none. A brief examination of each work will justify their conclusions.

---

69. The other three steps are: Find out what is the destination of those who follow this religion; notice what this religion legitimatizes; and look into the motives behind this religion and how it spread. Pérez de Ayala, *Catecismo,* 83.

The Qur'an

The *Catecismo's* approach to critiquing the religion of Muhammad from three angles—Muhammad, the Qur'an, and the sect of Muhammad—would have been beneficial in three ways.

1. To strengthen the Moor's resolve to leave his religion. He had a general sense of dissatisfaction with his religious beliefs when he came to Guadix. Although he did not specify what he was dissatisfied with, he admitted to the Teacher that it is very difficult for someone to forsake the religion of his ancestors. The Teacher's critique was one important piece of evidence for the Moor to move forward with his desire to become a Christian.

2. To prepare the Moor to use this same critique or a condensed version to explain to his co-religionists why he left and perhaps even persuade them to do likewise.

3. To equip the rectors, preachers and confessors in Ribera's diocese to minister to the Moriscos in Valencia. Ribera's cover letter to the *Catecismo* stated that the *Catecismo* shows "the clumsiness and blunders" (*torpeza y desatinos*) of the sect of Muhammad. The Qur'an claims that if it had come from someone other than Allah, it would have "much contradiction" (Q. 4:82); only Allah could have produced the Qur'an (Q. 10:37–38); and even if mankind and the *jinn* were to work together to produce the Qur'an, they would not have been able to (Q. 17:88).

The following section examines the "clumsiness, blunders and contradictions" that the authors of the catechisms and polemical treatises discovered in the Qur'an.

Catecismo

The *Catecismo* used a classification of the Qur'an from the Maghrib school of Qur'anic copyists inaugurated in Spain by Juan Andrés. This classification divided the Qur'an into four books: Book 1 (Q. 1–6), Book 2 (Q. 7–18), Book 3 (Q. 19–37) and Book 4 (Q. 38–113).[70]

---

70. Szpiech, Starczewska, and García-Arenal, *Journal of Transcultural Medieval Studies*, 99–132.

Errors, Lies, and Fables

The *Catecismo* only discusses what it considers to be major "errors, lies, and fables." There would not have been enough time for the Teacher to discuss all of them with the Moor.[71] The following sixteen were discussed:

(1) God has a body and members. His hands are as cold as ice. But this is impossible. If God were to have a body, he would be divisible, limited, and comprehensible; (2) God is the author of sins. But this is impossible because God is supreme goodness and justice; (3) Man has a portion of God's soul. But this is impossible. God is infinite and indivisible. Man is limited.[72]

(4) God does not receive a penitent more than once. But, this is contrary to the fact that God always receives those who genuinely want to convert; (5) God only forgives light sins, but not the gross ones. But, this is contrary to the mercy of God; (6) God does not forgive those who repent at their hour of death. But, this is contrary to God's promise in Ezekiel 17; (7) God is the cause of reprobation and the cause of predestination. He causes some to walk on the straight path and some to walk on the crooked path. But, this is contrary to the notion that men and women have a free will; (8) If God wanted to, all the people would be one; he makes some err and makes others believe. But, this is against human free will and against God's justice and desire for all to be saved; (9) God hardens the hearts of the unbelievers and causes them to make mistakes. But, this is against the goodness of God.[73]

(10) It is impossible for men to abstain from having sexual relations with women; (11) God gave Muhammad license to commit perjury and adultery; (12) God commanded all the angels—including Beelzebub—to bow down and worship Adam.[74]

(13) God forgave the sins of a group of demons because they heard the Qur'an and believed; (14) Animals will be resurrected on the day of judgment; (15) Paradise is a place for men to satisfy their physical and sexual appetites;[75] and (16) Hell will not last more than one thousand years. Afterwards, all the condemned will be released.[76]

---

71. Pérez de Ayala, *Catecismo*, 106–20.
72. Pérez de Ayala, *Catecismo*, 109.
73. Pérez de Ayala, *Catecismo*, 110.
74. Pérez de Ayala, *Catecismo*, 111.
75. Pérez de Ayala, *Catecismo*, 112.
76. Pérez de Ayala, *Catecismo*, 113.

Contradictions

The *Catecismo* discusses ten contradictions in the Qur'an.[77] (1) The Qur'an is clear and evident (Q. 12), but everyone who rejects it will face a grave torment (Q. 5); (2) Everyone who lives righteously—including Jews and Christians—can be saved through their own law (Q. 2, Q. 12), but God has abandoned the Jews because they are reprobates (Q. 3) and punishes them with fire coming out of their bellies.[78]

(3) Everything can be eaten with thanksgiving to God (Q. 2), but other passages forbid various types of food; (4) Muslims must not marry those who follow another law (Q. 3), but another passage says that men can marry Jewish women who believe in God and do not have friends (Q. 5); (5) God does not open the doors of paradise except to those who exert themselves in battle (Q. 5), but Q. 2 states that paradise is open to those who worship God and do good deeds; (6) Many believers and unbelievers walk on the straight path (Q. 54), but the latter will be thrown into the fire. However, unbelievers are not walking on the straight path. If they were, there would not be unbelievers whose destiny is the fire; (7) Q. 13 says that God forgives all fornicators and sinners who repent, but "Book 2, Q. 3" says that God does not forgive gross sins; (8) Q. 8 states that no one should pray for unbelievers, but Abraham prayed for this father—an idol worshiper—and God forgave him (Q. 26).[79]

(9) Bad angels use force to remove the souls of the evil ones and use grace to remove the souls of the good ones (Q. 61), but Q. 32 says that God is the one who removes the souls of those who die; and (10) Q. 3 says that the Qur'an removes contention and animosity, but "many parts" of the Qur'an urge the followers of Muhammad not to befriend those who contradict the Qur'an, but to fight them.[80]

Confusión o confutación

Absurdities

Andrés discusses four absurdities in the Qur'an. (1) King Solomon and his army were marching towards a river of ants. One of the ants shouted to the rest of the ants to run for cover or they would be crushed to death. The

---

77. Pérez de Ayala, *Catecismo*, 121–25.
78. Pérez de Ayala, *Catecismo*, 121.
79. Pérez de Ayala, *Catecismo*, 122.
80. Pérez de Ayala, *Catecismo*, 123.

king heard that ant's voice from a league away and disaster was avoided (Q. 27:17–44).[81]

(2) King Solomon had thrown demons into prison. As long as he was still alive, they would remain imprisoned and tormented. He instructed his people to embalm him after he died to look as if he were still alive. They did so, sat him on his throne, and put his staff in his hand. A worm came out of the ground, ate the staff, and the corpse crashed on to the floor. It was only then that the demons knew that King Solomon had died and they were free (Q. 34:14).[82]

(3) God created a tree in hell as big as hell itself. "Verily, it is a tree that springs out of the bottom of Hellfire, the shoots of its fruit stalks are like the heads of devils." Those condemned to hell will eat these heads and drink molten lead (Q. 37:62–66); and (4) God created the skies out of smoke. "He rose over towards the heaven when it was smoke, and said to it and to the earth: 'Come both of you willingly or unwillingly.' They both said: 'We come willingly'" (Q. 41:11).[83]

Contradictions

Andrés also discusses contradictions in the Qur'an.[84] (1) God cursed the devil and expelled him from paradise. The devil retaliated and said to God that he (the devil) would be man's perpetual mortal enemy. The Qur'an warns man repeatedly to be on guard against his enemy (Q. 2.28–39; 7.20–30; 38.77). But, the Qur'an contradicts itself by stating that God forgave the demons and promised them the glories of paradise because they had become friends with Muhammad, man, and God after hearing the recitation of the Qur'an (Q. 37.6–10; 72.1–28; 50.1–45).

(2) The Qur'an claims that it descended from heaven to earth during the month of Ramadan (Q. 2.185), but another passage says that it came in one night (Q. 44.3; 97.1). This contradiction remained during Muhammad's ten years in Mecca and thirteen years in Medina. Andres's verdict: the Qur'an was revealed over a period of twenty-three years—not in one night.

(3) Moors are forbidden from eating twelve different types of food (Q. 5.3), but another passage says that only four types of food are forbidden (Q. 6.145). Drinking wine was permitted (Q. 16.67). Moors had been

---

81. Ruiz García, *Juan Andrés*, 150.
82. Ruiz García, *Juan Andrés*, 153.
83. Ruiz García, *Juan Andrés*, 154.
84. Ruiz García, *Juan Andrés*, 195–98.

drinking it for twelve years before Muhammad "out of a whim" decided to proscribe it.

(4) The *taurat* and the *injil* are "true guidance" (Q. 2.4–5), but Jews and Christians in the same *sura* accuse each other of not following the right religion (Q. 2.113). This last passage also contradicts two other passages—Q. 5.44 and Q. 5.47. The first passage (Q. 5.44) states that God sent down the *taurat*—"therein was guidance and light"—which the prophets and the rabbis—entrusted by God to protect the *taurat*—used to judge for the Jews. There is a warning: those who do not judge by what God has revealed are the *kafirun* (the disbelievers). The second passage also has a warning: The people of the *injil* must also judge by what God has revealed or they will be the *fasiqun* (the rebellious).

Worthless Matter

Andrés also discusses some of what he regards as "worthless" matter in the Qur'an. (1) The wife is a tilth for her husband—"So go to your tilth, when or how you will . . ." (Q. 2.223); (2) If a husband divorces his wife for the first time, they can be reconciled only after she has gone through three menstrual cyles (Q. 2.228). If he divorces her a second time, he cannot take back the bridal money he gave her when they first got married (Q. 2.229). If he divorces her a third time, they can be reconciled only after she has married another man (Q. 2.230); (3) Dhul Qarnain kept walking towards the setting place of the sun until he found out that it is a spring of black muddy water. (Q. 18.86, 90);[85] and the Qur'an recorded events out of sequence. The story of Abram is before Noah's. The story of Joseph is before Abram's. The story of David is before Moses's. Miriam—the sister of Aaron—is the mother of Jesus. The virgin Mary was the sister of Aaron and Moses.[86]

Catecismo provechoso

Felipe

This catechism is a dialogue between Orozco—in the role of an anonymous priest (*religioso*)—and Felipe, a Christian who used to follow the sect of Muhammad. Their dialogue, recorded as Chapter II, began the morning after Felipe had spent a sleepless night thinking about eternal

---

85. Ruiz García, *Juan Andrés*, 202.
86. Ruiz García, *Juan Andrés*, 203–4.

life. Sunrise could not have come sooner for him to rush to the monastery to see Orozco. He wanted Orozco to tell him about "the greatness of this holy Christian law."[87]

Dreams Full of Vanities

Orozco replied by using Ecclesiastes to describe the sects of the heretics, Hebrews, Gentiles, and Moors as "vain and lies."[88] After Orozco explained why the first three sects were meaningless,[89] Felipe inquired about the sect of Muhammad, which he referred to as "dreams full of vanities that have deceived many."[90] His own parents were among the deceived. He wants to use Arabic to reason with them so that they may turn to Christ and receive the same mercy he has already received.

Felipe's dialogue with Orozco—recorded as Chapter III[91]—continues on the following day. Orozco mentions that Muhammad gave himself the title of "Messenger of God and Prophet sent to the world" so that he could do whatever he wanted.[92] He robbed and killed. Mecca sentenced him to death. Many were fooled into believing that he was a prophet. God who is supreme goodness would not have chosen him to be his prophet. Felipe said that if people knew the truth about Muhammad, they would curse him but worship Christ.[93]

The Law of Muhammad

The Law of Muhammad is tyrannical. He did not want anyone arguing about the Qur'an, but to use violence instead to protect it and to kill anyone who refused to believe him. Muhammad said that no one should be coerced to believe, but his actions did not match his words. By comparison, philosophers cherished to no end "the excellence and freedom of man." Even a Muslim cleric by the name of Abdallah believed that man is free and capable of

---

87. Orozco, *Catecismo provechoso*, 10 [l].
88. Orozco, *Catecismo provechoso*, 10 [r].
89. Orozco, *Catecismo provechoso*, 10 [r]–12 [r].
90. Orozco, *Catecismo provechoso*, 12 [r].
91. Orozco, *Catecismo provechoso*, 13 [l]–17 [r].
92. Orozco, *Catecismo provechoso*, 14 [l].
93. Orozco, *Catecismo provechoso*, 14 [r].

reasoning because "man is a miracle in the world endowed reason." Thus, it is an act of violence to force anyone to obey a law against his or her will.[94]

Experience

Muhammad said that he did not understand the entire Qur'an because only God can understand it. So, Muhammad was either a "madman" (*loco*) or "demon-possessed" (*endemoniado*) for talking about what he did not understand or could not explain. A law that cannot be understood is empty. Experience confirms what Saint Augustine said that the will cannot act on what the mind cannot understand. Muhammad also contradicted himself. At one time he claimed that he had been sent only to his people the Arabs, but later said that it was the whole world.[95]

There are twenty-three chapters in *Catecismo provechoso*, but only the above two—Chapters II and III—focuses on polemics. Additional comments are spread throughout the fourteen Articles of Faith beginning in Chapter VII,[96] but these two chapters suffice for the purposes of the present book. Orozco wrote at the end of Chapter III that what he presented in that chapter and the previous one is sufficient to show that "the laws given by this enemy of the truth and minister of the Antichrist are dreams full of vanities."[97]

Doctrina Christiana

Falsehoods, Lies, and Contradictions

Alba wrote, "If the Qur'an were Scripture from God, it would not have falsehoods, lies, and contradictions." Some of the errors that Alba mentioned: (1) God commanded the angels to prostrate before Adam. All of them obeyed except Iblis (Q. 2:34). Adam knew more than the angels (Q. 2:30–31). However, it is the angels who know more than Adam; (2) God created the earth and the seven heavens (Q. 2:29). But, astrologers and philosophers know that there are more than seven heavens; (3) God created everything then "rose over" towards heaven (Q. 2:29). But, this is impossible because God is immutable—"going up" and "coming down" do not apply to him; (4) The Qur'an is in error on the Incarnation of Christ

---

94. Orozco, *Catecismo provechoso*, 15 [r].
95. Orozco, *Catecismo provechoso*, 17 [r].
96. Orozco, *Catecismo provechoso*, 26 [r].
97. Orozco, *Catecismo provechoso*, 17 [l].

and for not knowing that God is triune—one in essence, three persons—Father, Son, and Holy Spirit; and (5) God "misleads whom he wills and guides whom he wills" (Q. 14:4). However, it is insulting to God that he should be charged for the sins that people commit.[98]

Antialcorano

Muhammad claimed to have travelled from Mecca to Jerusalem on Buraq—a white animal smaller than a mule and bigger than a donkey (Sahih Al-Bukhari 5:58:277). Chinchón used Sermon 16 in his *Antialcorano* to patiently, politely, and systematically dismantle everything that Muhammad claimed to have seen in his journey (Q. 17).[99]

(1) Muhammad had eleven wives living with him when an angel appeared before him to announce the journey. However, men and women in the past were involved in holy pursuits when God appeared to them—Abraham, Noah, Jacob, Moses, Joshua, David, and Mary the mother of Jesus. God would not have sent his angels (who are sinless spirits) to appear before such a "lustful and carnal" man as Muhammad.

(2) There is no such animal as Buraq. It never existed. If Moors claim that it was created specially so that Muhammad could make the trip, God could have easily sent him on a camel. He could have also made the trip riding the angel that had seventy pairs of wings. If God created Buraq so that Muhammad could go to Jerusalem, it makes no sense that it refused to be ridden until after Muhammad had promised that it would be the first animal to enter paradise.

(3) Animals will resurrect and there is a paradise for them. However, this is false. It is also false that Buraq will be the first animal to enter paradise. The first one was the ram that Abraham sacrificed.

(4) Adam, Abraham, Moses, and Christ entrusted themselves to Muhammad. However, there was no need for them to do so as if they needed to be forgiven. Christ was sinless, but Muhammad was not. Adam, Abraham, and Moses had already been forgiven, but not Muhammad.

(5) The first heaven was made of silver. The second heaven was made of gold. The third heaven was made of precious stones. However, God had no need for these materials to create the heavens. Muhammad came up with this idea to entice people who crave for riches to follow him. But, gold, silver and precious metals are the source of trouble. Wise men despise them and choose virtue instead.

98. Resines, *El Catecismo de Pedro Ramiro de Alba*, 169–72.
99. Pons Fuster, *Antialcorano. Diálogos Christianos*, 267–75.

(6) Stars in the first heaven hung from chains of gold as large as a mountain. However, those chains would have to be made of iron because iron is stronger than gold. If stars do hung from chains, they would be swinging back and forth creating astrological problems.

(7) Angels in the first heaven look like different animals—horses, bulls, goats, etc. However, angels are invisible spiritual beings like God; (8) There was a rooster in the first heaven whose large head reached the second heaven. However, the heavens have no need for roosters; (9) There was an angel who placed one of its hands on the east and another hand on the west. Its head touched the third heaven. However, as already mentioned, angels do not have bodies; (10) There was another angel with seventy thousand heads. Each head had seventy thousand tongues. Each tongue had seventy thousand voices. But, Muhammad told seventy thousand lies seventy thousand times; (11) God's hand was cold. However, if God has hands, he would have feet and a head; and (12) If God's hand was cold, it has to be said that he feels cold.

Chinchón finished by saying that he spent time discussing these lies because it caused him "great pain" to see Moors believe them simply because Muhammad said them. He exhorted them, "Be ashamed. You are men. God gave you understanding. Turn around and realize that you have been deceived until now." They should thank God for bringing them the knowledge of the truth. They have clearly seen that the more Muhammad talked, the more lies he told. Chinchón told them to forget "that bestial law and carnal sect." They should start liking the law that came from Christ because it is true, based on reason, and confirmed by miracles. They will be satisfied and joyful when they entrust themselves wholeheartedly to God with the faith of Jesus Christ—"true God and man"—who wants to take him (Chinchón) and the Moors to his holy kingdom.[100]

Confutación del alcorán y secta mahometana

Obregón wrote, "Truth never contradicts another truth. . . . Whenever something contradicts another, one of them by necessity has to be false. No falsehood can be from God who is truth itself." Falsehood and lies are from Satan, the father of lies. There are "many lies" in the Qur'an because of its "many contradictions." Just one contradiction or lie is sufficient to show that a law is not from God.[101] Obregón discusses these contradictions:

---

100. Pons Fuster, *Antialcorano. Diálogos Christianos*, 275.
101. Obregón, *Confutación del alcorán y secta mahometana*, 52 [r].

THE NEW *CATECISMO*: EXPERIENCE AND EVIDENCE   189

Was the Qur'an revealed in one night or in one month? The claim that God does not force anyone to become a Moor is contradicted by the fact that those who do not become Moors will have to be killed.[102] The devil tempts man because he is man's enemy, but cannot tempt Muhammad. However, the devil did tempt Muhammad.[103]

The heavens are made from smoke and the earth is held up by the horns of a bull. When the bull moves its head, the earth shakes. The heavens are made of water, fog, metal and precious stones.[104] All food—including wine—that God created is licit for eating is contradicted by the injunction against four kinds of forbidden food: meat from animals that die of themselves (Q. 5:3); blood (Q. 5:3); meat of pigs (Q. 2:173); and meat offered to idols (Q. 2:173).[105]

Catecheses mystagogicae

Lorca wrote that it is "easy to fight" the sect of Muhammad not only because of "the reprobation" of Muhammad, but also because of the contradictions in the sect.[106] It is necessary to look carefully into the Qur'an to "uproot (Muhammad's) pernicious lies from its dark place"[107] such as the following seven contradictions:

(1) Muhammad did not have authority to perform miracles, but later had it; (2) He said that he did not want to kill anyone yet came with the sword; (3) He told his followers to love Christians, but also to kill them; (4) He said that everyone who follows their own religion will be saved, but also said that only those who followed his sect can be saved; (5) Adultery is a grave sin, but sometimes it is not a sin; (6) No one should be harmed, but fighting, plundering, and robbing Christians are permitted; and (7) No one should be compelled to follow his sect, but it is licit to compel everyone to embrace it.

Lorca wrote that there are "many" contradictions in the Qur'an, but only summarized these seven without supplying the Qur'anic source.[108] A note on the margin of folio [94 v] informs readers to find out more about the contradictions by referencing Chapter 6 of *Antialchoranus* written by

102. Obregón, *Confutación del alcorán y secta mahometana*, 59 [l]–60 [r].
103. Obregón, *Confutación del alcorán y secta mahometana*, 61 [l]–61 [r].
104. Obregón, *Confutación del alcorán y secta mahometana*, 63 [r].
105. Obregón, *Confutación del alcorán y secta mahometana*, 65 [l]–65 [r].
106. Busic, "Saving the Lost Sheep," 477.
107. Busic, "Saving the Lost Sheep," 423.
108. Busic, "Saving the Lost Sheep," 466–67.

Riccoldo da Monte di Croce (ca. 1240s–1320). Lorca also confronted fifty-two errors by matching the catechism that critiqued the error; e.g., Abraham should be honored as the father of Muhammad and his Saracens (fourth catechism); baptism is only necessary for salvation for those who pass from Judaism to Muhammadism (ninth and fifth catechism); and Christ was not the natural son of God (first catechism).[109]

Catecismo del Sacromonte

This catechism is a dialogue between an anonymous priest and an also anonymous novice being trained by the priest. The novice is a recently baptized Morisco who's learning how to present the religion of Christ to his family who are followers of the sect of Muhammad. *Catecismo del Sacromonte* teaches that anyone who wishes to go to God needs three things just as a sailor needs three things to get to his destination: The truth taught by the church (North), faith that points to the North (a compass), and the Scriptures (a map).

The novice wants to know how to respond when Moors claim that the Qur'an is the map. The priest answers with a question: How would the novice respond when idolaters and Jews say to him that the map consists of their ceremonies and rites? The novice would say to them that if they cannot prove their claim, they are deceived. The priest agrees. Those who come claiming that the king sent them must provide evidence. Otherwise, they should not be believed but be punished for lying.[110]

The Qur'an states, "God is God and is not God except God." Q. 2:163: "And your God is One God. There is none who has the right to be worshiped but He, the Most Gracious, the Most Merciful." So what? It is not saying much. No one would deny that statement just as no one would deny these statements: "A man is a man and is not a man except a man," "A horse is a horse," and "A dog is a dog." The Qur'an not only has these "amusing" statements, but also has lies taken from the Talmud, which Muhammad corrupted even more.[111] The majesty of God and his marvelous deeds give men and women the faith to praise him more than what the Moors can because of the thinness of the Qur'an and Muhammad's carnality.[112]

Catecismo del Sacromonte regards the commandment "You shall not take the name of the LORD your God in vain, for the LORD will not leave

---

109. Busic, "Saving the Lost Sheep," 265–73.
110. Resines, *Catecismo del Sacromonte*, 191.
111. Resines, *Catecismo del Sacromonte*, 210.
112. Resines, *Catecismo del Sacromonte*, 224.

him unpunished who takes His name in vain" (Exod 20:7) as the second commandment.[113] Muhammad broke this commandment in at least two ways: First, he lied about what God did. Q. 19:28 is mistaken in saying that Mary—the mother of Jesus—was the sister of Moses and Aaron. Second, Muhammad portrayed God as inconsistent or contradicting himself. Q. 5:57–61 presents Moors as tolerant of those who mock their religious practices. They should not retaliate, but fear God and leave matters in his hands (let him be the one to turn Jews into monkeys and swine). However, this tolerance is limited. Q. 13:35 declares that the final destination of the disbelievers is the fire.[114]

Muhammad also broke the third commandment, which states that we should honor God in everything we do.[115] Every religious ceremony of the Moors comes from either the Jews or the Gentiles. The Friday prayer was a Gentile ceremony honoring the goddess Venus.[116] Muhammad instituted dietary laws to ingratiate himself to the Jews, but in the process contradicted himself. The passage with a long list of forbidden food is contradicted by another passage that everything can be eaten as long as Moors do not eat "extravagantly."[117]

The Sect of Muhammad

Catecismo

Pérez de Ayala critiques the sect of Muhammad from three viewpoints: The law of the sect of Muhammad is *not a divine revelation*; the sect of Muhammad is *against reason*; and *human experience* rejects the sect of Muhammad.

Not a Divine Revelation

God would not have revealed and miracles and reasons would not have substantiated the "lies and blasphemies" in the law of Muhammad.[118] By comparison, the law of Christ[119] is the true path to God because of its preaching,

113. Resines, *Catecismo del Sacromonte*, 270.
114. Resines, *Catecismo del Sacromonte*, 274.
115. Resines, *Catecismo del Sacromonte*, 276.
116. Resines, *Catecismo del Sacromonte*, 279.
117. Resines, *Catecismo del Sacromonte*, 279.
118. Pérez de Ayala, *Catecismo*, 165–187.
119. Also known as "the religion of Christ," "the evangelical law" or "the doctrine of Christ."

its Scriptures and its effects;[120] the dignity of Christ;[121] his fulfillment of Old Testament Messianic prophecies;[122] his divinity;[123] his miracles;[124] and people who have been transformed for following *Christ*.[125]

These reasons—or evidence—not only strengthen the faith of those who already follow this law, but could also convince the most stubborn follower of the law of Muhammad. But reasons are not mathematical proofs. The Spirit of God is involved. A person first believes the evidence then understands it. The Spirit of God follows with confirmation so that the person can know "without a shadow of a doubt" that this law is from God.

The *Catecismo* presents a "believe-understand-Holy Spirit confirmation" sequence, but there is no reason to think that this is how the Spirit always work. It is plausible for the sequence to be "Spirit confirmation-believe-understand-more confirmation." The Spirit of God is like the wind. It blows where it wishes. We hear its sound, but do not know where it comes from and where it is going. So is everyone who is born of the Spirit (John 3:8).

A human doctrine or law should be authenticated by natural reason. A divine doctrine or law should be verified by divine reasons. The law of Muhammad cannot be substantiated by either natural or divine reasons. There is no genuine testimony proving that it is a revelation from God. Thus, people with a free will should opt for not following it.[126]

Against Reason

taqiyya

The title of Dialogue I in Book One states that the *Catecismo* is "a reasoning"[127] (*un razonamiento*) between the Teacher who is fluent in Arabic and the Moor from Barbary. The Teacher does not use the word *taqiyya*, but that is exactly what he is referring to when he says that the sect of Muhammad is against reason.[128] Followers of this sect are permitted to hide what they believe when

120. Pérez de Ayala, *Catecismo*, 187–209.
121. Pérez de Ayala, *Catecismo*, 210–27.
122. Pérez de Ayala, *Catecismo*, 227–28.
123. Pérez de Ayala, *Catecismo*, 227–28.
124. Pérez de Ayala, *Catecismo*, 238–44.
125. Pérez de Ayala, *Catecismo*, 245–53.
126. Pérez de Ayala, *Catecismo*, 139–40.
127. Pérez de Ayala, *Catecismo*, 1.
128. Pérez de Ayala, *Catecismo*, 132–39.

they fear that it is risky to reveal their true religious beliefs. The Teacher gives five reasons why this type of dissimulation is wrong.

(1) If the religion of Muhammad were true, its followers would not need to pretend to be what they are not. God wants a person to worship him wholeheartedly; (2) Bad deeds reveal what is in a person's heart. A good tree bears good fruit; a bad tree bears bad fruit; (3) It is a serious insult against God to treat him the way we would not treat another person. We would not deny the honor or gratitude to someone who has been good to us. Who would be satisfied to have an ungrateful person as a friend? God loves us and takes care of us. In the face of danger, it would be better to die of hunger than to deny him and what we believe; (4) People cannot say that they love God above all else when they disavow him in the face of danger. They love what they do not want to lose more than they love him; and (5) There have been godly people throughout history who chose death instead of renouncing God. The Teacher also gives biblical reasons:

(a) Mal 1:6: The prophet rebuked the people of Israel. They called him "Father," but did not honor him. They called him "Master," but did not respect him; (b) Isa 29:13: The prophet spoke out against the double-mindedness of the Israelites. They honored God with their lip service, but their hearts were far from him; (c) Matt 10:32–33: Christ said that anyone who denied him in front of others, he would deny him before God; and (d) Rom 10:9: Paul said that we confess with our mouths and believe with our hearts.

The Teacher not only shows that the sect of Muhammad is against reason for teaching its followers to lie, but also discusses why the Christian religion is perfect—what is done externally matches what the heart believes. He entreats the Moor not to emulate the new converts. It would have been better for them not to have known the truth than to have known it then become traitors. They are "neither Moors nor Christians, but like Arabs without religion."[129]

Muhammad and his message

The sect of Muhammad is against reason also because of Muhammad and his message. He claimed to be God's messenger; that his law is the same law that was given to Abraham; and that God wants mankind to follow this law.

---

129. Pérez de Ayala, *Catecismo*, 139.

Moses and Christ

Every doctrine or law intended for people to follow must come with supporting evidence. It is not enough for a man—even if he were a saint—to say that he is a prophet sent by God. Moses did not just tell the people of Israel that God sent him to deliver them out of Egypt. He performed the signs of the plagues.

Christ did not just say that God sent him. He also performed miracles. Christ's apostles also performed miracles. Even the Qur'an says that Jesus the son of Maryam performed miracles. But the Qur'an states that Muhammad came not as a miracle worker, but as a warner. According to the Qur'an, he performed no miracles to verify his message. Thus, it is against reason to accept the doctrine of Muhammad as a revelation from God.[130]

Human Experience

Paradise is "a garden of delight" (Q. 37:43). Its dwellers will have all that they ask for (Q. 36:57). Their time will be spent on satisfying their appetites for food, drink and sex (Q. 2:2; 38:50-57; 47:15; 76:14; 18:32).[131] But, man's final destination is God himself—not pleasures.[132]

Experience teaches that people who pursue sensual appetites become blind to God and "the light of reason" and end up far away from the path to God.[133] Muhammad said that it is impossible for men to abstain from sex. But, this kind of thinking is against the experience of many prophets and holy men who were virgins and chaste.[134]

Muhammad could not perform miracles or use reason to persuade people to follow him so he resorted to the only methods he knew—threats, violence, and death. However, experience shows that people do not believe in something just because they are afraid.[135]

Muhammad claimed that he had come "to reform and temper" the law of Christ, which he (Muhammad) described as "too rigorous." However, Christ said that his yoke is easy and his burden is light (Matt 11:28-30). The experience of all who follow him testify that his words are true.[136]

---

130. Pérez de Ayala, *Catecismo*, 139-64.
131. Pérez de Ayala, *Catecismo*, 96-97.
132. Pérez de Ayala, *Catecismo*, 97.
133. Pérez de Ayala, *Catecismo*, 98.
134. Pérez de Ayala, *Catecismo*, 111.
135. Pérez de Ayala, *Catecismo*, 150.
136. Pérez de Ayala, *Catecismo*, 154-55.

Moors believe that Muhammad is mentioned in the Scriptures of the Christian religion. If that were the case, that Scripture would be the Book of Revelation, which describes a time of persecution, suffering and death on the earth. Experience shows that this is what happened with Muhammad's arrival.[137] The law of Muhammad is contrary to the law of Christ.[138] But, experience shows that the more closely one follows the law of Christ, the "more saintly" he or she is.[139]

Diálogos Christianos

The Old Testament

Are there "natural and moral reasons and facts" that certify that Muhammad was a prophet of God? His followers claim that his coming is foretold in the Old Testament. Pérez de Chinchón examines three prophecies. (1) Deut 18:18-20 gives three reasons why Muhammad is not the prophet referred to in this passage: (a) He does not meet the criterion in Ps 72:11 ("And let all kings bow down before him, All nations serve him."); (b) He does not meet the criterion in Ps 2:7 ("You are My Son, Today I have begotten You."); and (c) The prophet foretold in Deut 18:18-20 would not be a descendant of Ishmael;[140] (2) The two peoples hinted at in Gen 25:23 are the Jews and the Christians. Muhammad comes from a completely different line as alluded in the criterion in Ps 72:11; (3) Isa 54:1-4. The sons of the desolate one would be more numerous because of the preaching of the gospel throughout the whole world. Muhammad spread his religion through the sword so "sons of the desolate one" cannot be a reference to his followers.[141] According to Pérez de Chinchón, there are no "natural and moral reasons and facts" to vouch for Muhammad because he is not that prophet foretold in the Old Testament.

---

137. Pérez de Ayala, *Catecismo*, 156–57.
138. Pérez de Ayala, *Catecismo*, 173.
139. Pérez de Ayala, *Catecismo*, 171.
140. Pons Fuster, *Antialcorano. Diálogos Christianos*, 476.
141. Pons Fuster, *Antialcorano. Diálogos Christianos*, 477.

Catecismo provechoso

Identity and Mission

Orozco presents a succinct two-part description of the *identity* and the *mission* of Jesus Christ.[142] *Identity:* He is the Redeemer;[143] King of kings;[144] and giver of an "excellent treasure."[145] *Mission:* He loved humanity and suffered for its sake.[146] He rescues people from a "deep sea of errors"[147] and those who believe in him become God's "adopted children."[148] Although Orozco does not provide extensive background information about Muhammad probably because Felipe had been a Moor for thirty years, Orozco is sufficiently acquainted with Muhammad[149] that he can compare him with the identity and mission of Jesus Christ. Orozco concludes that Muhammad was "an enemy of the truth and a minister of the Antichrist."[150]

Catecismo del Sacromonte

The Ten Commandments

Are there "natural and moral reasons and facts" to demonstrate that Muhammad was a prophet of God? The priest is specific about how Muhammad broke each of the first eight of the Ten commandments.[151] When the novice asks about Muhammad's detailed violations of the last two commandments, the priest answers with "We do not want to walk on such a dirty quagmire."[152] Muhammad was not a prophet of God when his life and teaching are measured against the identity and mission of Jesus Christ (Orozco). He was not a prophet of God also because he violated all Ten Commandments (*Catecismo del Sacromonte*).

142. Orozco, *Catecismo provechoso*, 13 [l].
143. Orozco, *Catecismo provechoso*, 13 [r].
144. Orozco, *Catecismo provechoso*, 15 [l].
145. Orozco, *Catecismo provechoso*, 13 [r].
146. Orozco, *Catecismo provechoso*, 15 [l].
147. Orozco, *Catecismo provechoso*, 13 [r].
148. Orozco, *Catecismo provechoso*, 13 [r].
149. See "*Catecismo provechoso*" above in "Round Three, Event 1. Does the author of the catechism or polemical treatise have experience talking with and instructing Moriscos?"
150. Orozco, *Catecismo provechoso*, 13 [r].
151. Resines, *Catecismo del Sacromonte*, 261–316.
152. Resines, *Catecismo del Sacromonte*, 316.

Catecismo

Muhammad's Life

Unlike Orozco, the Teacher in Pérez de Ayala's *Catecismo* does offer a summary of the life of Muhammad even though the Moor—like Felipe—is well acquainted with the traditional account. Nevertheless, the summary—based for the purposes of accuracy on the Qur'an, the *sunna*, and the *sira*—is provided to prove how little credibility Muhammad deserves.[153]

Four parts of this summary are noteworthy.[154] First, the angel Gabriel is not the source of some of the material in the Qur'an, but two secretaries hired by Muhammad: Abdallah, a Jew from Mecca and Sergius from Alexandria who followed Arianism, Marcionism, Manichaeism, Nestorianism, and other heresies.[155] Second, Muhammad's escape to Mecca was prompted by his inability to perform a single miracle to prove that he was a prophet of God and the Meccans discovering that he was "full of thousand of lies and contradictions."[156] Third, the life of Muhammad after the *hijra* was marked by wars, robberies, and his betrayal and killing of the Jews who welcome him to Medina and offered him shelter.[157] Fourth, Muhammad's death from a "terrible illness"[158] and claim that he would come back to life after three days.[159]

There are two assertions—one at the beginning and one at the end of the summary—that act as bookends. The summary begins with the Teacher stating that Muhammad lived a "vicious and brutal life"[160] and ends with the Teacher pronouncing Muhammad to be a "false prophet."[161] The Teacher's care in providing evidence to support his critique of Muhammad and anything related to him is also customary with Pérez de Chinchón, Orozco, and *Catecismo del Sacromonte*.

---

153. Pérez de Ayala, *Catecismo*, 84.
154. The summary begins on page 84 and concludes on page 90.
155. Pérez de Ayala, *Catecismo*, 87–88.
156. Pérez de Ayala, *Catecismo*, 88.
157. Pérez de Ayala, *Catecismo*, 88–89.
158. The Teacher does not reveal the type of sickness.
159. Pérez de Ayala, *Catecismo*, 89.
160. Pérez de Ayala, *Catecismo*, 84.
161. Pérez de Ayala, *Catecismo*, 90.

Summary

Muhammad was not a prophet of God because of natural and moral reasons and facts.

Natural reasons and facts. The Old Testament did not foretell the coming of Muhammad (*Diálogos Christianos*). He fell short of the standard set by the *identity* of Jesus Christ (*Catecismo provechoso*) and was unable to perform miracles, contradicted himself, and died from an unspeakable death (*Catecismo*).

Moral reasons and facts. Muhammad violated all Ten Commandments (*Catecismo del Sacromonte*); was below the standard set by the *mission* of Jesus Christ (*Catecismo provechoso*); and fought in wars, robbed, betrayed, killed, and lied about being able to come back to life after death (*Catecismo*).

Conclusion

The authors of these four catechisms and polemical treatises evaluate Muhammad with the lens of two different authorities. Three of the authors use authorities of the religion of Christ: the Old Testament (*Diálogos Christianos*), the Ten Commandments (*Catecismo del Sacromonte*), and Jesus Christ (*Catecismo provechoso*). The Teacher's (*Catecismo*) use of authorities of the sect of Muhammad—the Qur'an, the *sunna*, and the *sira*—to prepare his summary on the life of Muhammad has two possible benefits not discernible in the other three catechisms and polemical treatises.

First, *interpretation* might not be an issue because Moors and Moriscos are well versed in the words and deeds of their prophet. The Teacher deliberately chose these authorities for his summary to avoid being accused of having built a straw man.[162] He does not have to interpret, but only tap these resources for information that the Moor already knows. By comparison, the use of authorities of the religion of Christ such as the Old Testament (*Diálogos Christianos*) might create a barrier to mutual understanding. Followers of the religion of Christ and members of the sect of Muhammad could read the same Old Testament prophecies yet draw opposite conclusions. A discussion on *how* to interpret these prophecies or other passages in the Scriptures of the Christian religion deemed critical of Muhammad (*methodology of interpretation*) might be necessary.

Second, the Teacher's summary of the life of Muhammad would benefit not only catechumens who previously were not members of the sect of

---

162. Pérez de Ayala, *Catecismo*, 84.

Muhammad, but even those who did.¹⁶³ Felipe said that if Moors know the truth about Muhammad—"a thug who lived a degenerate life"—they would become followers of Jesus Christ.¹⁶⁴ Third, the Teacher's summary may help Moors realize that even their authorities present a picture of Muhammad that does not support their claim that he was a prophet of God.

Results

Diálogos Christianos, Catecismo provechoso, Catecismo del Sacromonte, and *Catecismo* proceed to Event 4.

Round Three, Event 4. Does the catechism or polemical treatise use the format of a dialogue, "which is the clearest and most distinct way to teach when the one being instructed has questions and the teacher has answers"?

	Dialogue between
1. *Diálogos Christianos*	Pérez de Chinchón and his Arabic teacher, Joseph.
2. *Catecismo provechoso*	A priest (Orozco) and Felipe.
3. *Catecismo del Sacromonte*	A priest (anonymous) and a novice (anonymous).
4. *Catecismo*	A teacher (Pérez de Ayala's interpreter) and a Moor (anonymous).

Results

Diálogos Christianos, Catecismo provechoso, Catecismo del Sacromonte, and *Catecismo* proceed to Round 4, the final round.

---

163. A summary is not put forward in the case of Joseph (*Diálogos Christianos*), Felipe (*Catecismo provechoso*), and the novice (*Catecismo del Sacromonte*) probably because they previously belonged to the sect of Muhammad.

164. See "*Catecismo provechoso*" above in "Round Two, Event 3. Could the catechism or polemical treatise inflame the emotions of the Moriscos?" in Chapter 7.

Table 6. Results of Round Three, All Four Events

	1[165]	2[166]	3[167]	4[168]
Diálogos Christianos	✔	✔	✔	✔
Catecismo provechoso	✔	✔	✔	✔
Catecismo del Sacromonte	✔	✔	✔	✔
Catecismo	✔	✔	✔	✔

---

165. Event 1. Does the author of the catechism or polemical treatise have experience talking with and instructing Moriscos?

166. Event 2. Does the catechism or polemical treatise use "natural and moral reasons and facts" to show the "purity and beauty" of the religion of Christ?

167. Event 3. Does the catechism or polemical treatise use "natural and moral reasons and facts" to show the "clumsiness and blunders" of the sect of Muhammad?

168. Event 4. Does the catechism or polemical treatise use the format of a dialogue, "which is the clearest and most distinct way to teach when the one being instructed has questions and the teacher has answers"?

Chapter 9

The New *Catecismo*: Heart, Mind, and Behavior

Step 1

Round Four, Two Events

Round Four, Event 1. Is the catechism or polemical treatise aware of the Triple Challenge; that is, the confession, the beliefs, and the commandments that control the heart, the mind, and the behavior of the Moriscos?

First Challenge	Public Confession of Religious Faith	Heart
Second Challenge	Religious *Beliefs*	Mind
Third Challenge	Religious *Commandments*	Behavior[1]

Results

Diálogos Christianos, Catecismo provechoso, Catecismo del Sacromonte, and *Catecismo* are aware of the Triple Challenge. The rationale behind this answer is presented in the answer to the next event.[2]

---

1. Chapter 4 provides details of the three challenges.
2. Events 1 and 2 in Round 4 are inextricable. Both of them need to be asked. Given that it cannot be assumed that all catechisms and polemical treatises are aware of the Triple Challenge, Event 1 exists to differentiate them.

Round Four, Event 2. Does the catechism or polemical treatise grapple with the Triple Challenge?

The First Challenge: The Heart

Besides being aware of the Triple Challenge,[3] a catechism or polemical treatise also needs to show *how* it addresses the challenge.[4] *Diálogos Christianos*, *Catecismo provechoso*, *Catecismo del Sacromonte*, and *Catecismo* respond to both parts of The First Challenge, which consists of the public confession of faith in the *hearts* of the Moriscos: "There is no God but Allah" and "Muhammad is his prophet."[5]

"There is no God but Allah."

The conception of Allah in the hearts of Moriscos that He is the Creator, omniscient, omnipotent, judge, perfect, just, transcendent, self-existent, and incomprehensible gives the impression that Allah is similar if not identical to the God of the religion of Christ. However, *Diálogos Christianos*, *Catecismo provechoso*, *Catecismo del Sacromonte*, and *Catecismo* present God as "one absolutely perfect essence" who is "also triune in persons—Father, Son, and Holy Spirit. Not three lords, but one Lord. Not three Gods, but only one God." The triune nature of God is a crucial and uncompromising difference between Allah and the divine being worshiped by the followers of the religion of Christ. Despite this difference, *Diálogos Christianos*, *Catecismo provechoso*, *Catecismo del Sacromonte*, and *Catecismo* bridge the gap between both groups' understanding of the nature of God.[6]

"Muhammad is the Prophet of Allah"

If *Diálogos Christianos*, *Catecismo provechoso*, *Catecismo del Sacromonte*, and *Catecismo* understand the nature of God as triune, then Muhammad is the prophet of Allah but not the prophet of God. Even if their understanding

---

3. Event 1 of Round 4.

4. Given that it is not enough to know which author is aware of the challenge, Event 2 of Round 4 asks *how* he grapples with the challenge. In other words, *who* (Event 1) and *how* (Event 2).

5. See above "The First Challenge. The Profession of Faith of the Moriscos (Heart)" in "Chapter 4. The Religious Context of the *Catecismo*."

6. See above "Overview. The Trinity: A Common Basic Understanding" in "Chapter 5. The Trinity: Bridging the Gap."

were incorrect or incomplete, the authenticity of the prophethood of Muhammad does not depend on a flawless grasp of the nature of God. *Diálogos Christianos, Catecismo provechoso, Catecismo del Sacromonte,* and *Catecismo* present evidence—"natural and moral reasons and facts"—to support their assessment that Muhammad was not a prophet of God.[7]

Results

Diálogos Christianos, Catecismo provechoso, Catecismo del Sacromonte, and *Catecismo* proceed to The Second Challenge.

Round Four, Event 2

The Second Challenge: The Mind

In order to meet this challenge, *Diálogos Christianos, Catecismo provechoso, Catecismo del Sacromonte,* and *Catecismo* would have to replace the set of religious beliefs in the minds of the Moriscos[8] with a different set of beliefs. By the end of their dialogue, the Moor says to the Teacher: "Now that you have been the instrument of my conversion, be also the teacher of my instruction and teach me specifically *what I ought to know*[9] and do, and what the Christian religion teaches about walking this path well."[10]

The Moor has abandoned the sect of his ancestors for the religion of Christ. In the vocabulary of the *Catecismo provechoso,* Orozco would say that the Moor has been "baptized and washed in the blessed blood of our Savior Jesus Christ" and Felipe would no longer regard the Moor as a member of the sect of Muhammad, but an "adopted son of God" and a "member of the holy Roman Church."[11] What the Moor wants in effect is for the Teacher to teach him how to be a good follower of the religion of Christ; that is, how to be a good Catholic.

---

7. See above "Summary of Round 3, Event 3."

8. See "The Second Challenge. The Religious Beliefs of the Moriscos (Mind)" above in Chapter 4.

9. Emphasis added.

10. Pérez de Ayala, *Catecismo,* 252–53.

11. See "*Catecismo provechoso*" above in "Round 2. Event 3. Could the catechism or polemical treatise inflame the emotions of the Moriscos?" in Chapter 7.

Catecismo

Text of the Symbol

The Teacher instructs the Moor with the goal of replacing the latter's old set beliefs with the Symbol; that is, a new set of beliefs. The Moor's old set of beliefs include belief in Allah, death, hell and paradise, the day of judgment, the Qur'an and Muhammad, and the resurrection.[12] The new set of beliefs (fourteen articles) would require the Moor to say

> I believe in God Almighty the Father, Creator of heaven and the earth and in Jesus Christ his only Son our Lord; He was conceived by the Holy Spirit and was born of the virgin Mary; He suffered under the power of Pontius Pilate; was crucified, died, and buried; He descended to Hell and on the third day resurrected from the dead; He ascended to the heavens and is seated at the right hand of God Almighty the Father; and from there he will come to judge the living and the dead. I believe in the Holy Spirit, the Holy Catholic Church, the communion of the saints, the forgiveness of sins, the resurrection of the flesh, and eternal life.

Purpose of the Symbol

According to Pérez de Ayala, the purpose of this new set of beliefs—formally known as the Symbol of the Apostles, the Creed or the Articles of Faith—is what every follower of the Christian religion is obligated to believe. These beliefs are labeled "the Symbol" because they are the signs that differentiate "the soldiers of Christ" from those who follow false religions or sects.[13] According to Orozco, the purpose of the Symbol is to help "all the faithful know what they need to affirm, confess, and—if necessary—give their lives for the truth in each belief."[14]

The "obligation to believe" seems restrictive, but it is not for two reasons. First, God must "be loved, honored, and served" according to his will instead of a person's selfish desires. Second, obligation is a proper response that results from appreciating "God's being, power, goodness, and love" in sending his own Son to die on behalf of sinners.[15]

---

12. Thirteen articles grouped into seven categories. See "The Second Challenge: The Religious Beliefs of the Moriscos (Mind)" above in Chapter 4.
13. Pérez de Ayala, *Catecismo*, 270.
14. Orozco, *Catecismo provechoso*, 28 [l].
15. Pérez de Ayala, *Catecismo*, 272.

The "obligation to believe" the right set of beliefs was so paramount that the Symbol became one of the four key parts[16] of the new catechism published by the Catholic Church after the Council of Trent.[17] Thus, a catechism or polemical treatise would have to include the Symbol so that the right beliefs could replace the old beliefs of the Moriscos. The original broad question for this Round 4, Event 2 (Does the catechism or polemical treatise grapple with the Triple Challenge?) can be rephrased to ask specifically "Does the catechism or polemical treatise meet The Second Challenge by discussing the Symbol?"

Preliminary Results

Diálogos Christianos does not explain the Symbol, but *Catecismo provechoso*, *Catecismo del Sacromonte*, and *Catecismo* do grapple with The Second Challenge.

Diálogos Christianos

There are two possible reasons why Pérez de Chinchón does not discuss the Symbol in *Diálogos Christianos*. First, his work is a work of apologetics set out to prove through "human and divine reasons" the falsity of the sect of Muhammad and the truthfulness of the Christian faith.[18] While *Antialcorano* fights the enemy from afar, *Diálogos Christianos* engages in close combat to protect the Christian camp and invade enemy territory with a wide variety of weapons such as argumentation, cross-examination, harassment, indoctrination, and refutation.[19] Given the apologetics focus of *Diálogos Christianos* instead of instruction of new converts,[20] it seems reasonable for these dialogues not to discuss the Symbol. Second, when *The Roman Catechism* was published in late 1566, it became the model that made it necessary for all catechisms published after that year to follow in terms of content (the Symbol, the Lord's Prayer, the Decalogue, and the Sacraments).

When the year of publication of *Diálogos Christianos* (1535) is taken into account, it also seems reasonable for it not to be concerned with the

---

16. The other parts were the Lord's Prayer, the Decalogue, and the Sacraments.

17. This new catechism—*The Roman Catechism*—was published in late 1566 after Pérez de Ayala had already passed away on 5 August 1566.

18. Pons Fuster, *Antialcorano. Diálogos Christianos*, 399.

19. Pons Fuster, *Antialcorano. Diálogos Christianos*, 394.

20. See "*Diálogos Christianos*" above in Chapter 3.

Symbol. There are two reasonable responses to the potential criticism that the omission suggests that these dialogues are more suitable for finding fault with the sect of Muhammad and defending the Christian faith than instructing Moriscos on *how to live* as Catholics. First, Pérez de Chinchón would not have written *Diálogos Christianos* unless he believed in the Symbol. Second, if these dialogues are deficient, they might be so only when compared with Pérez de Ayala's *Catecismo* and when someone such as Ribera has to decide between the two.

Catecismo provechoso

The only difference between the Symbol presented in *Catecismo provechoso* and *Catecismo* is that Orozco combines articles 10 and 11 found in *Catecismo* into one article. The comparison can be seen below.

Catecismo

I believe in (10) the Holy Catholic Church; (11) the communion of the saints; (12) the forgiveness of sins; (13) the resurrection of the flesh, and (14) eternal life.

Catecismo provechoso

I believe in (9) the Holy Mother Church, Catholic, and the communion of saints; (10) the forgiveness of sins; (11) the resurrection of the flesh; and (12) eternal life.

The difference—twelve articles (*Catecismo provechoso*) compared with fourteen articles (*Catecismo*)—is not significant. According to both authors, the beliefs in the Symbol can be grouped into twelve in honor of Christ's twelve disciples.[21] What is more important is that not a single one of the fundamental beliefs in the Symbol[22] is missing from *Catecismo provechoso*. Its twelve articles confess exactly what is confessed in the *Catecismo*.

21. Pérez de Ayala, *Catecismo*, 271. Orozco, *Catecismo provechoso*, 28 [l]. There might be other reasons for this difference, but it is beyond the scope of this event to investigate further.

22. "I believe in God Almighty the Father, Creator of heaven and the earth and in Jesus Christ His only Son our Lord. He was conceived by the Holy Spirit and was born of the Virgin Mary. He suffered under the power of Pontius Pilate; was crucified, died, and was buried; descended to hell, and on the third day resurrected from the dead. He ascended to the heavens and is seated at the right hand of God Almighty the Father. From there he will come to judge the living and the dead. I believe in the Holy Spirit, the Holy Catholic Church, the communion of saints, the forgiveness of sins, the resurrection of the flesh, and eternal life."

Explanation of the Symbol

A common feature of both catechisms is their explanation in painstaking detail[23] of each article of the Symbol. Orozco dedicates 11 chapters (VIII to XVIII)[24] out of a total of twenty-three chapters in *Catecismo provechoso* (90 pages; 47.8 percent).[25] Pérez de Ayala allocates only one dialogue (Dialogue IX)[26] out of a total of forty-six dialogues in Book Two of the *Catecismo*, but that dialogue alone occupies 150 pages of the total of 442 pages (approximately 34 percent). This thoroughness may indicate that Orozco and Pérez de Ayala consider the Symbol to be vital in transforming the *mind* of the Moriscos so they can *think* like good Catholics.

Catecismo del Sacromonte

The table below shows how *Catecismo del Sacromonte* compares with the *Catecismo* and *Catecismo provechoso* in response to the questions: (1) Is the purpose of the Symbol stated? (2) Is the text of the Symbol provided? and (3) Is the Symbol explained?

Table 7. The Symbol

	Purpose of the Symbol	Text of the Symbol	Explanation of the Symbol
Catecismo	Yes	Yes	Yes. 34%
Catecismo provechoso	Yes	Yes	Yes. 47.8%
Catecismo del Sacromonte	Yes	Somewhat	No. 0.0125%

Purpose of the Symbol

According to *Catecismo del Sacromonte,* the Symbol summarizes the teachings of the Christian religion and gives instruction on the "divinity

---

23. With an emphasis on "painstaking."
24. Orozco, *Catecismo provechoso*, 29 [l]-83 [r].
25. Orozco, *Catecismo provechoso*. Chapter VIII (Article 2) to Chapter XVIII (Article 12). Orozco's explanation of Article 1 begins on page 19 [l] of Chapter VII.
26. Pérez de Ayala, *Catecismo,* 273–323.

of God"[27] and the "humanity of Christ" who is "the door and the path to eternal joy."[28]

Summary

The purpose of the Symbol is to fill the *mind* of the Moriscos with new knowledge: To know the difference between followers of Christ and followers of a false religion (*Catecismo*); to know what to die for (*Catecismo provechoso*); and to know the "divinity of God" and the "humanity of Christ" (*Catecismo del Sacromonte*).

Text of the Symbol

Catecismo del Sacromonte presents fourteen statements of belief in lieu of the text of the Symbol as seen in *Catecismo* and *Catecismo provechoso*. These statements are also found in *Catecismo provechoso*.[29] Both *Catecismo provechoso* and *Catecismo del Sacromonte*[30] organize these statements into two groups of seven articles each. *Catecismo provechoso* and *Catecismo del Sacromonte* present these articles to other catechumens besides the original ones—Felipe and the novice—as follows:

Catecismo provechoso

Seven articles on the divinity of Jesus Christ: Believe (1) in an omnipotent God; that (2) he is Father; (3) he is Son; (4) he is Holy Spirit; (5) he is Creator; (6) he is Savior; and (7) the one who glorifies.

Seven articles on the humanity of Jesus Christ: Believe that he was (8) conceived by the Holy Spirit; (9) born of the virgin Mary who was a virgin before and during her pregnancy and after childbirth; (10) he suffered and died for sinners; (11) he descended to hell and rescued the souls of the faithful who waited for his appearing; (12) he was raised on the third day; (13) he ascended to heaven and is seated at the right hand of the Father; (14) he will return to judge the living and the dead. Those who kept the commandments will be glorified. Those who did not will suffer eternal punishment.

Catecismo del Sacromonte

This catechism does not provide a specific or approximate wording for the first seven articles the way *Catecismo provechoso* does and offers to the

---

27. Orozco uses the expression "the divinity of Christ."
28. Resines, *Catecismo del Sacromonte*, 207.
29. Orozco, *Catecismo provechoso*, 27 [r]–28 [l].
30. Resines, *Catecismo del Sacromonte*, 207.

novice[31] only the following explanations in quotation marks: "The first article confesses the unity of God"; "The next three articles confess the trinity of the divine persons"; and "The next three articles confess the three types of work that only God can do—create out of nothing, justify the sinner, and glorify and bless." *Catecismo del Sacromonte* arranges these last seven articles the way *Catecismo provechoso* does and communicates their truths in wording similar to *Catecismo provechoso*'s.[32]

Another difference in the way *Catecismo provechoso* and *Catecismo del Sacromonte* handle the above fourteen statements is that Orozco goes further by formulating them into what has already been referred to as "the text of the Symbol."[33] A catechumen could find the entire text in the *Catecismo*[34] and *Catecismo provechoso*,[35] but not in *Catecismo del Sacromonte* except for the last seven articles.

Explanation of the Symbol

There are 160 pages in the transcription of *Catecismo del Sacromonte* of which just two pages (0.0125 percent) are allocated to the presentation of the fourteen statements of beliefs. This catechism lacks the full text of the Symbol and its discussion of the statements of beliefs is brief.

Final Results

Catecismo del Sacromonte stays behind while *Catecismo provechoso* and *Catecismo* proceed to The Third Challenge: Behavior.

---

31. Catechumens using *Catecismo del Sacromonte* would—for example—learn that "The first article confesses the unity of God." However, if they are ignorant of the text as stated in *Catechismo provechoso*, they would not be able to learn from *Catecismo del Sacromonte* that it is along the lines of "Believe in an omnipotent God."
32. Resines, *Catecismo del Sacromonte*, 207–8.
33. See "*Catecismo*" above in "Round Four, Event 2."
34. Pérez de Ayala, *Catecismo*, 271–72.
35. Orozco, *Catecismo provechoso*, 28 [r].

Round Four, Event 2

The Third Challenge: Behavior

In order to meet this challenge, the *Catecismo* and the *Catecismo provechoso* would have to replace the religious behavior of Felipe and the Moor with a new set of behaviors. This replacement is not instantaneous, but a lifetime process. It was mentioned previously that the Moor had asked the Teacher to teach him *what to do*.[36] The Moor can be understood to be asking what will replace his previous behavior as a Moor[37] or how should he behave now that he has become a member of the Roman Church. He also asks another weighty question:

> It is because of the goodness and mercy of God that a person can participate in the merits of Christ, be adopted for the glory of heaven, and obey like a child. If this person falls from this state, how can he be restored and reconciled to God? After having been received as a son and a servant of the house of God, it would seem a betrayal for him to deviate from his will and disobey him.[38]

New Questions

The general question "Does the catechism grapple with The Third Challenge?" can now be changed into three new questions:

1. Round Four, Event 2, Question 1: Do the *Catecismo* and the *Catecismo provechoso* teach Moors and Moriscos[39] how to behave as Catholics?
2. Round Four, Event 2, Question 2: Do these two catechisms teach them how to continue behaving as Catholics?
3. Round Four, Event 2, Question 3: Do these catechisms teach them what to do when they fail to behave as Catholics?

---

36. Pérez de Ayala, *Catecismo*, 252–53.

37. See "The Third Challenge. The Religious Commandments of the Moriscos (Behavior)" above in Chapter 4.

38. Pérez de Ayala, *Catecismo*, 423.

39. It would be inaccurate to continue referring to Felipe and the Moor as "Moor" or "Morisco" because both of them have already become "adopted sons of God" and "members of the Holy Roman Church." The "Moors" and "Moriscos" mentioned in these three questions refer to those who have not left the sect of Muhammad ("Moors") and those who have been baptized, but haven't fully embraced the Catholic faith ("Morisco").

Difference between Questions 2 and 3. The focus of Question 2 is what to do *before* sin strikes. The focus of Question 3 is what to do *after* sin strikes—particularly, when it has become habitual.

Round Four, Event 2, Question 1. Do the *Catecismo* and the *Catecismo provechoso* teach Moors and Moriscos how to behave as Catholics?

Both catechisms use the Lord's Prayer, the Ten Commandments, and the Sacraments to teach Moors and Moriscos three ways to behave as Catholics. First, the Lord's Prayer[40] are guidelines for Moors and Moriscos to know to whom they pray and what to pray for. Second, the Ten Commandments[41] are rules for them to know how to behave towards God and towards their neighbors. Third, the Sacraments (Baptism, Confirmation, Eucharist, Penance, Extreme Unction, Holy Orders, and Matrimony)[42] are their strength from God to live as Catholics from shortly after they are born (Baptism) until before they die (Extreme Unction). The next three sections provide brief descriptions of the Lord's Prayer, the Ten Commandments, and the Sacraments to highlight their role in the life of Moors and Moriscos who want to behave as Catholics.

The Lord's Prayer[43]

To whom to pray. Moors and Moriscos learn about *to whom they pray* and *what to ask for*. When they pray "Our Father" what does it mean that God is "Father"? God is our Father because he created us and adopted us (*Catecismo*).[44] "Father" refers to the Trinity yet one God. The one who prays addresses God as "Father"—not "king," "God," "Adonai" or "Lord" even

---

40. Orozco, *Catecismo provechoso*, 115 [l]. Pérez de Ayala, *Catecismo*, 329.

41. Orozco, *Catecismo provechoso*, 87 [r].
Note: The introductory material that Orozco wrote about the first three commandments—pages 73 [r] to 83 [l]—are missing from the digital copy of his catechism. The remainder of what he wrote about the first, the second, and the third commandment is found on pages 84[r], 85 [l], and 85 [r], respectively.
Pérez de Ayala, *Catecismo*, 345.

42. Orozco, *Catecismo provechoso*, 97 [r].
Pérez de Ayala, *Catecismo*, 369.

43. Additional information about the Lord's Prayer is available above in "The Solution: A Catechism From The Council of Trent" in Chapter 4.

44. Pérez de Ayala, *Catecismo*, 332.

though these are proper titles. But, God allows us to call him "Our Father" because of his tenderness towards us who are his children and he wants us to be confident when we pray to him (*Catecismo provechoso*).[45]

What to ask for. The Lord's Prayer contains seven petitions. Moors and Moriscos should pray for: (1) The name of God to be honored; (2) the coming of his kingdom; (3) God's will to be done on earth as it is done in heaven; God to (4) give them their daily bread; (5) forgive their sins; (6) not let them fall into temptation; and (7) set them free from all evil.[46]

The Ten Commandments[47]

These commandments teach Moors and Moriscos how to behave; that is, what to do and not to do.

What to do. Honor your father and mother (fifth commandment) and remember the sabbath (fourth).

What not to do. Have no foreign gods (first); do not make images and worship them (second); do not use the Lord's name in vain (third); do not murder (sixth); do not commit adultery (seventh); do not steal (eight); do not bear false testimony against your neighbors (ninth); and do not covet your neighbors' field, servants, oxen or anything that belongs to them (tenth).

Catecismo

The Ten Commandments (Exod 20:1–17) convey God's will regarding the obedience that he demands and the obedience that followers of Christ owe him.[48] The Teacher explains each commandment and concludes by saying that these commandments can be summed up as two commandments—"Love God above everything else" and "Love our neighbor as we love ourselves."[49] The Moor then asks a critical question—"Can these commandments be obeyed without God's favor?" The Teacher replies and says that God's favor is indispensable because sin makes it impossible for anyone to

---

45. Orozco, *Catecismo provechoso*, 115 [l].

46. Pérez de Ayala, *Catecismo*, 329–332.
Orozco, *Catecismo provechoso*, 117 [l]–129 [l].

47. Additional information about the Ten Commandments is available above in "What Christians Should Believe and The Roman Catechism" in Chapter 4.

48. Pérez de Ayala, *Catecismo*, 346.

49. Pérez de Ayala, *Catecismo*, 355.

love God more than self.[50] Christ said that without him one can do nothing.[51] The Moor's question and the Teacher's answer show that to behave as a Catholic does not require obedience to man-made rules, but reliance on divine favor to follow divine commandments.

Catecismo provechoso

The first three commandments direct the soul towards God.[52] The last seven commandments guide people to live in harmony with their neighbors.[53] The priest also tells Felipe—like the Teacher has told the Moor—that these ten commandments can be summarized into two commandments: "You shall love God with all your heart" and "You shall love your neighbor as yourself."[54] After the priest explains each commandment, Felipe makes three observations that show that he recognizes the magnitude of the Ten Commandments. First, what the commandments reveal about the author of these commandments. Felipe says that God is "supreme goodness and infinite wisdom."[55] Second, what the commandments reveal about their purpose. Felipe seems excited and grateful when he declares, "O divine law, holy law that directs souls to heaven."[56] Third, what the commandments say about those who do not possess them. Felipe laments, "Wretched are the heathen and the heretics who lack such a celestial law."[57] While the Moor's question and the Teacher's answer teach that God helps the Catholic obey his commandments, Felipe's observations notice that God is good and wise to have given such commandments so that people can go to heaven.

---

50. Pérez de Ayala, *Catecismo*, 355–56.

51. The Teacher does not provide the biblical requence. It is John 15:5: "Apart from Me you can do nothing."

52. Orozco, *Catecismo provechoso*, 87 [l].

53. Orozco, *Catecismo provechoso*, 87 [r].

54. Orozco, *Catecismo provechoso*, 93 [l].

55. Orozco, *Catecismo provechoso*, 93 [r].

56. Orozco, *Catecismo provechoso*, 94 [l].

57. Orozco, *Catecismo provechoso*, 93 [r].

Catecismo

The Sacraments

The Sacraments are "sacred signs" instituted by God to transmit the fruits of Christ's Passion and the effects of grace to the soul.[58] The Moor and the Moriscos receive strength through The Sacraments "to walk the path of God."[59] However, it is not incumbent upon them or all Catholics to receive all seven sacraments; for example, the two sacraments of Matrimony and Holy Orders are not required unless a Catholic chooses to get married or enter into vocational ministry. The sacraments of Baptism, Confirmation, Confession, Communion, and Extreme Unction are the common ones, but only three of them are necessary: Baptism (the soul of the recipient is washed of all sins—including original sin—and the recipient is made into a child of God),[60] Penitence (the sins of the penitent are absolved),[61] and Communion (takes place when followers of Christ experience a kind of spiritual communion during Mass as they contemplate their current stage in life and yearn to be better with God's help).[62] So, Moors and Moriscos who have become members of the Roman Church are required to observe no less than three of the sacraments.

Catecismo provechoso

There is no difference between Orozco's and Pérez de Ayala's understanding of the role that the sacraments can play in the life of the Moors and Moriscos. While Pérez de Ayala speaks of the sacraments as "sacred signs" that gives strength to Catholics "to walk the path of God," Orozco describes the sacraments as "divine cups" for drawing the grace of God out of the passion of Christ. The sacraments take the followers of Christ to their final perfection, which is to see the divine essence for which they were created.[63]

---

58. Pérez de Ayala, *Catecismo*, 370.
59. Pérez de Ayala, *Catecismo*, 372.
60. Pérez de Ayala, *Catecismo*, 372–74.
61. Pérez de Ayala, *Catecismo*, 382.
62. Pérez de Ayala, *Catecismo*, 399.
63. Orozco, *Catecismo provechoso*, 97 [r].

Summary

Orozco and Pérez de Ayala are in effect saying to Moors and Moriscos: "If you want to behave as a Catholic, this is how you should pray (The Lord's Prayer). This is what you should do and not do (The Ten Commandments). This is God's grace or strength for your entire life from the time after you are born until before you die (The Sacraments)."

Round Four, Event 2, Question 2. Do the *Catecismo* and the *Catecismo provechoso* teach Moors and Moriscos how to continue behaving as Catholics?

Catecismo

This question and the next one ("Do the *Catecismo* and the *Catecismo provechoso* teach Moors and Moriscos what to do when they fail to behave as Catholics?") are concerned with sin. Pérez de Ayala wrote five chapters to address this major issue. Each chapter answers one or more questions from the Moor. The content of these chapters can be condensed into the single heading of "How to Defeat Sin to Continue Behaving as a Catholic." The key content of each chapter is presented below and will be used to compare the answers to Questions 2 and 3 provided by *Catecismo provechoso*. It is possible to determine quickly what material is covered and how much of it is covered in these two catechisms.

How to Defeat Sin to Continue Behaving as a Catholic

The Moor (M) asks and the Teacher (T) answers.[64]

M: "What are the different types of sin?"

T: Original sin, mortal sin, and venial sin.

M: "Are there other types of sin?"

T: Sins out of ignorance, sins due to weakness, and sins out of malice.

M: "What are the different forms of sin?"

T: Sins of the heart, sins of the mouth, sins of deed, and sins of omission (or negligence).

M: "What are the mortal sins?"

---

64. Pérez de Ayala, *Catecismo*, 358–69.

T: Pride, avarice, lust, envy, gluttony, wrath, and sloth. A mortal sin is the deliberate or negligent withholding of the love due to God and neighbor. Mortal sin is also disobedience of God's commandments.

M: "How do I root out mortal sins?"

T: By the grace of God; by a virtue opposite to the mortal sin; and by the gifts and fruits of the Holy Spirit. The virtue opposite to the mortal sin: pride (humility), avarice (generosity), lust (chastity), envy (charity), gluttony (temperance), wrath (meekness), and sloth (hope). The gifts of the Holy Spirit "perfect the soul to pursue and obey the Spirit perfectly" are wisdom, intelligence, counsel, fortitude, science, piety, and reverence. The fruits of the Holy Spirit are charity, joy, peace, patience, forbearance, goodness, kindness, meekness, faith, modesty, continence, and chastity.

M: "What are venial sins?"

T: A state of disorder that people fall into lightly because of their weaknesses. These sins do not incur eternal punishment and can forgiven more easily than mortal sins.

M: "How can venial sins be forgiven?"

T: There are many ways, including but not limited to attending Mass, praying the Lord's Prayer, giving alms, and being remorseful.

M: "Are there sins more severe than the ones above?"

T: The sin against the Holy Spirit and sins that cry out to God for revenge against the perpetrator. The sin against the Holy Spirit is "the gravest mortal sin" and encompasses losing hope of the mercy of God; presuming to have received God's mercy; contesting Catholic truth; blasphemy; jealous over a neighbor being favored; unwilling to repent; and loathing God. The sins that fall under the category of sins that cry out to God for revenge against the perpetrator are involuntary homicide, sin against nature, oppression of the poor, widows, and orphans, and refusal to pay salary to a worker.

M: "What can help me fight against sin and follow the will of God?"

T: Theological virtues (faith, hope, and charity) and cardinal virtues (justice, fortitude, temperance, and prudence).

The Teacher's answers show that in order for Moors and Moriscos to be able to continue behaving as Catholics they must know *what* and *how*; that is, *what* is sin (types and forms) and *how* to prevent or overcome sin by relying on God (his grace, virtues, and the gifts and fruits of the Holy Spirit).

Catecismo provechoso

Orozco's discussion of sin covers the definition of mortal sin ("the fountain or root from which all vices flow"); types of mortal sins (pride, avarice, lust, envy, gluttony, wrath, and sloth); the remedies for mortal sins (the seven virtues—humility, generosity, chastity, temperance, meekness, and hope); and the gifts of the Holy Spirit (wisdom, intelligence, counsel, fortitude, science, piety, and reverence).[65]

Similarities

Orozco's presentation on mortal sins shares similarities with Pérez de Ayala's. First, both of them define mortal sins. Second, they explain each of the seven mortal sins and the virtues that combat them. Third, both also introduce and explain the gifts of the Holy Spirit.

Differences

There are also differences between Orozco's and Pérez de Ayala's discussion on the topic of sin. First, Orozco limits his discussion to mortal sins. Second, Felipe is quiet until the end when he comments that he is confident that he and other Christians will benefit from reading this catechism. By comparison, the Moor is an active participant who asks three questions on mortal sins. The discussion opens with, "How many mortal sins are there?" The rest of the dialogue is a response to his other two questions—"Which seven (mortal sins)?" and "What can be used to uproot these sins?"[66] Felipe's comment may encourage priests and Moriscos to use Orozco's catechism. However, the Moor's questions might be more instructive for priests who gain insight into what types of questions Moriscos are asking for which priests need to be prepared to answer.

Conclusion

Although Orozco's presentation is shorter than Pérez de Ayala's, there are no reasons to believe that Orozco does not regard sin—of which mortal sins is one of its manifestations with venial sins being the other one—as a serious problem. Orozco describes the gifts of the Holy Spirit as "excellent" and

---

65. Orozco, *Catecismo provechoso*, 107 [l]–113 [l].
66. Pérez de Ayala, *Catecismo*, 361–362.

"divine precious jewels." Given that the one who commits a mortal sin loses them, Orozco exhorts Felipe to beseech God to preserve those "treasures" in his soul. Orozco admits that he could have written more, but felt it necessary to bring his catechism to an end.[67] If he had continued to write, his exposition on sin may have been as wide-ranging as Pérez de Ayala's.

Round Four, Event 2, Question 3. Do the *Catecismo* and the *Catecismo provechoso* teach Moors and Moriscos what to do when they fail to behave as Catholics?

Catecismo

When servants of the house of God disobey God, how can they be restored and reconciled to him? The title of the chapter ("What to Do to Get Out of the Bad Life of Sin"[68]) and its content seem to indicate that the Teacher is not just trying to help the servant who commits the occasional sin, but also the one who lives in sin or is trapped by sin. According to the Teacher, disobedient servants can do six things:

First, they should not continue to cling to sin and sin as much they can. Second, they should not allow sin to age before repenting. Third, if they find themselves attached to sin, they should cry out to God and ask him to rescue them. Fourth, they should not stop doing all the good deeds they can at every opportunity. Fifth, they should ask good people for advice, doctrine, and model behavior. Sixth, when God grants them an opportunity to walk away from sin, they should ask him to increase that opportunity, listen to what he wants them to do, and take action.[69]

Catecismo provechoso

Orozco does not discuss this issue.

Summary

Does the *Catecismo* and the *Catecismo provechoso* teach the Moors and Moriscos:

---

67. Orozco, *Catecismo provechoso*, 111 [r]–112 [r].
68. Pérez de Ayala, *Catecismo*, 423.
69. Pérez de Ayala, *Catecismo*, 424–26.

How to behave as Catholics? Both works teach them how to behave as Catholics.

How to continue behaving as Catholics? *Catecismo*: yes; *Catecismo provechoso*: partially.

What to do when they fail to behave as Catholics? *Catecismo*: yes; *Catecismo provechoso*: no.

Catecismo succeeds at meeting The Third Challenge while *Catecismo provechoso* does not.

Table 8. Results of Round Four, All Two Events

	1^{70}	2^{71}
Diálogos Christianos	✔	
Catecismo provechoso	✔	
Catecismo del Sacromonte	✔	
Catecismo	✔	✔

Step 1

Twelve catechisms and polemical treatises (the Group of twelve) and the *Catecismo* participated in four rounds and sixteen events. Only *Catecismo* and *Catecismo provechoso* reached the last event (Round Four, Event 2).

Step 2

The analysis of *Catecismo* and *Catecismo provechoso* is found in Chapter 10. Both *Catecismo* and *Catecismo provechoso* will be analyzed, but this does not mean that they were tied after sixteen events. *Catecismo* is the only one of the thirteen catechisms and polemical treatises to have completed all four rounds successfully.

---

70. Event 1. Is the catechism or polemical treatise aware of the Triple Challenge; that is, the confession, the beliefs, and the commandments that control the heart, the mind, and the behavior of the Moriscos?

71. Event 2. Does the catechism or polemical treatise grapple with the Triple Challenge?

Chapter 10

The Content of the New *Catecismo*: Apologetics and Polemics

Step 2

STEP 1 (CHAPTERS 6 to 9) applies the criteria in Chapter 5 to assess the *Catecismo* and the Group of twelve. Chapter 10 analyzes the results from Step 1 for their content in two areas: apologetics and polemics. Step 3 uses the results from Step 2 to offer preliminary answers to two questions: (1) What was the potential of the *Catecismo* as an evangelistic tool addressed to Moriscos? and (2) Why did archbishop Juan de Ribera choose the *Catecismo* to bolster his own evangelistic task in 1599—thirty-three years after Pérez de Ayala had passed away and ten years before the decree of Philip III in 1609 that launched the process to expel the Moriscos from Spain? Chapter 11 covers this step.

The objective of Step 2 is to examine the apologetical and polemical contents of the competitors who reached Round 4; that is, *Catecismo* and *Catecismo provechoso*. However, *Diálogos Christianos, Catecismo del Sacromonte*, and *Antialcorano* have been included in this examination in order to intensify the contrast between the apologetical and polemical material in the *Catecismo*[1] and these four works; uncover the building blocks for narrow definitions of the terms apologetics and polemics; and

---

1. As previously stated, the *Catecismo* is the only catechism or polemical treatise to have successfully completed all four rounds and sixteen events. If Chapter 10 only had the *Catecismo*, no meaningful analysis would be possible. This explains the inclusion of *Catecismo provechoso*. Given that *Diálogos Christianos* and *Catecismo del Sacromonte* were strong enough competitors to reach Round Four, Event 2. The Second Challenge: The Mind, they have been added to the analysis.

provide a broader definition of both terms that matches with the realities of sixteenth-century Spain.[2]

Although *Antialcorano* is considered a polemical treatise, it has some apologetics material. By comparison, *Confusión o confutación*—which is also a polemical treatise—contains no apologetics material. *Antialcorano* was stopped at Round Two, Events 2 ("Is the tone of the catechism or polemical treatise 'charitable and friendly'?") and 3 ("Could the catechism or polemical treatise inflame the emotions of the Moriscos?"). *Diálogos Christianos* and *Catecismo del Sacromonte* were eliminated at Round Four, Event 2, The Second Challenge: The Mind ("Does the catechism or polemical treatise grapple with The Second Challenge by explaining the Symbol?").

Chapter 10 examines the apologetics and polemical material of *Catecismo*, *Catecismo provechoso*, *Diálogos Christianos*, *Catecismo del Sacromonte*, and *Antialcorano*. These five works will be examined for their apologetical approach to six topics: Jesus Christ (*Catecismo* and *Antialcorano*), faith (*Catecismo provechoso*), the Catholic Church (*Catecismo del Sacromonte*), the Christian law (*Catecismo provechoso*), the gospel (*Antialcorano*), the Scriptures (*Catecismo*, *Diálogos Christianos*, and *Catecismo del Sacromonte*), and testimonies (*Catecismo* and *Antialcorano*). The building blocks that each work uses for a narrow definition of the term "apologetics" are: *Catecismo* (the excellence and divinity of Christ, the Scriptures, and testimonies), *Catecismo provechoso* (the Christian law and faith), *Diálogos Christianos* (the Scriptures and testimonies), *Catecismo del Sacromonte* (the Scriptures and the Catholic Church), and *Antialcorano* (the sonship of Jesus Christ and the gospel). The narrow definitions are:

"Apologetics defends the excellence and divinity of Christ, the Scriptures, and the truth of the gospel through the testimonies of those who have embraced it" (*Catecismo*); "Apologetics is a defense of the Christian law and faith" (*Catecismo provechoso*); "Apologetics defends the Scriptures and testifies to the truthfulness of the Christian law" (*Diálogos Christianos*); "Apologetics is a defense of the Scriptures and the Catholic Church" (*Catecismo del Sacromonte*); and "Apologetics is concerned with defending the sonship of Christ and the gospel" (*Antialcorano*).

---

2. The broader definitions of "apologetics" and "polemics" are presented after each term has been discussed in this chapter.

APOLOGETICS

Jesus Christ

The foundation of apologetics in *Diálogos Christianos* consists of the Christian Scriptures and the testimonies of those who follow the Christian law. Apologetics in *Catecismo del Sacromonte* means a defense of the greatness of the Catholic Church and its teachings. Apologetics in the *Catecismo* begins with the statement "The Christian religion is the only path to God." In fact, this material does not begin until Dialogue XX of Book One of the *Catecismo*.[3] By the time this dialogue begins, the *Catecismo* has already presented two types of material that this present book has categorized as "pre-apologetics" and "polemics."

Catecismo

Chapter 3 above noted that the *Catecismo* is the only one of the catechisms and polemical treatises that offers "pre-apologetics" material.[4] This material is a lengthy argumentation covering three questions: (1) What is God? The *Catecismo* focuses on explaining God's nature (who is he and how is he one) and his sovereignty (God rules the universe he created); (2) What is man? Man is immortal and his soul is perfect; his final destination is God; true religion is the path to God; and man cannot rely on natural light to guide him to the true religion because of original sin and the corruption of his nature; and (3) What is the path to God? There is only path to God, but it is neither philosophy nor Jewish law.

When the *Catecismo* starts discussing apologetics it has already explored who is God, what is man, and demonstrated that three paths—philosophy, Jewish law, and the religion of Muhammad[5]—cannot lead to God. In contrast with the foundation of apologetics in *Diálogos Christianos*, the foundation of apologetics in the *Catecismo* is "the excellence and divinity of Christ."[6] The Teacher tells the Moor as their final dialogue (Dialogue XXV[7])

---

3. Pérez de Ayala, *Catecismo*, 165.

4. Book One of the *Catecismo* consists of twenty-five dialogues. The pre-apologetics material occupies 10 of those dialogues (Dialogues III, IV, V, VI, VII, VIII, IX, X, XI, and XII).

5. Seven of the twenty-five dialogues in Book One of the *Catecismo* are polemics (Dialogues XIII, XIV, XV, XVI, XVII, XVIII and XIX).

6. "The excellence and divinity of Christ" is also the foundation of the *Catecismo's* polemics.

7. Pérez de Ayala, *Catecismo*, 245–53.

is about to conclude: "I have wanted to take my time to prove this point about the excellence and divinity of Jesus Christ because it is the foundation of everything that we have been discussing."[8] The Teacher's proof of the excellence and divinity of Christ rests on the dignity of Christ, his messiahship, and miracles.[9] It is not possible to compare and contrast how *Diálogos Christianos* and the *Catecismo* view Jesus Christ because Chinchón does not touch on this point at all. A summary of the Teacher's proof of "the excellence and divinity of Christ" is provided below.

The Dignity of Christ

This dialogue begins when the Moor makes a request to the Teacher: "Now let's come to the end of this proposition that I am so interested in learning about, that is, to prove the truth and infallibility of the holy evangelical doctrine by the excellence of the person who gave it and ordered it to be disseminated."[10]

The essence of the Teacher's response: Christ taught the path to God and how to honor and serve God not just with actions, but also with thoughts. He performed miracles. He fasted and prayed. He was patient when insulted. He knew what was in people's hearts, which is something that only God can do. Everything he did, he gave God the glory. He drew people to the gospel by the power of the Spirit. His life matched what he taught. Not only the prophets and his disciples spoke of his dignity and excellence, but others also—Pontius Pilate, Tiberius, Josephus, and even Muhammad.[11]

The Messiahship of Christ

The Teacher makes this assertion: "It is clear that Messiah had to be God. It is also clear that Christ is the Messiah . . . which is proven by the fulfillment of the prophecies in the Old Testament and by the wonderful deeds that Christ did. It then follows that Christ is God."[12] However, the Moor is skeptical and

---

8. Pérez de Ayala, *Catecismo*, 250–51.
9. Pérez de Ayala, *Catecismo*, 210–44.
10. Pérez de Ayala, *Catecismo*, 210.
11. Pérez de Ayala, *Catecismo*, 210–27.
12. Pérez de Ayala, *Catecismo*, 228–29.

says: "It seems that you presuppose that the Messiah had to be God and not just a man.¹³ But I have heard the Jews say something different."¹⁴

The Teacher's defense of the divinity of the Messiah has two parts. Part One: The Old Testament declared that the Messiah is God. (Ps 2, 44, 71, 109; Isa 9, 11, 45, 51, 62, 66; and Jer 23). The Moor responds and says: "You have proven that the Messiah had to be God, but how do you prove that Jesus Christ was the Messiah?"¹⁵

Their next exchange—particularly the Moor's reaction—merits a verbatim quotation because it is evident that the Moor is not a passive and silent listener, but engages the Teacher. First, the Teacher makes this affirmation: "This can be clearly proven. If we follow the flow of the characteristics and signs written about the Messiah that they all converge in Christ, it is then proven that Jesus Christ was both man and God." The Moor says: "Please continue, Father. I am listening quite eagerly. It seems that your answers given in order are satisfying me."¹⁶

Part Two: The second part of the Teacher's defense in brief. He points to twenty-seven passages in the Old Testament¹⁷ and seven in the New Testament¹⁸ to show the specific characteristics and signs of the Messiah fulfilled in Christ; for example, that he was to be a descendant of Abraham, from the tribe of Judah, and born of a virgin. The Teacher concludes by saying that Jews and even Moors honor John the Baptist who declared that Christ is "The Lamb of God who takes away the sin of the world." (John 1:29.)¹⁹

The Miracles of Christ

This dialogue begins after the Moor points out to the Teacher: "Why have you not talked to me about the miracles of Christ? It would please me greatly for you to pause here because I have heard that there are some who have

---

13. The debate on the divinity of the Messiah continues today. See for example *Beyond Mere Christianity* by Brandon Toropov (2005) and *Jesus: Man, Messenger, Messiah* by Abu Zakariya (2017).

14. Pérez de Ayala, *Catecismo*, 229.

15. Pérez de Ayala, *Catecismo*, 232.

16. Pérez de Ayala, *Catecismo*, 232.

17. Gen 12, 18, 22; Deut 18; Pss 3, 5, 21, 68, 131; Isa 7, 9, 35, 40, 50, 53, 61; Jer 16, 31; Ezek 36, 39; Dan 7, 9; Joel 2; Mic 5; Zech 9.

18. Matt 3, 16, 20; Luke 3; John 1, 2, 3, 18.

19. Pérez de Ayala, *Catecismo*, 232–38.

slandered him."[20] The Teacher's response can be summarized as follows: First, he defines a miracle as "something that only God can do." He then discusses sixteen miracles of Jesus' miracles (raising the dead, giving sight to the blind, healing the paralytic, walking on water, casting out demons, calming the storm, etc). In more than one instance, Jesus demonstrated his power over nature by just saying a word. He did what no human can do. After he was baptized, God declared, "This is My beloved Son, in whom I am well-pleased." (Matt 3:17.) At his transfiguration, God said something similar: "This is My beloved Son, with whom I am well-pleased; listen to Him!" (Matt 17:8.) Even the Qur'an acknowledges that Jesus performed miracles. The Teacher finishes by saying: "If Jesus Christ is God, he cannot lie. Therefore, the evangelical law that he gave cannot be false."[21]

Antialcorano

Apologetics in *Antialcorano* means a defense of Christ and the gospel. The defense of Christ centers on his sonship, which the followers of the Muhammad have a fundamental difference with Christians.

The Sonship of Christ

Antialcorano explains the sonship in three ways: (1) Fire comes from another fire, a tree comes from another tree, and a human being comes from another human being. The sonship of Christ could be understood in a similar way, but with a significant difference. The Son has no beginning. He has been with God since the beginning. There was never a time when he began to be like God;[22] (2) The works of Christ show that he is the Son of God; and (3) The Scriptures. After Jesus was baptized, God declared, "This is my beloved Son." (Matt 3:13–17.) Peter said to Jesus directly, "You are the Christ, the Son of the Living God" (Matt 18:16). When the Jewish religious leaders asked Jesus whether or not he was the Son of God, he answered, "Yes, I am" (Luke 22:66–71).[23]

---

20. Pérez de Ayala, *Catecismo*, 240.
21. Pérez de Ayala, *Catecismo*, 240–44.
22. *Catecismo provechoso* and *Catecismo del Sacromonte* also use "fire" to explain the Sonship of Christ. See above "Jesus Christ: Bridging The Gap" in Chapter 6.
23. Pons Fuster, *Antialcorano. Diálogos Christianos*, 287–95.

Catecismo provechoso

Faith

The apologetics of *Catecismo provechoso* is not only a defense of the truthfulness of the Christian law, but also a defense of faith itself. Orozco asserts that faith is excellent. The starting point to appreciate the excellence of faith is that without faith it is impossible to please God (Heb 11). In what sense is this faith excellent? First, God does not accept good moral deeds, but gives faith to those who do them (for example, the Roman centurion Cornelius and the Ethiopian eunuch) that they find the path to him. Second, this faith is excellent because with it we know how to obey and serve God. Third, this faith is excellent because God gives it without measure so that we can do what our nature cannot do. Fourth, this faith is excellent because we are saved by faith in Christ and by our good moral deeds (Eph 2).[24]

In sum, Orozco's defense of faith is important because it notes that God gives people the faith that they do not have so that they can be saved and honor him. God does not just tell them that they do not have the right kind of faith, but gives it out liberally to those who want it. This giving of God separates the Christian law from all other philosophies and religions.

Catecismo del Sacromonte

The Catholic Church

The apologetics of *Catecismo del Sacromonte* is a defense of the Catholic Church and the Scriptures. Three aspects of the Church are defended: (1) The excellence of the Church. The Church is excellent because it provides everyone with three things that will guide them to God. Sailors rely on three things to reach their destination—the North, a compass, and a map. Anyone who desires to go to God has a North (the truth taught by the Church whose head is Peter's successor); a compass (the faith that God gives everyone who wants it and always points to the North); and a map (the Scriptures);[25] (2) The mysteries of the Church, which include the divinity and humanity of Christ, the fatherhood of God, the virgin birth, and the Trinity; and (3) The effects of faith; that is, a spiritual marriage between the soul and God; eternal

---

24. Orozco, *Catecismo provechoso*, 17–20.
25. Resines, *Catecismo del Sacromonte*, 189–92.

life or enjoying God begins now and continues after death; guidance as to what is good and what is bad; and victory over temptation.[26]

Catecismo provechoso

The Christian Law

The apologetics of Orozco is a defense of the truthfulness of the Christian Law. Orozco gives four reasons why it is true. One, demons, heresy, persecution, tyrants, and even sin inside the church have not been able to destroy the church because Christ promised "the gates of Hades will not overpower it." Two, the church is a solid pillar and support of the truth. Third, Christ promised to protect his church like a good shepherd guards his flock. Fourth, this Christ is unique. Jacob announced that he would arrive before the scepter departed from Judah; Daniel foretold that he would come "seven weeks and sixty-two weeks" after the decree was issued to rebuild Jerusalem; and Zechariah prophesied that he would be humble and arrive riding a donkey. In sum, the Christian law is true because the church exists and Christ's role in the church.[27]

Antialcorano

The Gospel

The apologetics of the *Antialcorano* is a defense of the gospel. Pérez de Chinchón makes and defends three assertions. One, the gospel is perfect because it contains the Ten Commandments for people to live by.[28] Two, the gospel is good because its witnesses include God, the angels, and holy men of old. Even the Qur'an says so although the gospel does not need it to be one of its witnesses.[29] Three, the gospel agrees with natural reason. People who live by the gospel are good. It stands to reason that the gospel is good.[30]

---

26. Resines, *Catecismo del Sacromonte*, 207–18.
27. Orozco, *Catecismo provechoso*, 9–13.
28. Pons Fuster, *Antialcorano. Diálogos Christianos*, 209–31.
29. Pons Fuster, *Antialcorano. Diálogos Christianos*, 329–36.
30. Pons Fuster, *Antialcorano. Diálogos Christianos*, 367–83.

Catecismo

The Scriptures

The *Catecismo*'s defense of the Scriptures can be condensed into three parts.[31]

1. The work of the Holy Spirit. Before the Scriptures had been written down, the Holy Spirit recorded them in the hearts of those who followed God. Later, this same Spirit guided the writing of the authors in such a manner that what they wrote did not deviate from what was already in their hearts. There is agreement in the Scriptures even though there were multiple authors who lived in diverse places in different time periods. However, this agreement does not mean agreement in every word or detail. Some authors left out what other writers wrote down. Perfect agreement does not prove lack of corruption because even a court of law would be suspicious if all the witnesses agreed in everything. Thus, the written Scriptures with the differences still show evidence of the handiwork of the Holy Spirit.

2. The antiquity of the message in the Scriptures. The core of the message is about the coming of one Messiah, one Redeemer, and one faith that saves everyone. Although the people of Israel believed in the Messiah who was to come and today we believe that he has come, it is still the same faith. This message is the oldest because it has been proclaimed since the beginning of the world. As an oracle of Apollo stated, "The goodness of a religion is measured by its antiquity."

3. The compilation of the Qur'an and the Scriptures. When Muhammad was alive, the Qur'an was recorded in "secret and suspect sheets."[32] After he died, his followers had to ask one his wives for what she had in her possession.[33] The lack of agreement in the Qur'an resembles "a cape patched together by a pauper."[34]

---

31. Pérez de Ayala, *Catecismo*, 187–90.

32. Pérez de Ayala did not reveal his source, but this is what is known: The edition of the Qur'anic text commissioned by Zayd bin Thabit (610–660 CE)—known as the Uthmanic codex—is based on oral material and text written on scraps of wood, palm leaves, bark and bones. Zayd himself recorded Muhammad's revelations on the shoulder blade of a camel. Leemhuis, "From Palm Leaves to the Internet," 145.

33. Although Pérez de Ayala did not provide a source, Muslim tradition speaks of people in Muhammad's community such as his wife Aisha who at the time of his death had copies of portions of his revelations. Donner, *The Cambridge Companion to the Qurʾān*, 31.

34. Pérez de Ayala, *Catecismo*, 190. It could be said that Pérez de Ayala drew this conclusion on the basis of his two preceding two statements.

Diálogos Christianos

Unlike the *Catecismo* which makes Christ the foundation of its apologetics, the apologetics of *Diálogos Christianos* is rooted in a defense of the Scriptures—a theme that is also part of the apologetics of the *Catecismo* and *Catecismo del Sacromonte*: "The gospel is true and excellent because of its Scriptures" (*Catecismo*); "Divine and natural reason show that the law of the prophets were true and complete when Christ came" and "Christians neither falsified nor corrupted the law of the prophets" (*Diálogos Christianos*); and "The integrity of the Scriptures" (*Catecismo del Sacromonte*).

The section below contrasts how the *Catecismo* and *Diálogos Christianos* defend the Scriptures. *Diálogos Christianos* defends the Scriptures by answering the question "Where would the corruption have come from?" and exploring four possible sources of corruption: (1) The one who gave the Scriptures; (2) The prophets who wrote the Scriptures; (3) Those who received the Scriptures; and (4) War, captivity and natural disasters.

Diálogos Christianos argues that it is against reason for any of these four answers to be in the positive because (1) It is unthinkable that God—who is absolute goodness and absolute truth—would corrupt or falsify the Scriptures that he gave; (2) Prophets had to be of good character for God to have chosen and equipped them to proclaim his message. If they had added, deleted or falsified the Scriptures, it would mean that he had made a mistake in choosing them; (3) Those who received the Scriptures—the people of Israel—corrupted them. But God had warned them not to add or take away from his commandments (Deut 4:2). Even though they sinned against him regularly, no one tried to change the commandments they disobeyed; and (4) The Scriptures were lost or distorted due to war, captivity or natural disasters. However, not everyone went to war, but those who did fight or were captured had the law hidden with them. Given that it is unreasonable that any of these answers can explain the corruption of the Scriptures, the Moors need to present evidence for the corruption. They also need to remember that even the Qur'an acknowledges that Jesus is the Messiah spoken of in these same Scriptures they say have been corrupted.[35]

Catecismo del Sacromonte

The priest explains to the novice why it was impossible for Christians and the Jews to have falsified their Scriptures:[36] (1) God declared that his word

---

35. Pons Fuster, *Antialcorano. Diálogos Christianos*, 434–44.
36. Resines, *Catecismo del Sacromonte*, 204.

stands forever (Isa 40:8; 1 Pet 1:25). It does not make sense that he would give the Scriptures then to allow them to be corrupted; (2) If the Jews had corrupted the Scriptures, God would have dealt severely with them just as he did when they committed other kinds of sins; (3) Jews and Christians living far apart from each other would have had to agreed to corrupt the Scriptures together. But, they did not get along at the time. Furthermore, there would be evidence of this collusion to alter the Scriptures; (4) Everything prophesied in the Old Testament about the first coming of Christ has been fulfilled in the New Testament; (5) The Spirit of God guided or inspired Christ's disciples and apostles to write down what Christ did not write; and (6) If the Scriptures had been corrupted, either the Old or the New Testament would have portions of the Talmud. They do not. By comparison, the Qur'an does.[37]

Catecismo and *Diálogos Christianos*

Testimonies

The gospel can also be defended with the testimonies of the people who believe it: "The gospel is true and excellent because of the virtues in those who obey it"[38] and "Testimonies from Christians verify the truth of the Christian law."[39] This section compares and contrasts these two assertions.

Transformed Lives (*Catecismo*)

God always sends a person to the right path when they ask him about it. An angel told the Roman centurion Cornelius ("a devout man who feared God and prayed to him continually") to look for Peter. When they met, Peter preached the gospel, Cornelius believed and was baptized (Acts 10). The Ethiopian eunuch was reading but not understanding Isaiah 53 when the Spirit of God sent him Philip. After Philip explained the passage, the eunuch believed and was baptized (Acts 8). Saul was on his way to Damascus when Jesus appeared to him and told him to find Ananias. After they met, Saul believed the gospel and shortly after started to preach it in the synagogues (Acts 9).[40]

---

37. Resines, *Catecismo del Sacromonte*, 205–6.
38. Pérez de Ayala, *Catecismo*, 245–53.
39. Pons Fuster, *Antialcorano. Diálogos Christianos*, 427–32.
40. Pérez de Ayala, *Catecismo*, 247.

These three examples show that gospel is true and excellent because when someone wants to know God, he does not lead them to a philosophy, the Jews or the religion of the Moors, but to his evangelical law. The *Catecismo* gives two more reasons why the gospel is true and excellent. One, experience shows that when people live in obedience to the evangelical law, they are more virtuous and spiritual. Two, history demonstrates that the Christian religion grows and strengthens under persecution because truth defends itself and prevails when it is oppressed.[41]

The Christian Law Is True (*Diálogos Christianos*)

Testimonies in the *Catecismo* refer to the lives of people who have been transformed by the gospel. By comparison, testimonies in *Diálogos Christianos* refer to the following five pieces of evidence that prove that the Christian law is true:[42] (1) The Jews had the Law of Moses and other prophetic writings in their entirety before Christ came the first time; (2) After he came, the Jews did not change what Moses and the prophets wrote. They had no reason; (3) The disciples and the apostles of Christ did not change what Moses and the prophets wrote; (4) The gospel emerges from the Law of Moses and those prophetic writings; and (5) It is impossible for the Qur'an and the law of Muhammad to have emerged from the Law of Moses and the other prophetic writings.[43]

Summary

Building Blocks

The building blocks that each work uses for a narrow definition of the term "apologetics" are: *Catecismo* (the excellence and divinity of Christ, the Scriptures, and testimonies), *Catecismo provechoso* (the Christian law and faith), *Diálogos Christianos* (the Scriptures and testimonies), *Catecismo del Sacromonte* (the Scriptures and the Catholic Church), and *Antialcorano* (the sonship of Jesus Christ and the gospel).

---

41. Pérez de Ayala, *Catecismo*, 247–49.

42. This section on the truthfulness of the Christian Law could have been assigned to "The Christian Law," but it is presented here to contrast how the *Catecismo* and *Diálogos Christianos* explain "testimonies."

43. Pons Fuster, *Diálogos Christianos*, 427–32.

Differences

Jesus Christ is a feature only in the apologetics of *Catecismo* and *Antialcorano*. However, only the Teacher states specifically that the foundation of his apologetics is "the excellence and divinity of Christ." *Catecismo* and *Antialcorano* explain the divinity or Sonship of Jesus Christ in terms of the dignity of Christ, the messiahship of Christ, and the miracles of Christ (*Catecismo*) and the sun and sunlight, the work that Christ did, and the Scriptures (*Antialcorano*). *Catecismo provechoso*, *Diálogos Christianos*, and *Catecismo del Sacromonte* have a different foundation for their apologetics, but there is no evidence to suggest that the divinity or the Sonship of Christ is unimportant in these works.

Common Features

The building blocks of apologetics of these five catechisms and polemical treatises have six common features: (1) Jesus Christ. Both his humanity[44] and divinity.[45] His divinity is synonymous with the phrase "Sonship of Jesus Christ" (*Antialcorano*); (2) The gospel (*Antialcorano*). This term and Christian Law (*Catecismo provechoso*) are synonymous because of the context of Chapter II of *Catecismo provechoso*.[46] "Gospel" can also be understood as the "good news" of Catholic doctrine embodied in the Creed, the Ten Commandments, the Sacraments, and the Lord's Prayer; (3) The Scriptures (*Catecismo, Diálogos Christianos*, and *Catecismo del Sacromonte*); (4) Christian Faith (*Catecismo provechoso*); (5) Testimonies (*Catecismo* and *Diálogos Christianos*); and (6) The Catholic Church (*Catecismo del Sacromonte*).

Connection

These six common features may be connected as follows: What can be known about the humanity and divinity of Jesus Christ is presented in the gospel/Christian law. This gospel/Christian law is not a collection of fabricated or imaginary stories, but is grounded in the Scriptures as taught and defended by the Catholic Church. Moors or Moriscos who wish to believe in Jesus Christ should exercise faith. The lives of those who exercise faith

---

44. The "excellence" portion of the phrase "the excellence and divinity of Christ" in the *Catecismo*.

45. The "divinity" portion of the phrase "the excellence and divinity of Christ" in the *Catecismo*.

46. Orozco, *Catecismo provechoso*, 10 [l].

have been changed (Testimonies: Catecismo). "Testimonies" refer to lives changed by the gospel (*Catecismo*) or evidence that the Christian law is truthful (*Diálogos Christianos*).

Basic Definition of Apologetics

This first part of Chapter 10 concludes with a definition of the concept "apologetics." The apostle Paul was commissioned for "the defense (ἀπολογίαν) of the gospel (τοῦ εὐαγγελίου)" (Phil 1:16). The Christians in Philippi worked with him in "the defense (τῇ ἀπολογίᾳ) and confirmation of the gospel" (Phil 1:7). The apostle Peter encouraged Christians living in Pontus, Galatia, Cappadocia, Asia, and Bithynia (1 Pet 3:1) to be ready at all times "to make a defense" (ἕτοιμοι πρὸς ἀπολογίαν) to anyone who asked them why they were Christians (1 Pet 3:15). The meaning of "defense (ἀπολογία)" in these three instances is "the speech act of attempting to prove some act or belief to be reasonable, necessary, or right; especially occurring in a court of law."[47]

Specific Definition

None of the authors in the Group of twelve or *Catecismo* offer a definition of apologetics. They are not before a court of law *per se*, but responding to the criticisms or attacks from Moors and Moriscos. Two things need proof: an act and a belief.

Belief

The *Catecismo* and others prove three cardinal beliefs. First, Jesus Christ is the Son of God. Second, the Trinity is not three gods, but one divine being in three persons. Third, the Scriptures have been carefully preserved since the time of the Old Testament. These catechisms and polemical treatises use "natural and moral reasons and facts"[48] to prove that it is "reasonable, necessary, *and* right" to believe that Jesus Christ is the Son of God;[49] God cannot be God without being triune and one;[50] and the Scriptures could not have been corrupted.[51]

---

47. Brannan, *Lexham Research Lexicon of the Greek New Testament*.
48. See Round One, Event 6 in Chapter 6 and Round Three, Event 2 in Chapter 8.
49. See "Jesus Christ: Bridging the Gap" above in Chapter 6.
50. See "The Trinity: A Common Misunderstanding" above in Chapter 6.
51. See "The Integrity of the Christian Scriptures: Bridging the Gap" in Chapter 6.

Act

The evidence for the act is provided not only by the authors, but also by the faithful. Both of them prove that it is "reasonable, necessary, *and* right" to behave (act) according to the teachings of the Roman Church as contained in the Creed, the Sacraments, the Ten Commandments, and the Lord's Prayer. Moors and Moriscos prove that they are no longer followers of the sect of Muhammad, but Catholics when they live by (act according to) these teachings. Two versions of the specific definition of apologetics in the context of Christian and Muslim relations in sixteenth-century Spain can now be presented.

Version 1 (drawing on the information above under "Summary"): "Apologetics is the use of the Scriptures as taught and defended by the Catholic Church to prove that it is 'reasonable, necessary and right' for Moors and Moriscos to believe in the humanity and divinity of Jesus Christ presented in the gospel/Christian law."

Version 2 (based on the above presentation on *belief* and *act*): "Apologetics is the use of 'natural and moral reasons and facts' to prove that it is 'reasonable, necessary and right' for Moors and Moriscos (1) to believe that Jesus Christ is God; that God is one being in three persons; and that the Scriptures have been carefully preserved and (2) to act according to the teachings of the Catholic Church embodied in the Creed, the Sacraments, the Ten Commandments, and the Lord's Prayer."

POLEMICS

Preparation

The *Catecismo* does not discuss Muhammad until Book One, Dialogue XIII.[52] The Teacher uses the preceding twelve dialogues ("pre-apologetics") to prepare for the sensitive phase of his conversation with the Moor. After the Moor confirms that his motivation for becoming a Christian is genuine, the Teacher gives him instructions on what to do before they start their discussions: (1) Ask God for light to open his mind and soften his heart; (2) Rely on God to forsake sin; and (3) Abandon the doctrines of his ancestors.[53]

At their next meeting, the Moor says that he complied with the first two instructions, but had difficulty with the third one. The Moor admits that it is "very difficult" for a man to "suddenly leave the errors and

---

52. Pérez de Ayala, *Catecismo*, 81–95.
53. Pérez de Ayala, *Catecismo*, 8–11.

THE CONTENT OF THE NEW *CATECISMO*: APOLOGETICS AND POLEMICS 235

opinions" of his ancestors[54] and that leaving would depend on what kind of information the Teacher will be giving him. Although he is not specific about the type of errors and opinions, the discussion above in Chapter 4 on The Triple Challenge[55] gives an idea. The Moor's admission alerts the Teacher and other priests expected to use this *Catecismo* that The Triple Challenge is indeed a formidable one.

Pre-Apologetics

After the Moor asks "Father, tell me briefly what order will your instruction follow,"[56] the Teacher answers with (1) Recognize that the beginning of health is knowing God. There is a God, he is one, and he rules the universe; (2) Know oneself and one's final destination. This final destination shows that there is only one God; (3) The path to God is the true religion. The truthfulness of this religion shows that it cannot be known naturally, but only by divine revelation. There cannot be many religions that are true—only one religion is true; (4) Examine the religions of the world and prove that the sect of Muhammad is false and the Christian religion is the only true religion; and (5) Learn what new converts need to know about the Christian religion.[57]

Pre-Polemics

The order of instruction above is what the present book has designated as "pre-apologetics" because it precedes the section on apologetics material. However, it would also be appropriate to label this same material as "pre-polemics." The pre-apologetics/pre-polemics material of the *Catecismo* is found in Dialogues III-XII of Book One. A sample of the content of some of the dialogues: What is God (Dialogue III), what is man (Dialogue V), philosophy is not the path to God (Dialogue XI), and Judaism is also not the path to God (Dialogue XII). The polemics material is presented in Dialogues XIII-XIX. A sample of the content of some of the dialogues: The sect of Muhammad is not the path to God (Dialogue XIII) and the sect of Muhammad is false because of the way it was spread (Dialogue XIX). The apologetics

---

54. Pérez de Ayala, *Catecismo*, 12.

55. The confession of the Moors (what is in their hearts); their beliefs (what is in their minds); and their behavior (what they have to obey).

56. Pérez de Ayala, *Catecismo*, 13.

57. Pérez de Ayala, *Catecismo*, 13-14.

material is covered in Dialogues XX-XXV. A sample of the content of some of the dialogues: The Christian religion is the only and necessary path to God (Dialogue XX) and the gospel is true because of the virtues of those who embraced it (Dialogue XXV).

Discussion of this material is indispensable. By the time the topics shift to Muhammad, the Qur'an, and the sect of Muhammad in Dialogue XIII, the Moor is receptive to continuing the discussion. The Moor reveals that he is "very satisfied" with the Teacher's reasons for why philosophy and Judaism are not the paths to God.

Preliminary Definition

The Moor does not define polemics. If he were asked, he would define it as "the destruction of the sect of Muhammad." In Dialogue XIII, he asks for "the reasons" the Prelate (Pérez de Ayala) uses "to destroy the sect" of his ancestors. The Teacher also does not define polemics. If he were asked, he would agree that polemics involves destruction, but also an examination of "the goodness or wickedness of the law of Muhammad." He tells the Moor, "Many things are necessary to . . . destroy and examine a law that is introduced as a religion."[58] Neither of the following preliminary definitions of polemics state that its purpose is to destroy Muhammad: "Polemics means the destruction of the religion of Muhammad." (The Moor.) "Polemics is the examination of the goodness or wickedness of the law or religion of Muhammad to destroy it." (The Teacher.) A revised definition of polemics is available at the end of this chapter.

Examination

According to the Teacher, the following should be examined: (1) The person who introduced the law;[59] (2) The destination of those who follow this law;[60] (3) What this law forbids and permits;[61] and (4) Reasons for this law and its mode of expansion.[62] The remainder of this chapter examines these four points.

---

58. Pérez de Ayala, *Catecismo*, 82–84.
59. Pérez de Ayala, *Catecismo*, 81–95.
60. Pérez de Ayala, *Catecismo*, 95–106.
61. Pérez de Ayala, *Catecismo*, 106–20, 125–32.
62. Pérez de Ayala, *Catecismo*, 139–64.

Muhammad: The Prophet Who Introduced a New Law

Catecismo

Muhammad was a false prophet because of his inability to perform miracles. He tried to excuse this inability by saying that God had only sent him to announce his message (sura 6 and sura 12). He came announcing "blasphemies, lies, discord, bloodshed." If he brought any happiness, it was the "beastly and carnal" type leading to "sadness and tears." Damned (*el maldito*) adulterer, perjurer, robber, murderer, blasphemer, and extremely ignorant of human and divine knowledge. He was a "complete idiot" who did not know history, philosophy of the Scriptures, but only knew how to fight and kill.[63] He did not even have a "shadow of the prophetic spirit."[64] Robber, violent, adulterous, and of the flesh. Lost and fickle.[65] His speech was crude (Dialogue XX). His "one thousand heresies" make him as much of a heretic as Arius, Eutyches, Mani, Marcion, Nestorius and Valentinus.[66] He was a false prophet also because he made the false claim that he had come "to reform and temper" law of Christ, which he (Muhammad) described as "too rigorous."[67] The Moor said that Muslims believe that Muhammad is mentioned in the Scriptures of the Christian religion. The Teacher retorted and said that if that were the case, Muhammad is mentioned in Revelation 6—the red horse. Revelation 12 speaks of the dragon that destroyed one-third of the word's population with its tail.[68] Muhammad was a false prophet because his entire doctrine was "deceptions and lies."[69] He was fearful that someone would find out the truth so he told his followers not to argue about his doctrines, but to defend them with the sword and not to talk to Christians and Jews for they were the only ones capable of exposing him.[70]

---

63. Pérez de Ayala, *Catecismo*, 206.
64. Pérez de Ayala, *Catecismo*, 159.
65. Pérez de Ayala, *Catecismo*, 173.
66. Pérez de Ayala, *Catecismo*, 88, 203.
67. Pérez de Ayala, *Catecismo*, 154, 171–72.
68. Pérez de Ayala, *Catecismo*, 157.
69. Pérez de Ayala, *Catecismo*, 159.
70. Pérez de Ayala, *Catecismo*, 161–62.

Confusión o confutación

Muhammad was a false prophet for being "the son of contradiction and discord"[71] and "spreading falsehood to ignorant Moors."[72] He was "perverse and evil" for deceiving simple people with "lies, senseless words, stupidities, mad words, blasphemies, tactless words, absurdities, and contradictions" in the Qur'an.[73]

Doctrina Christiana

This catechism has four parts. Only the fourth part focused on critiquing Muhammad because the objective of *Doctrina Christiana* was to instruct new Christians on what they must not believe and do. People who want to be good Christians must not believe that Muhammad was a "man of God," but "firmly believe" that he was a "very bad man, a liar, lustful and demon-possessed." He was illiterate[74] for he claimed that he could not read or write. He was an idolater who kissed and worshiped the black stone in Mecca and asked others to do likewise. He was not a prophet because he knew neither what happened in the past nor what will happen in the future. He was a murderer and a "tyrant" for taking kingdoms that were not his. He also took possession of women who belonged to other men; spoke heresies ("Believe in God and in Muhammad his messenger."); and claimed that his name was written on God's throne ("There are only God and Muhammad his messenger").[75]

Antialcorano

Chinchón exhorted his readers (canons, rectors, vicars and church leaders) to teach the newly baptized Moors in their dioceses in Aragón, Granada and Valencia to believe in Christ who was "chaste and truly fully God and fully

---

71. Ruiz García, *Juan Andrés*, 89.
72. Ruiz García, *Juan Andrés*, 92.
73. Ruiz García, *Juan Andrés*, 91.
74. The word *ummī* in the Qur'an means "illiterate," but Western scholars and many Muslim scholars refute the idea that Muhammad was illiterate. The plural—*ummiyyūn*—does not refer to those who cannot read, but to those who do not possess a sacred book. The statement that Muhammad was "the prophet to the *ummiyyūn*" means that he considered himself to be a prophet to the pagans, not to the Jews and the Christians, who already had a sacred text. Samir, *111 Questions on Islam*, Kindle location 538.
75. Resines, *El Catecismo de Pedro Ramiro de Alba*, 168.

man" instead of Muhammad who was "a killer, a liar, and a false prophet who taught a false law."[76] His claim to prophethood can be shown to be false when his life is compared with the life of Christ[77] and the lives of those who follow Christ.[78] The paradise he described is a place where men can satisfy their physical (eating and drinking) and sexual appetites to the fullest because he himself pursued these appetites, particularly the sexual ones for he had eleven wives.[79] It was a "great madness" of Muhammad to claim that he made a trip to the heavens where he learned that only he could intercede for others on the day of judgment, but Adam, Noah, Abraham, Moses, and John the Baptist would not be able to.[80] By comparison, *Confutación del alcorán y secta mahometana* refers to Muhammad as "damned Muhammad," demon-possessed, and an idolater. *Catecismo provechoso* describes Muhammad as an "uneducated, demon-possessed, liar; a thug and an idiot."[81]

Catecheses mystagogicae

Muhammad was a "false prophet";[82] a "minister of the devil"; a "nefarious prophet";[83] a "demonic man full of lies"; "completely wrapped up in errors"; an "abominable man who brings forth evil from the wickedness of his heart's treasure";[84] "that most false and lost little man . . . thoroughly armed with a diabolical spirit"; "this most impious and perverse prophet"; "seized by I know not what insanity";[85] a "most foul man (if he is to be called a man and not rather more appropriately a devil";[86] a "most vile merchant, a leader of thieves, a messenger of Satan, precursor of the Antichrist, the complement

---

76. Pons Fuster, *Antialcorano. Diálogos Christianos*, 271, 285.
77. Pons Fuster, *Antialcorano. Diálogos Christianos*, 247–59.
78. Pons Fuster, *Antialcorano. Diálogos Christianos*, 367–83.
79. Pons Fuster, *Antialcorano. Diálogos Christianos*, 166–67.
80. Pons Fuster, *Antialcorano. Diálogos Christianos*, 271.
81. Orozco, *Catecismo provechoso*, 13–16.
82. Busic, "Saving the Lost Sheep," 251, 261, 286, 308, 310.
83. Busic, "Saving the Lost Sheep," 251.
84. Busic, "Saving the Lost Sheep," 255.
85. Busic, "Saving the Lost Sheep," 258.
86. Busic, "Saving the Lost Sheep," 263.

of all falseness and heresy";[87] and "that most foul one of a dog."[88] His mouth was "blasphemous"[89] and he is "buried in hell."[90]

Catecismo del Sacromonte

Muhammad claimed to be the prophet of God who brought a new law. But, the law of Muhammad is "bad and unjust." God would not have given such a law. Muhammad lied. Prophets of God do not lie. The fact that a liar like Muhammad was a fool and an idiot is a "divine favor." If he had known how to read and write, he would have caused more damage than the heretics. God only allowed Satan to enter into the serpent instead of a beautiful animal like the eagle. It was a divine favor that God had not allowed Muhammad to be a nobleman, a philosopher or a theologian, but just a merchant. Otherwise, he would have done more harm.[91]

Muhammad was "very dirty, unjust and perverse" and commanded his followers not to wrangle over his law; not to believe the Christians and the Jews; not to talk to them; and to use force to defend his law because he was afraid that his lies would be discovered.[92] He was the "damned enemy of God"[93]—"arrogant, ambitious, and pretended to pursue peace with others," but betrayed the people of Medina after they had welcome him and his soldiers from Mecca. His sexual sins and his encouragement to his followers to do likewise disqualify him from being called "a messenger of God."[94]

Muhammad was "an abominable blasphemer and a traitor" who never confessed his sins or showed contrition and was worse than Lucifer for placing himself at the same level as God. Q. 4:80: "He who obeys the Messenger, has indeed obeyed Allah, but he who turns away, then We have not sent you as a watcher over them (Hilali & Khan)."[95] The devil taught him to use brute force to defend his law.[96]

---

87. Busic, "Saving the Lost Sheep," 275.
88. Busic, "Saving the Lost Sheep," 276.
89. Busic, "Saving the Lost Sheep," 255.
90. Busic, "Saving the Lost Sheep," 251.
91. Resines, *Catecismo del Sacromonte*, 206.
92. Resines, *Catecismo del Sacromonte*, 247.
93. Resines, *Catecismo del Sacromonte*, 247, 250.
94. Resines, *Catecismo del Sacromonte*, 249.
95. Resines, *Catecismo del Sacromonte*, 250.
96. Resines, *Catecismo del Sacromonte*, 305.

Summary

The catechisms and polemical treatises sought to prove that Muhammad lacked the credentials to be the founder of a doctrine, a sect or a religion that anyone should follow. The harshest critique comes from Lorca's *Catecheses mystagogicae*. The other authors are gentle by comparison. Their verdict is unanimous: Muhammad was a false prophet.

Paradise

Catecismo

Description

This section focuses on describing the paradise that the Law of Muhammad designed for men. The next section concentrates on evaluating it. The Teacher uses what is recorded in the Qur'an and is careful not to inject his own interpretation or commentary. Paradise has women with "big and clear eyes"; beautiful virgins with white skin;[97] all types of fruits and fountains flowing with milk and honey; and beds of gold, garments of fine brocade, jewelry, and even some animals[98]. If there were no women, the "blessing of paradise would be incomplete without carnal pleasures."[99] This paradise satisfies all of the physical and sensual wants of a man. He will be able to drink and eat as much as he craves and even get married.

Evaluation

Although the Teacher claims that he can give an "infinite number"[100] of reasons for why the Law of Muhammad should not be followed, he makes his final evaluation from a wide and narrow angle.

Wide Angle

Man's blessing consists of the "absolute perfection" of his "soul and its powers"; that is, his "understanding and will." Man was "created so perfectly" that

---

97. Pérez de Ayala, *Catecismo*, 95.
98. Pérez de Ayala, *Catecismo*, 97.
99. Pérez de Ayala, *Catecismo*, 102.
100. Pérez de Ayala, *Catecismo*, 97.

his destination cannot be the same as the one for brute animals. Both of them should have separate destinations. The blessing of man should bring him "tranquility and happiness"—not "discontent and tiredness" caused by appetites that are difficult to be satisfied fully. So, the blessing of man should be spiritual instead of physical, which requires food and drink. If there is marriage and eating and drinking in paradise as Muhammad taught, there would be "digestions and egestions, sleeping, offspring and sickness."[101]

If blessing on earth includes unlimited eating and drinking, there is no need to go to paradise because food and drink are in abundant supply on earth. Eating and drinking in paradise are superfluous because hunger and thirst will not exist. Marriages will be pointless because everyone will live forever and there will no need to preserve the human race. If Muhammad had intended for physical delights to be understood in the "mystical sense," he should have said so. However, the Qur'an is silent.[102]

The Qur'an reveals that every kind of fruit—including grapes and pomegranates—abounds in paradise together with rivers of honey, milk, wine, and fresh water (Q. 47:15; Q. 44:55). Eating, drinking, marriage to *houris*, and sexuality are an indispensable part of the anthropocentric imagery of paradise.[103] Q. 2:25 declares what people will eat in paradise:

> And give glad tidings to those who believe and do righteous good deeds, that for them will be gardens under which rivers flow (paradise). Every time they will be provided with a fruit therefrom, they will say: "This is what we were provided with before," and they will be given things in resemblance (i.e. in the same form but different in taste) and they shall have therein purified mates or wives, (having no menses, stools, urine, etc.) and they will abide therein forever.

Narrow Angle

Not only secular philosophers and religions, but also philosophers of the sect of Muhammad condemn Muhammad's teaching on paradise. Philosophers say that a man who is debauched and carnal is the type of man who thinks and teaches that such a paradise exists. Condemnation also comes from religions, but the Teacher does not elaborate. The Teacher mentions three of the philosophers of the sect of Muhammad who reprehend Muhammad's

---

101. Pérez de Ayala, *Catecismo*, 98–99.
102. Pérez de Ayala, *Catecismo*, 99.
103. Wild, "Paradise," 487.

depiction of paradise: Ibn Sina or Avicenna, Aben Ruyz, and Al-Ghazali. The Law of Muhammad underlines corporal pleasure, but "wise theologians" strive for blessing through understanding instead of pleasure (Ibn Sina). The Law of Muhammad is problematic because it places men in paradise who are simultaneously "eternal, corruptible and reproducible" (Aben Ruyz). Al-Ghazali is mentioned, but no details are given regarding the specifics of his criticism of the Law of Muhammad.[104]

Response

The Moor informs the Teacher that he (the Moor) understands that Muhammad erred and asks the Teacher not to "waste more words" on this topic, but to proceed to next one.[105]

The Law of Muhammad: Permissions and Proscriptions

Catecismo

The Law of Muhammad contains "doctrines that are toxic to good morals."[106] The Teacher refers specifically to marriage, divorce, fornication, sodomy, vengeance, and war and violence. The section below highlights the Teacher's understanding of those doctrines and his evaluation of each.

Marriage

Men can have four wives at the same time. The Teacher explains why this is against "nature and reason" and against God. Even Gentiles recognize that having many wives simultaneously causes jealousy and frequent discord; dissipates the man's property; and is a bad way to raise children. Polygamy is also against what God ordained. He gave Adam only one female companion. The Moor rebuts by saying that he has heard that many good men in old times had more than one wife. The Teacher uses the lives of four men—Abraham, Lamech, King David, and King Solomon—to demonstrate why polygamy is against the will of God. By the time the Teacher

---

104. Pérez de Ayala, *Catecismo*, 105–6.
105. Pérez de Ayala, *Catecismo*, 106.
106. Pérez de Ayala, *Catecismo*, 113.

finishes his explanation, the Moor admits that his doubts on this matter have been removed.[107]

Divorce

A husband can divorce his wife and marry another woman. A wife can divorce her husband and marry another man. The Teacher explains that this permission is "against God" and "against nature." It is against God because he wants the husband and the wife to be one flesh. It is against nature because the license to divorce instills in the husband a craving for many women and destroys marital fidelity and love. The ease of divorce gives a husband an excuse to find any fault in his wife just so he can divorce her. Divorce was never licit in God's plan. Moses permitted divorce to avoid a greater evil; that is, husbands killing their wives.[108]

Fornication

The Law of Muhammad sanctions fornication. Q. 23:1 and 6 states: "The believers have prospered . . . who guard their private parts, except from their wives or what their right (hands) own—surely then they are not (to be) blamed" (Droge). The Teacher comments that the chastity ("guard private parts") spoken of in this *sura* is an "amusing chastity" (*donoso castidad*) that "mocks the virtue of continence" and opens the door to sodomy.[109] The expression "what their right (hands) own" refers to female slaves (cf. Q. 4:3, 24).[110]

Sodomy

Q. 2:223: "Your women are (like) a field for you, so come to your field when you wish, and send forward (something) for yourselves" (Droge). The Teacher interprets this *ayah* as teaching sodomy—a "brutal sin" that is "against nature."[111] The phrase "send forward (something) for yourselves"

---

107. Pérez de Ayala, *Catecismo*, 114–18.
108. Pérez de Ayala, *Catecismo*, 118–19.
109. Pérez de Ayala, *Catecismo*, 119.
110. Droge, *The Qur'ān: A New Annotated Translation*, 24.
111. Pérez de Ayala, *Catecismo*, 119.

probably means children, but is usually interpreted as doing or saying something pious before sexual intercourse.[112]

Vengeance

All injuries should be dealt with according to *lex talionis* (Q. 2:178–79). But, the Teacher remarks that this is "against all charity" and "the peace of the republic."[113]

War and Violence

God only opens the doors of paradise to those who have exerted themselves in battle. Those who follow a different law than Muhammad's should be killed. However, the Teacher mentions that war and violence are contrary to the "humanity and benevolence" that people owe each other in their capacity as human beings.[114]

Response

As mentioned previously, the Moor only reacts after the Teacher has finished evaluating what the Law of Muhammad teaches about marriage. He is silent after hearing what the Teacher said about divorce, fornication, sodomy, vengeance, and war and violence. If he were asked, he might have also said that his doubts about these matters have been removed.

The Law of Muhammad: Reasons and Mode of Expansion

Catecismo

The notion of "reasons" refers to the two types of reasons or questions that people with a free will need to think about or ask before they accept and follow a law. If a law or doctrine is of human origin, it should be rooted in "natural and human reasons." If a law has "divine or supernatural" origin, it

---

112. Droge, *The Qurʾān: A New Annotated Translation*, 24.
113. Pérez de Ayala, *Catecismo*, 120.
114. Pérez de Ayala, *Catecismo*, 120.

should be grounded on "divine reasons." The Teacher examines whether or not the Law of Muhammad has both types of reasons.[115]

Divine Reasons

The Law of Muhammad was not revealed by God for it lacks an authentic testimony of God. The Moor asks the first one of the two crucial questions: "Is it not enough for God to say that the law comes from him?"[116] Yes, it is enough, but even God had to prove himself. It is not enough to believe the person who makes claims. Muhammad claimed that God had sent him and that the Qur'an contains the doctrines of God yet threatened anyone who rejected him (Muhammad) and his claims. However, there must be testimony—reasons—to persuade reasonable people with freedom of the will to believe. Even if Muhammad had been a saint, he would still lack the authority to issue a new law in the name of God—especially when this new law intends to repeal what God has already revealed. Claims must be accompanied by miracles, which are deeds that only God is capable of doing. Otherwise, anyone can claim that God had chosen him to be his messenger.[117] The Teacher compares Moses, Jesus, and Jesus' apostles with Muhammad.

Moses, Jesus, and Jesus' Apostles

Moses performed miracles to prove that God had chosen him to lead the people of Israel out of Egypt.[118] Jesus performed miracles. People saw them and believed that he had come according to the will of God. He had done so many miracles that John could not write them all. The purpose of those that he did record in his gospel is to help people believe that Jesus is the Christ, the Son of God, and that believing in him they may have life (John 20:30–31).[119] The apostles of Jesus also did miracles (Acts 2, 3, 10, 28).[120] By comparison, Muhammad excused his inability to perform miracles. He claimed that God sent him to be his messenger—not a miracle worker. The messenger just declares God's precepts and does not do miracles (Q. 6:37, 48, 109; Q. 2:119). But, God—who is "supreme truth and goodness"—would

---

115. Pérez de Ayala, *Catecismo*, 139.
116. Pérez de Ayala, *Catecismo*, 140.
117. Pérez de Ayala, *Catecismo*, 142–43.
118. Pérez de Ayala, *Catecismo*, 142–43.
119. Pérez de Ayala, *Catecismo*, 144.
120. Pérez de Ayala, *Catecismo*, 147.

not have validated the "blasphemous and carnal law" of Muhammad—"a robber and an adulterer"—with miracles.[121]

Natural Reasons

Muhammad was unable to provide divine reasons so the Moor asks the second crucial question: "By what means was Muhammad able to persuade so many people?" The Teacher's answer: violence (robbery, death, and bloodshed) and license for the flesh.[122] These two modes of expansion also indicate that the Law of Muhammad has no natural reasons to compel people with a free will to follow.[123]

Experience teaches that no one believes out of fear. But, Moors counter by saying that Christians also fight. The Teacher replies: Christians do fight, but only to defend themselves. They have the right to protect themselves from those who disturb them; to free themselves from vexations; and to recover what was taken away from them. The Church never uses physical force, but uses persuasion to convince people to believe.[124]

When asked for natural reasons, Moors say that they are Moors because of their parents. But, a Christian who is a Christian because his or her parents are Christians, is not a Christian. They do not believe in God, but in their parents to whom they are still attached to. On the day of judgment, the Moors will not be able to justify themselves for not believing in the gospel. Everyone can use reason and free will to determine whether or not what is preached to them is helpful or harmful. If the father throws himself out of a window, should his son do likewise? If the father travels on the wrong road, should the son travel on that same road even when everyone is telling him that it is the wrong road?[125]

Response

The Law of Muhammad lacks divine reasons and its mode of expansion confirms that it also lacks natural and human reasons. The Moor does not

---

121. Pérez de Ayala, *Catecismo*, 148.
122. See above "The Law of Muhammad: Permissions and Proscriptions."
123. Pérez de Ayala, *Catecismo*, 150–52.
124. Pérez de Ayala, *Catecismo*, 150–52.
125. Pérez de Ayala, *Catecismo*, 152–53.

disagree or try to counter argue. He says to the Teacher, "I am pleased with how well you disputed against my sect. Your rationale is persuasive."[126]

Definition of Polemics

The material presented in the discussion above can now be brought together to provide the following definition of polemics in the context of Christian and Muslim relations in sixteenth-century Spain: "Polemics is the examination or evaluation of four key components of the Law of Muhammad: (1) Muhammad, the one who introduced this law; (2) paradise, the destination of those who follow this law; (3) the permissions and proscriptions of this law; and (4) the reasons behind this law and how it expanded."

Apologetics and Polemics: The Connection

We continue to adopt the analogy of competitive sports presented in Chapters 5 to 9. Apologetics and polemics may be viewed as "defense" and "offense," respectively. Apologetics concentrates on defending Christian *belief* and Catholic *behavior* against the attacks (criticisms) of the Moors and Moriscos. Polemics focuses on putting Moors and Moriscos on the defensive by attacking (examining or evaluating) the Law of Muhammad. The action of putting the other side on the defensive (attacking)—playing offense—does not have to be offensive provided the catechism or polemical treatise is "charitable and friendly"[127] and does not inflame the emotions of the Moors or Moriscos.[128]

---

126. Pérez de Ayala, *Catecismo*, 158.

127. Round Two, Event 2. Is the tone of the catechism or polemical treatise "charitable and friendly"?

128. Round Two, Event 3. Could the catechism or polemical treatise inflame the emotions of the Moriscos?

Chapter 11

Juan de Ribera's *Catecismo*

Martín Pérez de Ayala's Legacy

Step 3

STEP 3 IS THE final step of the process used to evaluate the *Catecismo*. The objectives of the previous steps:

> Step 1: Apply the sixteen criteria to assess the *Catecismo* and the Group of twelve.
>
> Step 2: Analyze the results from Step 1 for apologetical and polemical content.

The objective of Step 3 is to use the results from Step 2 to offer preliminary answers to two questions: What was the potential of the *Catecismo* as an evangelistic tool addressed to Moriscos and why did archbishop Juan de Ribera choose the *Catecismo* to bolster his own evangelistic task in 1599—thirty-three years after Pérez de Ayala had passed away and ten years before the decree of Philip III in 1609 that launched the process to expel the Moriscos from Spain?

The answers draw on: (1) The results of the four rounds presented in Chapters 6 to 9; (2) Extra features; (3) The situation in Valencia before and during the time of Ribera; and (4) Ribera's vision.

Results After Four Rounds

The *Catecismo* meets the following sixteen criteria (each criterion is an event):

Round One. Six Events

(1) The *Catecismo* is not written for children; (2) it is addressed to rectors, preachers, and confessors; (3) it is a handbook and a primer on both Catholic doctrine and Muhammad, his doctrines, and his sect; (4) presents apologetic material that addresses the usual objections raised by Islamic clerics; (5) gives an exposition on the life and doctrines of Muhammad; and (6) introduces theological concepts adapted to the abilities and talents of the Moriscos.

Round Two. Four Events

(7) The *Catecismo* discusses all the material needed to teach the gospel to an unbeliever—especially, someone who comes from the sect of Muhammad; (8) the tone of the *Catecismo* is "charitable and friendly"; (9) does not inflame the emotions of the Moriscos; and (10) uses "common and ordinary terms" to preach "intelligible doctrine" so that Moriscos know what they must believe and do.

Round Three. Four Events

(11) The Teacher (Pérez de Ayala) has experience talking with and instructing Moriscos; *Catecismo* (12) uses "natural and moral reasons and facts" to show the "purity and beauty" of the religion of Christ; (13) employs "natural and moral reasons and facts" to show the "clumsiness and blunders" of the sect of Muhammad; and (14) uses the format of a dialogue.

Round Four. Two Events

The *Catecismo* (15) is aware of The Triple Challenge and (16) grapples with all three challenges.

Extra Features

This section presents extra features that further differentiate the *Catecismo* from *Catecismo provechoso*. In the parlance of competitive sports, the goal posts have not been moved. The *Catecismo* has already won all four rounds. These extra features are not criteria introduced at the last-minute to help the *Catecismo* cross the finish line, but show how strong a competitor the *Catecismo* is. The extra features are: (1) Religious Background of the Catechumen; (2) Introduction to Polemics; (3) The Eucharist; and (4) Felipe and the Moor: Insight into the Triple Challenge.

Religious Background of the Catechumen

The only catechisms and polemical treatises that use the format of a dialogue are *Diálogos Christianos*, *Catecismo provechoso*, *Catecismo del Sacromonte*, and *Catecismo*.[1] Of the four dialogue participants—Joseph (*Diálogos Christianos*), Felipe (*Catecismo provechoso*), the novice (*Catecismo del Sacromonte*), and the Moor (*Catecismo*)—only the Moor is still a Moor when the dialogue begins. The other three used to be Moors, but have already become "adopted children of God" and followers of the Christian religion. They and the Moor are not interested in discussing the same areas. This difference is noticeable in the case of Felipe.[2] Given that the Moor is still a Moor,[3] his dialogue with the Teacher would have helped a priest using the *Catechism* gain insight into the ways a Moor thinks about Muhammad and his sect; misconceptions that a Moor has about the Christian religion; barriers that a Moor must overcome before becoming a follower of the religion of Christ; questions that Moors ask for which the priest must be prepared to answer; and how to communicate the Christian religion so that a Moor can understand; that is, close the gap.[4]

Many priests prior to Ribera's arrival in Valencia were poorly educated and ill-equipped for their ministry to Moriscos.[5] The *Catecismo* not only taught a priest about *how* a Moor thinks, but also about his own Christian religion (doctrine *and* practice).

Introduction to Polemics

Another feature that further distinguishes the *Catecismo* from *Catecismo provechoso* is the manner in which polemics is discussed. Manner not only refers to *what* is discussed, but also *when* the discussion takes place. The Triple Challenge informs priests that Moriscos have the highest regards for

 1. See "Round Three, Event 4" above in Chapter 8.
 2. See the extra feature "Felipe and the Moor: Insight Into The Triple Challenge."
 3. From the very beginning of the *Catecismo*, the Moor and the Teacher are identified with the letters "D" for "discipulo" (disciple) and "M" for "Maestro" (teacher), respectively. It would have been more accurate to have given different letters to the Moor; for example, "MB" for "Moro de Berberia" (Moor from the Berber region) for he is a Moor throughout Book One of the *Catecismo* and does not abandon the sect of his forefathers until Dialogue XXV when he says to the Teacher, "I'm convinced and persuaded to receive your holy faith," Pérez de Ayala, *Catecismo*, 252. The Moor would be identified with the letters "MB" in Book One and "D" in Book Two.
 4. See the extra feature "Felipe and The Moor: Insight Into The Triple Challenge."
 5. See the next section—"The Situation in Valencia Before and After Ribera's Arrival."

everything related to their sect, its religious text, its teachings, and its founder. Discussion cannot be premature, but entered into cautiously and pursued carefully. As already noted above, the present book has classified some of the material in the *Catecismo* as "pre-polemics." The presentation below sharpens the contrast between *Catecismo provechoso* and the *Catecismo*.

Catecismo provechoso

Pre-Polemics Material. None.

Polemics Material. 2 chapters. "All sects are false" (Chapter II) and "The Catholic faith condemns the sect of Muhammand (Chapter III).

Catecismo

Pre-Polemics Material. 9 dialogues. "Who is God and how is he one?" (Dialogue XIII); "God governs the universe and takes care of it" (Dialogue IV); "What is man and the perfection and immortality of his soul" (Dialogue V); "Only God and nothing created can be the end of man. True religion is the path to him" (Dialogue VI); "Why man after the disorder of sin cannot find the true path and aim at the true religion by depending on natural light" (Dialogue VII); "Original sin, the corruption of human nature, and what philosophers know about sin" (Dialogue VIII); "Causes and effects of sin and vice" (Dialogue IX); "Evidence that the doctrine of philosophers is false and not the path to God" (Dialogue XI); and "Evidence that the Jewish law cannot be the path to God" (Dialogue XII).

Polemics Material. 7 dialogues. "The sect of Muhammad cannot be the path of God and the vicious life of its lawgiver" (Dialogue XIII); "The Law of Muhammad is false because the end and the blessing that it promises are false" (Dialogue XIV); "The Qur'an contains errors, lies, and fables" (Dialogue XV); "There are many places in the Qur'an where Muhammad contradicts himself" (Dialogue XVI); "The Law of Muhammad is bad because its content is bad" (Dialogue XVII); "The Law of Muhammad is weak and false because its followers are permitted to lie about what they actually believe" (Dialogue XVIII); and "The Law of Muhammad is false because of the way it was preached" (Dialogue XIX).

Catecismo provechoso—like the other catechisms and polemical treatises in the Group of twelve—lacks pre-apologetics material. This material in the *Catecismo* is a gentle, lengthy, and necessary introduction that prepares the Moor for a substantial discussion on everything that a Moor or Morisco believes in firmly. When the discourse on polemics finally begins with Dialogue XIII, the Moor can mention to the Teacher "What you are about to say is not intended to hurt or offend."

The Eucharist

Apostle of the Eucharist. What distinguishes Ribera from other servants of God was his devotion to the Eucharist. This sacrament motivated his actions. Every day he allocated long periods of time to meditate on its significance and draw inspiration and encouragement. His dedication was a role model for the reformation of his clergy and the consecration of his diocesans. He started the habit in his family and diocese of using the greeting "Blessed and praised be this Holiest Sacrament." His affection for this *Misterium Fidei* can be seen in his pastorals, circulars, and numerous practices.[6]

Ribera was an apostle of the Eucharist. The source of his adherence was his love for Christ. The petition *Tibi post haec Fili mihi ultra quid faciam* ("What more can I do for you?") was his personal motto and coat of arms. He used it in furniture, garments, sacred ornaments, facades of buildings, books, and much more.[7]

The most visible expression of Ribera's fidelity to the Eucharist is his Real Colegio de Corpus Christ. The college is regarded as "The greatest monument in the world today of the sternness of Catholic worship."[8] By founding the college and building it with his own funds, Ribera became one of the few bishops to respond promptly to the urging of the Council of Trent to build diocesan seminaries. He explained the purpose of the college's chapel as follows: "I have endeavored to build a chapel in this city so that it can be a testimony of the truth to the ignorant and the faithful few that we ought to be dedicated (to this Holiest Sacrament)."[9] Construction of the chapel took eighteen years (1586–1604) while construction of the college and seminary took twenty-three years (1586–1610). The entire project also showcases Ribera's unstinting support for the fine arts. He commissioned well-known and talented guilders, silversmiths, sculptors, tilers, stonemasons, and glaziers to interpret his vision for the chapel, the college and the seminary.[10]

Ribera was accustomed to spending three to four hours at a time in the chapel even during the winter. He would kneel or stand and be without a chair, a pillow or a bonnet. On one occasion his steward urged him to retire after seeing him in the cold on his knees from morning until evening.

---

6. Boronat y Barrachina, *El B. Juan de Ribera*, 24–25.
7. Boronat y Barrachina, *El B. Juan de Ribera*, 25.
8. Boronat y Barrachina, *El B. Juan de Ribera*, 27.
9. Boronat y Barrachina, *El B. Juan de Ribera*, 262.
10. Robres Lluch, *San Juan de Ribera*, 260–61.

Ribera replied, "Do not be afraid. No one has ever been hurt for honoring God even though what your warm-hearted solicitude sees is discomfort."[11]

Catecismo provechoso and *Catecismo*

Three differences in the explanation of the Eucharist in these two catechisms can be noted: (1) The *amount of material* covered. The *Catecismo provechoso* is briefer than the *Catecismo*; (2) The *content of the material* covered. This difference is a function of the first one. The brevity of presentation impacts what can be covered; and (3) The level of involvement of Felipe (*Catecismo provechoso*) and the Moor (*Catecismo*) in their instruction.

The first and the second differences can be covered simultaneously by highlighting all the material found in the *Catecismo provechoso*. Orozco makes four points: (1) The meaning of this sacrament; (2) The equivalent of participating in this sacrament;[12] (3) The effects of taking the wafer; and (4) The manner in which the wafer should be received.[13]

The third difference sharpens the contrast between these two catechisms. Felipe is silent during his instruction. The Moor, on the other hand, asks eight questions. The following section has three parts: (1) The list of questions that the Moor asks, which brings to the fore the variation between both catechisms; (2) The similarities between both catechisms; and (3) Ribera's choice.

Questions from the Moor about the Eucharist.[14] (1) "What are the main things that must be believed about this sacrament?" (2) "Who confirms that this is indeed so?" (3) "Are only the body and the blood in the bread and the wine?" (4) "What else should be believed about this sacrament?" (5) "How should I prepare myself to receive this sacrament?" (6) "How does this sacrament—which is life—become death to the one who receives it in an unworthy manner?" (7) "How often should I take communion in a year?" and (8) "What are the fruits for and the effects on those who receive this sacrament properly?"

Similarities. *Catecismo provechoso* and *Catecismo* overlap in four areas: (1) The meaning of the sacrament; (2) The sacrament and the remission of sins; (3) The effect of participating in the sacrament; and (4) Preparation to participate in the sacrament.

---

11. Ximenez, *Vida y Virtudes*, 119.
12. Orozco, *Catecismo provechoso*, 100 [l].
13. Orozco, *Catecismo provechoso*, 100 [r].
14. Pérez de Ayala, *Catecismo*, 376–82.

Meaning. The sacrament is "the fount of all grace."[15] In answer to the Moor's request "Now tell me about the Eucharist," the Teacher says that it is "a sacred sign of the grace of Christ communicated in actuality through the bread and the wine that unites the faithful to Christ."[16]

Remission of sins. The faithful worship the real presence of Christ in the bread and the wine.[17] The Moor asks, "What else should be believed about this sacrament?" The Teacher says, "The blood and the body of Christ are true food offered for the remission of the sins of the living and the dead."[18]

Effect. The faithful is moved to "love, glorify, and give thanks to their Creator, their Redeemer, and the One who glorifies them."[19] The Moor asks, "What are the fruits for and the effects on those who receive this sacrament?" The Teacher says, "Union with God; light for knowing and understanding the truth; strength of will against sin; reduction in the desire to sin; aid towards Christian perfection; ability to walk the hard path of life; and firm hope to receive the divine promises."[20]

Preparation. The faithful must receive it with "a clear conscience."[21] The Moor asks, "How should I prepare myself to receive this sacrament?" The Teacher says, "Be armed with a living faith; search and examine your conscience; and find out if you have offended someone and need to be reconciled. There should be no hatred or rancor towards your neighbor."[22]

Ribera's choice. Ribera would agree with the content of *Catecismo provechoso* and *Catecismo*. Which of the two catechisms might he have chosen? Given (1) Ribera's intense devotion to the Eucharist; (2) The *Catecismo's* more detailed discussion of this sacrament; and (3) The potential of the Moor's questions to act as teaching aids. Pastors interested in being more effective in their ministry to Moriscos would know what questions Moriscos are asking about the Eucharist. The pastors could also ask these same questions to their Morisco flock. The *Catecismo's* approach would have been able to engage pastors and Moriscos more than the *Catecismo provechoso* whereby the pastor teaches and the Moriscos listen. Ribera would have chosen the *Catecismo* over the *Catecismo provechoso*.

15. Orozco, *Catecismo provechoso*, 100 [l].
16. Pérez de Ayala, *Catecismo*, 377.
17. Orozco, *Catecismo provechoso*, 100 [l].
18. Pérez de Ayala, *Catecismo*, 378–79.
19. Orozco, *Catecismo provechoso*, 100 [r].
20. Pérez de Ayala, *Catecismo*, 382.
21. Orozco, *Catecismo provechoso*, 100 [r].
22. Pérez de Ayala, *Catecismo*, 379–80.

Felipe and the Moor: Insight into the Triple Challenge

The Triple Challenge[23] was a daunting barrier. The Moor and Felipe may be regarded as living examples of this challenge. Which one of them could have helped a priest in sixteenth-century Spain to understand what influences a Moor or a Morisco to leave the sect of Muhammad?[24] What issues does he wrestle with? What questions does he ask? What does he want to know before he makes the decision to become a follower of the religion of Christ and a member of the Roman Church? These questions help a priest understand his flock and can be condensed into one question: "Which one—Felipe or the Moor—provides insight into *the thinking process* of someone considering leaving the sect of Muhammad for the religion of Christ?" The goal of the next section is to answer this question, which in turn will further differentiate the *Catecismo* and *Catecismo provechoso*. This section is divided into Felipe's questions and statements, the Moor's questions and statements, summary, and Ribera's choice.

Felipe's Questions and Statements

The content of three of the chapters in *Catecismo provechoso*[25] has been categorized as "apologetics" and "polemics."[26] The distribution of questions and statements in these chapters:

> Apologetics. Two chapters (II and IV); one question; eleven statements.
>
> Polemics. Two chapters (II[27] and III); two questions; five statements.

These questions and the main ideas in the statements are presented below. They are followed by a section titled "Remarks," which focuses on aspects of The Triple Challenge that users of the catechism should be aware of.

---

23. The confession of the Moors (what is in their hearts); their beliefs (what is in their minds); and their behavior (what they have to obey).

24. The only difference between the Moors and the Moriscos was that one had been "baptized" (Moriscos) and the other had not (Moors). But, for all practical purposes, Moriscos were still Moors.

25. *Catecismo provechoso* consists of twenty-three chapters and the Lord's Prayer.

26. See above "Alonzo de Orozo: Content" in "Chapter 3. Overview of The *Catecismo* and Other Catechisms and Polemical Treatises in Sixteenth-Century Spain."

27. Some of the material in Chapter II has been categorized as "apologetics" and some as "polemics." See above "Alonzo de Orozo: Content" in "Chapter 3. Overview of The *Catecismo* and Other Catechisms and Polemical Treatises in Sixteenth-Century Spain."

Felipe only asks three questions.[28] One of them is apologetical in nature; two of them are polemical.

Apologetical Question. "What can the creation do to fight against the Holy Church whose foundation is Christ?"[29]

Polemical Questions. "What can you say about the dreams full of vanities that Muhammad used to deceive many souls?"[30] and "I would very much like to know how that happened?"[31] Felipe wants to know how Lucifer and his angels were cast out of heaven.

All of Felipe's statements express agreement with what the priest says. Felipe—unlike the Moor[32]—never challenges or questions what the priest says. The main ideas in these statements:

(1) Felipe's first statement is to declare that it is an "important matter of the soul" for him to be "very attentive" to hear about "the greatness of this Holy Christian law";[33] (2) No one should doubt such an evident truth as God having created everything with his power and governing his creation with wisdom;[34] (3) It is "a great pity" that the Jews—chosen by God to be his—are blind;[35] (4) He requests (not a question) the priest to declare "the lies and vanities" of the followers of the "miserable Muhammad";[36] (5) If the Moors know the truth about Muhammad, they would "worship Jesus Christ, King and Lord of everything created";[37] (6) People owe a debt of gratitude to Christ for what he did for them on the cross. No king on the earth has done so much for his subjects;[38] (7) Christian patience brings peace between the offender and the offended. Evil is borne out of the desire for vengeance;[39] (8) The Qur'an is "fickle" and has "no value";[40] (9) People cannot gain eternal glory through good moral acts;[41] (10) Those who receive God's favor are blessed;[42]

---

28. The Moor asks 33 questions. Please see below.
29. Orozco, *Catecismo provechoso*, 11 [r].
30. Orozco, *Catecismo provechoso*, 12 [r].
31. Orozco, *Catecismo provechoso*, 19 [r].
32. Please see below.
33. Orozco, *Catecismo provechoso*, 10 [l]–10 [r].
34. Orozco, *Catecismo provechoso*, 11 [l].
35. Orozco, *Catecismo provechoso*, 12 [r].
36. Orozco, *Catecismo provechoso*, 13 [r].
37. Orozco, *Catecismo provechoso*, 14 [l]–14 [r].
38. Orozco, *Catecismo provechoso*, 15 [l].
39. Orozco, *Catecismo provechoso*, 16 [r].
40. Orozco, *Catecismo provechoso*, 17 [l].
41. Orozco, *Catecismo provechoso*, 17 [l].
42. Orozco, *Catecismo provechoso*, 18 [l]–18 [r].

(11) Felipe blesses Christ for making him his disciple;[43] (12) The humble person who believes in God and loves and obey him will enter heaven and be blessed;[44] (13) Faith is only granted to angels and men;[45] (14) It is daring or presumptuous to choose a path that God did not set out;[46] (15) There are three reasons why the Christian faith is great.[47]

Remarks

Felipe had been a Moor for thirty years. His questions and statements reveal that he is more interested in matters related to the religion of Christ than the sect of Muhammad. Only Felipe's two polemical questions and statements 4, 5 and 8 fall into the areas that occupy one-third[48] of the Triple Challenge; specifically, death, hell, paradise, Muhammad, and the Qur'an. Felipe's statements 1, 2, 3, 6, 7, 9, 10, 11, 12, 13, 14 and 15 focus on matters that are important in the religion of Christ.[49] Sixty three percent of Felipe's questions and statements are related to apologetics while 37 percent concentrate on polemics. We will return to this distribution in the "Synopsis" section below after discussing the Moor's questions and statements.

The Moor's Questions and Statements

The content of the twenty-five dialogues in Book One of the *Catecismo* has been categorized as "pre-apologetics" (or "pre-polemics"), "polemics," and "apologetics."[50] The distribution of questions and statements in these dialogues:

> Pre-Polemics. Twelve dialogues (III–XII); twenty-five questions; twenty-five statements.
>
> Polemics. Seven dialogues (XIII–XIX); five questions; twelve statements.

---

43. Orozco, *Catecismo provechoso*, 18 [r].
44. Orozco, *Catecismo provechoso*, 19 [r].
45. Orozco, *Catecismo provechoso*, 19 [r].
46. Orozco, *Catecismo provechoso*, 20 [l].
47. Orozco, *Catecismo provechoso*, 20 [l].
48. See "The Second Challenge: The Religious Beliefs of The Moriscos (Mind)" above in Chapter 4.
49. Statements 10, 12, and 14 refer to the God of the religion of Christ—not the one of the sect of Muhammad.
50. See Chapter 3 above.

Apologetics. Six dialogues (XX–XXV); five questions; twenty-one statements.

All of the statements and questions are presented below. Reading them in sequence is like listening to an audio recording or watching a video of the Moor's *thinking process* as he evaluates vital information that will help him decide whether or not to leave the sect of Muhammad for the religion of Christ and the Roman Church.

Pre-Polemics

The sequence of the Moor's statements and questions in the following dialogues:

Dialogue III[51]

Statements. This dialogue begins with two statements: "Let's start with the knowledge of God" and "I want to understand what Christians mean by God."

Question. "Who is this whom you call God?"

Statements. "You presuppose that God is one, but this is not true." Dialogue III concludes when the Moor states: "There cannot be but one God."

Dialogue IV[52]

Statement. This dialogue begins with the Moor making a statement as to why he doubts the God providentially cares for the creation.

Questions. "What natural reasons prove that God providentially cares for the universe?" and "You have proven that God providentially cares for the universe. But, how do you answer the doubts that I raised?"

Statement. Dialogue IV concludes when the Moor states, "Blessed be God. My doubts have been answered."

Dialogue V[53]

Statement. This dialogue starts with "Tell me what is man."

---

51. Pérez de Ayala, *Catecismo*, 15–20.
52. Pérez de Ayala, *Catecismo*, 20–30.
53. Pérez de Ayala, *Catecismo*, 30–33.

Questions. (1) "Man has two natures?" (2) "What are the consequences of having two natures?" (3) "How is the creature similar to God?" (4) "Where is it said that the soul is spiritual and immortal?"; (5) "What can man do that brute animals cannot?"

Dialogue VI

Questions. (1) "Does man have an end and an aim?" (2) "What is the end and the aim of man?" (3) "What is the end of man? Is it honor, delight, indolence, health, wealth, nobility or science?" (4) "What is the true end of man?" (5) "Is there a path for man to reach this end who is God and enjoy him this way?" (6) "What would that path be?" (7) "What is true religion?" (8) "Did the world always have this path open to reach God?"[54]

Dialogue VII[55]

Question. "Can man by his own natural strength find the true path to God or the true religion?"

Statement. "Philosophers using natural light only teach about virtue."

Question. "How is it possible for philosophers not to understand sin for they teach about virtue, which is the opposite of sin?"

Statement. "You say that sin matters. I want to have a thorough understanding."

Dialogue VIII

Statements. (1) "Tell me the how the Christian religion and philosophers differ on the matter of sin." (2) "I will listen humbly." (3) "Doctrine and experience teach that sin is real." (4) "I want to know what philosophers are missing according to the Christian religion."[56]

Dialogue IX[57]

Statement. "Use the least amount words possible to help me understand thoroughly."

---

54. Pérez de Ayala, *Catecismo*, 33–36
55. Pérez de Ayala, *Catecismo*, 36–42.
56. Pérez de Ayala, *Catecismo*, 42–47.
57. Pérez de Ayala, *Catecismo*, 47–54.

Question. "I understand, but tell me: where does this disarray within man comes from?"

Statements. "I understand" and "It will please me if you could summarize what we have discussed so far."

Dialogue X[58]

Statement. "I want to better understand that only by being a Christian one can go to God."

Questions. (1) "What about the philosopher, the Moor and the Jew—but, particularly the Moor and the Jew—who believe that they can go to God because of the way they live?" (2) "God gave reason to man. How can it not be the path to God?" (3) "God gave the law to Moses. How can this not be the path to God for the Jews?"

Statements. "God is behind the discord between Christians, Moors and Jews" and "Good and bad religions cause division."

Question. "Are there not many ways of living in the Christian religion?"

Statements. (1) "It would appear that you have shown that there cannot be many religions." (2) "You have proven that there are contradictions and falsehoods in what Muhammad said." (3) "Discuss the path that leads to God according to philosophers, Jews, Moors, and Christians."

Dialogue XI[59]

This dialogue closes with the Moor stating, "Now I understand that philosophers do not know and do not teach the straight path of God."

Dialogue XII[60]

Statement. "I have heard that the path to God of the Jews will last forever."

Questions. "How is it that the path of the Jews cannot last forever?" and "If the path of the Jews is bad and imperfect, why did God give it? If it is good, why did he take it away?"

Statement. This dialogue concludes when the Moor states, "I am well persuaded and have discarded any good opinion I had of the path of the Jews."

58. Pérez de Ayala, *Catecismo*, 54–65.
59. Pérez de Ayala, *Catecismo*, 65–68.
60. Pérez de Ayala, *Catecismo*, 69–81.

Polemics

Dialogue XIII[61]

Statements. "Now tell me what reasons does the Prelate use to destroy the sect of my forefathers" and "What you are about to say is not intended to hurt or insult me. Use reason and what agrees with what the learned and saints know."

Dialogue XIV[62]

Statement. "If body and soul will be in heaven, it is necessary for the body to have food and drink."

Question. "Could Muhammad have been speaking in a spiritual sense when he spoke of food and drink (in paradise)?"

Statement. This dialogue concludes when the Moor states, "There is no need to waste more words on this matter. I also understand Muhammad's error."

Dialogue XV[63]

Statements. "I have heard that good men in previous times had more than one wife yet did not offend God. What they did became licit" and "You have removed my doubts on this matter. Now tell me about the doctrine of Muhammad."

Dialogue XVI[64]

The Moor makes no statements and does not ask questions.

Dialogue XVII[65]

Statements. "Muhammad preached constancy, abstinence, fasting, alms, and other good things." This dialogue concludes when the Moor states, "I am pleased that you have so faithfully recounted the main points of the doctrine of Muhammad and that you have used good reasons to prove that it has mistakes and fables."

---

61. Pérez de Ayala, *Catecismo*, 81–95.
62. Pérez de Ayala, *Catecismo*, 95–106.
63. Pérez de Ayala, *Catecismo*, 106–20.
64. Pérez de Ayala, *Catecismo*, 120–25.
65. Pérez de Ayala, *Catecismo*, 125–32.

Dialogue XVIII[66]

Statement. "Fear is a valid excuse for Moors to pretend to be what they are not."

Dialogue XIX[67]

Questions. (1) "Is it not enough for God to say that he is the one who revealed the new law or doctrine?" (2) "How did Muhammad manage to persuade so many people?" (3) "Did Moses not fight against those who followed another law? Did Christians not fight for their law?"

Statements. (1) "Moors say that Muhammad is mentioned in the Scriptures of the Christians." (2) "I am pleased to see how well you have presented the details of this sect that I have followed until now and how well you disputed against it. I have to confess that your reasons are strong." (3) "I am happy with what you said to destroy the sect of Muhammad. Now I need to be persuaded about the faith and the religion of Christ, which Gentiles, Moors, and Jews contradict."

Question. "How have you already proven that the religion of Christ is the true religion and the only path to God?"

Statement. Dialogue XIX concludes when the Moor states, "I will be pleased to hear what else you will use to prove that the religion of Christ is the true religion and the only path to God."

Apologetics

Dialogue XX[68]

Statements. (1) "I would very much like to start the instruction on the Christian religion." (2) "May he illumine me for without him we walk blindly." (3) "There are difficult things in the gospel that are difficult to follow such as treat enemies well; be chaste; and do not resist evil."

---

66. Pérez de Ayala, *Catecismo*, 132–39.
67. Pérez de Ayala, *Catecismo*, 139–64.
68. Pérez de Ayala, *Catecismo*, 165–87.

Dialogue XXI[69]

Statements. "There are saints among us who fast and pray. They do not quarrel with others or take what belongs to them" and "My doubts about the gospel being confirmed by the miracles of Christ and his disciples have been removed."

Question. "But, when you speak of the gospel, is this the same gospel that Christ preached?"

Statements. "I have heard that the Qur'an says that this is not the same gospel that Christ preached, but that it has been corrupted and falsified" and "I thank God that I no longer think that the gospel has been corrupted and falsified."

Dialogue XXII[70]

Statements. (1) "Let's talk about something that I am also very interested in: to prove the truth and infallibility of the gospel with the excellence of the one who gave it and ordered it disseminated"; (2) "I place myself in the hands of God to listen attentively"; (3) "Tell me everything about Jesus Christ whom the Qur'an refers to as 'Jesus son of Maryam;'" (4) "I have heard that the Jews found faults in his life."

Questions. "Did enchanters and the disciples of Christ not perform miracles yet divinity is not attributed to them?" and "Why did Muhammad deny the divinity of Christ even after learning about his miracles?"

Dialogue XXIII[71]

Statement. "You presuppose that the Messiah had to be God instead of only a man. But, I have heard the Jews say something else."

Question. "You have proven that the Messiah had to be God. But, how can it be proven that Jesus Christ was the Messiah?"

Statement. "Proceed with the signs that point to Christ. I am listening carefully. You are convincing me."

Dialogue XXIV[72]

---

69. Pérez de Ayala, *Catecismo*, 187–209.
70. Pérez de Ayala, *Catecismo*, 210–27.
71. Pérez de Ayala, *Catecismo*, 227–38.
72. Pérez de Ayala, *Catecismo*, 238–44.

Question. This dialogue starts when the Moor asks, "Why have you not talked about the miracles of Christ?"

Statement. "I would be very pleased if you talked about the miracles of Christ. I have heard that some tried to slander him."

Dialogo XXV[73]

Statements. "Tell me about the clear sign that shows that this evangelical doctrine is true and the path that God wants men to take to reach him. I am listening carefully" and "I am greatly comforted by your many reasons. I am convinced and persuaded to receive your holy faith. I thank God that you have been the instrument of my conversion. Now teach me specifically what I ought to know and do, and what the Christian religion teaches about walking this path well."

Remarks

The Moor is actively engaged in a discussion on faith, religion, and truth. Unlike Felipe who either agrees or supports what the priest (Orozco) says, the questions and statements of the Moor indicate the following:

1. He does not hesitate to challenge the Teacher by stating, "You presuppose that God is one, but this is not true."[74]
2. He shows that he has an open mind when he says, "I will listen humbly."[75]
3. He is well-informed even if he had not received a formal education. On more than one occasion he asserts, "I have heard."[76]
4. He defends Muhammad when he declares (1) "Could Muhammad have been speaking in a spiritual sense?"[77] (2) "Muhammad preached constancy."[78] (3) "Fear is a valid excuse."[79]
5. He declares, "I am greatly comforted by your many reasons."

---

73. Pérez de Ayala, *Catecismo*, 245–53.
74. Dialogue III.
75. Dialogues VIII, XX, XXII, and XXV.
76. Dialogues XII, XV, XXI, XXII, XXIII, and XXIV.
77. Dialogue XIV.
78. Dialogue XVII.
79. Dialogue XVIII.

This is an indication that he understands and accepts the Teacher's "natural and moral reasons and facts." By the time the Moor admits and says, "I am convinced and persuaded to receive your holy faith," we have listened to or read his dialogues with the Teacher and witnessed how they successfully navigated the first two challenges of the Triple Challenge. When the Moor makes the request "Now teach me specifically what I ought to know and do," he and the Teacher are ready to embark on the third and final challenge.[80]

Summary

The tables below compare the number and distribution of questions and statements in the *Catecismo provechoso* and the *Catecismo*.

Table 9. Questions and Statements

Questions

	Pre-Polemics	Polemics	Apologetics	Total
Catecismo provechoso	0	2	1	3
Catecismo	25	5	5	35

Statements

	Pre-Polemics	Polemics	Apologetics	Total
Catecismo provechoso	0	5	11	16
Catecismo	25	12	21	58

Both *Catecismo provechoso* and the *Catecismo* meet the criteria in Round Three, Event 4 ("Does the catechism or polemical treatise use the format of a dialogue?"). The two tables make two points.

1. There is more dialogue (questions and statements) in the *Catecismo*. As noted above, the Moor's *thinking process* can be detected and followed. Four observations can be made to explain why is there more

---

80. Book Two of the *Catecismo* discusses The Third Challenge. See also above "Round Four, Event 2" in "Chapter 9. The New Catechism: Heart, Mind and Behavior."

dialogue on pre-polemics (25) than on polemics (12) in the *Catecismo*. First, it is the Moor who initiates this entire series of dialogues by saying, "Let's start with the knowledge of God because he is the beginning of all things, and is the destination of the true religion that we are searching for."[81] Second, the discussion on "Who is God?" leads into a discussion on why there cannot be many paths to God.[82] The Teacher spends time proving that *all* paths—not just the religion of Muhammad—are not paths to God. Third, time spent on the foundation—pre-polemics—benefits the discussion of polemics and apologetics. Fourth, the dialogues cover essential topics in polemics[83] even though there are less questions and statements from the Moor.

2. The *Catecismo* has a breadth of material (pre-polemics, polemics, and apologetics) that *Catecismo provechoso* does not have. (The rest of the Group of twelve also lacks pre-polemics material.)

Ribera's Choice

Given the above information, the question "Which one—Felipe or the Moor—provides insight into *the thinking process* of someone considering leaving the sect of Muhammad for the religion of Christ?" can now be answered. The *Catecismo* can help a priest who wants to understand the hurdles that a Moor or Morisco has to overcome to become a follower of the Christian religion and a member of the Roman Church.

The Situation in Valencia before Ribera's Arrival

The Diocese of Valencia

Three well-regarded bishops preceded Ribera at the archbishopric of Valencia: Tomás de Villanueva (1544–55), the charitable reformer and founder of the Colegio Mayor de la Presentación in Valencia for poor students and candidates for the altar; Francisco de Navarra (1556–63) whose irreproachable

---

81. Pérez de Ayala, *Catecismo*, 15.
82. Pérez de Ayala, *Catecismo*, 54–65.
83. The life of Muhammad; paradise; lies, errors and contradictions in the Qur'an; Moors can hide what they actually believe; and the way the sect of Muhammad was spread.

conduct would have gained him sainthood, but for not having performed miracles; and Pérez de Ayala (1564–66).[84]

Valencia and its Moriscos after the Council of Trent and prior to Ribera's arrival[85]

The War of the Alpujarras resulted in Moriscos from Granada being scattered to Valencia and Aragón, which swelled their *aljamas* (Moorish quarters) and stiffened further the resistance in those kingdoms.[86] The overall picture of Valencia was grim. Law breakers were punished as harshly as in medieval times. Culprits were dragged through the streets then dismembered. Ears and hands were cut off depending on the type of crime committed. Common folk were hanged. Nobles were decapitated. Even the clergy fought amongst themselves and sometimes killed each other. Many followed self-proclaimed "pseudo-prophets" and "visionaries." Demon-possession was not uncommon. Duels were frequent. The cavalry had lost its military prestige.[87] A large number of Ribera's sheep consisted of "incorrigible Christians" and "skinflint Moriscos" who lived *sicut equus et mulus*.[88]

Ribera was only thirty six years old when he was appointed to the archbishopric of Valencia in late 1568. His sole episcopal experience was a six-and-half-years stint as bishop of Badajoz (27 May 1562–3 December 1568). Philip II appointed Ribera in spite of his youth because the plan to bring Moriscos into the Catholic Church required someone who could stay for as long as it would take to see the plan bear fruit. Moriscos were considered apostates or obdurate infidels. They were "as Christians as Muhammad" and acted in concert with the Turks. Many of them worked for masters who preferred that they stayed away from the Catholic Church. Their condition had barely changed from previous years. Times had become much more dangerous by the time Ribera arrived in Valencia.[89]

The War of the Alpujarras had put the capital in a stage of siege and imminent danger. The Moriscos had made a commitment to support the *monfies*[90] in Granada. Even some among the nobility—strong advocates of

---

84. Robres Lluch, *San Juan de Ribera*, 82.
85. Ribera took over the archbishopric of Valencia on 21 March 1569.
86. Danvila y Collado, *La expulsión de los moriscos españoles*, 173.
87. Robres Lluch, *San Juan de Ribera*, 105–7.
88. Robres Lluch, *San Juan de Ribera*, 113.
89. Robres Lluch, *San Juan de Ribera*, 390–91.
90. Baroja, *Los moriscos del Reino de Granada*, 149, 162, 164. "Monfí" from the Arabic word منفي, which means "banished, exile, outcast." The *monfies* were Morisco bandits living in the highlands of Granada.

spreading Islamic doctrine—were prepared to protect them. The Inquisition in its inimitable way persuaded the less fanatical ones from switching sides, but a strong hand to impose civil and ecclesiastical order was still lacking. The Valencia that welcome Ribera when he arrived on 21 March 1569 to become its archbishop was unhinged.[91]

There were approximately sixty thousand to eighty thousand Moriscos in the Kingdom of Valencia when Ribera arrived. The kingdom's three provinces—Alicante, Castellón and Valencia—occupied a total area of 13,211 km2 of which approximately 82 percent belonged to Valencia.[92] The Inquisition in Valencia was also active against Muslims scholars and doctrinaires and their sympathizers. Between 1567 and 1579, at least eighty-six people were put on trial for being agents, conspirators or spies. Among them were not only Moriscos, but also French and even Spaniards. The Holy Office discovered friars and masters protecting their Morisco vassals and labeled them heretics.[93]

Ribera and the Moriscos in Valencia

Challenges

Ribera faced three challenges in implementing his program of evangelization.

1. The geography of Valencia was inhospitable. Scarcity of roads and bridges forced him to think of a more rational way to distribute the new parishes he wanted to build.
2. The low salary for parish priests had not improved in more than forty years to meet the rise in cost of living. Consequently, churches had been abandoned or remained vacant because of the lack of qualified priests.
3. The religious ignorance of the Moriscos because of the shortage of rectors and the difficulty of requiring the few who were available to fulfill even their most basic duties of preaching, administering the sacraments, and living in their parishes. Preaching to the Moriscos had been neither sustained nor well-planned. Given the limited resources, it was near impossible to implement a peaceful and systematic

---

91. Boronat y Barrachina, *Los moriscos españoles y su expulsión*, 261–63. Cited in Robres Lluch, *San Juan de Ribera*, 391.
92. Robres Lluch, *San Juan de Ribera*, 391–92.
93. Robres Lluch, *San Juan de Ribera*, 393.

program of attracting into the Catholic Church a group of Moriscos who had just lost the War of the Alpujarras.[94]

The *potential* of the *Catecismo* as an evangelistic tool addressed to Moriscos is gauged against the repercussions of this all-out war of such ferocity and rapacity that the Kingdom of Granada was left in ruins.[95] The deportation of approximately eighty thousand Moriscos from Granada to Castilla worsened relations between them and old Christians. Moriscos clung to their religion and continued to be an indomitable foe. The monarchy and church leaders considered three radical solutions: Morisco ghettos, gradual extinction or expulsion. Gradual extinction would have meant sending Moriscos in their prime (aged eighteen to forty) to the galleys; abducting all children under the age of six and giving them to the care of old Christians; and proscribing marriages between Moriscos. Expulsion had the strongest advocates and was approved in principle. Although immediate implementation was halted because of the resistance of masters who employed Moriscos and the difficulty in mobilizing the necessary resources for such a large scale operation,[96] relations between old Christians and Moriscos were tainted by contempt, hatred and fear.[97] (The potential of the *Catecismo* is discussed further in Chapter 12.)

Solutions

In 1574, Ribera started to meet these three challenges. The plan was to inject new funds into existing parishes and build as many new ones as needed. However, he needed money and priests willing to leave the comfort of living in the cities in exchange for living with people many viewed as barbarians and infidels. There were 190 parishes in Valencia when Ribera arrived in 1569. The last one was built in 1534. He wanted to build twenty-two new ones, which would give his diocese a total of 212 parishes for meeting the spiritual needs of the Moriscos at a ratio of approximately 283 to 377 Moriscos per parish. A papal bull from Pope Gregory XIII stipulated the various sources of funds. However, resistance from those who were satisfied with

---

94. Robres Lluch, *San Juan de Ribera*, 396–404.

95. Domínguez Ortiz and Vincent, *Historia de los moriscos*, 37.

96. Domínguez Ortiz and Vincent, *Historia de los moriscos*, 69–71. Several sections of the present book ("Conversion and Rebellion" and "Aftermath of the War of the Alpujarras" in Chapter 4 and "Valencia and its Moriscos After the Council of Trent and Prior to Ribera's Arrival" and "Edict of Reprieve" in Chapter 11) provide additional information about the Moriscos after they lost the War of the Alpujarras.

97. Domínguez Ortiz and Vincent, *Historia de los moriscos*, 129.

the *status quo* was fierce. In the end, Ribera used his own money—172 thousand pounds in twenty-five years (1578–1603). Starting from 1576, he also used his own funds to pay for salaries.⁹⁸

Ribera exhausted all possible means to instruct the Moriscos and put the right people in charge; for example, the Dominican priest Domingo Anadón preached to the Moriscos with such zeal that he would invite them, "Bring me any dead of your choice and I will resurrect them on the testimony of the faith that I am preaching to you." Ribera himself went regularly to places where Moriscos congregated and preached to them. He also spent hours talking with Muslim clerics alone. When his servants wondered why he took such risks, he answered, "Brothers, what can they do to me?"⁹⁹

Mission Trips and Preaching

Ribera also organized "periodic mission trips." On 16 July 1599, he wrote a pastoral letter with instructions for his priests and preachers to work together. They were to take only the barest of necessities and travel to Morisco areas. Preaching—lasting from half-an-hour to no more than three-fourth of an hour and for a period of at least fifteen days at each parish—was to take place before men went to work at five o'clock in the morning. Preaching to women and their children was to be done separately and in the presence of a priest. He also promised to go personally to preach and reward the diligent rectors and discipline the slackers.¹⁰⁰

New Policy, Unfulfilled Hope

Edict of Reprieve

A soft policy that would have ramifications for Valencia began on 23 April 1570 when an eloquently written edict of reprieve was issued to the Moriscos who fought in the War of the Alpujarras. The edict began with these words:

> The King . . . having understood that the majority of the new Christians who rose up against this Kingdom of Granada did so not on their own will but were compelled and hard-pressed

---

98. Domínguez Ortiz and Vincent, *Historia de los moriscos*, 129.

99. Domínguez Ortiz and Vincent, *Historia de los moriscos*, 129.

100. Ximenez, *Vida del Beato Juan de Ribera*, 448–50. Cited in Robres Lluch, *San Juan de Ribera*, 404–5.

and induced by certain main actors and ringleaders and warlords amongst them who for their private aims sought to help themselves to the property of the common folk while offering no benefits in return and so ensured that they would rise up.

The edict also acknowledged that the Moriscos had endured "violence, bloodshed, thievery, and many other great evils" because of the war and concluded with an offer of "great clemency." What happened in Granada was also happening in Valencia. Masters extracted higher duties and tributes from their Morisco vassals than from old Christians because Moriscos lived in and cultivated the lands of their masters. This edict of reprieve led to the issue of a specific one on 30 September of the same year for Moriscos in Valencia.[101]

Ribera and the Edict of Reprieve

Ribera played a role in this edict of reprieve. In August of 1570, the armies of Selim II defeated the Christian forces in Nicosia, Cyprus. Fifteen thousand Christians were killed and two thousand were enslaved. The victors had Famagusta—the island's second largest city—in their sight. If it were to fall, the last Christian bulwark in the East would have been destroyed. Pope Pius V—the defender of the Christian faith—was worried. While the Christian forces were regrouping, Ribera sent an envoy to Rome to advise the Pope to use restraint and avoid harassing the Moriscos who had become allies of the Turks after representatives of the Moriscos went to Constantinople in the spring of 1569 to request assistance. Pressure on Cyprus was removed on 7 October 1571 when the navy of the Holy League won a decisive victory over the fleet of the Turks at the Battle of Lepanto.[102]

New Accord

News of the defeat had not reached Valencia when Philip II and the inquisitor general approved an expansive accord on October 12 between the *aljamas* (Moorish quarters) of Valencia and the Supreme Inquisition. The accord limited the reach of the Inquisition. The *aljamas* would pay a fixed amount of money for salaries that would not increase even after other Moorish quarters signed on to the accord later. Ribera had encouraged Philip II to

---

101. Danvila y Collado, *La expulsión de los moriscos españoles*, 180–81. Cited in Robres Lluch, *San Juan de Ribera*, 394.

102. Robres Lluch, *San Juan de Ribera*, 394–95.

approve it. Its lack of an expiration date signaled an official change in policy and the start of a period of tolerance.[103]

Grace and Mercy

The accord represented a triumph in Morisco policy where kindness was preferred over terror. The Holy Office of the Inquisition agreed to the following: (1) Never confiscate the property of new converts and their descendants for the crimes of heresy and apostasy committed in the past or in the future; (2) Grant leniency to Islamic scholars and anyone else who in any way followed the sect of Muhammad; those who relapsed more than once after having been charged for such crimes; inmates in the jails of the Holy Office; and *tagarinos* (Moriscos from Aragon[104]) who had lived ten years in the kingdom of Valencia; (3) Cap the financial penalty for committing such crimes; and (4) New converts living outside the kingdom of Valencia had up to a year to return and confess their errors and receive the benefits of this edict of grace.[105]

Ribera's Vision

Ribera wrote a second letter on 16 July 1599 addressed to preachers. It is noteworthy that he was still committed to the evangelization of the Moriscos seventeen years after the Junta of Lisboa had deliberated on their expulsion. Both letters reveal his vision and approach despite his admission that there had been very little fruit. The following highlights what he wrote in his second letter:[106]

The Goal of Preaching. "The goal of preaching is to see the new Christians of the Moors of Valencia obey the gospel. Few of them have left the sect of Muhammad. None of them are at a point to receive the Holy Sacrament of Penitence. They show no enthusiasm during the Mass; oppose anything that is Christian; and continue to follow their religion. Their excuse is that they have not been instructed in the Catholic faith. Given that they are regarded as new plants, steps were adopted to instruct them with gentleness. His Majesty, Pope Clement, and the Inquisition agreed to absolve anyone from the crimes

103. Robres Lluch, *San Juan de Ribera*, 394–95.
104. Ehlers, *Between Christians and Moriscos*, 20.
105. Danvila y Collado, *La expulsión de los moriscos españoles*, 184–90. Cited in Robres Lluch, *San Juan de Ribera*, 396.
106. Ximenez, *Vida del Beato Juan de Ribera*, 450–63.

of apostasy and heresy. Thus, a burden was lifted from the souls and the bodies of these new Christians. They have not been penalized into obeying the gospel, which they should obey anyway because they have been baptized. In an effort to save their souls and help them live as Catholics, rectors were sent, new parishes built, and too remote parishes demolished. Now preachers will also visit them in accordance with the wishes of His Majesty. The are eight means to fulfill his aspirations."

Unwavering Apostolic Calling. "The first and most important means is for preachers, rectors and other ministers to be convinced that their apostolic task is difficult, but not impossible. Those who enter into this labor thinking that it is not demanding, sin for being wet behind their ears. There is no satisfaction when the battle is sweet and easy. What God said is proof enough that your job is indeed not easy—*Si mutare potest Aethiops pellem suam, aut pardus varietates suas, et vos poteritis benefacere, cum didiceritis malum.*[107] You are taking care of people who hate us. A longstanding gap separates us from them because we have not been charitable or friendly towards them. They think that we treat them like slaves. They stick together as the prophet said—*Unusquisque proximo suo auxiliabitur, et fratri suo dicet: Confortare.*"[108]

Evidence of Conversion. "Second, new converts should take their conversion and instruction seriously. The charge from the leaders of the *aljamas* that new converts remained in the sect of Muhammad because the Church failed to instruct them is without merit. Instruction has not ceased. This second means also keeps us from being fooled. New converts are in the habit of saying that they are Christians when in fact they are not. We need to look for evidence such as their asking for the sacrament of Extreme Unction."

Edict of Reprieve. "Third, persuade new converts to take advantage of the edict of grace (reprieve) so that among other benefits they can escape the penalties for the crimes of apostasy and heresy."

Invite others to join the church. "If the wealthiest among them embrace the Catholic faith, they could encourage their co-religionists to join them."

Taxes. "Fifth, it is beyond the scope of your pastoral duties to discuss taxes or duties (*zofres*)."[109]

---

107. Jer 13:25: "Can the Ethiopian change his skin or the leopard his spots. Then you also can do good who are accustomed to doing evil."

108. Isa 41:6: "Each one helps his neighbor and says to his brother, 'Be strong!'"

109. Ximenez, *Vida del Beato Juan de Ribera*, 459.

Gentleness and Kindness. "Sixth, it is always best not to inflame the emotions of the new converts during private and public conversations by saying something bad about their sect. The apostle Paul did not chastise the Athenians when he saw their altar dedicated to an unknown God, but took the opportunity to share the gospel. We should begin with soft approaches. If they bear no fruit, we may proceed with stronger and more rigorous approaches to show listeners that our gentleness and kindness can be seen in our words and deeds.

"Their harshness is their choice and against us—*Quid vultis in virga veniam ad vos, an in charitate et spiritu mansuetudinis?*[110] The apostle attributed the rod to the will of the Corinthians and kindness and meekness to his own. Christ instructed his apostles that when first entering a town or village they should extend a peace greeting, heal the sick, eat what was offered to them, and stay with their hosts."

Impeccable Behavior. "Seventh, abide by a strict code of behavior. Do not enter the house of Moriscos when women are present;[111] the church is the best place to teach; go with the rector or an old Christian when visiting the sick; do not accept gifts; and avoid the pursuit of such indecent pleasures as dancing, hunting and similar ones because they are incompatible with the office of salt, light and the torch."

Keeping and Losing Morisco Servants. "Eight, some masters apparently prefer that their servants remain in spiritual darkness for fear of losing their labor once they start to follow Catholic teaching. However, this impression is a false one. The only way for masters to keep their servants is for the latter to become Catholics. Otherwise, they would indeed run the risk of losing them. Furthermore, Morisco servants have become so attached to their masters that it would be to their benefit for preachers to pay them a visit and keep contact with their masters."

Another Catechism

Ribera concluded his letter by mentioning that he was printing a catechism— "the doctrine that is preached should be simple and conveyed in ordinary and common terms given that what is taught are the articles and the commandments. The sense and the meaning of the words should also be easy to understand and act upon. There is more to discuss about this matter, but I will not do so here and instead refer to a catechism that I am printing. It

---

110. 1 Cor 4:21: "What do you desire? Shall I come to you with a rod, or with love and a spirit of gentleness?"

111. An indication that preachers are sensitive to Islamic culture.

deals at length with teaching that is adapted to the capacity of these people. Until the printing is finished, what I have said here should suffice. Valencia, 16 of July of 1599. The Patriarch Archbishop of Valencia."[112] This catechism is characterized by the preaching of "simple doctrine" using "ordinary and common terms" so that Moriscos can understand and put into practice. Ribera is referring to Pérez de Ayala's *Catecismo*.

Problem and Solution

The content of his letter can be divided into two main parts. The first part is *a somber assessment of the problem*. The Moriscos are still attached to their religion. They show no signs of having accepted the teachings of the Roman Church; specifically, the sacraments of Penitence, the Mass, and Extreme Unction. The second part of the letter discusses the solution. It concentrates on *the behavior of priests and masters*. Ribera reminds priests of their duties (continue to preach the gospel and evangelize using soft approaches; do not force Moriscos to believe; be charitable and kind); exhorts them to be convinced of their call to this demanding ministry; and admonishes them to be above reproach (do not respond to the Moriscos' harshness with hardness, but imitate the response of the apostle Paul; abide by a strict code of personal behavior). He reproves masters for being unconcerned about the spiritual condition of their Morisco servants thinking that they will stop working for them after they become Catholics.

Ribera's Choice

1. What was the potential of the *Catecismo* as an evangelistic tool addressed to Moriscos? The *Catecismo* had the potential because it meets all 16 criteria in Chapters 6 to 9 and has extra features that differentiates it further from *Catecismo provechoso*, its nearest competitor.

2. Why did Ribera choose the *Catecismo* to bolster his own evangelistic task in 1599—thirty-three years after Pérez de Ayala had passed away and ten years before the decree of Philip III in 1609 that launched the process to expel the Moriscos from Spain? The *Catecismo* has unmatched breadth of content: pre-polemics/pre-apologetics, polemics, apologetics, knowledge, and *praxis*. Book One of the *Catecismo* covers pre-polemics/pre-apologetics, and polemics. Book Two discusses knowledge and *praxis*.

112. Ximenez, *Vida del Beato Juan de Ribera*, 463.

Table 10. Final Results

	Pre-Polemics	Polemics	Apologetics	Knowledge	Praxis
Breve doctrina y enseñanza				✔	✔
Confusión o confutación		✔			
Doctrina Christiana (Alba)		✔ (brief)		✔	✔
Antialcorano		✔	✔		
Diálogos Christianos			✔		
Confutación del Alcorán y secta Mahometana		✔			
Doctrina Cristiana (Ayala)				✔	✔
Catecismo provechoso		✔ (brief)	✔		
Catecheses mystagogicae		✔			
Sacromonte		✔	✔	✔	✔
Doctrina Cristiana (Ripalda)				✔	✔
Doctrina cristiana (Astete)				✔	✔
Catecismo	✔	✔	✔	✔	✔

Given the following situation in Valencia before and after Ribera's arrival: (1) The overall picture of Valencia was grim. The area was unhinged. Times were dangerous; (2) The condition of the Moriscos. They were "incorrigible Christians"; "skinflint Moriscos"; as Christian as Muhammad; and "obdurate infidels"; (3) The condition of the clergy. There were insufficient priests. The need was urgent for qualified and trained priests. There was also an urgent need to build more churches.

Despite the meagre results, Ribera remained committed to seeing his vision become reality; that is, clergy certain of their calling, trained for ministry to Moriscos, and living by a strict code of behavior; Moriscos showing specific signs of genuine conversion; and mission characterized by gentleness and kindness.

Ribera chose the *Catecismo* because it meets all the criteria; it has extra features; its comprehensive content (pre-polemics, polemics, apologetics, knowledge, and *praxis*); the situation in Valencia before and after Ribera arrived; and Ribera's vision.

This chapter closes with a response to García Cárcel. He refers to the *Catecismo* as "the *Catecismo* of Ribera-Ayala" and gives reasons for why he believes it is the work of Ribera. The tone of the first part of the *Catecismo* is colloquial, but the second part is emphatic and dogmatic. In the *Catecismo* Ribera distorts the meaning that Pérez de Ayala intended to give to his *Doctrina Cristiana*. First, *the Catecismo*—unlike *Doctrina Cristiana*—is not addressed to Moriscos directly, but to priests responsible for teaching them Catholic doctrine. Second, the religious emphasis of the *Catecismo* shows a lack of cultural sensitivity to the Moriscos. Finally, the erudite language in some of the chapters betrays Ribera's claim in his cover letter of the *Catecismo* that Pérez de Ayala wrote it in simple language.[113]

The perspective of the present book is different from the one held by García Cárcel. If the *Catecismo* reflects the conversations between Pérez de Ayala and Moriscos, the colloquial tone of the first part is natural. The emphatic and dogmatic tone of the second part is to be expected because there is less dialogue than the first part. The Teacher is teaching and the Moor is listening. The Moor makes requests ("I would very much like to start the instruction on the Christian religion"; "Tell me") and promises to be quiet ("I am listening carefully").[114] The *Catecismo* is addressed to priests because they were poorly educated and ill-equipped for their catechetical work. They had to learn first before they could teach the Moriscos.[115] If the *Catecismo* lacks cultural sensitivity, the Moor would not have said to the Teacher: "What you are about to say is not intended to hurt or insult me."[116]

---

113. García Cárcel, "Estudio crítico del catecismo de Ribera-Ayala," 161–68.

114. The Moor says, "Tell me about the clear sign that shows that this evangelical doctrine is true and the path that God wants men to take to reach him. I am listening carefully"; "I place myself in the hands of God to listen attentively"; "Tell me everything about Jesus Christ whom the Qur'an refers to as 'Jesus son of Maryam;'" "I would be very pleased if you talked about the miracles of Christ"; and "I am greatly comforted by your many reasons. I am convinced and persuaded to receive your holy faith. I thank God that you have been the instrument of my conversion. Now teach me specifically what I ought to know and do, and what the Christian religion teaches about walking this path well." See the sections "The Moor's Questions and Statements" and "Apologetics" in this chapter.

115. See the section "Religious Background of the Catechumen" in this chapter.

116. The Moor also says, "I am pleased that you have so faithfully recounted the main points of the doctrine of Muhammad and that you have used good reasons to prove that it has mistakes and fables"; "I am pleased to see how well you have presented the details of this sect that I have followed until now and how well you disputed against

On the use of erudite language in some of the chapters, García Cárcel does not specify which ones. However, its use would be appropriate depending on the subject matter. Ribera wrote in the cover letter that Pérez de Ayala uses simple language with such care to match the Moriscos' talents that even the learned could find truth about Catholic doctrine in the *Catecismo*.[117] The Moor in the *Catecismo* might not have received a classical education, but is able to discuss weighty matters such as the meaning of God, philosophy, and religion with the Teacher. If this Moor is a composite of the Moors with whom Pérez de Ayala conversed, the *Catecismo* was intended to be understood even though some chapters employ erudite language.

---

it. I have to confess that your reasons are strong"; and "I am happy with what you said to destroy the sect of Muhammad." See the sections "The Moor's Questions and Statements" and "Polemics" in this chapter.

117. Pérez de Ayala, *Catecismo*, 3.

Chapter 12

Reflections

Reflections on the Past: Potential and Effectiveness

THE MONARCHY AND THE Catholic Church of sixteenth-century Spain had difficulty persuading Moriscos to become genuine Catholics. Despite the challenges, the authorities continued to pursue the path of evangelization. High hopes must have accompanied the preparation of the *Catecismo*. The word "effective" comes to mind in this reflection of what happened in late 1599 when the catechism was finally published. The definition of "effective" ("adequate to accomplish a purpose; producing the intended or expected result"[1]) raises two questions:

1. Was the *Catecismo* adequate to accomplish the purpose of evangelizing the Moriscos while simultaneously equipping priests to instruct Moors or Moriscos in the Christian religion and teach them the doctrines of the Catholic Church? This question can be rephrased as "*Could* the Catecismo get the job done?" The answer is affirmative.

2. Did the *Catecismo* produce the intended or expected result? Pons Fuster writes that if preachers had started to preach to the Moriscos starting from the dialogues on Muhammad and his doctrines, the usefulness of the *Catecismo* would have been null because of the "offensive and disparaging" tone of these dialogues.[2] The present book holds another view. First, only seven of the twenty-five dialogues in Book One of the *Catecismo* concentrate on Muhammad and Islam. These seven dialogues are preceded by nine dialogues on pre-polemics material that prepare Moriscos to hear a critique of Muhammad and

---

1. www.dictionary.com. Accessed on 13/10/2019 at 09:25:21.

2. Pons Fuster, "El patriarca Juan de Ribera y el Catecismo para instrucción de los nuevos convertidos," 211.

their religion. Given that the material in the *Catecismo* is presented in the form of a handbook and a primer,[3] it would be reasonable to expect preachers to present the material in order; that is, start from these nine dialogues and finish them before preaching against Muhammad and the religion of the Moriscos.[4] Second, although the tone of the *Catecismo* is not charitable or friendly towards the Moriscos,[5] the *Catecismo* does not inflame the emotions of the Moriscos.[6] Third, if the *Catecismo* can be regarded as a distillation of the experience that Pérez de Ayala gained from regular dialogues with Moriscos over the years and if the Moor in the *Catecismo* can be viewed as a composite of different Moors instead of just one Moor, preachers who followed the sequence—pre-polemics first, polemics afterwards—would have had grounds for hoping that some Moors might respond as this Moor responded; that is, agreement with the critique against Muhammad and their religion followed by conversion to the Catholic faith.[7]

Escolano—in the last sentence of Chapter 39 of his chronicle of Valencia titled *Segunda parte de la década primera de la historia de la insigne, y coronada ciudad y Reyno de Valencia*—opines that the *Catecismo* had no effect.[8] Chapter 39 is a reprint of the entire letter that Ribera wrote on 16 July 1599 to the preachers of his archdiocese.[9] The reprint occupies fifteen columns (seven-and-a-half pages), but the last sentence—consisting of just thirty-eight Spanish words at the end of the reprint—reads as follows: "The ministers of the word of God went to their mission with this (*Catecismo*)[10], but they returned home without making an impact because of the

3. See the criterion "Round One, Event 3" in Chapter 6.
4. See "Introduction to Polemics" in Chapter 11.
5. See the criterion "Round 2, Event 2" in Chapter 7.
6. See the criterion "Round Two, Event 3" in Chapter 7.
7. The Moor says to the Teacher, "You have been the instrument of my conversion, be also the teacher of my instruction and teach me specifically what I ought to know and do, and what the Christian religion teaches about walking this path well." Pérez de Ayala, *Catecismo*, 253. See also the criterion "Round Four, Event 2. The Second Challenge: The Mind" in Chapter 9.
8. Escolano, *Segunda parte*, cols. 1783-98.
9. The present book uses this same letter as seen in Ximenez's *Vida del Beato Juan de Ribera* to develop the criteria that the *Catecismo* should meet. See "Criteria" in Chapter 5 and "Round Two, Four Events" in Chapter 7. The title in Escolano's Chapter 39 is "A letter from the Patriarch Archbishop of Valencia with documents for those who were in charge of the instruction of Moriscos in the year fifteen hundred and ninety nine."
10. Escolano refers to the *Catecismo* as "carta de navegar"; that is, "navigation letter" or "sailing chart."

discontentment of the Moriscos."[11] The present book does not consider this sentence to be a judgment against the usefulness of the *Catecismo*. First, the sentence is also not a verdict against the ministers. Second, Chapter 39 does not analyze the strengths and weaknesses of the *Catecismo* to reach a verdict. This chapter reprints Ribera's letter, which is a double exhortation to Ribera's preachers and rectors to work "very hard" because their mission—although difficult—is not impossible and they will derive no satisfaction from their labors if they see themselves as fighting an easy battle.[12] Ribera uses his letter to give instructions on how preachers and rectors should fulfill their pastoral duties. Specifically, he is concerned with the goal of their preaching, their attitude towards the Moriscos, their dialogue with Moriscos, and how they should teach Christian doctrine.[13] Third, Escolano offers the discontentment of the Moriscos as the single cause for a lack of impact. If it had been the *Catecismo*, it would be reasonable to expect Escolano to have written, "but they returned home without making an impact because the *Catecismo* failed to deliver." However, that is not what he wrote. Fourth, if it had been the ministers, neither the last sentence in Chapter 39 nor the chapter itself explain their inability to make an impact. It is in Chapter 38 that we learn that Moriscos held on to their beliefs and practices despite an edict of grace published in 1574 that gave them time to confess and be absolved without any repercussions.[14] A second edict of grace published in 1599 also failed notwithstanding Ribera's personal involvement in preaching together with other upright priests.[15] Fifth, Escolano does not elaborate on the nature of the discontentment of the Moriscos. If he had, he might have noted that the efforts of the church and the monarchy to evangelize the Moriscos, the reverberations of the War of the Alpujarras, and the impact of the Inquisition were some of the causes of the Moriscos' distress. Relations between both groups deteriorated to such a degree that Moriscos declared defiantly, "We will not become Christians even if we were cut to pieces"[16] and "A cup of glass is more precious than the *crisma*[17] of the Christian."[18]

11. Escolano, *Segunda parte*, col. 1797.
12. Escolano, *Segunda parte*, col. 1786.
13. See the section "Criteria" in Chapter 5.
14. Escolano, *Segunda parte*, col. 1781.
15. Escolano, *Segunda parte*, col. 1782.
16. "Que no se volverían cristianos aunque les cortasen con unas tijeras y les hiziesen pedazos."
17. "Más estimaría una taza de vidrio que la crisma de un cristiano." *Crisma* was the oil and balsam used to anoint those who received baptism, confirmation, or ordination.
18. García Cárcel, "La Inquisición y los Moriscos Valencianos. Anatomía de una represión," 412.

These circumstances would have made it difficult for ministers to be fruitful in their ministry to Moriscos.

Ribera's plan to evangelize the Moriscos of Valencia rested on repairing old parishes and constructing new ones to give priests a permanent and active presence among the Moriscos. Philip II, on the other hand, favored a series of missional campaigns that would compensate for the deficient network of parishes and the Moriscos' lack of Christian education. Ribera's plan required financing, well-trained priests, and repressive measures against Moriscos to be handled by civil authorities instead of priests to reduce friction between Moriscos and their pastors. By comparison, Philip II's plan involved the issuing of edicts of grace to reconcile recalcitrant Moriscos to the Church without confiscation of property; a benevolent attitude not only towards Moriscos, but also their masters; no persecution by the Inquisition of Moriscos receiving Christian education; and no prohibition on the use of Arabic language and wearing of traditional garb. Neither plan made much progress because Philip II and Ribera could not reach an agreement on which one to implement. The publication of edicts of grace and the funding for parishes required approval from Rome, which did not arrive on time before the death of Philip II in 1598.[19]

The reception of Philip III to the publication of the *Catecismo* is difficult to know. His father was never in favor of the expulsion of the Moriscos despite the memoranda urging him to do so. He continued to encourage the launch of missional campaigns. Philip III was influenced by three personages: his wife Margarita of Austria who hated Islam and Muslims; his prime minister, the duke of Lerma, who wanted a "victory" for the Spanish Crown after the defeat of Algiers; and Archbishop Ribera who was in favor of expulsion after the failure of the last evangelistic campaign in Valencia. Given such pressure, Philip III never endorsed any new efforts to evangelize the Moriscos. His decision in 1602 was to expel the Moriscos from Valencia.[20]

Given the animosity between Moriscos and Christians and the complexities of executing a plan to evangelize the former, it would have been prodigious task for any catechism to succeed at attracting Moriscos into the Catholic Church. It is impossible to know the answer to the question "Did the *Catecismo* produce the intended or expected result?" Jesus illustrated the work of the Spirit of God in bringing people into the kingdom of God. He said, "The wind blows where it wishes and you hear the sound of it, but do not know where it comes from and where it is going" (John

---

19. Sánchez-Blanco, *Heroicas decisiones*, 313–23, 353–60, 421–29.

20. Sánchez-Blanco, *Tríptico de la expulsión de los moriscos*, http://books.openedition.org/pulm/1135, 19–52.

3:8.) There are no historical records of how the Spirit of God worked in the hearts and minds of the Moriscos during the time of Ribera. There is no written feedback from priests, Ribera and other church authorities, the king, or the Moriscos.

No Morisco left behind a private letter or a journal entry saying, "I discarded the religion of my forefathers and became a follower of the Christian religion and a member of the Roman Church after reading and studying the *Catecismo*." Moriscos may have been influenced by priests using the *Catecismo* without acknowledging that they were doing so. There are no official reports from either ecclesiastical or royal authorities stating, "The *Catecismo* of our beloved archbishop Martín Pérez de Ayala was used during evangelistic campaigns held in Valencia during the year 1600 under the leadership of our Lord's humble servant archbishop Juan de Ribera. As a result of using the *Catecismo*, 800 Moriscos confessed that they no longer wished to be identified as Moriscos, but as 'adopted children of God' and 'members of the Roman Church.'" The *Catecismo* had the *potential* ("adequate to accomplish its purpose") even though its *effectiveness* ("to produce the intended or expected result") is impossible to know.

Reflections for the Present: Timeless Principles

Over 420 years have passed since Ribera published Pérez de Ayala's *Catecismo* in 1599. The Triple Challenge remains. The modern version may not be identical to the version of sixteenth-century Spain. However, the core is intact; that is, the confession (heart); the beliefs about Allah, the Qur'an, Muhammad, and Muhammad's teachings (mind); and what is permitted and forbidden in public and in private (behavior).

What timeless principles can be extracted from the *Catecismo* for the twenty-first century? The principles are introduced below in alphabetical order. There is no connection between the order in which they appear and their degree of importance. All these principles are equally valuable.

Attitude

Pérez de Ayala addresses the Moriscos as "most beloved children in Christ."[21] He refers to himself as "your pastor and spiritual father."[22] He desires their

---

21. "hijos muy amados en Cristo."
22. "vuestro Pastor y padre espiritual."

salvation with all his heart.²³ The Teacher—his translator—shares the same attitude. The Moor wants to know what reasons does Pérez de Ayala use "to destroy" his religion. The Teacher says that he will be sharing damaging information, but does not want the Moor to think that he is doing so "to hurt or insult" him. If it were necessary, he would take the blood out of his heart for the sake of converting him to the true light.²⁴ This type of attitude is called for today. There is no need to hurt or insult the other party.

Balance

Both apologetics and polemics are necessary. Polemics (offense) without apologetics (defense) is insufficient. A follower of Muhammad needs to know *who* and *what* are the alternatives to Muhammad and his doctrine. This is where purely polemical works like *Confusión o confutación* and *Confutación del alcorán y secta mahometana* fall short.

Criteria

Some of the sixteen criteria used in evaluating the catechisms and polemical treatises are relevant for today.

Respond to criticisms.²⁵ Today's followers of Muhammad and those of the sixteenth century have similar criticisms; for example, the divinity of Christ, the Trinity, and the corruption of the Christian Scriptures. Pérez de Ayala addressed those criticisms with the Qur'an, the *sunna*, the *sira*, and information from historians and Christian learned men who lived during and after the time of Muhammad.²⁶ Today those same criticisms and new ones should be tackled with the latest scholarship.

Preach the gospel.²⁷ If the gospel is good news and the alternative to Muhammad and his teachings, those who live by the gospel should preach it in word and in deed like Pérez de Ayala did. The other criteria also offer

---

23. "que de todas entrañas desea vuestra salvación." Pérez de Ayala, *Doctrina Cristiana*, 3.

24. "que la sangre del corazón nos sacaríamos si fuese menester para convertirlos a la verdadera luz." Pérez de Ayala, *Catecismo*, 83.

25. Round One, Event 4. Does the catechism or polemical treatise have apologetic material that addresses the usual objections raised by Islamic clerics?

26. Pérez de Ayala, *Catecismo*, 84.

27. Round Two, Event 1. Does the catechism or polemical treatise discuss all the material needed to teach the gospel to an unbeliever—especially someone who comes from the sect of Muhammad?

food for reflection: (1) Is our tone "charitable and friendly"?[28] (2) Do we "inflame the emotions" of the other party?[29] (3) Do we use "natural and moral reasons and facts"?[30] (4) Are we aware of the twenty-first century version of the Triple Challenge?[31] (5) Do we know how to grapple with this modern version of the Triple Challenge?

Pérez de Ayala showed the "clumsiness and blunders" of the sect of Muhammad by using its own sources—the Qur'an, the *sunna*, and the *sira*. He even used the Qur'an to support the "divinity and excellences" of Christ. It is possible and necessary to examine or evaluate Muhammad and his doctrine by just using "natural and moral reasons and facts" (polemics).

Foundation

The foundation of apologetics is "the excellence and divinity of Christ"; specifically, his dignity, his messiahship, and his miracles.[32] If Christ is the alternative to Muhammad, there must be clarity about Christ's identity.

Goal

The goal of apologetics is "to prove that it is reasonable, necessary, and right" to believe in Christ and the Christian religion. The goal of polemics is not—as the Moor believed—"to destroy the Law of Muhammad," but "to examine and evaluate it."

---

28. Round Two, Event 2. Is the tone of the catechism or polemical treatise "charitable and friendly"?

29. Round Two, Event 3. Could the catechism or polemical treatise inflame the emotions of the Moriscos?

30. Round Three, Event 2. Does the catechism or polemical treatise use "natural and moral reasons and facts" to show the "purity and beauty" of the religion of Christ?
Round Three, Event 3. Does the catechism or polemical treatise use "natural and moral reasons and facts" to show the "clumsiness and blunders" of the sect of Muhammad?

31. Round Four, Event 1. Is the catechism or polemical treatise aware of the Triple Challenge; that is, the confession, the beliefs, and the commandments that control the heart, the mind, and the behavior of the Moriscos? Round Four, Event 2. Does the catechism or polemical treatise grapple with the Triple Challenge?

32. See "The Excellence and Divinity of Christ" in Chapter 10.

Meaning

If someone had asked Pérez de Ayala what does it mean to be a Christian and a Catholic or what does it mean to be a Christian and a member of the Roman Church, he might have said "Have you read Book Two of the *Catecismo*?" The knowledge he wrote in those pages enabled him to respond to everything the Moor asked and said (thirty-five questions and fifty-eight statements). Irrespective of our doctrinal persuasion—Catholic or Protestant—can we explain to the other party what we believe?

Target

The target of polemics is not a person—Muhammad—but what he taught; specifically, what happens to those who follow him; what his law allows and forbids; and how his law was disseminated. Polemics does evaluate the life of Muhammad, but—according to the definition of "polemics" in Chapter 10— this is only 25 percent of polemics. Evaluation of the remaining 75 percent would be the indirect way to examine the life of Muhammad that might not inflame the emotions of those who have the highest regard for him.[33]

Reflections for the Future

The preparation of the present book was akin to the filming of a movie. There is always something left on the cutting floor that the movie director can use in a special edition to be shown later. The research that went into this book has opened another window into areas that can help us further understand what happened in Spain in the sixteenth century.

Miguel de Cervantes (1547–1616). It would be enriching to learn how he saw Islam through the eyes of his literary character *Don Quijote*. Cervantes was injured in the Battle of Lepanto and spent several years as a slave in North Africa. Rodrigo Díaz de Vivar (1048–99) also known as *El Cid*. Although he lived some 500 years before Pérez de Ayala, he was an important figure in *La Reconquista*. He is buried in Valencia. It is likely that Pérez de Ayala met Martin Luther at the Diet of Worms (1521). It would be rewarding to investigate points of contact between both of them in terms of their theology as seen through the pages of the catechisms they wrote.

---

33. Round Two, Event 3. Could the catechism or polemical inflame the emotions of the Moriscos?

Maps

Map 1

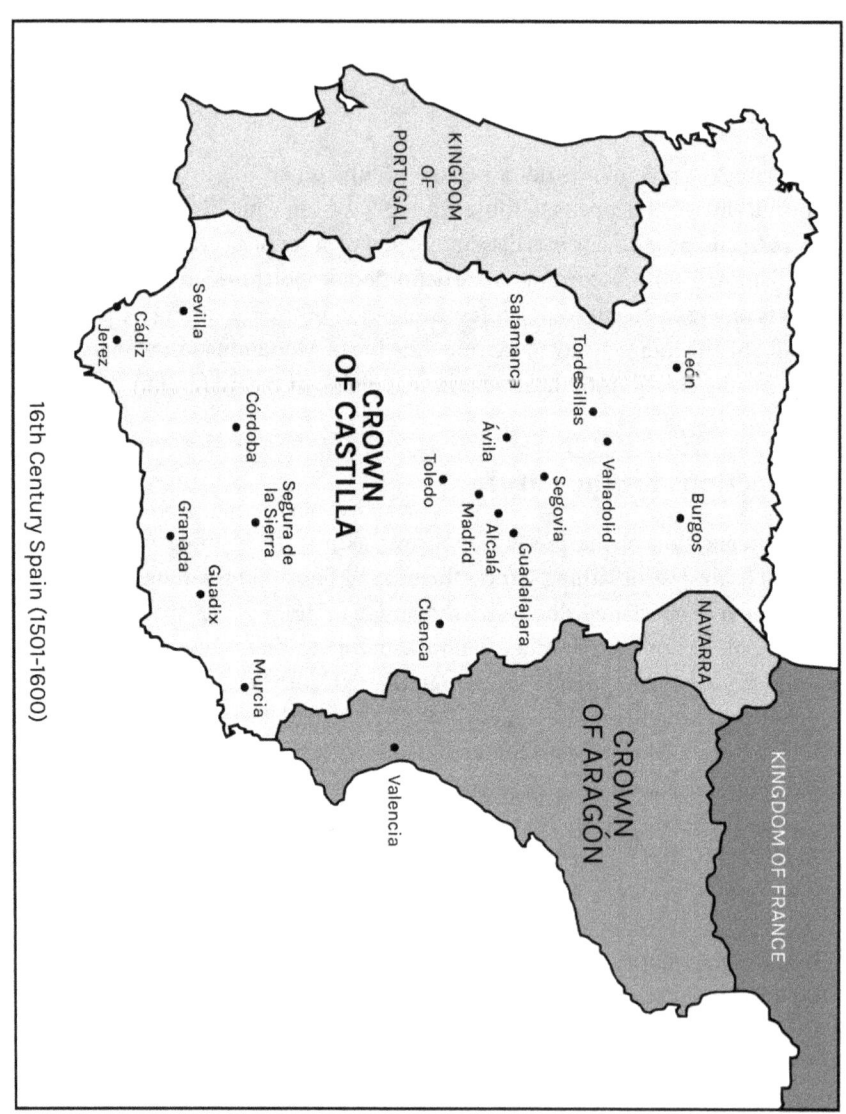

Map 2

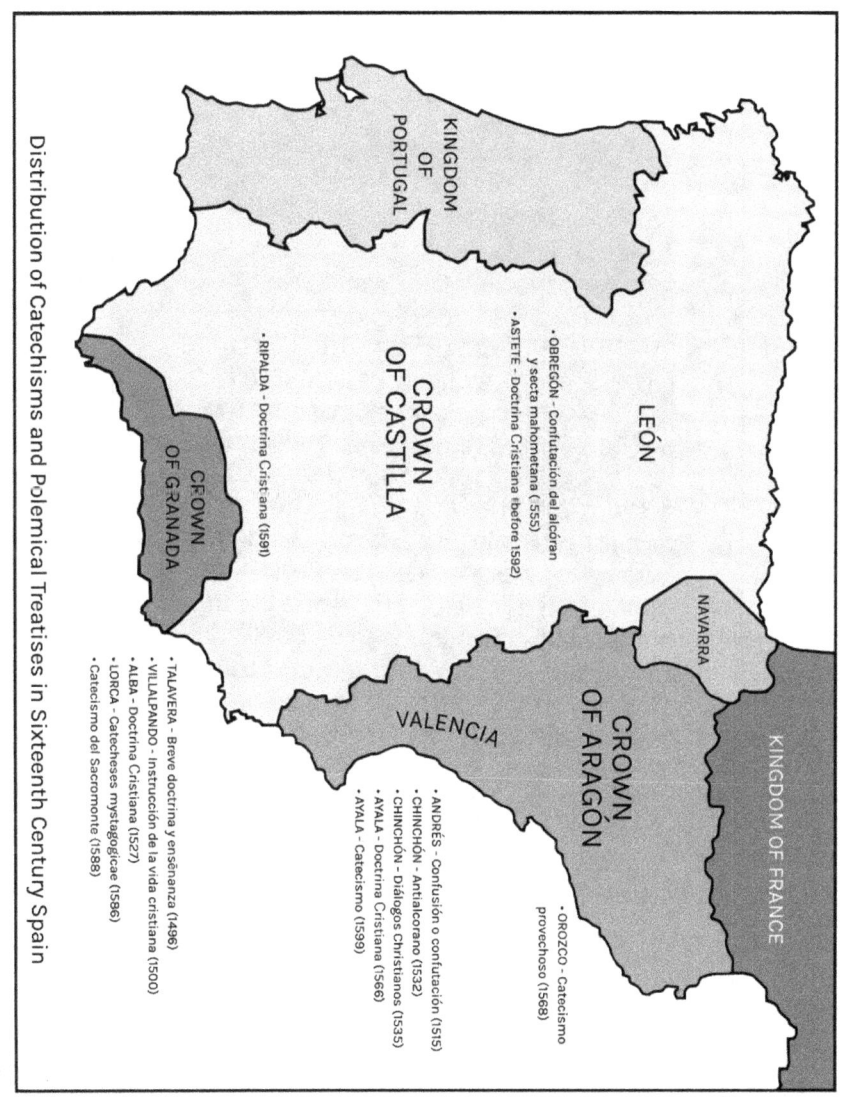

Appendices

Appendix 1

The first page of Hernando de Talavera's
Breve doctrina y enseñanza[1]

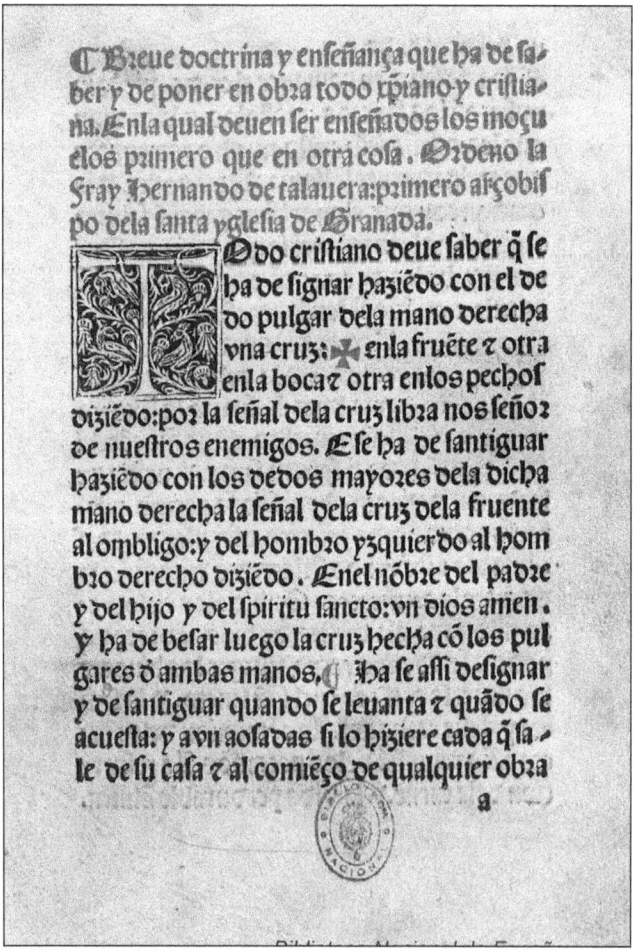

1. A digital copy of Hernando de Talavera's *Breve doctrina y enseñanza* is archived at the Biblioteca Digital Hispánica http://bdh.bne.es/

Appendix 2

The title page of Lope Obregón's
Confutación del alcorán y secta mahometana[2]

2. A digital copy of Lope Obregón's *Confutación del alcorán y secta mahometana* is archived at Sächsische Landesbibliothek-Staats-und Universitätsbibliothek Dresden (SLUB) https://digital.slub-dresden.de/en/ Public Domain Mark 1.0.

Appendix 3

The title page of Martín Pérez de Ayala's
Doctrina cristiana[3]

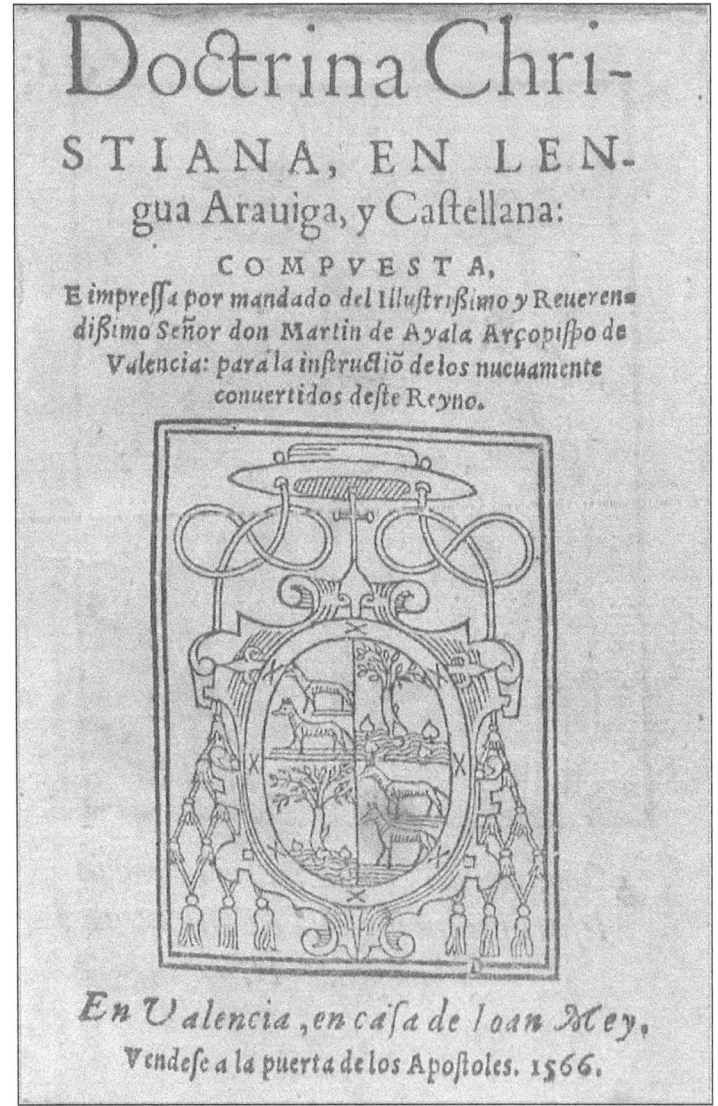

3. A digital copy of Martín Pérez de Ayala's *Doctrina cristiana* is archived at the Biblioteca Digital Hispánica http://bdh.bne.es/

Appendix 4

The title page of Alonso de Orozco's
Catecismo provechoso[4]

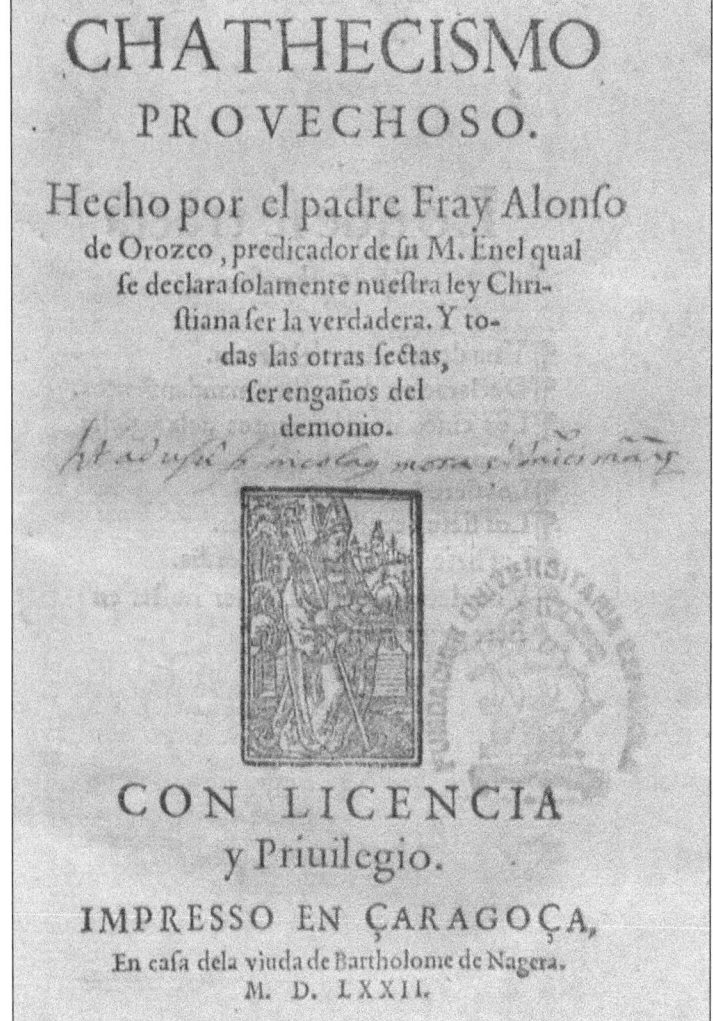

4. A digital copy of Alonso de Orozco's *Catecismo provechoso* is archived at La Biblioteca Virtual de Madrid https://bibliotecavirtualmadrid.comunidad.madrid/

Appendix 5

The title page of Gaspar Astete's
Catecismo de la doctrina christiana[5]

> # CATECISMO
> ## DE LA DOCTRINA CHRISTIANA,
> ESCRITO POR EL P. GASPAR ASTETE,
> y añadido para su mayor declaracion con varias preguntas, y respuestas,
>
> POR EL LICENCIADO DON GABRIEL Menendez de Luarca, Colegial que fue en el Insigne de San Pelayo de la Universidad de Salamanca, y Catedrático de Filosofía, y Teología en ella; y al presente Canónigo Penitenciario de la Santa Iglesia Catedral de Segovia:
>
> QUIEN PARA LA MAYOR INSTRUCCION y provecho espiritual de los Fieles, nuevamente aumentado lo da à luz juntamente con el Librito intitulado: *Vida Christiana, ó práctica facil de entablarla con medios, y verdades fundamentales*,
>
> ESCRITO POR EL P. GERONIMO DUTARI; y una breve explicacion de la Bula de la Santa Cruzada.
>
> CON LICENCIA:
>
> En Valladolid en la Imprenta de Don Manuel Santos Matute. Año de 1787.

---

5. A digital copy of Gaspar Astete's *Catecismo de la doctrina christiana* is archived at Hathi Trust Digital Library https://www.hathitrust.org. Public Domain Google-Digitized.

Appendix 6

The title page of Martín Pérez de Ayala's
Catecismo[6]

6. A digital copy of Martín Pérez de Ayala's *Catecismo* is archived at the Biblioteca Valenciana Digital https://www.bivaldi.gva.es/ Public Domain Mark (PDM).

Appendix 7

Ribera's cover letter to Martín Pérez de Ayala's *Catecismo*[7]

CARTA DEL PATRIARCHA y Arçobispo de Valencia,

D. Iuan de Ribera, a los Rectores, Predicadores, y Confessores de su Arçobispado.

VENERABLES Padres, Este Catechismo llego a mis manos sin nombre de autor, pero con opinion que era compuesto por el Reuerendissimo señor Don Martin de Ayala Arçobispo desta santa Iglesia: la qual opinion se confirmo con tantas conjecturas, que vino a ser certeza. Porque no solo se hallo entre los papeles del señor Arçobispo, y escrito de mano del Reuerendiss. Don Iuan Baptista Perez, que era en aquel tiempo su Secretario, y despues fue Obispo de Segorue; pero (lo que mas es, y deue quitar toda duda,) estaua en muchas partes enmendado y añadido con sobrepuestos de la misma letra del señor Arçobispo. Los quadernos estauan sin orden, y muchas cosas con necessidad

¶ 2   de ma-

---

7. A digital copy of Martín Pérez de Ayala's *Catecismo* is archived at the Biblioteca Valenciana Digital https://www.bivaldi.gva.es/ Public Domain Mark (PDM).

de mayor explicacion, como suele acontecer a las obras
que no gozan de la vltima mano de sus autores; y assi fue
menester gastar algunos meses en disponer las materias y
capitulos, y assi mismo en añadir y mudar palabras y clau
sulas para mayor claridad de la doctrina. Lo qual hize jū
tamente cō algunas personas doctas, assi de las que tēgo en
mi compañia, como de otras fuera de mi casa. Para reco-
mendacion de la obra basta hauer certificado del Autor:
porq̃ allende de sus muchas letras, de las quales son testi-
gos otras obras que hizo, fue siempre estimada en mucho
su persona, assi por la Magestad del Rey nuestro señor
Don Phelipe segũdo que haya sancta gloria, como por todos los demas que le conocieron. Particularmente quando
se celebrò el sancto Concilio de Trento, fue de mucho peso
su parecer ante todos los Padres que se hallaron en el. Y
(lo que importa mucho) tuuo particular noticia de las cosas que tocan a los nueuamente conuertidos de Moros, por
hauer sido Obispo de Guadix, donde auia muchos en
su tiempo: y con esta ocasion començo a componer alli este
Catechismo. Despues fue trasladado al Obispado de Se-
gouia, y como alli no los hay, suspendio la escriptura:
pero siendo a lo vltimo promouido a este Arçobispado, en
el qual militaua la misma ocasion y necessidad q̃ en Guadix, boluio a continuar la obra. De manera que no solo
concurrierō letras y prudencia en el señor Arçobispo, pero
tambien

tambien experiencia y entera noticia de las neceſsidades
deſta gente; y aſsi conſta con quanta verdad he dicho,
que baſta ſaber el Autor, para eſtimar la obra. En ella ſe
tratan todas las materias neceſſarias para inſtruyr vn in-
fiel a la Fe del Euangelio; y particularmente al que hu-
uiere ſeguido la ſecta de Mahoma. Porq̃ no ſolo mueſtra
con razones y conueniencias naturales y morales la pure-
za y hermoſura de nueſtra ſanta Fe; pero haze demonſ-
traciones de la torpeza, y deſatinos que hay en la ſecta
de Mahoma. Y en lo vno y lo otro procede con tanta claridad de razones y conceptos, y con tan llano eſtilo, que
ſe conoce bien el cuydado y diligencia que puſo en con-
menſurar y acomodar la eſcritura al talento de los que
hauian de ſer enſeñados. Pero de tal manera haze eſto,
que tambien los doctos hallaran aechadas las verda-
des de nueſtra ſanta religion, y prouadas con lugares
de la ſanta Eſcriptura, y de los ſantos Padres que la de-
clararon. Por eſta miſma razon fue muy a propoſito que
fueſſe en forma de dialogo eſte Catechiſmo, pues es la mas
clara y diſtincta manera de enſeñar quando hay preguntas del diſcipulo, y reſpueſtas del maeſtro; como lo obſer-
uaron muchos de los antiguos y modernos, aſsi ſantos, como doctores, guardando eſta miſma forma, enſeñando ver
dades, o confutando mentiras. Eſto ſe vee en S. Auguſtin
en diuerſas materias, tratadas en el ſexto tomo de ſus
¶ 3   obras,

obras, en S. Gregorio Magno, en S. Iustino, y S. Vigilio Martyres, y en otros muchos, que por ser tantos, y tan notorias sus obras, dexo de referir. Resta agora Padres, que os aproucheys deste Catechismo, como de medio tan importante para el descargo de vuestro oficio, y aprouechamiento de vuestros feligreses, leyendolo muchas vezes, y haziendolo muy familiar, y aun teniendolo (si fuere possible) de memoria. Esto os encargo mucho, y que en pago de la buena obra que haueys recebido del señor Arçobispo, os acordeys de encomēdarle a nuestro Señor, y que hagays lo mismo por mi. El os tenga en su gracia, y os dè la que haueys menester para satisfazer enteramente a vuestro ministerio. Dada en nuestro Palacio Arçobispal de Valencia, a 27. de Octubre, 1599.

El Patriarcha Arçobispo de Valencia.

Appendix 8

The first page of Pérez de Ayala's journal
Vida de D. Martin Perez de Ayala[8]

8. A digital copy of Martín Pérez de Ayala's journal *Vida de D. Martin Perez de Ayala* is archived at the Biblioteca Digital Hispánica http://bdh.bne.es/

Appendix 9

The table of contents of Pérez de Ayala's journal
Vida de D. Martin Perez de Ayala[9]

---

9. A digital copy of Martín Pérez de Ayala's journal *Vida de D. Martin Perez de Ayala* is archived at the Biblioteca Digital Hispánica http://bdh.bne.es/

Bibliography

"Alonso de Orozco: Biography (1500–1591)." https://bit.ly/3Lflcj5

Andrés, Gregorio de. "La biblioteca de un teólogo renacentista: Martín Pérez de Ayala." *Helmantica: Revista de Filología Clásica y Hebrea* 27.82 (1979) 91–111.

Andrés, Melquíades. *La teología española en el siglo XVI*. Madrid: Biblioteca de Autores Cristianos, 1976.

Aparicio López, Teófilo. "Alonso de Orozco. Asceta y místico del Siglo de Oro español." *Estudio Agustiniano* 37.3 (2002) 523–48.

Astete, Gaspar. *Catecismo de la doctrina cristiana escrito por el P. Gaspar Astete y añadido para su mayor declaración con varias preguntas y respuestas por el Licenciado Don Gabriel Menendez de Luarca*. Valladolid: Imprenta de Don Manuel Santos Matute, 1787.

Bernabé Pons, Luis F. *Los moriscos: conflicto, expulsión y diáspora*. Madrid: Los Libros de la Catarata, 2009.

———. "Taqiyya, niyya y el islam de los moriscos." *Al-Qanṭara* XXXIV.2 (2013) 491–527.

———. "Una visión propicia del mundo: España y los Moriscos de Granada." In *Averroes dialogado y otros momentos literarios y sociales de la interacción cristiano-musulmana en España e Italia. Un seminario interdisciplinar*, 89–137. Kassel: Edition Reichenberger, 1998.

Boronat y Barrachina, Pascual. *El B. Juan de Ribera y el R. Colegio de Corpus Christi. Estudio histórico*. Valencia: Imprenta de F. Vives y Mora, 1904.

———. *Los moriscos españoles y su expulsión. Estudio histórico-crítico. Tomo I*. 2 vols. Valencia: Francisco Vives y Mora, 1901.

———. *Los moriscos españoles y su expulsión. Estudio histórico-crítico. Tomo II*. 2 vols. Valencia: Francisco Vives y Mora, 1901.

Brannan, Rick, ed. *Lexham Research Lexicon of the Greek New Testament*. Bellingham, WA: Lexham, 2020.

Buckley, Theodore Alois. *The Catechism of the Council of Trent (Illustrated)*. London: Aeterna, 2014. Kindle edition.

Bunes Ibarra, Miguel Ángel de. "El enfrentamiento con el Islam en el Siglo de Oro: los Antialcoranes." In *Iglesia y literatura: la formación ideológica de España*, 41–58. Madrid: Ediciones de la Universidad Autónoma de Madrid, 1988.

Busic, Jason. "Pedro Guerra de Lorca." In *Christian-Muslim Relations: A Bibliographical History. Volume 6. Western Europe (1500-1600)*, edited by David Thomas and John Chesworth, 250-58. Leiden: Brill, 2014.

———. "Saving the Lost Sheep: Mission and Culture in Pedro de Guerra Lorca's *Catequeses mystagogicae pro advenis ex secta mahometana: ad parochos, & potestates (1586)*." PhD diss., The Ohio State University, 2009.

Cantarino, Vicente. "Notas para la polémica contra el Islam en España." In *Spanien und der Orient im frühen und hohen Mitteralter*, 126-41. Mainz: Verlag Phillip von Zabern, 1991.

Cardaillac, Louis. *Moriscos y cristianos. Un enfrentamiento político (1492-1640)*. Madrid: Fondo de Cultura Económica, 1979.

———. "Un aspecto de las relaciones entre moriscos y cristianos: polémica y taqiyya." In *Actas del Coloquio Internacional Sobre Literatura Aljamiada y Morisca*, 107-22. Barcelona: Editorial Gredos, 1978.

Caro Baroja, Julio. *Los moriscos del Reino de Granada. Ensayo de historia social*. Madrid: Instituto de Estudios Políticos, 1957.

Carrasco Manchado, Ana Isabel. "Antonio García de Villalpando." In *Christian-Muslim Relations: A Bibliographical History. Volume 6. Western Europe (1500-1600)*, edited by David Thomas and John Chesworth, 49-53. Leiden: Brill, 2014.

Chesworth, John, and Luis F. Bernabé Pons. "The Young Man of Arévalo." In *Christian-Muslim Relations: A Bibliographical History. Volume 6. Western Europe (1500-1600)*, edited by David Thomas and John Chesworth, 159-68. Leiden: Brill, 2014.

Clugnet, León. "St. Martin of Tours." In *The Catholic Encyclopedia*. New York: Appleton, 1910. www.newadvent.org/cathen/09732b.htm.

Cowans, Jon. *Early Modern Spain: A Documentary History*. Philadelphia: University of Pennsylvania Press, 2003.

Danvila y Collado, Manuel. *La expulsión de los moriscos españoles*. Madrid: Librería de Fernando Fé, 1889.

Doeswyck, Peter J. *The Ever-Changing Church: Its Origin and Development. A History of the Doctrines and Practices of the Roman Catholic Church, Based on the Original Sources of the Middle Ages, Presented Especially for the Benefit of Those Who Contemplate Merger with Rome*. Volume 2. Long Beach: Knights of Christ, 1962.

Domínguez Ortiz, Antonio, and Bernard Vincent. *Historia de los moriscos: Vida y tragedia de una minoría*. Madrid: Alianza Editorial, S.A., 1985.

Donner, Fred M. "The Historical Context." In *The Cambridge Companion to the Qur'ān*, edited by Jane Dammen McAuliffe, 23-39. Cambridge: Cambridge University Press, 2006.

Droge, Arthur J. *The Qur'ān: A New Annotated Translation*. Comparative Islamic Series. Sheffield, UK: Equinox, 2012.

Ehlers, Benjamin. *Between Christians and Moriscos: Juan de Ribera and Religious Reform in Valencia, 1568-1614*. Baltimore: Johns Hopkins University Press, 2006.

Escolano, Gaspar. "Libro decimo. Capitulo XXXIX. Contiene una carta del Patriarca Arçobispo de Valencia con documentos a los que se encargaron de la instruccion de los Moriscos en el año mil quinientos nouenta y nueue." In *Segunda parte de la década primera de la historia de la insigne, y coronada ciudad y Reyno de Valencia*, 1783-97. Valencia: Pedro Patricio Mey, 1611.

Framiñán de Miguel, Ma. Jesús. "Manuales para el adoctrinamiento de neoconversos en el siglo XVI." *Criticón* 93 (2005) 25-37.

———. "Martín Pérez de Ayala." In *Christian-Muslim Relations: A Bibliographical History. Volume 6. Western Europe (1500-1600)*, edited by David Thomas and John Chesworth, 207-14. Leiden: Brill, 2014.
Frederiks, Martha. "Introduction: Christians, Muslims and Empires in the 16th Century." In *Christian-Muslim Relations: A Bibliographical History. Volume 6. Western Europe (1500-1600)*, edited by David Thomas and John Chesworth, 1-10. Leiden: Brill, 2014.
Gallego y Burín, Antonio, and Alfonso Gámir Sandoval. *Los moriscos del Reino de Granada según el Sínodo de Guadix de 1554*. Granada: Universidad de Granada, 1968.
García Cárcel, Ricardo. "Estudio crítico del catecismo de Ribera-Ayala." In *Les Morisques et leur temps*, 159-68. Paris: Éditions du Centre national de la recherche scientifique, 1983.
———. *Herejía y sociedad en el siglo xvi: la Inquisición en Valencia, 1530-1690*. Barcelona: Ediciones Península, 1980.
———. "La Inquisición y los moriscos valencianos. Anatomía de una represión." *Actas de las Jornadas de Cultura Arabe e Islámica (1978)*, 401-17. Madrid: Instituto Hispano-Arabe de Cultura Madrid, 1981.
García-Ferrer, María Julieta. *Fray Hernando de Talavera y Granada*. 1st ed. Granada: Editorial Universidad de Granada, 2007.
García y García-Estévez, Ángel. "Sínodo diocesano celebrado en Segovia el año 1661 por el Obispo D. Francisco de Zárate y Terán." *Salmanticensis* 54 (2007) 123-80.
Gómez, Jesús. "Catecismos dialogados españoles (siglo XVI)." In *Iglesia y Literatura: la formación ideológica de España*, 117-28. Madrid: Universidad Autónoma de Madrid, 1988.
González Novalín, José Luis. *El inquisidor general Fernando de Valdés (1483-1568): Su vida y su obra*. Oviedo, Spain: Universidad de Oviedo, 2008.
Griffith, Sidney H. "Holy Spirit." In *Encyclopedia of the Qurʾān*, Volume 2, edited by Jane Dammen McAuliffe, 442-44. Leiden: Brill, 2002.
Guardia Guardia, Simón. "Doctrina teológica del Sínodo de Guadix de 1554." *Boletín del Instituto de Estudios "Pedro Suárez": Estudios sobre las comarcas de Guadix, Baza y Huéscar* 14 (2001) 9-38.
Guillaume, A. "The Story of Baḥīrā." In *The Life of Muhammad: A Translation of Ibn Isḥāq's Sīrat Rasūl Allāh*, 79-81. Oxford: Oxford University Press, 2012.
Gutiérrez, Constancio. *Españoles en Trento*. Valladolid, Spain: Industrias Gráficas Diario-Dia, 1951.
Harvey, Leonard P. "Crypto-Islam in Sixteenth-Century Spain." In *Actas del Primer Congreso de Estudios Árabes e Islámicos*, 163-79. 1962. Reprint, Madrid: Comité Permanente del Congreso de Estudios Árabes e Islámicos, 1964.
———. "An Explicit Reference to the Lawfulness of the Exercise of taqīya by Moriscos." *Aljamía*, 8 (1996) 40-43.
———. "Una referencia explícita de la legalidad de la práctica de la taqiyya por los moriscos." *Sharq al-Andalus* 12 (1995) 561-63.
Iannuzzi, Isabella. "Hernando de Talavera." In *Christian-Muslim Relations: A Bibliographical History. Volume 6. Western Europe (1500-1600)*, edited by David Thomas and John Chesworth, 60-66. Leiden: Brill, 2014.

Iogna-Prat, Dominique, and John Tolan. "Peter of Cluny." In *Christian-Muslim Relations: A Bibliographical History. Volume 3 (1050–1200)*, 604–9. Leiden: Brill, 2011.

Janer, Florencio. *Condición social de los moriscos de España: Causas de su expulsión, y consecuencias que esta produjo en el orden económico y político*. Madrid: Real Academia de la Historia, 1857.

Kleinschmidt, Harald. *Charles V: The World Emperor*. Stroud, UK: History, 2012. Kindle edition.

Leemhuis, Fred. "From Palm Leaves to the Internet." In *The Cambridge Companion to the Qurʾān*, edited by Jane Dammen McAuliffe, 145–61. Cambridge: Oxford University Press, 2006.

Longás, Pedro. *Vida religiosa de los moriscos*. Madrid: Imprenta Ibérica. E. Maestre, 1915.

Lutz, H. "Morone, Giovanni." In *New Catholic Encyclopedia*, Volume 9, 899–900. 2nd ed. Farmington Hills, MI: Gale Research, 2003.

Medina, F. B. "Apostolado morisco." In *Diccionario histórico de la Compañía de Jesús*, Volume 3, edited by Charles E. O'Neill and Joaquín M. Domínguez, 2746–49. Madrid: Universidad Pontificia Comillas, 2001.

Mols, R. "Borromeo, Charles, St." In *New Catholic Encyclopedia*, Volume 2, 539–41. 2nd ed. Farmington Hills, MI: Gale Research, 2002.

Morgado García, Arturo. "El clero en la España de los siglos XVI y XVII. Estado de la cuestión y últimas tendencias." *Manuscrits*, 25 (2007) 75–100.

Newby, Gordon D. "Baḥīrā." In *A Concise Encyclopedia of Islam*, 39–40. Oxford: Oneworld, 2002.

Obregón, Lope. *Confutación del alcorán y secta mahometana, sacado de sus propios libros, y de la vida del mesmo Mahoma*. Granada, 1555. https://bit.ly/44LcuQA

O'Malley, John W. *Trent: What Happened at the Council*. Cambridge: Harvard University Press, 2013.

Orozco, Alonso de. *Catecismo Provechoso*. Zaragoza: Casa de la Viuda de Bartholome de Nagera, 1572. https://bit.ly/3Z9QMod

Pedraza, Amalia García. "El otro morisco: Algunas reflexiones sobre el estudio de la religiosidad morisca a través de fuentes notariales." *Sharq al-Andalus* 12 (1995) 223–34.

Penn, Michael Philip. *Envisioning Islam: Syriac Christians and the Early Muslim World*. Philadelphia: University of Pennsylvania Press, 2015.

Pérez de Ayala, Martín. *Catecismo para la instrucción de los nuevamente convertidos de moros*. Valencia: Casa de Pedro Patricio Mey, 1599. https://bit.ly/3EAEnQC

———. *Doctrina cristiana en lengua arábiga y castellana para instrucción de los moriscos del Ilustrísimo Sr. D. Martín Pérez de Ayala, Arzobispo de Valencia*. Valencia: Imprenta Hijos de F. Vives Mora, 1911. https://bit.ly/3LldT9v

———. "Vida de D. Martín Pérez de Ayala, del Orden de Santiago, Arzobispo de Valencia." https://bit.ly/3RidgRU

Plans, Juan Belda. "La obra reformadora de Martín Pérez de Ayala como Arzobispo de Valencia (1565-1566)." *Corrientes Espirituales en la Valencia del Siglo XVI (1550-1600)*, 211–17.

Pons Fuster, Francisco. *Antialcorano. Diálogos Christianos. Conversión y evangelización de moriscos. Bernardo Pérez de Chinchón*. Alicante: Publicaciones Universidad de Alicante, 2000.

———. "Bernardo Pérez de Chinchón." In *Christian-Muslim Relations: A Bibliographical History. Volume 6. Western Europe (1500-1600)*, edited by David Thomas and John Chesworth, 119-24. Leiden: Brill, 2014.

———. "El patriarca Juan de Ribera y el Catecismo para instrucción de los nuevos convertidos." *Studia Philologica Valentina* 15.12 (2013) 189-220.

Ramón Guerrero, José. "Catecismos de autores españoles en la primera mitad del siglo XVI (1500-1559)." *Repertorio de historia de las ciencias eclesiásticas en España* 2 (1971) 225-60.

Resines, Luis. "Alonso de Orozco." In *Christian-Muslim Relations: A Bibliographical History. Volume 6. Western Europe (1500-1600)*, edited by David Thomas and John Chesworth, 219-23. Leiden: Brill, 2014.

———. "Catecismo del Sacromonte." In *Christian-Muslim Relations: A Bibliographical History. Volume 6. Western Europe (1500-1600)*, edited by David Thomas and John Chesworth, 265-67. Leiden: Brill, 2014.

———. *Catecismo del Sacromonte y Doctrina Cristiana de Fr. Pedro de Feria: conversión y evangelización de moriscos e indios*. Madrid: Consejo Superior de Investigaciones Científicas, 2002.

———. *La Catequesis en España: Historia y Textos*. Madrid: Biblioteca de Autores Cristianos, 1997.

———. *El Catecismo de Pedro Ramiro de Alba*. Granada: Universidad de Granada, 2015.

———. "Lectura crítica de los catecismos de Astete y Ripalda. Primera Parte." *Estudio Agustiniano* 16.1 (1981) 73-131.

———. "Lectura crítica de los catecismos de Astete y Ripalda. Segunda Parte." *Estudio Agustiniano* 16.2 (1981) 241-97.

———. "Los catecismos del XVI y su modo de presentar la fe." *Anuario de historia de la Iglesia*, 3 (1994) 197-214.

———. "Pedro Ramírez de Alba." In *Christian-Muslim Relations: A Bibliographical History. Volume 6. Western Europe (1500-1600)*, edited by David Thomas and John Chesworth, 93-95. Leiden: Brill, 2014.

Robres Lluch, Ramón. *San Juan de Ribera. Patriarca de Antioquía, Arzobispo y Virrey de Valencia. Un obispo según el ideal de Trento*. Barcelona: Imprenta Clarasó, 1960.

Roggema, Barbara. *The Legend of Sergius Baḥīrā: Eastern Christian Apologetics and Apocalyptic in Response to Islam*. History of Christian-Muslim Relations. Leiden: Brill, 2009.

Rubio, Diego. "La *taqiyya* en las fuentes cristianas: indicios de su presencia entre los moriscos." *Al-Qantara: Revista de Estudios Árabes* 34.2 (2013) 529-46.

Ruiz García, Elisa. *Juan Andrés. Confusión o confutación de la secta mahomética y del Alcorán. Estudio preliminar, edición y notas*. Mérida: Editora Regional de Extremadura, 2003.

Samir, Samir Khalil. *111 Questions on Islam*. San Francisco: Ignatius, 2008.

Sánchez-Blanco, Rafael Benítez. *Heroicas decisiones: la monarquía católica y los moriscos valencianos*. Valencia: Institutió Alfons el Magnànim, 2001.

———. *Tríptico de la expulsión de los moriscos: El triunfo de la razón de estado*. Montpellier: Presses universitaires de la Méditerranée, 2012.

Sánchez Hernández, Antonio. "Catecismos para la instrucción religiosa de los Moriscos." PhD diss., Universidad Pontificia de Salamanca, 1955.

Schroeder, H. J., trans. *The Canons and Decrees of the Council of Trent*. Charlotte: TAN Books, 2014. Kindle edition.

Serrano y Sanz, Manuel. *Autobiografías y memorias coleccionadas é ilustradas*. Madrid: Bailly Bailliére é hijos, 1905. https://bit.ly/3EB4nv4

———. "Discurso de la vida del Ilustrísimo y Reverendísimo Señor Martín de Ayala, Arzobispo de Valencia, hasta nueve días antes que Dios Nuestro Señor le llevase consigo escrito por sí mismo." In *Autobiografías y Memorias Coleccionadas é Ilustradas*. Madrid: Bailly Bailliére é hijos, 210–38. 1905. https://bit.ly/44Oys4Y

Spiteri, Laurence. *The Catholic Counter-Reformation (At Your Fingertips)*. St. Paul: Alba House, 2010. Kindle edition.

———. *A History of the Roman Catholic Church until the Council of Trent (At Your Fingertips*. Staten Island: St Pauls, 2008. Kindle edition.

Szpiech, Ryan. "Lope Obregón." In *Christian–Muslim Relations: A Bibliographical History. Volume 6. Western Europe (1500–1600)*, edited by David Thomas and John Chesworth, 169–75. Leiden: Brill, 2014.

Szpiech, Ryan, Katarzyna K. Starczewska, and Mercedes García-Arenal. "'Deleytaste del dulce sono y no pensaste en las palabras.' Rendering Arabic in the Antialcoranes." *Journal of Transcultural Medieval Studies* 5.1 (2018) 99–132.

Talavera, Hernando de. "Breve doctrina y enseñanza que ha de saber y poner en obra todo cristiano y cristiana. En la cual deben ser enseñados, los mozuelos primero que en otra cosa." In *Breve y muy provechosa doctrina de lo que deber saber todo cristiano con otros tratados muy provechosos compuesto por el Arzobispo de Granada*. Granada: Meinardo Ungut y Juan Pegnitzer, 1496. https://bit.ly/3PJdYXn

Tejada y Ramiro, Juan. *Colección de cánones y de todos los Concilios de la Iglesia Española. Parte Segunda. Tomo V*. Madrid: Imprenta de Don Pedro Montero, 1855.

Tolan, John. "Nicholas of Cusa." In *Christian–Muslim Relations: A Bibliographical History. Volume 5 (1350–1500)*, edited by David Thomas and Alex Mallett, 421–28. Leiden: Brill, 2013.

———. "Petrus Alfonsi." In *Christian–Muslim Relations: A Bibliographical History. Volume 3 (1050–1200)*, edited by David Thomas and Alex Mallett, 356–62. Leiden: Brill, 2011.

Toropov, Brandon. *Beyond Mere Christianity: C. S. Lewis & the Betrayal of Christianity*. Riyadh: Darussalam, 2005.

Waterworth, J., trans. *The Canons and Decrees of The Sacred and Ecumenical Council of Trent*. London: Dolman, 1848.

Wild, Stefan. "Paradise." In *The Qur'an: An Encyclopedia*, edited by Oliver Leaman, 486–88. Abingdon, UK: Routledge, 2006.

Ximenez, Juan. *Vida del Beato Juan de Ribera*. Valencia: Joseph de Orga, 1798.

———. *Vida, y Virtudes del Venerable Siervo de Dios el Ilustrísimo y Excelentísimo Señor D. Juan de Ribera*. Roma: Imprenta de Roque Bernabó, 1734.

Zakariya, Abu. *Jesus: Man, Messenger, Messiah*. London: iERA, 2017.

Zwartjes, Otto. "Pedro de Alcalá." In *Christian–Muslim Relations: A Bibliographical History. Volume 6. Western Europe (1500–1600)*, edited by David Thomas and John Chesworth, 73–78. Leiden: Brill, 2014.

Index

Aaron, 184, 191
'Abd Allah, Ibn, 43. See also Andrés, Juan
Abdallah, 185, 197
Abdia, 47
Abel, 139, 139n88
Abraham, 139, 139n88, 182, 187, 190, 224, 239, 243
Abram, 184
Abu Talib. See Sergius
Adam, 131, 139, 181, 186, 187, 239, 243
Aisha, 228n33
Álava y Esquivel, Diego, 46, 113
Alba, Pedro Ramiro de, 3, 10, 32, 34, 38, 44, 53, 66, 73–74, 93, 114, 115, 116, 117, 150, 186, 277
Albert of Brandenburg, 13
Alcalá, Pedro de, 3, 4, 98
Alexander VI, Pope, 96
Alfonsi, Petrus, 96
Alfonso X, King of Castilla, 29
Alfonso XI, King of Castila, 29
Al-Ghazali, 243
al-Magrawi al-Wahrani, Ubaydallah Ahmd Ben Bu Jumua, 79
Ambrosius, 149n120
Anadón, Domingo, 271
Ananias, 230
Andrés, Gergorio de, 12n18, 30n96
Andrés, Juan, 2, 4, 5, 32, 33, 38, 39, 42–44, 46, 93, 96, 99, 100–101, 113, 114, 116, 120, 121, 122, 125, 149, 152, 154, 163, 163n70, 183, 184

Andrés, Melquíades, 100n126
Aparicio López, Teófilo, 48n32, 48n34
Arávigo, Joseph, 124n30
Arias, Diego Jiménez, 91
Arius, 237
Astete, Gaspar, 1, 3, 32, 35, 37, 38, 39, 52–53, 52n43, 53n46, 66, 92, 93, 94, 95, 115, 116, 150, 277, 294, 294n5
Athanasius, 149n120
Augustine, 149n120, 186
Ávalos, Gaspar de, 10, 20
Avicenna. See Ibn Sina (Avicenna)

Bahira. See Sergius
Baroja, 268n90
Basil the Great, 149n120
Bernabé Pons, Luis F., 33n12, 79n56, 80n59, 80n61, 82n64, 85n74, 86n82
Betolaza, Juan Pérez de, 95
Bleda, Jaime, 99
Boabdil, Sultan of Granada, 75, 83
Boronat y Barrachina, Pascual, 102n2, 102n4, 103n5, 103nn8–9, 253nn6–9, 269n91
Borromeo, Charles (Carlos/Carlo), 15, 66
Brannan, Rick, 233n47
Buckley, Theodore Alois, 67n20, 68nn21–25, 69n26
Bunes Ibarra, Miguel Ángel de, 99n119, 99nn121–22, 100nn123–25, 100n127

Busic, Jason, 50nn36–37, 74n42, 75nn43–44, 113n2, 189nn106–8, 190n109, 239nn82–86, 240nn87–90

Calixtus III, Pope, 96
Calvin, John, 91
Canisius, Peter, 92, 94
Cantarino, Vicente, 96n114, 98n118
Cardaillac, Louis, 84nn67–69
Carrasco Manchado, Ana Isabel, 42n17
Cervantes, Miguel de, 287
Charles I, King of Spain (Charles V, Holy Roman Emperor), 1, 2, 7, 8, 10, 11, 12, 19, 20, 23, 24, 28, 29, 34, 44, 48, 76, 77, 78, 82, 83, 114, 167, 168, 174
Chesworth, John, 31n1, 44n26, 80n61
Chinchón, Bernardo Pérez de. *See* Pérez de Chinchón, Bernardo
Cisneros, Francisco Jiménez de, 6, 33, 34, 41, 42, 76, 90, 91
Clement, Pope, 273
Clement VII, Pope, 34, 77
Clugnet, León, 9n10
Cluny, Peter of (Peter the Venerable), 96, 97, 100
Conelius, 154, 175, 226, 230
Cowans, Jon, 75n45
Cyprian, 149n120

Daniel, 227
Danvila y Collado, Manuel, 268n86, 272n101, 273n105
David, 129, 139n88, 146, 178, 184, 187, 243
De Soto, Domingo, 91, 92, 93
De Soto, Pedro, 91, 92
Desprats, Guillén, 113
Dhul Qarnain, 184
Díaz de Vivar, Rodrigo (El Cid), 287
Doeswyck, Peter J., 21n58
Domínguez Ortiz, Antonio, 33n13, 34n14, 35n15, 82n65, 84n71, 85nn72–73, 85nn75–77, 85nn79–80, 270nn95–97, 271nn98–99
Doña Juana, 48

Donner, Fred M., 228n33
Dorador, Bartolomé, 12
Droge, Arthur J., 74nn38–41, 121n23, 244, 244n110

Ehlers, Benjamin, 273n104
El Cid. *See* Díaz de Vivar, Rodrigo (El Cid)
Elijah, 139, 139n88
Erasmus, Desiderius, 65
Escolano, Gaspar, 281n8, 281nn9–10, 282, 282nn11–12, 282nn14–15
Espina, Alfonso, 99
Eutyches, 237
Eve, 139
Ezekiel, 146, 147

Felipe, 37, 71, 72, 158, 159, 160, 161, 162, 165, 172, 184, 185, 196, 197, 199, 199n163, 203, 208, 210, 210n39, 213, 217, 218, 251, 254, 256, 257, 258, 267
Ferdinand II of Aragón, 6, 33, 41, 42, 43, 75, 76, 83, 98, 113
Ferdinand V, King of Aragón, 29
Figuerola, Juan Martín, 46
Flórez, Andrés, 91, 92, 93, 95
Framiñán de Miguel, Ma. Jesús, 1n1, 3n4, 4, 4n14, 4n20, 5, 6n1, 8n5, 114n6
Francis I of France, 20
Francisco, 37
Fredericks, Martha, 6n2, 7nn3–4, 33n11
Fuente, Constantino Ponce de la. *See* Ponce de la Fuente, Constantino

Gabriel, 171, 197
Gallego y Burín, Antonio, 86n83, 87nn84–87
García, Martín, 43, 113
García Cárcel, Ricardo, 4, 4nn15–16, 103n6, 278, 278n113, 279, 282n18
García de Villalpando, Antonio. *See* Villalpando, Antonio García de
García y García-Estévez, Ángel, 14nn25–27
García-Arenal, Mercedes, 180n70

INDEX   311

García-Ferrer, Maria Julietta, 76n46
Gay, Juan, 113
Gayangos, Pascual de, 55n3
Gergorian of Nazianzus, 149n120
Gómez, Jesus, 91n102, 92nn103–5,
　93nn106–7, 94n108, 94n110,
　95n111
González de Santalla, Tirso, 4
Gregory of Nyssa, 149n120
Gregory XIII, Pope, 270
Guardia Guardia, Simón, 88nn90–92,
　89nn93–96
Guerra de Lorca, Pedro. *See* Lorca,
　Pedro Guerra de
Guerrero, Pedro, 27n76
Guillaume, A., 171n25
Guise, Charles de, 13
Gutiérrez, Contancio, 9n7, 9n9,
　19nn47–51, 20n53

Hagenbach, Pedro, 42
Harvey, Leonard P., 79n56, 80nn57–58,
　80n60, 81n62
Henry VIII, King of England, 65
Hieronymus, 149n120
Hilali, 240

Iannuzzi, Isabella, 41n16
Ibn Sina (Avicenna), 243
Innocent VIII, Pope, 96
Ionga-Prat, Dominique, 97n116
Isabella of Castilla, Queen, 6, 29, 33, 41,
　42, 43, 75, 76, 83, 98, 113
Isaiah, 129, 138, 148
Ishmael, 195

Jacob, 187, 227
James of Aragón, 18
Janer, Florencio, 83n66, 84n70, 86n81
Jean de Lorraine, 13
Jeremiah, 129, 146, 147
Jesus Christ, 22, 23, 24, 27, 29, 36, 37,
　40, 44, 45, 48, 63, 67, 68, 69, 70,
　71, 72, 73, 74, 80, 88–89, 113,
　119, 120, 121, 122, 123, 124,
　125, 126, 127, 129, 131, 132,
　133, 134, 137, 138, 139, 141,
　142, 144, 145, 147, 148, 151,
　153, 155, 159, 159n46, 160,
　160n46, 165, 173, 175, 176, 177,
　178, 184, 185, 187, 188, 190,
　191, 192, 193, 194, 195, 196,
　198, 199, 200n166, 202, 203,
　204, 206n22, 208, 210, 213, 214,
　221, 222, 222n6, 223–25, 227,
　229, 230, 231, 232, 232n44, 233,
　234, 237, 239, 246, 257, 259,
　263, 264, 278n114, 286, 286n30
Jiménez Arias, Diego. *See* Arias, Diego
　Jiménez
Jiménez de Cisneros, Francisco. *See*
　Cisneros, Francisco Jiménez de
John (the Evangelist/Revelator), 128,
　145, 246
John Paul II, Pope, 48
John the Baptist, 129, 224, 239
Jonah, 153
Joseph (Jacob's son), 125, 130, 134, 136,
　155, 156, 160, 161, 163, 164,
　165, 168, 169, 174, 184, 199,
　199n163, 251
Josephus, 223
Joshua, 187
Juan de Segovia, 97, 98
Juana I of Castilla, 76
Julius III, Pope, 19
Juttlar, Jerónimo, 95

Khan, 240
Kleinschmidt, Harald, 20n55

Lamark, Ehrard de, 113
Lamech, 243
Ledesma, Santiago, 92
Leemhuis, Fred, 228n32
León, Luis de, 63
Loaces, Fernando de, 28
Longás, Pedro, 55nn1–3, 56nn4–5,
　58n6, 60n7, 76nn47–48,
　77nn49–51, 78nn52–54
Lorca, Pedro Guerra de, 3, 4, 32, 35,
　49–50, 66, 74–75, 93, 104, 189,
　190, 241
Luarca, Gabriel Menéndez de. *See*
　Menéndez de Luarca, Gabriel
Lucifer. *See* Satan

Luke, 128, 145
Luther, Martin, 13, 21, 22, 65, 90, 91, 287
Lutz, H., 20n56

Mani, 237
Marcion, 237
Margarita of Austria, 283
Mark, 134, 145
Marqués, Juan, 42
Martin, bishop of Tours, 9
Mary, 68, 71, 80, 121, 147, 184, 187, 191, 204, 206n22, 208
Maryam, 194
Matthew, 128, 145
McAuliffe, 122n25
Medina, F. B., 4, 4n17
Sultan Mehmed the Conqueror (Mehmed II), 96, 98
Méndez, Francisco, 42
Mendoza, Diego de, 21
Mendoza, Francisco, 20
Menéndez de Luarca, Gabriel, 52n43, 114n10
Mols, R., 15n30
Monte di Croce, Riccoldo da, 190
Monzón, Cortes de, 34
More, Thomas, 65
Morgado García, Arturo, 64nn10–11
Morone, Giovanni, 20, 20n56
Moses, 139n88, 144, 146, 173, 184, 187, 191, 194, 231, 239, 246, 263
Muhammad, 1, 17, 30, 32n4, 32nn6–7, 32n9, 36–37, 39, 40, 41, 43, 44, 45, 46, 47, 50, 51, 54, 56, 59, 61, 73, 75, 80, 81, 96, 97, 100, 101, 103, 105, 106n14, 107, 108, 115, 116, 117, 118, 120, 121, 122, 123, 125, 127, 128, 128n45, 131, 133, 136, 141, 143, 144, 148, 149, 150n125, 152, 154, 155, 157, 158, 158n36, 159, 160, 162, 163, 164, 166n78, 168, 169, 170, 171, 172, 173, 174, 179, 180, 181, 182, 183, 184, 185, 186, 187, 188, 189, 190, 191, 192, 193, 194, 195, 196, 197, 198, 199, 199n163, 200n167, 202, 203, 204, 206, 210n39, 222, 223, 225, 228, 228n32, 228n33, 231, 234, 235, 236, 237, 238, 238n74, 239, 240, 241, 242, 243, 244, 245, 246, 247, 248, 250, 252, 256, 257, 258, 258n49, 259, 261, 262, 263, 265, 267, 267n83, 268, 273, 274, 277, 279n116, 280, 284, 285, 285n27, 286, 286n30, 287
Sultan Muhammad XII, 6
Sultan Murad II, 96, 98

Navarra, Francisco de, 267
Nestorius, 237
Newby, Gordon D., 170n24
Nicholas of Cusa, 96, 97–98
Nicholas V, Pope, 96
Noah, 139, 139n88, 184, 187, 239

Obregón, Lope, 2, 3, 4, 32, 34, 46–47, 96, 99, 101, 104, 116, 149, 188, 188n101, 189nn102–5, 291, 291n2
Obregón, Sebastián de, 29
O'Malley, John W., 13nn20–21, 13n24, 25nn69–70, 26n71, 26n74, 27n78, 27n80, 27n82
Origen of Alexandria, 149n120
Orozco, Alonso de, 2–3, 32, 35, 48–49, 66, 71, 71nn27–28, 93, 104, 126, 126nn38–39, 130, 130nn50–51, 137, 137nn76–81, 138, 138nn82–87, 139, 139nn88–90, 141, 142, 156nn24–27, 157, 159nn37–39, 159nn40–45, 170, 170nn18–19, 170nn21–23, 171, 171nn26–27, 172, 174, 174n36, 174n39, 175, 175n41, 176, 176nn42–43, 177, 177n56, 179, 184–85, 185nn87–93, 186, 186nn94–97, 196, 196nn142–148, 196n150, 197, 199, 204, 204n14, 206n21, 207, 207nn24–25, 208n27, 208n29, 209, 209n35, 211nn40–42, 212n45, 213nn52–57, 214, 214n63, 215, 217, 217n65, 218, 218n67, 226,

226n24, 227, 232n46, 239n81, 254nn12–13, 255n15, 255n17, 255n19, 255n21, 257nn29–31, 257nn33–42, 258nn43–47, 265, 293, 293n4

Pascual, Pedro, 30
Paul (apostle), 21, 128, 145, 152, 154, 233, 275. *See also* Saul of Tarsus
Paul II, Pope, 96
Paul III, Pope, 19
Pedraza, Amalia García, 79n55
Penn, Michael Philip, 171n25
Pérez de Betolaza, Juan. *See* Betolaza, Juan Pérez de
Pérez de Chinchón, Bernardo, 2, 3, 4, 5, 32, 34, 37, 39, 44–46, 91, 93, 99, 101, 116, 122–23, 124, 125, 129–30, 131, 132, 133–34, 134n65, 135, 136, 136n71, 141, 142, 143, 144, 144n108, 145, 149, 152, 153, 154, 155, 156, 157, 160, 161, 163, 164, 168, 169, 174, 174nn36–37, 174n39, 177, 178, 179, 187, 188, 195, 197, 199, 205, 206, 223, 238
Perkins, W., 91
Peter (apostle), 27, 128, 131, 145, 148, 153, 225, 226, 230, 233
Peter of Cluny. *See* Cluny, Peter of (Peter the Venerable)
Philip (apostle), 230
Philip II, King of Spain, 1, 2, 7, 8, 14–15, 16, 28, 29, 30, 35, 48, 49, 81, 82, 85, 102, 102n3, 103, 104, 111, 114, 116, 168, 174, 272, 283
Philip III, King of Spain, 2, 7, 28, 35, 81, 220, 249, 276, 283
Pius II, Pope, 96
Pius III, Pope, 23
Pius IV, Pope, 19, 25, 66
Pius V, Pope, 74, 272
Plans, Juan Belda, 16nn34–35, 17n38
Ponce de la Fuente, Constantino, 91, 93
Pons Fuster, Francisco, 5, 5n21, 45n27, 120n19, 123nn26–28, 124nn29–31, 125nn32–36, 130n47, 130n50, 131n55, 132nn56–58,

133nn59–61, 134nn62–64, 135n66, 135nn68–70, 136nn72–75, 143n105, 144n107, 144n109, 145n110, 146nn112–113, 147n114, 147n116, 153nn2–6, 155nn15–22, 156n23, 163n68, 164nn73–76, 168nn5–7, 169nn9–16, 178nn58–68, 187n99, 188n100, 195nn140–141, 205nn18–19, 225n23, 227nn28–30, 229n35, 231n43, 239nn76–80, 280, 280n2
Pontius Pilate, 68, 206n22, 223

Ramiro de Alba, Pedro. *See* Alba, Pedro Ramiro de
Ramón Guerrero, José, 90nn99–100, 91n101
Resines, Luis, 4, 4nn18–19, 5, 32n10, 44n25, 50n38, 51nn39–41, 52nn42–43, 53nn44–45, 63nn8–9, 72nn29–33, 73nn34–36, 74n37, 94n109, 95nn112–13, 114n5, 114n8, 117n13, 117nn15–16, 118nn17–18, 126n40, 127n41, 130nn48–49, 139nn91–92, 140nn93–95, 148nn117–18, 156n28, 160nn47–51, 161nn52–55, 173nn30–34, 174n35, 176nn44–46, 187n98, 190nn110–12, 191nn113–18, 196nn151–52, 208n28, 208n30, 209n32, 226n25, 227n26, 229n36, 230n37, 238n75, 240nn91–96
Ribera, Juan de, 2, 4, 6, 8–9, 15, 25, 28–30, 31, 33, 35, 36, 39, 54, 66, 82–83, 85n78, 86, 89, 93, 100, 102, 103–4, 105, 106, 110, 111, 168, 174, 206, 220, 249, 253, 254, 255, 256, 267, 268, 268n85, 269, 270, 271, 272, 273, 275, 276, 277, 278, 279, 281, 282, 283, 284
Ripalda, Jerónimo de, 1, 3, 32, 35, 37, 38, 39, 52, 54, 66, 89, 91, 93, 94, 95, 112, 150, 277
Robert of Ketton, 97

Robres Lluch, Ramón, 28n88, 29nn89–93, 30nn94–95, 102n1, 105nn11–12, 253n10, 268n84, 268nn87–89, 269nn92–93, 270n94, 271n100, 272nn101–2, 273n103, 273n105
Roggema, Barbara, 171n25
Rubio, Diego, 81n63
Ruiz García, Elisa, 42nn18–19, 43nn20–24, 121nn20–22, 122n24, 152n1, 154nn13–14, 163nn66–67, 163nn69–70, 164nn71–72, 183nn81–84, 184nn85–86, 238nn71–73

Salvatierra, Martín de, 81
Sánchez Hernández, Antonio, 3, 3nn5–7, 3n9, 3nn11–12, 4n13, 5
Sánchez-Blanco, Rafael Benítez, 283nn19–20
Sandoval, Alfonso Gámir, 86n83, 87nn84–87
Santalla, Tirso González de. See González de Santalla, Tirso
Satan, 170, 239, 240
Saul of Tarsus, 177, 230. See also Paul (apostle)
Schroeder, H. J., 66nn16–18
Segovia, Juan de. See Juan de Segovia
Selim II, 272
Sergius, 47, 170, 171, 197
Serrano y Saz, Manuel, 10n14
Sixtus IV, Pope, 96
Solomon, 129, 139, 139n88, 182, 183, 243
Soto, Domingo de. See De Soto, Domingo
Soto, Pedro de. See De Soto, Pedro
Spiteri, Laurence, 65nn12–14, 66n15, 66n19
Starczewska, Katarzyna K., 180n70
Szpiech, Ryan, 46n29, 180n70

Talavera, Hernando de, 2, 4, 6, 31, 33, 41–42, 44, 66, 75–76, 79, 90, 91, 93, 100, 113, 290, 290n1

Tejada y Ramiro, Juan, 16n34, 16n36, 17n37, 17nn39–40, 18nn41–44
Tertulian, 149n120
Theodoret of Cyrus, 149n120
Thomas (apostle), 131, 134
Thomas, David, 31n1, 44n26
Tiberius, 223
Tolan, John, 96n115, 97n116, 98n117
Toropov, Brandon, 224n13

Urbanus Regius, 91
Urrea, Martín, 20

Valdés, Fernando de, 15, 15n29
Valdés, Juan de, 91, 93
Valencia, de Pedro, 81
Valentinus, 237
Villalpando, Antonio García de, 2, 32, 33, 42
Villanueva, Tomás de, 267
Vincent, Bernard, 33n13, 34n14, 35n15, 82n65, 84n71, 85nn72–73, 85nn75–77, 85nn79–80, 270nn95–97, 271nn98–99
Virgin Mary. See Mary
Vivar, Rodrigo Díaz de. See Díaz de Vivar, Rodrigo (El Cid)

Waterworth, J., 13nn22–23, 21n58, 21n60, 22nn61–64, 23n65, 26nn72–73, 27n79, 27n81, 27nn83–85
Wild, Stefan, 242n103
William Duke of Cleves, 20

Ximenez, Juan, 104n10, 254n11, 271n100, 273n106, 274n109, 276n112, 281nn9–10

Zakariya, Abu, 224n13
Zayad bi Thabit, 228n32
Zechariah, 227
Zumárraga, Juan de, 63
Zumilla, Joseph, 37
Zwarties, Otto, 99n120